Subversion 2.0

DISRUPTIVE TECHNOLOGY AND INTERNATIONAL SECURITY

Series editors

BENJAMIN JENSEN
Marine Corps University and Center for Strategic and International Studies

JACQUELYN SCHNEIDER
Hoover Institution, Stanford University

BRANDON VALERIANO
Seton Hall University

OTHER BOOKS IN THE SERIES:

Repression in the Digital Age: Surveillance, Censorship, and the Dynamics of State Violence
Anita R. Gohdes

Leveraging Latency: How the Weak Compel the Strong with Nuclear Technology
Tristan A. Volpe

Subversion 2.0

Leaderlessness, the Internet, and the Fringes of Global Society

CHRISTOPHER WHYTE

OXFORD
UNIVERSITY PRESS

Oxford University Press is a department of the University of Oxford. It furthers
the University's objective of excellence in research, scholarship, and education
by publishing worldwide. Oxford is a registered trade mark of Oxford University
Press in the UK and certain other countries.

Published in the United States of America by Oxford University Press
198 Madison Avenue, New York, NY 10016, United States of America.

© Oxford University Press 2024

All rights reserved. No part of this publication may be reproduced, stored in
a retrieval system, or transmitted, in any form or by any means, without the
prior permission in writing of Oxford University Press, or as expressly permitted
by law, by license, or under terms agreed with the appropriate reproduction
rights organization. Inquiries concerning reproduction outside the scope of the
above should be sent to the Rights Department, Oxford University Press, at the
address above.

You must not circulate this work in any other form
and you must impose this same condition on any acquirer.

Library of Congress Cataloging-in-Publication Data
Names: Whyte, Christopher, 1988– author.
Title: Subversion 2.0 : Leaderlessness, the Internet, and the
Fringes of Global Society / Christopher Whyte.
Other titles: Subversion two point zero
Description: New York, NY : Oxford University Press, [2024] |
Series: Disruptive technology and international security series |
Includes bibliographical references and index.
Identifiers: LCCN 2024009028 (print) | LCCN 2024009029 (ebook) |
ISBN 9780197773369 (paperback) | ISBN 9780197773352 (hardback) |
ISBN 9780197773383 (epub)
Subjects: LCSH: Conspiracy theories. | Internet—Social aspects. |
Web 2.0. | Elite (Social sciences)
Classification: LCC HV6275 .W48 2024 (print) | LCC HV6275 (ebook) |
DDC 001.9—dc23/eng/20240422
LC record available at https://lccn.loc.gov/2024009028
LC ebook record available at https://lccn.loc.gov/2024009029

DOI: 10.1093/oso/9780197773352.001.0001

The manufacturer's authorized representative in the EU for product safety is
Oxford University Press España S.A. of Parque Empresarial San Fernando de Henares,
Avenida de Castilla, 2 – 28830 Madrid (www.oup.es/en or product.safety@oup.com).
OUP España S.A. also acts as importer into Spain of products made by the manufacturer.

Links to third party websites are provided by Oxford in good faith and
for information only. Oxford disclaims any responsibility for the materials
contained in any third party website referenced in this work.

Contents

Acknowledgments	vii
Preface	ix
Introduction	1
1. Information Technologies at the Fringe	22
2. Illegitimacy and the Logic of Subversion	36
3. Fringe 1.0: Information Control and the Early Web	68
4. Subversion Found: The Curious Case of Falun Gong	93
5. Fringe 2.0: Cyber Cultism and the Effects of Networked Subversion	117
6. The Landscape of Subversion in the Digital Age	147
7. Leaderlessness at the Fringes: Explaining When Subversives Hack	186
8. Leaderlessness, Subversion, and the Fringe 3.0	218
Appendix A: Additional Evidence and Diagnostic Testing	239
Notes	243
Index	267

Acknowledgments

It is said that the phrase "May you live in interesting times" is a kind of curse. After all, "interesting" might indicate instability, unwanted change, poverty, insecurity, and any number of other conditions not in the interests of whoever is being cursed. With this book, however, interesting times have helped the research within and the theory I offer evolve beyond the simplistic toward something I hope is insightful.

I began this project in 2015, nine years before the publication of this book. In that time, my work has taken me from an initial focus on cyberattacks by nonstate actors to a more holistic focus on fringe antagonism and the relationship between evolving web technologies and the modern machinations of subversion. I have conducted dozens of interviews and layered various kinds of data analyses to study in-depth what are truly complicated phenomena. And I have delayed publication of this book on three separate occasions so as to add nuance as real-world events—Unite the Right in 2017, incel-based violence in 2018 and 2020, the insurrection of January 6, 2021, and more—have added new dimensionality to the study of these issues.

The years I have spent building the analyses in this book have been filled with incredible encouragement, assistance, and support from family, friends, and colleagues. The book that is now published would look much different without such input and generosity. In particular, colleagues like Christopher Colligan, Miguel Alberto Gomez, David Webber, Brian Mazanec, Karl Grindal, Brandon Valeriano, Ben Jensen, and Ugochukwu Etudo have acted as sounding boards or have otherwise inspired me with their work to refine the contribution made here. Various research assistants, most notably Lauren Williams, John Senhoff, and Cate LeRoux, have helped to gather, transcribe, and make sense of information recorded in interviews. And my close colleagues at the Wilder School have encouraged me in this project (which I presented in an early form during my very first visit to the institution in 2017) and others, creating a collegial and open environment within which my scholarship has thrived. I am particularly thankful at VCU to Will Pelfrey, Jim Keck, and Maureen Moslow-Benway for their mentorship.

This project comes from a dissertation that I wrote many years ago, though the resemblance this book bears to that document is arguably minimal. That minimal resemblance, however, is not in spite of the support given to me by my dissertation advisors—Trevor Thrall, Eric McGlinchey, and Ed Rhodes—but rather directly because of it. I owe my advisors at George Mason University, including Hugh Sockett, a great deal for their patience, thoughtfulness, and encouragement. I see in this book the fruits of that support, particularly on the part of Trevor Thrall, who has supported me long after my graduation all those years ago.

Finally, I could not have completed this work without my family, at least two members of which did not exist when I started out in 2015. To Rupert and Willie, you keep me sane and are nothing short of the best friends a man could have. Rose, my wonderful daughter, your smile keeps me going under even the toughest conditions. And Susan, my long-suffering and ever-patient wife, your love has always proved the difference between what I could accomplish and what I do accomplish. I love you.

Preface

In 1983, a man named Louis Beam revolutionized the methodology of White supremacist advocacy in the United States. Beam, the Grand Dragon of the Texas branch of the Ku Klux Klan, was a different breed of activist—if any leaders of the KKK up until Beam could truly be called "activist"—than those who preceded him. More than just militant in his outlook on race, he was intelligent and ideologically ambitious. What really set him apart, however, was how shrewd he was regarding the rapidly transforming media environment of the late 20th century. In contrast with his predecessors and most of his peers, Beam derided the burning of crosses and sporadic race violence from behind the banner of the Klan. Although he certainly sanctioned such activities as appropriate, he recognized that they were unhelpful to the broader cause of White nationalism when undertaken in isolation. Political violence, he realized, must be married to compelling sociopolitical communication to be effective. The successful countercultural social movement—what White supremacy had clearly become over the course of the 20th century—had to engage, persuade, and mobilize points of resistance spread across an entire national populace. Otherwise, the cause would never be anything more than a fringe movement stuck at society's periphery.

The strategy and theory of subversive victory for which Beam became a strong proponent was called "leaderless resistance." The roots of the strategy are not entirely clear. Beam, in interviews, attributed it in part to the Central Intelligence Agency. But there are also clear historical links to resistance strategies popular among communists across Europe and Asia in the years following the Russian Revolution, as well as to the shape of resistance movements in Ireland, Nepal, and elsewhere. The basic idea of this theory of subversive victory was that the successful countercultural social movement would operate on two distinct levels and, most important, would strive to maintain separation between the practical manifestations of the cause on both fronts. On one level, the movement would be constituted of cells that engaged the population with the goal of provoking fear or prompting reflection on the validity of White nationalism. These cells would be highly militarized and largely detached from one another and would not shy away from transgression, even when such courses of action involved violence. The other level would be the public-facing institutions linked to the cause, from advocacy organizations to publishing houses and, eventually, political parties. This arm of the movement would disavow all knowledge of the cells' activities and would generally seek to blend into the prevailing sociopolitical fabric of mainstream society.

The purpose of this setup was twofold. First, separating public advocacy from violence extended the expected lifespan of the main organization (or network of organizations). Keeping both arms separate from one another allowed for plausible deniability in the eyes of the public and for legal and logistical protections for the public-facing organization in the eyes of the law.[1] Second, the separation of cells and figureheads allowed for the construction of contrarian narratives surrounding the cause itself. The public-facing effort could ingratiate itself with and spread its ideology to the mainstream, first among limited, receptive demographics and later to a wide audience, all the while labeling the cells acting on behalf of the broader cause "zealots" and "lone wolves." The intended effect would be to make the two levels of advocacy both separate and synonymous in the public eye. As Beam intended it, the mainstream manifestation of White supremacy would not be guilty of rogue extremism. At the same time, the public organization clearly represented those extremists on an ideological level, as well as thousands of others who either acted or might potentially act antagonistically based on their beliefs. Thus, if enacted correctly, the strategy would result in a legitimate presence in the prevailing sociopolitical discourse and a growing belief among the broader population that supporters of the cause were everywhere and could be anyone.

Few citizens care about the totality of a given ideology or political cause. Instead, most people are persuaded and activated only around those single issues where personal interests and advocacy intersect. The operational goal of those who attempt subversion is the social construction of issues, concepts, and symbols that work with this dynamic; that is, they appear compatible with mainstream predispositions but do not evoke the sensation of something taboo. Leaderless resistance is one of the most effective versions of such a strategy. The idea is, quite simply, that the *de jure* separation from extremism should allow front organizations to dissemble and use single issues to reorient national conversations to benefit a cause. One need only look to the historical example of the Nazi Party in interwar Germany to see the desired effect of a public outlook that converges with a fringe position. In short, under leaderless resistance, White nationalism could—given enough time—move from an outlying, taboo perspective to a pervasive undercurrent and, finally, to a set of values nestled in the heart of a national rebirth.

This book explores leaderlessness as a feature of efforts at the fringes of global society to subvert and transform the values, institutions, and norms of the status quo. Quite different from the explicit approach outlined by Louis Beam, as a strategy to be applied by White supremacists, however, the leaderless condition analyzed in this book is at least partially unintended, the side effect of a world transformed both by the unprecedented interconnectivity of the internet and by the shape of systems that have empowered individuals to leverage the web's potential for social coordination. Today, just over two decades into the 21st century, interactions between fringe social movements and society's mainstream are more visible and more regular than at any time in the past century. Moreover, according to various surveys and studies, the effects of countercultural communities' attempts to alter the status quo are greater than at any time since the rise of National Socialism in Germany during the interwar years of the 20th century. These effects include acts of domestic terror as well as the dangerous spread of conspiratorial ideas to immense and unexpectedly persuadable audiences. They also include the democratization of tools—many of which are digital in nature—for creating or encouraging widespread disruption. This book argues that the internet has altered the functional elements of the subversive enterprise so completely that leaderlessness is, for now, the organic shape of a multitude of fringe activities today and takes up the charge of making sense of such developments.

Introduction

On a Wednesday morning in early January 2021, a large crowd gathered in the heart of Washington, D.C., to attend a rally arranged by loyalists to President Donald J. Trump. Those who gathered did so to protest the congressional certification of votes that would guarantee the inauguration of his opponent, Joe Biden. Angered by the belief that forces of entrenched corruption had stolen the election from their preferred candidate, the assembled crowd marched down Pennsylvania Avenue toward the U.S. Capitol Building. At that point, what might initially have been viewed as yet another controversial protest in a year of unprecedented protest activity in America quickly became something else entirely. Around 1:30 p.m., the growing mob, originally held back by barricades, began to push forward. Police units were forced back, first from the fences and gates that had been put up to aid with crowd control and then up the Capitol steps and into the building itself. As the world watched events unfold live on television, the erstwhile protestors invaded congressional offices, chased staff around the building, and loitered on the Senate floor. Perhaps most shocking, images and videos of the events on Capitol Hill show some individuals, including several seen earlier in the day constructing makeshift gallows on the National Mall, wielding zip-tie handcuffs as they hunted for specific members of Congress. In the ensuing chaos, five Americans lost their lives. One of those, a Capitol police officer named Brian Sicknick, was killed under circumstances that few could have imagined possible prior to January 6: beaten to death by insurrectionists on the most hallowed grounds of the American republic.

It seems likely that the storming of the Capitol Building will be remembered by generations to come as a moment that defined an era. Although it is not yet clear whether these events will constitute some kind of societal turning point or a catalyst for further long-term discord, the attempted insurrection of January 6 has thrown into sharp contrast the form and nature of what has defined so much social strife in America and across the West in the early 21st century: the social subversion shaped and underwritten by the internet. This is a book about subversion, both as a force in the modern world and as something given a new format by the web and web technologies. As a starting point, one really need to go no further than the events of January 6 to better understand the ways in which new media and new information technologies have altered the dynamics of social movement advocacy not only in the mainstream of global society but also at its fringes. After all, is it possible that an attempted American insurrection driven by countercultural narratives and conspiracy theories would have occurred in early 2021 without the internet?

Answering this question is not as simple as it may seem. Certainly, the role of the web in driving the events of January 6 seems clear enough at first glance, even when seen alongside powerful evidence of direct provocation from Trump and other leaders on the political right.[1] Widespread planning to descend on D.C. took place in the open across a diverse set of mainstream and alternative virtual spaces in the weeks following the president's electoral loss to Biden. Across countless posts and comments, such planning included calls for transgressive disruption and subverting the process of Congressional certification. What's more, many thousands of online voices called on Americans to "drop the hammer" and embrace violent tactics, up to the point of prospectively executing key leaders of the political left. And even when coordination on platforms like Reddit, MeWe, Gab, and Parler trended toward less aggressive phraseology, the rallying cries were the same: "Stop the steal," make a "last stand" for democracy, and, echoing the conspiratorial rhetoric that could be seen on many protesters' regalia, "The Storm comes."

The results appear to speak for themselves. On the day, a strikingly small subset of slogans dominated the chants of a crowd that—broad labels like "rightwing" or "pro-Trump" aside—reflected an immense diversity of ideologies, conspiracy theories, and individual backgrounds. Thugs in combat gear sporting militia insignia joined others in North Face jackets, sports jerseys, and homemade cosplay regalia as they roamed the Capitol, loitered in staff offices, and hunted for specific members of Congress. Protestors sporting generic libertarian and anarchist symbols—like the Gadsden and Betsy Ross flags—rallied with QAnon adherents, Three Percenters, Oath Keepers, neo-Nazis, and Proud Boys around those same shared phrases that flooded spaces like TheDonald.win (formerly r/The_Donald), MeWe, Parler, and members-only Discord servers. The parallels between the online and physical outrage against America's left on January 6 were, in other words, obvious to the point of tautological.

And yet the parallel tells us only that the web played a critical role in shaping fringe advocacy, enabling coordination across diverse social movements and ensuring crowd turnout in Washington. It does not tell us *why* the internet today appears to be such a powerful enabler of counterculture and subversive intention in those areas of society, that is, society's fringes, that are most commonly defined by fragmentation, ideological infighting, and pariahism. It does not tell us, beyond the general argument that the web reduces barriers to exposure for diverse kinds of information, why fringe rhetoric, advocacy, and antagonism seem to characterize mainstream politics in the 21st century in a way that was the exception in the past rather than the rule. Neither does it explain the rising incidence of so much social antagonism and violence with clear roots in ideas that either originate or entirely exist in alternative web spaces. The remainder of *Subversion 2.0* is dedicated to answering these questions.

Leaderlessness: A Novel Evolution of Leaderless Resistance

This book's core research question is simple: What explains the meteoric rise in visibility of fringe elements and their voices in mainstream societal discourse during the first decades of the 21st century? Clearly, something has made the relationship between fringe advocacy and the sociopolitical processes of mainstream society increasingly sensitive and mutually responsive. This book argues that this something is the emergence of a condition of leaderlessness as the default format of subversive activity in the world today.

What this book calls "leaderlessness" is a phenomenon that looks, in broad terms, like Louis Beam's articulation of leaderless resistance. Both are characterized by a clear separation between the levels of subversive causes. On one level, public-facing elements of advocacy, such as political parties and celebrity commentators, reflect the agency of fringe ideologies in a format and framing that is palatable—or, at least, digestible—to the mainstream. The other level, by contrast, contains the raw substance of fringe causes in the discourse and actions of elements beyond the mainstream. However, in the 21st century, this separation between levels is generally not something engineered by the leaders and planners of a fringe cause, despite clear evidence that the two nonetheless influence one another. Rather, as this book illustrates, separation between fringe advocacy and mainstream representation in recent years is a unique outcome of the interaction between the dynamics of the subversive enterprise and the contours of the Web 2.0 era.

At its core, leaderlessness is characterized by an evolving and uneven feedback loop linking fringe spaces to mainstream elite rhetoric and popular discourse. Cult-like conditions in conspiratorial, restrictive virtual spaces simplify, standardize, and amplify extreme narratives. These narratives are then rapidly filtered into mainstream settings thanks to a series of sociotechnological conditions present in the Web 2.0 era. As a result, fringe narratives and symbols often become the lens through which social and political elites interpret information and find meaning that they then spread through public speech. Finally, this public speech is projected back to subversive spaces and communities, where it is interpreted and used to further perpetuate fringe narratives.

However, a range of factors create an imbalance in the link between the two levels wherein public figures and their rhetoric don't necessarily become a meaningful element of subversive narratives simply because they publicly react to them. Rather, elite speech is subject to a host of information controls that characterize discourse in fringe environments. The result is a filtering process that generally translates to public figures having a severely limited ability to shape the evolution and impact of subversive ideas, as well as their own meaningfulness to fringe narratives. This is as true for persons sympathetic to extreme ideologies as for those set against them. It is common for elites who are adopted as symbols for fringe advocacy to see their speech associated with some amount of notoriety or attention, only to find their influence waning or changing without a corresponding change in behavior. In reality, it is the evolving conditions in subversive community spaces that so often dictate when public figures and their speech become more or less meaningful to a circulating set of narratives. Most worrying, those same processes at the fringe also occasionally construct the conditions for something much worse: extreme behavior triggered by the words of a public figure that have been given meaning by underlying subversive narratives.

The Interaction of Subversion and Web 2.0

The feedback loop at the heart of this book entails the interaction of two features of fringe-mainstream interaction in the 21st century: (1) the unique fashion in which social forces interested in subversion utilize information technologies and (2) the contours of internet socialization over the past two decades. For the first feature, a clear starting point is the immense body of research that illustrates how new information technologies and media formats expand opportunities for advocacy and contestation as much for nonstate actors as for nation-states. A key position held by many studies is that while the internet has opened new space for activism and antagonism for nonstate actors broadly, its utility is generally as much a function of sociopolitical position and perspective as of the technology itself. With terrorists, for instance, the internet has been far more useful for recruitment, funding, and radicalization than for core terroristic activities. This is quite simply because coercion is difficult using purely digital means. After all, cyberattacks don't directly kill, and nonviolent disruption rarely delivers the spectacle that terrorists desire. For those aiming to bring attention to scandal and corruption without violence, hacking is much more appealing (leading to hacktivism).

With subversive actors and movements, being situated at society's fringes—on the outside looking in, so to speak—creates the imperative to generate and exercise influence without being seen to do so. This translates into a tendency to use new information and communication technologies (ICT) to manipulate information environments and generate social influence that can be leveraged toward persuasive outcomes without direct engagement. In retrospect, the long history of modern information technology usage by fringe elements isn't predominantly characterized by a focus on conventional activism or support for violence, as many might think. Rather, it is dominated by an emphasis on efforts to entice new followers and to craft narratives and conditions compatible with mainstream consumption.

The emergence of Web 2.0 around the turn of the 21st century flips the directionality of the relationship between the fringe and the mainstream. Subversive social movements traditionally follow the mainstream in attempting to insinuate a peripheral idea or ideology, relying on emergent trends and media conditions to craft persuasive messaging. The linearity of that relationship has changed in the Web 2.0 era. Starting in the late 1990s, a series of commercial takeovers and market developments shifted the sociotechnological basis of internet usage from one centered on large-scale user consumption of static information (i.e., Web 1.0) to one defined by user-created content, dynamic media, and mass audience participation (i.e., Web 2.0). At this point, all aspects of the information on the internet—its creation, alteration, annotation, framing, and contextualization—rapidly began to flow both ways between platform owners and users, rather than just from the former to the latter. Two decades on, fringe narratives possess unprecedented potency and virulence vis-à-vis those areas of the global information environment where mainstream internet users engage. As this book explains, this situation is driven by a range of factors, including the ubiquity of user-side media controls and moderator capabilities, visibility algorithms that favor extreme information, profit-oriented platform management decision-making, and the general porousness of conventional social media spaces such as Facebook and X (formerly Twitter).

Today fringe narratives are linked to public voices, mainstream news organizations, and popular social web communities via a series of interacting media ecosystems and their underlying architectures, both algorithmic and human. Fringe communities, which are typically restrictive and prone to information manipulation, simplify extreme talking points and prepare them for filtration into mainstream spaces along a number of lines. Social and political elites are, resultantly, forced to be much more sensitive to fringe narratives than in eras past. Indeed, the dispersed nature of fringe infiltration of mainstream societal discourse prevents public voices from ignoring extreme narratives even where they are explicit. Because they are found everywhere, engagement is necessary. This is in stark contrast to eras past, when occasionally encountering a fringe perspective simply incentivized elites to dissemble and dismiss.

At the same time, fringe spaces and their denizens are selectively sensitive to the rhetoric of these elites. Elite rhetoric is often meaningful for those occupying fringe spaces, but only insofar as such speech resonates with the meaning-making that occurs in those spaces. Where public figures take on meaning in fringe narratives, their words and actions become far more likely to inspire extreme acts, from hate speech and targeted slander to violence. Herein lies a singularly important distinction between the "leaderlessness" of fringe advocacy in the 21st century and leaderless subversion practices of the past. The capacity of elites—even prominent figures associated with fringe narratives, such as Donald Trump or France's Marine Le Pen—to shape subversive activities and outcomes is constrained by the very sociotechnological architecture that makes extreme persons and communities responsive to elite rhetoric. Likewise, the potency of fringe narratives as a meaning-making precursor to mainstream social and political discourse is not predetermined by the existence of the internet, but rather is similarly sensitive to the commercial, social, and technological realities of web usage.

Figure I.1 summarizes the relationship between fringe advocacy and the information environment of democratic states in simple terms. In the

INTRODUCTION 7

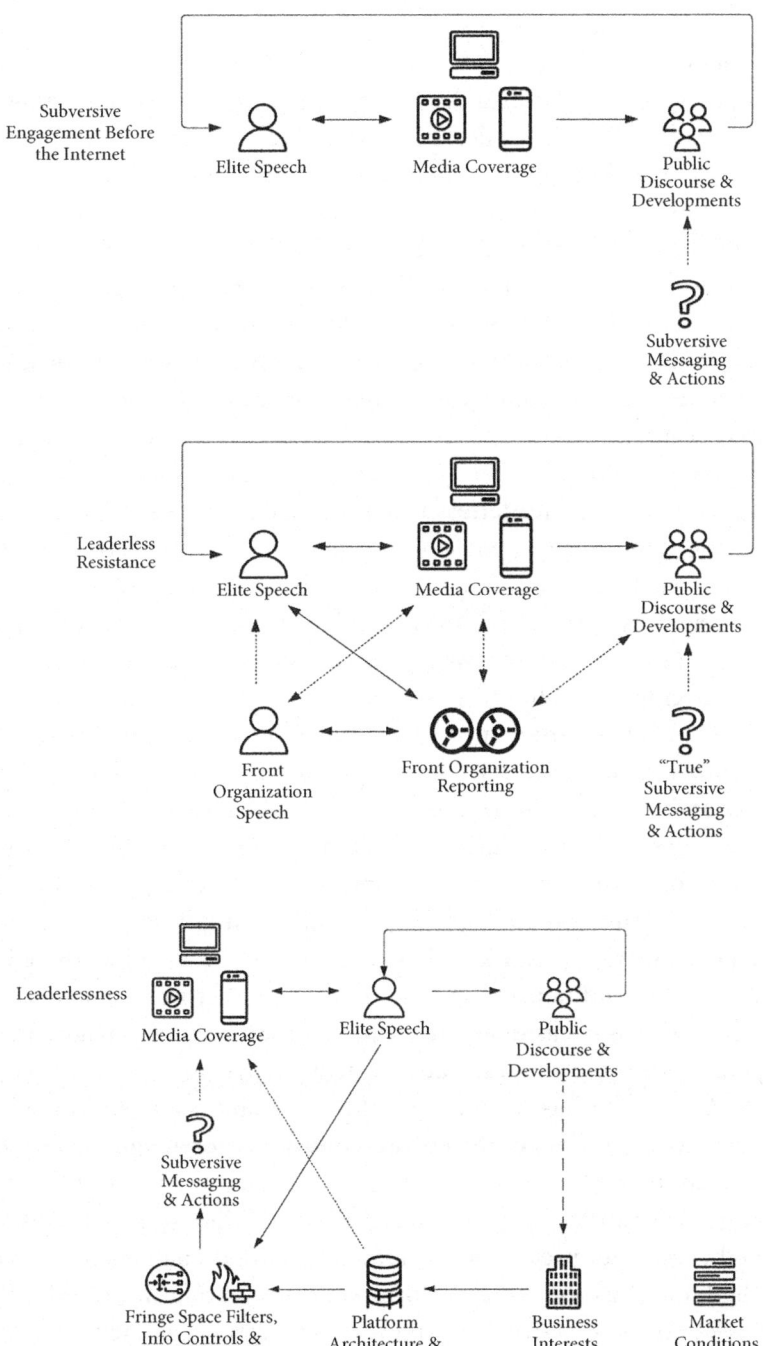

Figure I.1 Fringe advocacy and the information environment.

first scenario, democratic discourse is a function of three elements: (1) elite rhetoric that drives media coverage, (2) media coverage that shapes both elite speech and public discourse, and (3) public discourse that also influences elite speech. Under this base scenario of subversion attempted before the era of the internet, subversive movements are constrained in their capability to directly shape elite speech or media coverage and so must take steps (rhetoric, advocacy, disruption, etc.) to enter the information environment as an element of public conversation. Where a subversive cause adheres to the principles of leaderless resistance, this effort to enter and shape the information environment is split between those front organizations and persons who attempt to ingratiate themselves with the status quo and the raw substance of the fringe cause (i.e., militants, general sympathizers, etc.).

The condition of leaderlessness splits subversive efforts in a similar fashion, but not generally by design. Instead, subversive narratives emerge from fringe spaces where information is filtered, shaped, and manipulated by a series of controls. Algorithms and social interaction connects these narratives with mainstream web spaces, influencing media coverage and elite response. At this stage, fragments and themes of fringe narratives are regular elements of the mainstream information environment and public discourse. Elite speech, influenced by media dynamics and public discourse, is then reflected back in fringe spaces and communities as the most critical representation of how the mainstream responds to subversive ideas. That representation is warped, however, by the same information controls that originally simplified and amplified extreme content. The result is that elites who associate with fringe ideas often find their influence fragile in hard-to-predict ways. Furthermore, their influence is occasionally more potent than intended, triggering extreme acts by those indoctrinated in fringe environments. In this way, the feedback loop has not only heightened public exposure to subversive narratives but also created the conditions for heightened acts of extremism linked to them. Unfortunately, as later chapters of this book explain, such extremism is not necessarily sufficient to prompt changes to the business and technology architectures that enable subversion in the digital age, as the concerns of private actors that underwrite these processes are as sensitive to business considerations as they are to civic outcry.

Thinking More Clearly about Information Technology, Subversion, and Society's "Fringes"

The condition described here—leaderlessness underwritten by a unique combination of subversive agency and sociotechnological circumstances—offers a compelling explanation for why fringe elements and their voices have become increasingly and unprecedentedly more visible in mainstream discourse in the first decades of the 21st century. Simply put, subversive narratives today exist as part of a feedback loop with mainstream discourse in which fringe information controls matter more in shaping extreme public speech than do the designs of public figures. This contrasts with the subversive advocacy of eras past, which was forced to take points from public speech to create new opportunities for the rise of societal extremism.

The chapters of this book tell the story of this condition's emergence and its features. They do so by combining in-depth case investigations, interview-aided reporting, and large-N data analyses to build the case that leaderlessness has contributed greatly to the rise of global populism and the growing harshness of democratic politics in recent years. More directly, this book makes a strong case that the framework of leaderlessness allows for the prediction of when and how extreme rhetoric translates to extremist activity, from hateful digital expressions to disruptive activism and political violence.

Information Technologies at the Fringe. The next chapters of this book build the foundation for effectively characterizing and analyzing content and advocacy that aim to radically change society. However, the context for the study contained in this book is web technologies and changes to the global information environment that have occurred since the late 20th century. In that, there is a clear starting point for thinking about how and why nonstate actors and social movements are today more visible in their influence on civil society.

Chapters 1 and 2 establish the underlying premise of the book: that the ongoing information revolution, based around the internet, has changed the landscape and tools of operation for nonstate actors operating at societal fringes in much the same way it has for those in the mainstream. Organizations and movements that seek to dramatically alter the shape of society are faced with the same changes to the global information environment, the same new opportunities for activism, and the same emergent toolkits for contestation as are political parties, grassroots lobbying campaigns, and concerned citizens.² Such groups and communities must not only attempt to harness new abilities to mobilize and affect change; they must also strategize with the dynamics of a digitally augmented public sphere in mind.

In direct contrast with what is most often the norm among participatory political forces in society's mainstream, however, movements at the fringe must often move beyond acts of digital activism to circumvent user service policies and the rule of law, to violate moral norms, and to disrupt the status quo. At the same time, in contrast with the actions of hacktivists or cyberterrorists, such transgressions are rarely undertaken for explicitly coercive purposes. In other words, the rise of the internet has meant a dramatically different process of strategic evolution and tactical reimagining for those at the fringes of global society than has been seen with conventional activists, protest movements, and other cyber dissidents. In this way, technology does not determine the character of nonstate advocacy—or the rise of the leaderlessness phenomenon—but rather is an intervening variable.

Subversion and the "Fringes" of Global Society. So far, this book has used the term "fringe" liberally. But what does it mean to say that a social movement or organization is part of society's "fringe"? And why—beyond thinking more clearly about the events of January 6 in isolation—is understanding of how those at the "fringes" of global society use information technology particularly significant? This book understands fringe groups and social movements in the context of *subversion*. Though the term often conjures images of sedition and societal sabotage, subversion is simply a type of strategy for addressing prevailing power structures and relationships. In order to change society, most sociopolitical actors either directly contest the status quo or "flee" from it. Contestation involves either evolutionary or revolutionary acts taken to directly change the status quo, such as voting or attempting to overthrow a government, whereas "fleeing" power involves, via actions like secession or emigration, seeking out alternative social and political spaces where different logics of power might be considered.

By contrast, subversion is fundamentally a strategy of what some scholars have labeled "fleeing in place."³ It is an effort to displace prevailing norms and power structures without directly challenging them, that is, to "escape" power by seeking its dissolution. Subversive actors are those who fundamentally seek to *dis*empower the status quo, most often by detaching the loyalties of a population from one set of symbols and institutions so that they might be transferred to something else. Therein lies the key difference between strategies of subversion and coercion aimed at the imposition of costs on an adversary; whereas coercion is concerned with dynamics of relational power, subversion targets power that emerges from perceptions of legitimacy.

In essence, subversion is an approach to moving ideas, symbols, and their agents from societal fringes into the mainstream. It is not defined by specific ideas beyond the reality that subversive causes invariably run counter to society's prevailing norms and perspectives. In this way, this book is not exclusively about the far right in global society in the 21st century. Nor is it solely about fundamentalist Islam, militant environmentalism, or a host of other viewpoints that have motivated nonstate organizations and social movements to engage society's mainstream elements through conflict. The selection criteria for study is simply an emphasis on subversion as the primary method of approach to contesting the status quo and changing society.

In practice, the strategy of subversion emphasizes the erosion of what makes the status quo the status quo and, inevitably, due to the intrinsic "otherness" of fringe causes, entails attempts to socially construct narratives, symbols, concepts, and figureheads that court popular interest without incurring outrage. Indeed, it is this core feature of the subversive enterprise more than any other that most clearly sheds light on how many at the fringes of global society have turned to new web technologies. Although terrorist or insurgent organizations may also attempt to craft persuasive messaging or sell a particular vision of society, their additional focus on coercive contestation, that is, on the use of force to compel change in society, sets them apart from those who seek to subvert without violence, except as a desirable side effect, accident, last recourse, or final step. Those actors are society's fifth columns—not the literal saboteurs that Emilio Mola Vidal famously argued would open the gates of Madrid for his armies from within, but the vanguard of sociopolitical transformation that attempts to create through the construction of new shared understandings of issues the conditions necessary for a sea change.[4]

Why This Book Matters

The diverse crowd of individuals who stormed the Capitol Building on January 6, 2021—some of America's "fringe" elements—are subversive actors, as are countless other communities and organizations around the world. Studying the broader landscape of subversion in the age of the internet is obviously significant because it sheds light on why events in Washington unfolded as they did.

Predicting Fringe Antagonism. As important, however, better knowledge about the subversive enterprise and how it works in the age of the internet will allow researchers and policymakers to more clearly see where else we might expect similar acts of fringe antagonism to occur in the future. The years immediately preceding the writing of this book have sadly been filled with instances of violent extremism and nonviolent antagonism of unprecedented scope. In North America, fringe extremists have plotted to kidnap elected officials, attack religious facilities, and target individuals symbolic of a particular grievance or fringe belief. In Europe, law enforcement has interceded on numerous occasions to stop armed plots against political targets and catch individuals intending harm to women, minorities, and celebrities. In many cases, there are clear links to engagement in online spaces, fringe narratives found in those spaces, and other persons with extensive involvement in extreme communities. As Chapter 1 discusses, research has shown that these links exist even when individuals involved in violent extremism were initially radicalized offline. The framework advanced in this book explains the power of such narratives even for those not often found online. Moreover, it offers a clear idea of why fringe meaning-making sometimes—but not always—produces extreme disruption or violence; simply, these acts are often triggered by elite speech given power and meaning in fringe spaces.

This book is also important because it explores the concept of subversion in depth. Subversion is an understudied concept in the social sciences, a focus on it coming in and out of vogue over the past seventy or so years. Subversion is not simply the attempt to dissemble or use clandestine methods to gain influence, as is often portrayed. It is a unique strategy to contest the power of the status quo and has distinct analytic utility for scholars and practitioners alike.

An Intersectional Theory of Fringe Effects. One of the most prominent perspectives on foreign policymaking and geopolitics in the international relations field, neoclassical realism, holds that comprehending the actions of nation-states means understanding the interaction of cognitive (e.g., decision-makers' perception), domestic (e.g., the structure of political institutions), and systematic (e.g., the balance of power) variables. This stands opposite theories that conventionally emphasize one or another. The theory of leaderlessness proposed in this book takes a similar approach to understanding the behaviors and outcomes of subversion in the digital age. Simply, the format of most domestic subversive activity in the world today specifically emerges from the *interaction* of preferences common to fringe actors and the architecture, both technical and socioeconomic, of the Web 2.0 era.

This interactive character sets the theory of *Subversion 2.0* apart from other relevant scholarship on fringe activities, cognition, and strategy, albeit in a highly complementary fashion. The chapters to come describe many relevant literatures in an effort to build a foundation for answering the book's core research question and contextualize the subversive enterprise over the past several decades of the digital age. While the arguments presented here draw extensively from the findings of bodies of work across communications, extremism studies, and social movement studies, I find two common shortcomings. First, some work that narrowly focuses on fringe or extreme behavior and the internet suffers from a level of analysis limitation where individuals or specific social processes are emphasized at the expense of technical considerations. Second, work that resolves this shortcoming, such as that in the social movements field of study, often offers broad prescriptions that lack contextualization around uncommon circumstances (in this case, that of subversive advocacy). This book attempts to find a middle ground between these challenges and offer a theoretical view of societal fringe behavior that, akin to much work on actor networks, emphasizes the explanatory power of interactions between technosocial structures and sociotechnical preferences.

New Evidence. Finally, this book matters because of the way it draws a rich, evidence-driven picture of how subversion prompts particular uses of information technologies. In narrow terms, no previous study has systematically gathered and employed data on how nonviolent subversive actors and movements have used the web for activism and antagonism. Later chapters of this book provide a first-of-its-kind account of the hacking, disinformation, and activist activities of an incredibly diverse range of fringe actors spread across the globe. This exploration should serve as a first step for new study of the digital activities of such actors, who are often overlooked in favor of an analytic focus on terrorists, hacktivists, or violent extremists.

More generally, the tendency toward information manipulation and social control in fringe spaces drives a mode of problematic behavior that directly clashes with the architecture and underlying business designs of many modern social information systems. Even in spite of immense turmoil and punctuated violence brought about by web platforms and those who use them to find extreme voices, Western societies continue to have trouble exerting influence on private actors to change their systems with democratic security in mind. Major companies like Reddit, Meta, X (Twitter), and Google have taken many steps to minimize opportunities for misinformation and malicious use on their platforms. However, information search and presentation algorithms continue to favor extreme speech to drive user engagement. And fringe narratives, cultivated on alternative platforms and regurgitated by elites, still readily end up in discourse hosted on these conventional sites. This book casts the challenge of regulating technology providers in a new light and acts as a basis for assessing the viability of certain common antifringe tactics—such as banning extreme accounts from mainstream platforms—in the long term.

Plan of the Book: Tracing the Experience of Subversion Online

The book is set up to move readers from general principles, assumptions, and examples to theory based in both statistical and narrative evidence. Chapter 1 situates our study of subversive social movements and actors in the immense literature on the internet, activism, and advocacy. Simply, what arguments exist that link the internet to fringe actors in society? I outline common folk theories that link the two and then discuss the foundations of such ideas in scholarship on social movements and digital-age extremism.

Chapter 2 sets the scope of the book's study by introducing subversion as a framework necessary for thinking about societal fringe actors in generalizable terms, something that is imperative if a generalizable answer to the research question is to be clearly specified. The chapter sets about defining subversion as a distinct conceptual phenomenon that is often cited but remarkably understudied by scholars in political science, international relations, and communications studies. The term "subversion" often conveys a particular, derogatory meaning. However, subversion is simply one form of challenging power via the manipulation of its constituting bases. Subversive organizations and social movements differ from pedestrian political advocacy actors in that they aim for radical changes in prevailing sentiment and popular thought regarding the legitimacy of the status quo. In practice, they attempt to catalyze such changes by detaching the loyalties of mainstream society from status quo symbols and institutions and transferring them to something else. Such groups and movements are, by definition, at the fringe of mainstream society, contextually defined. As such, they are primed toward strategies of social construction that deceptively represent and advance their perspectives without inspiring broad-scope outrage, backlash, or the sensation of taboo.

Chapter 2 then introduces the book's empirical strategy. The challenge in empirically answering the book's core research question—What explains the rising visibility of fringe narratives and actions in mainstream society?—requires considering not only possible existing answers via a literature review but also clear parameters for understanding degrees of subversive interaction with society. The conceptual framework of subversion more fully sets the parameters of what kinds of nonstate elements constitute the fringes of global society than is commonly found in other work and opens the doorway to clear empirical examination of a diversity of such actors. As such, this book chooses to focus on variations in how subversives use ICT for different tasks, such as conventional activism, information manipulation, and disruption, as a means for exploring the rising interaction of fringe and mainstream.

Tracing Subversion amid Evolving Web Developments. The next three chapters are dedicated to elaborating on the global landscape of social subversion over the past several decades and the role of information technologies in changing the character of the subversive enterprise. Over the past several decades, an incredibly diverse universe of nonstate groups and social movements—from far-right groups and conspiracy theory communities across the West to radical conservationist outfits and cultist movements like Eastern Lightning in China—have moved to the web in great numbers. Beyond simply using ICT for organization and outreach, many of these actors antagonize via digital means with some frequency. From vandalizing websites to stealing membership information on opposing social movements, subversive antagonism in the digital age is a diverse phenomenon. Moreover, many such movements are expanded by and shaped in the crucible of online spaces that take advantage of algorithmic tools to tailor membership experiences, curtail discourse, and drive narrative construction. Taken together, these developments form the basis of a subversive enterprise that, in practice, looks dramatically different today than in eras past.

Case studies in Chapters 3 through 5 build nuance and context for later statistical explorations of the shape of digital-age subversion via in-depth, interview-aided explorations of the experiences of subversive social movements in the context of changing technology. Specifically, the cases presented in these chapters examine the ways in which fringe social movements and organizations interact with societal issues, leadership, and public imagery across a range of evolving internet-enabled settings, in particular, what I term the shift from Fringe 1.0 to Fringe 2.0, from the early 1990s to the present day. In doing so, the design of these case analyses reflects the need to consider shifting sociotechnical opportunities and context vis-à-vis the internet, an imperative that lends itself less to conventional case study selection and more to an examination of web usage over time. To this point, subversive actors have clearly changed how they use the internet in terms of both the types of tools utilized and the frequency with which web technologies are used to antagonize, reflecting changing geopolitical (i.e., trends in globalization and democratization) and sociotechnical (i.e., new hardware, software, and services undergirding global internet usage) conditions. Figure I.2, built from data presented in Chapter 6, illustrates such patterns in showing how the antagonistic use of the internet by society's fringe elements has ebbed and flowed with changes in global conditions.

Through case examinations, I illustrate how commonplace it has been for subversive elements within global society to utilize web technologies to construct manipulative information conditions. More important, I demonstrate

Figure I.2 Digital antagonism by fringe elements around the world by decade.

the tendency toward such behavior and the draw for fringe elements toward the social control features of different web technologies. Chapter 3 examines early efforts by several networks disillusioned with elements of modern global society to craft tools and coordination methods from nascent web technologies. Here, the analysis offers an illustrative context by focusing on the experiences of White supremacists in the days of Web 1.0, of individuals responsible for the formation of Electronic Disturbance Theater and the Strano Network, and of RedHack, an unusual left-libertarian Turkish collective whose operations have consistently centered on a grievance of mainstream illegitimacy. In these cases, the lessons of early web usage for subversion are evident, not least the recognition by key figures that activation of dispersed populations required leaning into the tools for automation, information manipulation, and social coordination more so than those tied directly to disruption.

In Chapter 4, *Subversion 2.0* shifts to the curious case of Falun Gong. The chapter explores the early experience of protest and coordination-in-exile among elements of the extensive community of Falun Gong practitioners. This well-known spiritual movement-cum-organization provides a fascinating test of the notion that subversive strategies themselves push certain fringe social movements toward information manipulation practices, as early efforts to create political "cracking" tools like Freegate stands in stark contrast to later efforts to transform a major publication of the cause in the West, the *Epoch Times*, toward a misinformation and manipulation operation not dissimilar to those seen in the political warfare efforts of Russia, Iran, and other state actors since 2014. These efforts are extensive, regularly select figureheads around which to construct positive narratives, and have even been expanded to communities on Discord and applications like SafeChat that attempt to co-opt alternative fringe communities, such as pro-Trump MAGA (Make America Great Again) and militia-oriented groups.

Chapter 5 picks up where the case of Falun Gong ends by focusing broadly on what might be thought of as "Fringe 2.0" or the shape of the fringe given the social turn in web technologies of the 2000s and 2010s. Here, the focus is the broad constellation of far-right and associated conspiracy theory communities operating in diverse virtual settings across the West. The chapter recounts the mobilization and activation of fringe antagonism across several subreddits with global membership, including two spaces focused on medical skepticism and the incel ideology. Here, I develop and illustrate the idea of reflexive evolution at the fringes, building from the notion that alternative spaces influence mainstream platforms to suggest that this process also acts as a focusing lens for those fringe spaces. Seeing the influence of broad fringe themes in the mainstream prompts subversive communities and groups to anchor their rhetoric on specific issues and voices in an effort to activate the population they have influence over.

A Note on Case Selection and Methods. The rationale for focusing on the causes, ideologies, and actors discussed through Chapter 5 is discussed in full in Chapter 2. Off the bat, however, it is important to note that these particular fringe elements of global society are selected for three distinct reasons. First, this book focuses on elements whose primary focus is subversive advocacy and transformation rather than the deployment of coercive methods for changing society. It is for this reason that some traditional focal cases of extremism—such as that of global Al Qaeda or the Islamic State—are not covered in depth, though the analysis here is certainly relevant for thinking about the dispersed manifestations thereof. Second, a diverse set of ideologies is considered to illustrate how operational lessons and behaviors among subversives that use the internet have emerged in common over time, implying that the common focus on subversion is more explanatorily significant than understanding the technology or the specifics of a cause. And finally, case selection includes elements that have turned to embrace subversion as a strategy over time, particularly Falun Gong. This methodological choice to explore variation in subversive character as well as changes in external sociotechnical conditions further strengthens the book's key underlying assertion. Simply put, it is the trappings of subversion as a strategic focus that prompts certain behavioral tendencies and has interacted in unique fashion with evolving web technologies to create today's ubiquitous condition of leaderlessness.

Marshaling Data to Investigate Fringe Digital Antagonism. Moving from case study analysis to large-N testing, Chapter 6 returns to the book's theoretical framework in relating digital antagonism to the rhetoric of figureheads linked to different fringe social movements. It then outlines a unique data collection effort and sets out to describe the landscape of antagonistic digital actions at society's fringes. *Subversion 2.0* specifically looks to an expanded version of an existing data set, the Global Digital Activism Data Set (GDADS), as a basis for testing hypotheses that link the subversive campaigns of fringe social movements to antagonistic digital acts. The GDADS has been published in two tranches and contains almost 1,800 entries (1,180 in the initial tranche, 426 in the second, and more than 200 additional entries in a supplementary data set) describing such campaigns.[5] The data set covers digital activism in more than 150 countries and spans three decades, from 1982 to 2012. In addition to qualitative information on digital activist campaigns and basic descriptive measurements of different actions involved in the activist effort (website usage, blog usage, chat/IM coordination, email coordination, e-petition used, etc.), the GDADS includes detailed data on the intended purposes of different campaign actions and variables on environmental conditions, such as regime type and the rule of law. All data is documented and freely available, all sources are cataloged, and the project behind GDADS provides summary case information for every digital activist campaign covered. I add data to the original GDADS effort, taking advantage of the well-documented coding procedures of the project, in the form of almost 1,700 additional digital activist episodes and organizations through 2019.

The data set used in this book builds from this data resource. I identify over 500 subversive social movements and organizations in the expanded digital activism archive engaged in digital activist efforts, from blogging and email campaigns to e-petitions and citizen journalism, before enriching the set with data on antagonistic digital actions. The coding of this data covers incidents across the range of tasks subversive organizations undertake to mobilize, to name, shame and disrupt threats to progress in the form of societal opponents, and to enhance their information environment. Specifically, I code more than 20 types of disruptive and circumventive web activities, including, among others, the simple use of websites for illegal and unconstitutional purposes (such as inciting protest against state laws), several categories of website-blocking actions, scripting attacks, DDoS attacks, malware employments, unauthorized data collection actions, email spear phishing, website defacement, and unauthorized hardware installations. The result is a data set of episodes that allows for the first real empirical exploration of subversive group employment of information technologies. Matched with a range of independent variable information, both original and drawn from locations such as Polity IV and World Bank indices, this data set allows both broad-scope descriptive and statistical analysis.

Chapter 7 engages in statistical testing designed to validate the theoretical framework presented in Chapter 6. It does so inductively, using the new data set to assess hypotheses related to diverse potential explanations for subversive community activities. Evidence presented in Chapter 7 provides robust support for the idea that proxies and peripheral members of a movement, lacking direct command oversight, in essence, decide whether or not to antagonize based on their reading of prevailing group objectives and chosen tactics. Where figures significant to fringe movements make nonparticipatory statements, they demonstrably act to incentivize civil disobedience and implicitly condone greater antagonism by members. Where grievances or criticisms are muted—or where emphasis is placed on change through participatory methods—incentives for antagonism are reduced. Thus, it follows that the use of the web to harass, circumvent, and manipulate closely ebbs and emerges in response to the expression of group objectives.

Finally, Chapter 8 returns to the leaderlessness phenomenon and the motivating case of the January 6 insurrection. It examines the case and context of the QAnon conspiracy theory, the broader network of far-right information sources in the months surrounding the 2020 presidential election, and the critical question of the role of public figures. In short, was the rhetoric of figures like Donald Trump and Rudy Giuliani consistently provocative of fringe antagonism, or was the effect of rhetoric shaped by the architecture of digital discourse in fringe spaces? And what has been their role in the months since, as deplatforming and other backlash has increasingly forced the fringe back to society's fringes?

Chapter 8 concludes the book by tracing the implications of this study's argument for democratic functionality and national security. Much as the examination of subversion in the age of the internet is necessarily complex, answering this question implies tackling many complex and crosscutting issues. The final sections of the chapter take up these issues.

It is worth ending this introductory chapter by noting that *Subversion 2.0* suggests that some optimism about the influence of fringe ideologies and personas may be warranted. After all, the description in this book of technology's impact fundamentally rejects the neutrality of the medium itself. The ability to build restrictive spaces around cult-like characteristics, for instance, is substantially a function of two very human processes, namely the design decisions undergirding so many digital platforms and the management strategies employed by technology firms, private businesses, and hosting services. This suggests that some optimism about the prospects of democracy in the digital age is well-founded. Although subversion is a force on the rise in world politics in the 21st century, it is far from the case that the events of January 6 are a bellwether of things to come. Given responsible courtship of new technological standards and public-private partnerships rooted in communally agreed priorities for compassionate civil discourse, democracies might find themselves in possession of the tools to limit the threat posed by new forms of leaderless fringe advocacy and antagonism to global society's processes of political participation.

1
Information Technologies at the Fringe

The idea that leaderlessness is, for the time being, the organic shape of a multitude of fringe activities in the world emerges from two efforts: a novel conceptual exploration of subversion and an in-depth multimethod empirical analysis of how subversive actors use information technologies, both of which are arrayed in the chapters to come. The theory proposed in this book goes beyond existing arguments about how the internet has impacted civil society and extreme actors due to its tight conceptual focus on subversion and emphasis on interacting sociotechnical factors.

Nevertheless, the leaderlessness argument is based on a large body of existing scholarship that offers a robust foundation for addressing the increased interaction between fringe and mainstream. In particular, an immense volume of work in communications studies, the science, technology, and society field, information systems, and political science addresses the interplay of web technologies and sociopolitical contestation. The goal of this chapter is to assess these literatures and in doing so build the case that effectively answering the book's core research question means constructing a view of fringe activities both informed by the framework of subversion and empirically centered on explaining variation in how subversive actors use information technologies.

As such, this chapter undertakes two tasks. First, it validates the book's premise that there has been an increasing interaction between the fringe and mainstream strata of society in recent years. This effort is undertaken briefly here and expanded upon in subsequent chapters; for example, the case studies in Chapters 3 through 5 engage many of the literatures mentioned above that will not be examined here. The book is structured this way so as to initially lay the foundations for studying digital-age fringe advocacy here and thereafter provide a rich exploration of subversive actors and conditions in the age of the internet so that large-scale testing aimed at the implications of the leaderlessness hypothesis can proceed in the book's later chapters.

The second task this chapter undertakes is to situate the book's study of fringe social movements and actors in the immense literature on the internet, activism, and extremism. It highlights arguments relevant to the research question and notes where the leaderlessness theory complements existing work. There is a clear need, I argue, to think about *fringe* actors more systematically and with greater conceptual clarity than is typical in work on social movements and digital-age extremism. From the outset, such scholarship has formed the basis for broadly understanding the interplay between social forces and web technologies in this research project. But work on social movements and the internet rarely offers analysis *only* on actors focused on subversive objectives, instead offering possible answers as to why radicalization around fringe perspectives might be more likely in the digital age *in the aggregate*. This necessitates a secondary conceptual focus on subversion to apply the lessons of existing scholarship. Chapter 2 provides this lens. Likewise, scholarship on extremism that considers fringe interaction with the mainstream describes extreme utilization of web technologies around bottom-up logics of radicalization. However, the focus of so much extremism scholarship tends to be narrowly set on its most visible and worrisome aspects, such as acts of violence, the *process* of radicalization of individuals toward violence, and the general utility of ICT for organizing extreme behavior. Given that this book is interested not just in explaining political violence but in a broader convergence of the fringe and mainstream society, we also require an empirical strategy that does not solely emphasize violence and its correlates. This chapter thus lays the foundation for introducing just such a strategy in Chapter 2, which also describes my approach to case selection and data gathering in later chapters.

Taken together, the relevant findings and shortcomings of existing scholarship assessed in this chapter amount to the need for a sociotechnical theory of fringe activities in the digital age. In line with many of the assumptions of actor-network theory,[1] the leaderlessness argument presented in *Subversion 2.0* constitutes exactly such a perspective.

Social Movements, the Internet, and Technological Neutrality

Exactly how the proliferation of web technologies around the globe has brought fringe advocacy into closer contact with mainstream sociopolitical discourse in recent years is far from clear. That said, there exist numerous arguments about the relationship between the internet, social advocacy, and extremism that serve as a good starting point for this book's investigation. Such arguments can be found in both popular and scholarly settings. Perhaps not surprisingly, popular discourse tends to oversimplify and generally struggles to find explanations for linking fringe activity to mainstream developments that aren't mechanically vague. For instance, media coverage of events as divergent as the January 6 Capitol attack, the 2018 attack on the Tree of Life synagogue in Pittsburgh, and cases of ISIS brides often points to the internet as a relatively unidimensional instrument for radicalization. When journalists attempt to report on how algorithms aid radicalization, the tactic favored is often a deep dive on a single platform, service, or web space that highlights to the general population the narrow conditions that seem to help explain one act or incident. At other times, developments involving highly visible entities like Al Qaeda, the Three Percenters, Blood & Honour, or the Atomwaffen Division often evoke descriptions of how digital environments are intentionally operationalized to activate radicalized persons.

This kind of situational analysis is understandable, but it often leads to unsatisfying popular arguments for what explains the increased exposure of mainstream societal discourse to fringe influences. For example, some might argue that the internet has simply made it more likely that individuals will find and be attracted to fringe ideas. Others might say that the internet has made it easier for political leaders to map fringe environments and command them for parochial gain. Yet others may argue that fringe ideas just appear more prevalent in modern democratic discourse because the internet makes minor incidents and outlandish rhetoric more visible. These arguments are commonplace in high-level punditry and even some expert analyses.

Importantly, there *are* valid points to be made in support of these kinds of arguments. Many such points emerge from social science research, particularly psychological studies, that tie advances in information technologies to changes in how humans perceive society and form preferences. However, as explanations for the prevalence of a new fringe presence in society's mainstream, arguments along these lines are limiting. Many reduce the interplay between internet and society to singular effects. Some fixate on the availability of new tools for information search, advocacy, and disruption as the primary motivator of novel behavior. Others build on this kind of technological determinism and make the all-too-common assumption that elites directly drive extreme fringe behavior because of their conventional power to set public agendas. In such a telling, the internet simply intervenes to extend a conventional sociopolitical dynamic.

Folk theories like these often play off of just one of the various complexities that underwrite this book's core research question about the interaction of fringe and mainstream discourse in the 21st century. They also selectively reference existing explanations for how the internet has impacted social movements and nonstate advocacy put forth in scientific research. Such explanations are in no way impotent for answering this question. In fact, the theory of leaderlessness proposed here is highly complementary to such explanations. But just as folk theories often reflect some piece of new data or inference while ignoring the broader body of knowledge, so too does this book's narrow focus on fringe activities risk misspecification if not effectively contextualized around what existing scholarship tells us. As such, the following sections clarify the stance that *Subversion 2.0* assumes toward the role of web technologies in evolving social advocacy among countercultural and subversive communities worldwide.

The Rising Interaction of the Fringe and the Rest

In the broadest sense, the idea that fringe effects are more distinctly felt in mainstream sociopolitical discourse and politics is evident in polling data gathered over the past two decades. According to surveys taken by Pew,[2] CNN, and Forbes, the number of Americans claiming to be concerned about radical, adversarial political interests has nearly quadrupled since 2006. At the same time, Gallup polling since 2019 shows that the number of respondents who would allow their actions to be driven by some element of conspiracy theory has skyrocketed, despite the limited number of respondents who could identify prominent fringe ideologies by name.[3] In 2020, for instance, 33% of North Americans stated they would not receive a vaccine for COVID-19 even if approved by the government. Of greater concern, a whopping 44% of U.S. Republicans agreed that Bill Gates was attempting to use the vaccine rollout to implant microchips in recipients to track their movements. Moreover, nearly 40% of Republicans (with nearly 30% of Americans overall concurring) stated *after* the January 6 insurrectionist attempt that political violence might be needed to correct politicians' shortcomings, and another 53% of self-identifying conservatives believed that Joe Biden, two months after his inauguration, was not the president of the United States.[4] Much psychology research has shown how some predispositions or mental capacities, given sufficient exposure to nonconformist viewpoints, are conducive to belief in conspiracy and sensational rhetoric. Taken together, these developments suggest a rising tide of fringe interactions with the public information environment in Western democracies. Alongside these developments, several studies have shown that the coverage of fringe, countercultural discourse by mainstream media organizations has increased significantly since 2000. Work in the computational social sciences has demonstrated how mainstream social media platforms like X (Twitter) and Facebook are increasingly influenced by alternative communities that produce content—including on counterhegemonic topics as diverse as pro-Christian secessionism, racial supremacy, and conspiracies to dominate society through control of the medical and technology fields—and funnel it toward easier-to-access digital spaces.[5]

The Transformation of Social Movements in the Age of the Internet

How has the internet changed the character of social movements over recent decades? Writers like Denning, Garrett, Earl, and Kimport have characterized the impact of the web on social advocacy in terms of novel affordances. The internet mitigates the impact of geographic distance and boundaries for its users, at the same time that it presents pathways making it possible to bypass the traditional gatekeepers of information dissemination, avoid the scrutiny of government, and access a wealth of data. Likewise, the internet contributes to a breakdown of traditional mechanisms of engagement in society, meaning that elites and significant stakeholders in socioeconomic developments are often directly accessible via web platforms. More broadly, web technologies dramatically reduce the expected costs of social advocacy in logistical and financial terms as well as reputational or social terms owing to the opportunities for independent publication and pseudonymity.

Of course, these mechanical descriptions of the impact of the internet on social movements do not effectively capture the extent to which social advocacy has evolved in an age of unparalleled interconnectedness. Many scholars have taken up the complex task of reconciling the changes to global society brought about by web technologies with the shifting microfoundations of social movements. They address questions of personalization and individuation, collective action versus connective action, geographical and temporal fluidity, community transformation, and the changing nature of social power. These studies plug into this book in several interesting ways.

The work of Manuel Castells stands out in the literature on the complexities of social advocacy in the age of the internet. In work going back several decades, Castells[6] holds that the internet has an erosive effect on network relationships typically associated with both social movements and formal organizations within societies' public and private sectors.[7] This erosion of strict interrelation presents a challenge for researchers, he argues, as conventional assumptions about things like executive control or functional differentiation across elements of an institution are no longer safe. Regarding social movements specifically, Castells argues that "social movements in the Internet age are now typified by individuation and autonomy, a multiplicity of networks and spaces, and collectively nurtured affect."[8] In essence, the internet encourages individuals to become the subjects of their own lives via participation in digital settings, sidestepping feelings of social invisibility by creating digital existences that reify physical circumstances. Funke and Wolfson support this notion, arguing that the leaderless and polysemic quality of internet-facilitated social advocacy is sufficient to characterize the phenomenon as being about the struggle of the individual.[9] Thus social transformation through internet-enabled advocacy is a story about the "change of collective imagination" as activists explore new forms of self-expression reified in digital-physical interactions.[10] It's worth noting that this reference to leaderlessness is distinct from the emergent strategic dynamic theorized in this book. However, the "polysemic quality" Castells, Funke, and Wolfson describe is highly relevant insofar as it explains[11] the susceptibility of individuals to being "captured" within fringe virtual spaces and the incentives that the architects of such spaces have to manipulate how individuals engage in their space.

This book puts forward the basic proposition that fringe actors have been impacted by the internet, which must be understood within the context of the subversive enterprise. Supporting this proposition, some scholars have pushed back against Castells's approach, arguing that web-enabled changes to social movement communications cannot always be seen across different settings. Bennet and Segerberg based their differentiation of the concepts of collective versus connective action around this critique.[12] Social movement studies, they note, were traditionally focused on how movements gained supporters and then enabled those supporters to share techniques and information, that is, their "repertoires of dissent," on how to effectively contest the forces in society they oppose. Castells, they argue, is correct to focus on the degradation of network ties in modern social movements, but not about the generalizability of individuation effects. To Bennet, Segerberg, and others, the traditional focus on leaders and structures to explain supporter interactions does not make as much sense as it used to, given that *connective* relationships—often leveraged via shared experiences, media, and some collective logistical structure—produced widely variable successes in sharing repertoires of dissent across cases. Successful connective action still requires some amount of street-level coordination, but it is the value-laden substance of interactions that produce scalable effects. This implies that, while collective and connective action logics do not compete per se, the trend in the age of the internet has increasingly been toward "intentionally broad and polysemic" modes of discourse that stray away from individualized messaging. This does not mean, however, that internet-enabled social movements remove individual needs or interests from the act of advocacy, just from the coordinative elements thereof. As Papacharissi and others have argued, internet-age connective social movements are unique in their promotion of individualized affect as both a driver of individuals' engagement and a key feature of resulting narratives that favor storytelling.[13]

Perhaps of most relevance to this book's focus on fringe elements of global society, Fenton's warning that it is a mistake to suggest that the internet's effects are entirely or even largely "liberatory" or democracy-friendly simply because it focuses on the individual and connective logics of engagement.[14] Joining others in pushing back against the tendency to think of web technologies as "liberation technologies,"[15] Fenton argues that technology is always "enmeshed with the systems of power in which they exist" (135). That is, the logics of social advocacy that appear liberatory in their basic elements remain organically open to co-optation by commercial interests, broader mechanisms of neoliberal or alternative political-economic systems, or authoritarian machinations. This argument constitutes two important points for *Subversion 2.0*. First, the impact of the internet on social movements may be simultaneously empowering of the individual in democratic societies and broadly conducive to countercultural interests. And second, these connective social movements may themselves be further susceptible to co-optation by external interests. Fenton argues that more "democratic" or progressive connective social movements tend to actively engage the government in a participatory fashion, a feature that, as later empirical analysis demonstrates, is almost entirely absent in subversive social movements.[16]

Taken together, Cloud argues, these evolutions of thinking about social movements transformed by the internet amount to three broad features of web-enabled social movements.[17] First, social movements are increasingly less defined by the logic of collective action mapped out by researchers during the 20th century and more by individuated logics of connective engagement. Second, internet-era social advocacy has the ability to sidestep traditional gatekeepers of information dissemination, yet the messaging and entrenched narrative power of media entities and other outlets retain a substantial role in the process of shaping social advocacy. For leaderlessness, this is an important point because it underwrites the incentives of elites to respond to fringe narratives found across the conventional and new media ecosystem. Finally, modes of social engagement continue to diversify as web technologies themselves diversify in form and function. Such diversification means that the networks of a much larger range of social issues and ideologies than might conventionally be expected increasingly overlap, including those dominated by radical or extreme perspectives.

Connective Advocacy at the Fringes of Global Society

Subversion 2.0 argues that subversive advocacy has a greater impact on mainstream sociopolitical discourse in the 21st century because the feedback loop described in the introduction has enabled fringe organizers to construct public figures around whom antagonistic actions are catalyzed. This argument aligns with the idea that social movements today are driven by processes of individuation and logics of connective action. Consistent with Fenton, however, I argue that this individual-level analytic assumption is insufficient to generalize about trends in social movement tactics or selection of tools. Technology is not neutral. It is shaped by societal narratives and by the functional choices of those who leverage power within social networks, as this book posits. Public figures have been given the power to activate fringe advocacy in many cases not by their own intrinsic sociopolitical appeal but by a process in which network conditions (e.g., the management policies of social media services or the privacy architecture of certain virtual spaces) have enabled fringe communities and those who organize those spaces to spread extreme narratives to mainstream settings and then socially construct public figures toward different ends.

To summarize, the immense body of work on digital-age social movements offers several plausible explanations for the rise of fringe advocacy in the eyes of the average citizen. One explanation might simply be that the trend toward individuation in social engagement increases the likelihood that individuals will not only find fringe causes but will also let their ideas and assumptions shape their real-world interactions. While this tells part of this book's story, it doesn't offer a mechanical explanation for the punctuated disruption, antagonism, and even violence that characterizes the trend.

Another explanation might be that connective evolutions of fringe advocacy in line with the broader transformation of social movements make it easier for fringe leaders to map out the dispersed elements of society that are susceptible to subversion.[18] Such an argument suggests one of two possibilities. First, the increasing emergence of fringe causes in mainstream social discourse essentially amounts to a straightforward "command and control made easier by the internet" proposition.[19] Alternatively, leaders and celebrities are more able to marshal previously hard-to-access social networks for parochial gain than in the past.[20]

These arguments essentially constitute the alternative explanations that the following chapters set out to assess. Both are reasonable in their own way, yet they also reflect logics that are increasingly dismissed as inaccurate by scholars of social movements and political extremism. The former smacks of technological determinism and the latter reflects a top-down understanding of social movements that belies some basic facts. While the rhetoric of prominent political voices is often a feature of antagonistic actions of denizens and frequenters of society's fringe spaces, this is not always the case. Indeed, prominent mainstream political rhetoric linked to fringe extremism is often associated only with the most extreme, visible manifestations of a subversive cause, from the occasional rally that captures national attention to sporadic violence. In reality, there is a large amount of activity where fringe movements interact in a more limited way with elements of the mainstream. In such activity, the role of leaders as commanding part of the fringe is far from clear-cut. Thus, without further exploration of the antagonisms at the fringes of global society, we risk oversimplification of the relationship between internet-age social movements and social behavior and predigital notions of how social movement advocacy and disruption take place, where connective actions are simply co-opted by prevailing power structures.

Digital Extremism: Exposure, Radicalization, and Web Facilitation

While the literature on social movements and the internet is the body of social science work most relevant to this book's core research question, other research offers argumentation and evidence related to the design of its empirical strategy. Several bear mention, including work on the psychology of conspiracy theories and on misinformation and disinformation centered on social media platforms. The latter largely belongs to the business studies field of information systems and has produced much of the knowledge about how conspiratorial and mainstream web spaces work in the Web 2.0 era. Chapter 5 relies on this literature to illustrate the evolution toward the leaderlessness condition. The remainder of this chapter, by contrast, demonstrates how the theory of the book both speaks to and extends work that has centered more narrowly on fringe actors and the internet in the context of *extremism*.

What Does It Mean to Be Extreme?

There is a great amount of conceptual imprecision about what extremism is. Scholars regularly disagree about the interchangeability and intersubjectivity of terms such as "extremism," "radicalization," "violent extremism," and "terrorism," among others.[21] These terms are inherently open to interpretation, with an intrinsic quality of relative judgment. As Schmid notes, extreme is only extreme relative to whatever one considers normal.[22] Indeed, Schmid's writings form the basis of the nomenclature used in this book insofar as the difference between "normal" areas of sociopolitical perspective and the "fringe" is meaningful for classification purposes.[23] Notions of what looks ordinary and extraordinary in society will change over time, but the fact that extremely divergent positions exist and are tied to distinct forms of behavior relative to the baseline of society validates explorations that treat society's fringe—its spaces, occupants, and strategies—as distinct.[24]

For this reason, most researchers ignore the idea that extremism is inherently subjective as unhelpful to an empirical analysis of extreme behavior.[25] This is a tendency that this book fully endorses, as the parameters of who counts as "other" enough to be studied will invariably be called into question if one selects a morally loaded set of factors to work with. I argue that a different path toward understanding fringe actors than the one typically chosen by extremism researchers is needed to assess a research question as broad as that of *Subversion 2.0*.

Most researchers, recognizing the pitfalls in subjective parameterization of extremism, tend to adopt process- or activity-based perspectives on extreme behavior.[26] Work on extremism might be divided into several subareas that are generally defined by specific actions or particular beliefs. Wibtrope summarizes the extremism studies field as containing three distinct tracks of research based on these two selection parameters.[27] One area focuses on those with extreme beliefs who rely on extreme methods to affect change.[28] Another area centers on those with extreme views who do not use extreme means to achieve their objectives.[29] A final, smaller area of study centers on actors who hold mainstream views but use extreme methods to pursue their objectives.[30] The result of this partition of the field is that scholars often treat the areas of focus as functionally discrete. Violence and activism are activities defined by their direct effects rather than by their relevance to a particular concept of fringe success.[31]

This focus on the means and outcomes of extreme behavior, rather than the underlying intention or strategic concept, is even more evident in work on radicalization.[32] Radicalization scholars emphasize the process of psychological and affective transformation, with various authors[33] noting that this produces a propensity for both violent and nonviolent actions. That said, as Winter et al. note,[34] definitions of radicalization often emphasize the end result of violence or other kinds of physical force. This inherently situates radicalization as something tied to coercion or support for coercive methods in service of extreme beliefs and objectives. For this reason, the empirical strategy in the following chapters does not closely mimic methodological strategies common in the field of extremism studies.

There are many significant findings—particularly on the topic of radicalization—relevant to my broad focus on the increasing proximity of fringe influence and society's mainstream. In contrast with the arguments of researchers[35] who considered radicalization as driven by conventional organizations that recruit members, for instance, one prominent theory[36] argues that individuals tend to be radicalized via bottom-up processes.[37] Specifically, the social network tends to be the factor most closely associated with the development of radical viewpoints. Traditional organizations, by contrast, are often successful at radicalizing only small numbers of motivated individuals and struggle to radicalize audiences en masse. This is so often the case because organizations and extremist leaders regularly fail to instill the necessary feeling of "otherness" that sits at the heart of the radical transformation of preferences and identity beyond those already susceptible to extreme messaging. This argument is complemented by work that centers on socialization toward extremist viewpoints. Wiktorowicz, for instance, argues that radicalization usually happens slowly and hinges on cumulative changes in a person's experiences, such as information consumption and traumas.[38] In other words, radicalization is rarely something that happens all at once. Explanations of the growing willingness to consider fringe narratives as relevant to mainstream society lie less in the actions of specific extremist organizations or movements and more in how conditions for exposure have changed over time and, potentially, been driven by macrobehaviors at the fringe.

The Repertoire of Digital Extremism

The digital extremism subfield—often called "online extremism"—is the convergence of the study of political violence, radicalization, and extreme political behavior with an examination of the information revolution. The landscape of the subfield is surprisingly simplistic. For about two decades, researchers have generally made one argument: that the internet has been an instrumental upgrade to extremism and terrorism. Gerstenfeld, for instance, argues that extremists have been empowered by the web to more readily network with sympathetic persons, reach audiences beyond their conventional geographic range, actively recruit members to extremist causes, and manage relations with the general public.[39] Weimann makes similar arguments, noting that the internet has meant the same opportunities for extremists as it has for activists[40]—that is, to harass, propagandize, organize, and spread information, network and recruit, raise funds, and coordinate violence.[41]

The wide array of work on the internet, extremism, and terrorism describes how particular groups and causes use web technologies for each of the above tasks. The next chapters engage much of this literature in some detail. Significantly, digital extremism scholarship tends toward the same focus on actions and tools as does the broader extremism studies field. Excellent work on the Islamic State's use of the web to propagandize and attract foreign fighters, for example, deftly makes the case that the internet has become a force multiplier for terrorist organizations.[42] Likewise, Geeraerts,[43] Shortland,[44] and Hoskins and O'Loughlin[45] establish the idea that virtual social spaces offer extremist organizations opportunities for radicalization to the point where distinguishing between online and offline is increasingly analytically unhelpful. These are highly relevant points to any exploration of the internet's impact on society's fringe elements, but not directly useful for answering the much broader research question of what has driven the convergent fringe and mainstream.

Online, Offline, and Back Again

Of relevance to our research question, by contrast, is how extreme narratives and influence conveyed online spread to internet users of every kind, from individuals who rarely leave virtual social spaces to those who use networked devices minimally. Recent research on exposure to extreme ideas and content has furthered a long-standing argument[46] that thinking about influence in online versus offline terms constitutes a false dichotomy.[47] In ethnographic research on radicalized persons, Gaudette, Scrivens, and Venkatesh demonstrate that the internet sits at the heart of most radicalization experiences.[48] About a third of the subjects studied in their project were directly radicalized by digital content. While that may seem relatively low, for the remainder of subjects the connection to the web was only one or two steps removed from the initial source of radical perspective (e.g., an acquaintance convincing them of an extreme argument and directing them to an online location for more information). More important, the online settings that radicalized individuals were found to correlate to the degree of radicalization. All participants began to spend more time online, and the amount of time spent in fringe web spaces corresponded directly to how extreme the resulting beliefs were.[49] Specifically, Gaudette, Scrivens, and Venkatesh report that direct social exposure to in-group culture, music, and mentors in online spaces—all elements that were emphasized and pushed toward new users—became key pillars of the radicalization experience.[50] This finding backs up other research, which I engage in Chapters 3 and 5, that considers the social conditions of extremist communities as indicators of proneness toward accepting extreme narratives and ideas as credible or at least tolerable points for discussion. And finally, Gaudette, Scrivens, and Venkatesh illustrate how extreme internet users see the web as an intervening and enabling feature of their particular movement, a connecting substrate that is as much about giving meaning to social community and activities (e.g., rallies, concerts, parties) offline as about moving extremism online.[51]

Toward Subversion

To summarize the chapter, the literatures on social movements, extremism, and the internet tell us a great amount about how web technologies have impacted civil society and its fringes in the past several decades. Fenton's argument that technology is always "enmeshed with the systems of power in which they exist" reflects the view taken in this book that technology is never a neutral game changer that drives changes in sociopolitical contestation in a static fashion. Social movements today are driven by processes of individuation and logics of connective action. This, by itself, would be a sound basis for answering a question similar to that proposed in the introduction: What explains the more diverse footprint of radicalization and susceptibility to fringe ideas in the age of the internet? However, this book addresses the idea that fringe narratives and actions are generally more visible and frequent in the 21st century, not simply palatable to a more diverse, dispersed audience.

Likewise, the literature on digital extremism tells us that radicalization most often derives from bottom-up processes, that the internet generally offers new tools and opportunities to nonstate actors, and that extremist spaces are singularly potent when it comes to the radicalization of individuals even with a limited online presence. Much as social movements scholarship has built knowledge by focusing on specific actors or types of organizations (like the protest movement), these lessons emerge from examining individuals, organizations, or causes and punctuated extremist acts (often of violence).

The next chapters take a complementary approach to studying fringe activities, narratives, and use of ICT. Chapter 2 introduces subversion as a conceptual framework amenable to drawing a line around much of what is referred to as "fringe." Understanding the fringe in terms of a shared strategy—as distinct from tactics or preferred techniques—sidesteps the traditional challenge of defining just how "other" something has to be to qualify as extremist. It also bypasses the challenge of building knowledge about extremist behavior by starting with a specific action, tactic, or process, namely, that applying the lessons of such studies to broad research questions is difficult. By focusing on subversion, this book produces theory and tenders an empirical approach that offers a compelling idea of why fringe and mainstream seem so destined for collision in the 21st century, as well as ideas about what might be done to limit the fallout of such a clash.

2
Illegitimacy and the Logic of Subversion

This chapter attempts to cut through the substantial conceptual and empirical confusion about fringe activities in the digital age that is often found in both scholarly and public discourse. As the previous chapter noted, answering the broad research question of this book in a generalizable and defensible fashion means adopting a framework that considers what diverse fringe actors, social movements, and spaces have in common beyond the general condition of "otherness" in contemporary society. Here, I delineate subversion as such a framework. Contrary to common thought, subversion is not ideological or necessarily extreme across all social contexts. Rather, it is a strategic posture and a practical way to approach sociopolitical change that is distinct from coercive or participatory alternatives. Subversion mutually characterizes what are often labeled "fringe" elements in global society and, as such, has unique implications for our understanding of fringe advocacy, antagonism, and use of web technologies.

I begin this effort by defining and contextualizing subversion. Subversion is a purposive effort to compromise the perceived legitimacy of prevailing status quo forces. In world politics, governmental and social authorities often employ coercive power to shape circumstances in line with their interests. Often, however, coercion is not desirable. In democratic nations, in particular, coercive action can appear heavy-handed or even antithetical to the trappings of liberal participationism. With authoritarian regimes, overt coercion might risk the provocation of social unrest. As a result, authorities often rely on normative power to craft favorable conditions for operation. Such power is based on the degree to which constituents consider a given set of societal circumstances to be legitimate, and that legitimacy is based on the existence of symbols—including institutions, cultural practices, and specific personas—that are fashioned to generate and sustain shared meaning about the credibility of the status quo.

Subversion is the strategic counter to power harvested from perceived legitimacy on the part of a given constituent population. Whereas coercion involves the imposition of cost in order to alter the behavior of others, subversion involves the degradation of the credibility, legitimacy, and perceived relevance of symbols of the status quo. In practice, the strategy involves detaching the loyalties of a population toward those institutions, belief systems, and agents of prevailing authority that contribute to a broad recognition of the status quo as legitimate. *Subversion 2.0*'s focus is on those nonstate social movements and organizations attempting to do just that.

The second task this chapter undertakes is to preview the ways in which subversive elements of global society have used the internet and web technologies over the past several decades. I particularly emphasize the way fringe circumstances and the subversive perspective on affecting sociopolitical change broadly drive such actors toward tactics of social construction. Fringe entities interested in transforming the mainstream must overcome the certainty of negative feedback associated with direct actions they might take to contest the status quo, from conventional activism to political violence. Practically, of course, subversion entails case-by-case instances of both. But to bring those activities into effect as part of a sea change in public perspective requires the construction of a rhetorical apparatus that appeals to elements of the broader population, as well as the building of tools relevant to shaping and directing a necessarily dispersed program of social advocacy.

This book argues that this categorical imperative of fringe elements of society has been translated to an emphasis on the social use of web technologies for antagonistic purposes and, most recently, the tendency to use such features to socially construct the conditions for widespread subversion. This dynamic sits at the heart of what today presents as a new form of leaderless resistance among fringe actors, a leaderlessness buttressed by the architecture and management of web platforms more so than by the intent of subversive leaders.

Finally, this chapter outlines the empirical strategy that guides the investigation of growing proximity between fringe and mainstream information environments. Given the tactical focus on noncoercive, nonviolent methods of engagement that the strategy of subversion compels, it is not surprising that most fringe activities parallel modes of activism found in mainstream societal discourse, albeit often involving substance not necessarily palatable or permitted in such settings. However, subversive actors sometimes use the web antagonistically to launch cyberattacks, vandalize web spaces, steal information, or threaten others. These unusual deviations from expected modes of sociopolitical engagement present an opportunity to study the determinants of subversives' use of web technologies. As such, the following chapters focus on exactly *how* subversives of all stripes have been affected by the internet and have in turn used it to affect change. Chapters 3 through 5 do so narratively, building understanding of what drives subversive internet usage across time and diverse cases, while Chapters 6 and 7 marshal large-*N* data to illustrate the shared drivers of digital antagonism among fringe actors.

What Is Subversion?

As a starting point, the empirical scope of this book's study is quite obviously broad. This is true not only in terms of the ideologies and social contexts involved but also in terms of how cohesive the fringe elements under investigation are. In the chapters to come, both case studies and statistical analyses sometimes focus on reasonably well-organized groups that are tied to one or other fringe causes, particularly hacker outfits like decocidio #Θ, Fallaga Team, and RedHack. Groups like these reflect the diversity of organized subversive elements that have looked to the web to effect change in recent years. Decocidio #Θ, a hacker collective linked to the radical environmentalist group Earth First!, shut down the main website of the European Climate Exchange in 2010 as a protest of steps being taken in the West to combat climate change. Fallaga Team, much like the United Islamic Cyber Force and other Islamist hacker groups, hack in support of "Al Jihad Électronique," a broad-scope manifesto only tangentially linked to the direct actions of Islamic terrorists that emphasizes the spread of fundamentalist Muslim teachings as an approach to vacating the cultural power of the West. And RedHack, a Turkish Marxist-Leninist collective that I examine in Chapter 3, acts to disrupt the functions of the Erdoğan government with a specific focus on delegitimizing prevailing institutions and the symbols thereof.

Elsewhere, the activism and antagonism of fringe elements that is felt by the mainstream is much less attributable to self-named affiliates of a given cause. On top of narratives that are injected into normal societal discourse, recent years have seen a groundswell in actions taken by fringe-inspired individuals and small groups absent the trappings of an organized front. In no fewer than thirteen European countries since 2012, for instance, anonymous Euroskeptical hackers have harassed progressive political actors and stolen private data for later release. In Chad, Bangladesh, Sudan, Turkmenistan, and other countries, pro-LGBTQ activists have repeatedly posted banned website content designed to aid persecuted individuals. And in some cases, subversive actors attempting to troll and dox their societal opponents have self-identified only via an expressed affiliation with niche religious movements, cults, or contextually extreme social positions. In many ways, these acts of digital antagonism parallel those acts of violence from the blue, such as the August 2019 anti-Hispanic mass shooting in El Paso, Texas, or the September 2017 Black nationalist shooting in Antioch, Tennessee, in retaliation for the 2015 murder of African Americans by a White supremacist in Charleston, South Carolina—that are of greatest concern to Western law enforcement entities.

These social forces of different shapes and motivations can be understood by their common association with the subversive enterprise. Admittedly, this argument is far from an analytical silver bullet given the substantial amount of conceptual confusion regarding subversion found in popular and scholarly conversation. If asked to identify the most visible manifestations of actions by "fringe" or "subversive" elements of society in recent years, the average consumer of news media coverage today—at least in North America—would likely point to events like the January 6 insurrection or the infamous 2017 Unite the Right rally in Charlottesville, Virginia. Alternatively, they might reference the repetition of one or other conspiracy theory by a friend, family member, or more distant acquaintance, from flat-eartherism to QAnon. Elsewhere in the Western world, respondents might point to the active ties that resurgent far-right politicians in Europe like Hungary's Viktor Orbán or Poland's Mateusz Morawiecki have to hate groups and conspiracy theories. And those living under the thumb of authoritarian regimes may either simply avoid answering or perhaps point to the actions of the wide array of organizations and social movements—from Iran's Green Party to the Chinese religious sect Eastern Lightning—that are explicitly labeled seditious, undesirable, or even an "evil cult" by the state.

These possibilities aside, of course, it seems just as likely that if asked to suggest a label for these events and interlinkages on their own, the same respondents might opt for nomenclature suggestive of something other than "subversion," such as domestic terror, radical dissidence, separatism, racism, or hate. So what is subversion? "Subversion" is a term often used to describe fringe narratives and advocacy, but exactly what is subversive about these things isn't always clear. Unfortunately, this problem of conceptual and empirical ambiguity involving subversion is often avoided by scholars, pundits, and practitioners because its visible manifestations are open to broad interpretation. Why, for example, would we classify a mass shooter who clearly prioritized political violence and spectacle as methods of sociopolitical contestation as a "subversive"? Instead, it is far more common that such fringe activities are characterized either in line with the prevailing priorities of mainstream discourse or in such a fashion that the most extreme attributes of a case (e.g., an act of violence) can be presented as touchstones for the layperson. When one is only considering the events surrounding the insurrectionist efforts of January 6, for instance, it becomes almost expected that we should frame the incident as domestic terror catalyzed by conspiracy theories harnessed by a megalomaniac political leader. But when looking at the complex network of interwoven narratives, social interests, and political coordination that undergird the buildup to the attack on the Capitol Building stretching back some years, it can—again, at least for the average citizen—be remarkably difficult to know what it is we're seeing. Likewise, when thinking about the footprint of a conspiracy theory like the QAnon movement or various medical skepticism platforms, it can be easy to dismiss their felt effects as not necessarily part of some sociopolitical strategy but rather something environmental and even generally uncoordinated.

Conceptualizing Subversion

Scholars often use the term "subversion" to describe the functional manifestations of everything from insurgency and domestic terrorism to state-backed intelligence operations. At times, of course, this use of the term is appropriate, as many such activities are in the most general sense aimed at undermining existing power structures. And yet so many references to subversive intent or enterprise are anecdotal rather than scientific, a specter of societal threat that is enduringly hard to define but recognizable enough that many might claim they "know it when [they] see it."

Such a definitional situation is not particularly surprising. Though it often presents as something nebulous, subversion is a feature of the modern political experience, a thing often referenced as a bogeyman by patriotic ideologues or explicitly disparaged by authoritarian rulers. From the point of view of the state, subversion has been a regular and at times prominent attribute of world affairs for hundreds of years, not least in the form of systematic struggles undertaken against societies' countercultural elements as they attempt to somehow achieve broad transformation of prevailing conditions. Students of American history know well the episodic regularity with which elected officials have responded to perceived threats from foreign ideologies with the establishment of countersubversive institutions tasked with assuring the continued integrity of "American" values. The second president of the United States, John Adams, famously signed into law the Alien and Sedition Acts in 1798[1] as a response to the dual fear of a coup d'état and subversion emanating from the ranks of foreign-born immigrants of radical persuasion.[2] Likewise in the 1930s, despite there being no law officially banning contestation in the form suggested, Congress formally recognized and enabled what would become the House Un-American Activities Committee. This investigative body was awarded broad oversight authority to examine cases of disloyalty and subversion, motivated specifically by the actions of the American Communist Party and a range of quasi-fascist oligarchic organizations.[3]

This section explores conceptual confusion about subversion, adjudicates on the range of efforts that have been made to define the phenomenon in scholarship over the past century, and contextualizes the felt effects thereof in world politics. In doing so, we necessarily start off by treating subversion in broad strokes, placing it in historical context before narrowing toward practical considerations.

Conceptual Confusion about Subversion in History and Scholarship

If prompted, a majority of historians and scholars would likely agree that subversion is more clearly linked to normative than material outcomes. This point seems uncontroversial; subversion is about hearts and minds, as well as the sociocultural context within which they operate. And yet a survey of history through the lens of subversion—or, at least, descriptive usage of the term—makes the task of parsing the phenomenon apart from other forms of political activity difficult. Indeed, such a survey is likely to lead one to broadly characterize the thing as being about sedition or revolution, concepts that are defined more by their functional connotations than their relation to prevailing societal conditions. In so many ways, this is unsurprising, perhaps most particularly as history's most prominent subversive causes invariably transformed into something else. Subversive dissidence often slips into what we would ultimately categorize as related forms of political advocacy or counterestablishment activities: revisionist political violence, crime, or mundane activism aimed at modification rather than transformation. We need look no farther than Nazism in the interwar years in Germany not only to see how subversion can transform the mainstream but also to see how the subversive movement itself can shed its initial trappings—often via the brutal culling of unsavory elements of the cause, as happened on the Night of the Long Knives in 1934—to become a mainstream political force. Likewise, subversion is not infrequently co-opted and shaped to serve others' political interests. This was the case with the Russian Empire's efforts to use Hungarian unrest to destabilize national power in 1888, as it quite arguably was with the CIA-backed activities of Kuomintang Nationalists operating to persuade and incite sedition in mainland China in the 1950s.[4]

Conversely, episodes of subversion across human history have often been understudied or missed entirely *specifically because* they were not tied to more visible forms of sociopolitical contestation, like foreign covert actions or rebellion. The corporatization of Spain and the subversive replacement of the authority of the "Old Kingdoms," as described in Ortega y Gasset's classic *Invertebrate Spain*,[5] illustrate well how limited interests in replacing the prevailing normative status quo so often produces subversion defined by delegitimizing the mainstream without actual structural transformation. In this way, it is sorely tempting to define subversion as something both limited and all-encompassing. We might simply argue that, unlike concepts such as revolution and insurgency, subversion is straightforwardly any effort to transform the ideational status quo to something that would be considered illegitimate by what came before. For a cause to be subversive demands neither structural transformation—though that development is often bound up in a specific effort—nor a totality of vision. Subversion can encompass a limited platform and set of ambitions insofar as it may address issues that characterize a society writ large but are not strictly codified or considered in law, such as social expectations regarding sexual orientation or religion. Given this definition, almost any type of anti–status quo actor in world politics might be reasonably labeled "subversive."

Though such a definition is clearly analytically unsatisfying, it serves a rough approximation of the state of conceptual debate over what constitutes subversion in modern human history. For scholars of world politics, subversion has consistently posed as both a compelling and somewhat inaccessible topic for study. On the one hand, it presents as an interesting phenomenon for the same reasons that insurgency and civil warfare are popular topics of study among international relations (IR) and comparative politics researchers (i.e., they are common and impactful forces in societies across the world, the understanding of which would undoubtedly improve our abilities to comprehend and predict patterns of political transformation). At the same time, again, subversion is persistently difficult to tease apart from other manifestations of political advocacy and contention. Despite the apparently normative nature of the subversive enterprise, conditions of ideational transformation often produce violent outcomes in revolutionary, insurgent, or terroristic activity. Likewise, subversion often succeeds in normalizing a countercultural perspective or involves an eventual compromise of position between extreme bodies of thought, thus producing conditions that might be sorted into more routine categories of political contestation and activism.

IR scholars and their predecessors in the political philosophy and historical analytic traditions have focused on subversion as a discrete political phenomenon at particular intervals in the past two centuries. The common thread among them is the link between subversive efforts in specific national situations and the manifestation of attempts to effect normative transformation in a transnational format. Many of the global schisms highlighted prominently by scholars in the English School and related literatures particularly correlate with surges of scholarly and philosophical focus on subversion. A range of the earliest historical accounts and assessments of subversion, largely as encouraged by great powers interested in gaining new support abroad, date to the years following the Crimean War. This period, though still commonly labeled by students of IR as the era of the Concert of Vienna, saw remarkable normative divisions appear across Europe in the form of broad populist influences on policy agendas in France and the United Kingdom against conservative consolidation and commitment to the spirit (but not the letter) of consultation agreements with Western Europe in Russia, the Ottoman Empire, and Poland.[6] Subversive activity between 1860 and the early years of the 20th century were a common focus of political commentators describing efforts by the continental powers to effect protective insulation through the manipulation of border states. Some years later, T. E. Lawrence and others would describe the patronage of subversive efforts in the 1910s and 1920s aimed at, among other things, producing favorable operating conditions for colonial powers in Africa, the Middle East, and Asia.[7] Most recently, though still some decades in the past at the time of writing, IR scholars have made broad efforts to describe subversion as a discrete political phenomenon in the context of the Cold War. With only a handful of exceptions—including a range of works that broadly label subversion as one tool available to separatist organizations in Ireland, India, and other postcolonial nations—the bulk of available scholarship and theoretical work on subversive behavior dates from the midpoint of the global struggle between communism and liberal capitalism and focuses on state-sponsored efforts at subversion. Kahin and Kahin's description of Eisenhower's sponsorship of a clandestine subversive campaign in Indonesia, for instance, is one of the few robust explorations of the subversive phenomenon in modern context.[8]

In short, though the counterculture has been a compelling focus for scholarship in the post-Westphalian era, the difficulties in separating subversion from related manifestations of political contention have enduringly set complex challenges for researchers. By and large, only meaningful interface with state strategies and threats in the context of transnational ideological conflict has prompted a groundswell of scholarly attention to the phenomenon as different from—though linked to—terrorism, insurgency, and civil activism.[9] Even in such cases, however, the phenomenon often receives attention only as an adjunct tool or aim of statecraft.

Digging Deeper: What Are Subversive Outcomes?

Triangulating an effective method of separating subversion in practice from the outcomes of alternative approaches to sociopolitical engagement means starting at the end. In other words, defining successful subversion is a critical step toward deconstructing the characteristics of the subversive enterprise at work.

The word "subversion" describes a particular kind of outcome. In the broadest sense, subversion is the successful manipulation of expectations and sociopolitical processes such that previously taboo issues and outcomes—or those beyond reproach in contemporary society—become legitimately considerable. Subversion is about hearts and minds insofar as it describes persuasion of a population to a position radically juxtaposed to what was formerly the norm (e.g., persuading an American audience that apple pie and baseball are fundamentally "un-American"). In applying this understanding of subversion to the vignettes above, it is not difficult to grasp the general shape of the subversive enterprise in practice. And yet such an understanding *only* suggests an image of the practical manifestations of subversion and lacks tie-in to an underlying logic of the phenomenon. This dynamic is reflected in past efforts to construct a defensible definition of the term.

Specifically, many past efforts to problematize and define subversion suffer somewhat from the context of their investigatory scope. Studies of subversive actors often take place as a component part of projects focused primarily on political extremism, civil militancy, terrorism, and insurgency. But while it is certainly the case that there are common linkages between such phenomena and subversion, it would be inaccurate to assume that these political activities are synonymous with subversive activities. Terrorists, for example, do attempt subversion. However, subversive behavior is relatively rare, and terrorists, focused as they often are on forcing policy changes on the part of national or international authorities, must often undertake activities broadly designed to alienate—rather than persuade or organically realign—elements of a population. The result of debating subversion by means of a focus on terror or insurgent violence is that studies often assume the perspective of the researchers or the intended audience in making a definition of subversion particularly relevant to the topic at hand. Favoring particular applications in this way can misstate the core set of outcomes implied by the term.

Much literature on the nature of insurgent activities in civil conflict provides good examples of the effort to label subversion in the context of closely related categories of political behavior. Kitson, for instance, advocates the use of the term to describe all elements of modern warfare that involve navigating the interaction of government and social processes to achieve political goals.[10] Trinquier goes even further in aligning subversion as primarily related to the insurgent enterprise and synonymous with modern warfare, an "interlocking systems of actions, political, economic, psychological and military that aims at the overthrow of established authority in a country."[11] Treatments of the specter of global communist subversion of political processes during the Cold War, while somewhat less adamant about the link between overthrow and the ideational transformation implied by the vignettes above, also tend to cast subversive activities as entirely aimed at the destruction of extant political systems. Bezmenov broadly labels subversion as a "destructive, aggressive activity aimed to destroy the country, nation, or geographical area of your enemy,"[12] a description remarkably reminiscent of the U.S. Department of Defense's own recent categorization of the phenomenon as any effort to lend "aid, comfort, and moral support to individuals, groups, or organizations that advocate the overthrow of incumbent governments by force and violence."[13] And yet more efforts over the past few years to define the concept suffer from a limitation of perspective, such as the need to consider subversion as sedition in order to produce a meaningful legal definition.[14]

The challenge for a study attempting to analyze the functional correlates of subversion is, thus, the task of stripping away the biases of work that considers the phenomenon as one component part of a broader actor toolkit or the larger set of threats that states face.[15] Though his reference to state-sponsored subversion weighs in the telling, Paul Blackstock offers the definition of subversion perhaps most free of such bias in arguing that it "is the undermining or detachment of the loyalties of significant political and social groups within the victimized state, and their transference, under ideal conditions, to the symbols and institutions of the aggressor."[16] Blackstock's definition is well articulated for a number of reasons. First, it detaches an understanding of subversion as being explicitly tied to the overthrow—violent or otherwise—of governments or subgovernmental institutions. This is important because, as noted, subversion is not always seditious. Modern history is full of cases—from LGBTQ movements in culturally oppressive regimes to White supremacist movements in Central and Eastern Europe—in which subversion either occurs or is attempted without a stated ambition for structural transformation or violence. Subversion is about ideas and perspectives that are often, but not necessarily, reflected in structures. Second, in referencing the loyalties of individuals, Blackstock links ideational perspectives to a population's preferences. Again, this is critical because subversion takes place under conditions of contestation. Subversive activities are inherently undertaken in an effort to effect a polar shift in the political and social preferences of a population. In short, there must be contest; otherwise, there is no struggle. Finally, Blackstock's definition does well to describe the transformation of ideational conditions and the transfer of normative loyalties to the "symbols and institutions" of the subversive force insofar as it describes subversive efforts as bound up in the unique sociopolitical spaces of particular cultures and nations. No subversive effort is identical to another, even when the cause and the argument are the same. Even in the overconnected world of the 21st century, attempts at subversion naturally take place across different theaters of the global public sphere that boast unique characteristics and challenges.

As Blackstock's definition retains clear reference to the use of subversion as a tool of statecraft, this book offers an adapted version of his definition as the basis for investigating subversion in the digital age:

> Subversion is a transformation of the normative status quo among a significant community or population characterized by the detachment and transference of prevailing political and social group loyalties to the symbols and institutions of the subversive force. Though subversive actors and movements need not consider prevailing conditions to be entirely illegitimate, successful subversion is itself characterized by the establishment of a status quo position that would previously have been considered illegitimate.

In short, subversion describes ideational transformation via the specific—but broadly interpretable—process of preference transference reflected in loyalty to new alternative symbols or institutions. The final identifier—"the subversive force"—is phrased so as to avoid being too specific about the origins of such symbols or institutions, as subversion originates with particular sociopolitical actors but by definition presents as an ideational phenomenon that can be understood only in context. After all, ideas that take hold in the public imagination have a life of their own beyond (but potentially in line with) what is intended by the originating actor and manifest based on a range of broad societal inputs (treatment by other civil society groups, exogenous shocks, government engagement, etc.).

It is important to note the second sentence of the offered definition. This addition to the modified form of Blackstock's original definition is significant because it enables a line to be drawn between persuasive efforts that are subversive and those that are merely radically progressive. It is certainly the case that not all subversive organizations consider the prevailing status quo to be wholly illegitimate. Indeed, in many cases it is one part of ideational conditions that appears as the objectionable segment of society, and the subversive effort is built around an effort to replace a single part (thus changing the characteristic of the whole). The suggested subversion of West Germany by Johannes Agnoli in the mid-20th century is an example of one such agenda, where Marxist ideology as a replacement for Western progressive liberal thought would nevertheless attempt to accommodate traditional national cultural and linguistic traits as a means of normative advancement.

However, successful subversion implies a new set of prevailing norms that would by definition be considered illegitimate by the old regime. Thus, the subversive movement is interested in transformation and not addition or adaptation.

The actual form that subversive efforts take is discussed further in the remainder of this chapter. First, however, it is important to note that the definition offered above is articulated as a starting point from which we might set appropriate parameters for the identification of subversive episodes and actors in world politics. In particular, the definition (1) retains Blackstock's focus on the subversive enterprise as being about ideation and not explicitly about structural overthrow and political violence. It also (2) keeps the earlier emphasis on preference contestation as a critically important factor in differentiating subversion from the tolerated expression of uncontroversial thought in a given society or polity. Finally, it (3) broadly defines the scope of subversion as necessarily tied to social and political dynamics at the level of major societal communities, whether they be provincial, national, or supranational. Of course, this bounding of subversion to large-scale units is not meant to disallow consideration of efforts whose aim is subnational subversion (such as those undertaken by nonviolent independence movements in Balochistan, Tibet, and elsewhere). Rather, the intention is to communicate the notion that subversion is the replacement of imagined community symbols and related institutions with alternative versions, and that this process naturally implies an identifiable population bound together by significant normative and/or structural constructs.

The Context of Subversion

How is this conceptual conversation tied to real social and political contestation? Subversion takes many forms and occurs in a variety of unique contexts. Despite the fact that subversion has most commonly been attempted throughout human history by groups and movements not linked to governments—by definition, in many cases—scholarship on the phenomenon in this context is limited. By contrast, subversive efforts undertaken or directly supported by governments are actually relatively well studied by modern social scientists. Scholars who have studied government-sponsored subversion scholars—Laurence Beilenson and Paul Blackstock, for instance—break the subversive enterprise into two broad categories (*internal* and *external*) in order to distinguish their research program on statecraft from direct consideration of subversion as it more commonly occurs.

Traditionally, *internal subversion* involves attempts to create the conditions necessary for subversive transformation by dissidents residing within a country,[17] while *external subversion* describes the actions of states in attempting to influence conditions abroad.[18] External subversion is a common tool of statecraft and is often used to achieve ancillary aims for states (or specific rulers) interested in effecting political change abroad through more traditional means, including conquest and the securing of favorable treaty arrangements. Louis XIV, for instance, employed subversion via the encouragement of corruption and the manipulation of cultural practices for years in advance of his military campaigns in central Europe. Centuries before, the competing leaderships of the fragmented Eastern and Western Roman Empires did much the same, extending influence into less well connected parts of the European continent in an attempt to subvert both cultural and formal political loyalties along the frontier. Ivan III would encourage sedition in Russia in the 16th century from abroad as preparation for the internal campaign to throw off the Mongol yoke, as would the Habsburgs, the English, the British, the Nazis, the Bolsheviks, and others at various times over the past several hundred years as an aid to broader strategies of domination. The logic, in each case, was fairly simple: conquest and/or superior positions in international relations is made much easier by the acquiescence of a target's population and ruling elites. And the employment of subversive tactics by governments is not merely an artifact of the premodern international system. Forcible regime promotion through subversive (among other) techniques has received some recent attention by scholars[19] inspired by events in, inter alia, Iraq (2003), Afghanistan (in both 1979 and 2001), Panama (1989), Angola (1975), Lebanon (1975–1976), and Cambodia (1970).[20] In short, and in defense of scholars who have eschewed consideration of internal subversion, external subversion is a common characteristic of the international system.

As this section is essentially a discussion of a key differentiation in how subversion is problematized for examination in scholarship on world politics, it seems impossible to avoid noting actions taken by a range of states in recent years to affect normative political outcomes abroad through influence operations. Perhaps the most visible and offensive actor in this regard is the Russian Federation, which, under the leadership of President Vladimir Putin and his administration associates, has demonstrably utilized cyber techniques alongside traditional intelligence methods to interfere in the regular function of political processes in more than 20 democracies across Europe and North America, notably peaking with interference in the U.S. presidential campaign in 2015–2016.[21] According to the U.S. intelligence community and the report of an American special counsel tasked with investigating the extent of such interference—and with corroborating reports made by British, German, French, and other security services—Russia continues to sponsor a range of sophisticated and coordinated attacks against information infrastructure in the Western world with the clear purpose of manipulating or directly disrupting political discourse. Specifically, Russian state-connected sources have been responsible for establishing disinformation outlets, setting up fake media outlets, using targeted social media doxxing for destabilization operations, and disseminating information meant to alter perceptions of news media credibility.[22]: That said, the core focus of this book on society's fringes lines up clearly with the concept of internal subversion. In the chapters that follow, I certainly consider some subversive actors and social movements that have received support from foreign states. In this way, it is certainly the case that this project's outputs have meaning for other studies that seek to better operationalize information threats from states and from state-sponsored entities in the form of influence operations. This will be discussed further in the book's final chapter. But answering the research question posed at the beginning of this book necessitates focus on the relationship between subversive actors and their target audiences. As such, what follows is *not* primarily a study of the specific foreign policy tools and machinations of governments seeking to achieve subversive outcomes abroad.

Internal subversion is a broad and multifaceted enterprise that can occur for a number of reasons. These are explored further below. It is again, however, important to reinforce the point about the goals and desired outcomes of those actors that qualify for inclusion in the internal subversion category: success in subversive activities does *not* always mean the structural overthrow of existing regimes and/or governing institutions. In other words, subversion is not always seditious. In saying this, I depart quite radically—but uncontroversially—from the treatments of scholars like Blackstock,[23] Beisinger,[24] Pike,[25] Varon,[26] and Selznik,[27] whose inspiration for studying subversion as a political phenomenon was the threat of global communist revolution. Not only is the universe of cases of subversion in modern history less monolithic in terms of the sources of possible subversive inspiration than was that portrayed by Cold War–era studies of the phenomenon, but it is simply not the case that attempted subversion *has* to involve structural overthrow. As a variety of analysts and researchers might attest to, this clarification is critical not only because of the greater conceptual accuracy involved but because a great number of actors in intelligence communities and defense claim normative goals and work in a participationist—if contextually objectionable—manner to achieve their goals. Normative transformation often does involve radical structural change, but it also often targets sentiments or practices that can be reformatted and accommodated by extant political institutions (or modified versions thereof). Without making such a clarification, we risk a critical mismatch between theoretical and empirical foundations such that the scholarly production of knowledge might be incomplete.

Subversion as a Power Strategy

If subversion is a transformation of the normative status quo that involves the detachment and transference of prevailing political and social group loyalties to the symbols and institutions of the subversive force, then what are the practical objectives and targets of a subversive organization or social movement? More simply put, what defines the logistical and targeting strategies of subversive elements of global society? While this chapter has thus far provided context of and perspectives on subversion among scholars of world politics, the discerning mind will yet note the challenges involved in studying the thing. These challenges are primarily bound up in a nebulous ability to differentiate subversive activities from the more commonly examined forces of extremism or dissidence in modern society. In particular, given that subsequent chapters focus on how subversives use the internet, how are these actors and their actions to be differentiated from the hacktivists, digital activists, proponents of cyber disobedience, and others who have been more often written about by social scientists?

In this section, I clarify the scope of subversion and subversive action as distinct from coercive sociopolitical behaviors because of the overarching focus on *legitimacy* and its dissolution. In doing so, I outline the parameters by which subsequent chapters understand subversive actors and activities relative to other extremism. Simply put, subversion is not an exercise in the material contestation of power, though its manifestation certainly has implications therefor. Rather, subversion is the normative contestation of *what constitutes* material power via a range of material actions. Subversives are those whose operational focus is on degrading the normative foundations of the status quo rather than attempting to alter it by force or participation.

Subversion, Not Coercion

Coercion is the use of threats, of direct forceful action, and of other forms of cost imposition to alter the behavior of an opposing force, often a government.[28] In the digital age, coercion is the prevailing perspective applied by scholars, journalists, policymakers, and researchers when attempting to categorize and analyze conflict and contestation enabled by the web.[29] Hacktivists exploit information systems to coerce social or political forces to change their approach to one or more issues by imposing either financial or reputational costs on targets, often via the process of naming and shaming. Digital activism is an adjunct of coercion as well, albeit often a more legitimate form, wherein citizens attempt to publicize, mobilize, and expose facts in order to galvanize protest, lobbying, or direct participationist action (i.e., voting).

Subversion 2.0 argues that the fringes of global society are by definition constituted of elements whose primary objective is not coercive change. Nevertheless, most of the actors described in this book have been—or, in some cases of understudied actors, would be—labeled as hacktivists, digital activists, cyberterrorists, patriotic hackers, or otherwise in both media reporting and digital studies scholarship. In large part, this tendency toward such categorization is a function of the prevailing zeitgeist that sees differentiation among "hackers" only in terms of the methods employed and the event-specific tactics being chosen. To understand why some purveyors of digital antagonism are different from others, we have to move beyond such limiting observations and root our understanding in the macro logic and intentionality of the organizations and social movements involved.

Pierce and Williams[30] present a rare perspective on subversion as distinct from coercion. They argue that actors faced with a prevailing power dynamic or set of relationships that they do not favor must select from one of three basic strategies of resistance. The first they describe is an approximation of the broad body of thought on coercion in the political science and IR fields. Actors may choose to directly contest objectionable power dynamics, either by force or as part of codified processes for ensuring willed political change. In other words, actors may choose to attempt forceful alteration of their environment via actions like terrorism, military action, or costly disobedience. Likewise, they may attempt to "force" such change by taking part in approved, regulated forms of political contestation, including voting, lobbying, or volunteering for social or political campaigns. The second dynamic Pierce and Williams describe is that of "fleeing" power: when faced with a prevailing power dynamic that is hostile or otherwise unacceptable, an actor may attempt to leave to find an environment where other logics of political or social relationship are possible. Repressed minorities in authoritarian regimes may emigrate to more liberal countries where their existence or subsistence is less likely to be threatened. Religious movements may endorse a similar flight among members to find space conducive to religious freedom, as the Puritans of the 17th century did in colonizing what is now the northeast coast of the United States. In terms of international affairs, a state may attempt to insulate itself from the felt power of global or regional opponents so as to minimize the influence that others have via the medium of international law and institutions, trade, and so on.

By contrast, they argue, subversion is an approach to resistance that attempts "fleeing in place." This approach to addressing power does not directly contest prevailing systems or relationships; rather subversion targets the foundations of power. Functionally, the idea is that material action should address either the material or ideational underpinnings of prevailing power dynamics so as to make further exercise or accumulation of power difficult. Subversion does not aim to displace a prevailing set of conditions as a primary effect of subversive action, but rather tries to change the logic of social and political relations under such conditions. In doing so, subversion creates space for sociopolitical thought and behavior that might have been unthinkable in the previous environment.

Though this argument does a reasonable job in offering a way to differentiate between coercion and subversion in the abstract, it falls just short of providing a robust defense to a simple criticism: that attempts to target the foundations of prevailing power systems is simply the strategy of degradation, which entails harassment of an opponent as a means of rebalancing power relationships via limited action. Degradation, despite its focus on indirect contestation, is nevertheless an element of coercive enterprise. So how is subversion actually different from coercion?

If there is one thing that past work on subversion agrees on, it is that subversion is primarily defined by its normative focus on power. In Pierce and Williams's framing of subversion as *functionally* different from coercive or "fleeing" strategies for resisting power, I argue, it is this normative character that defines subversion as an exclusive category of strategy. Specifically, subversive elements of society do not think of power in terms of its material manifestations but rather understand power as a function of *legitimacy*. Legitimacy, as it is often defined in IR scholarship, "refers to the belief by an actor that a rule or institution ought to be obeyed" or that "the actions of an entity [such as a government or political establishment] are desirable, proper, or appropriate within some socially constructed system of norms, values, beliefs, and definitions."[31] Naturally, legitimacy is a subjective, normative formation in human society. Here again, we intersect with the notion that subversion is not something defined by particular ideologies or perspectives on contemporary society. Subversive actors work not according to a categorical imperative but according to a conditional imperative.

In practice, the strategy of subversion is based on the manner in which legitimate institutions and formations in society generate symbols. These symbols function as resources for those whose belief legitimizes such institutions insofar as they provide cognitive and affective reinforcement that certain behaviors are desired, appropriate, and even necessary. Among other things, these might include objects significantly linked to a belief system, such as a flag or a figurehead or a religious marking, or a meaningful process, such as the exercise of voting rights. Thus subversion, as an attempt to "mitigate or destroy the capacity to accumulate power (35)" that stands as an alternative approach to coercive contestation whose logic is based on relational and material understanding of power held over others, is an enterprise fundamentally defined by internalization of standards on the part of individual actors.[32]

This grounding of our understanding of subversion as a process of challenging legitimacy provides a much-needed way to differentiate some hacktivists, digital activists, and cyber dissidents from others. More specifically, it allows us to differentiate the universe of subversive hackers, trolls, and activists from the rest such that an investigation of the patterns of antagonism at the fringes of global society is possible. The data collection effort described in Chapter 6 is based on the observation of an articulated targeting of the symbolism and legitimacy of a political force, whether that be a particular element or subject in mainstream society or some broader criticism.

For instance, both statements made and interviews offered anonymously by members of Fallaga Team, the Islamist hacker outfit mentioned at the start of this chapter, have framed the group's strategy as based on countering the "illegitimacy of the Israeli State" and combating elements of global society that they believe "challenge the fact of Islam's truth." Similarly, statements and manifestos of numerous radical environmentalist movements like Earth First! cite the moral bankruptcy of modern society and a lack of "legitimate ethical authority" as a rationale for efforts "not to terrorize" but to "vacate the point of view that" abuse of the planet is permissible.

The Practical Shape of Subversion

To return to fundamentals in the form of action taken by subversive elements of society on the web, what does subversion look like in practice? If the logic of subversion as targeting the legitimacy of social and political forces provides the basis for differentiating the intentions of some antagonists from others, what distinct forms of behavior and organizational formations might we expect to find populating the landscape of global digital subversion? As might be expected, a broad range of literatures—(1) those on the sociology of ideational transformation and (2) those that have considered subversion as a tool for political advocacy and statecraft—agree that the subversive enterprise is a functionally participationist process, albeit with inclinations toward counterculture and dissemination, in which a social movement attempts to persuade a population to dissolve loyalty to a particular set of preferences in favor of another. This is not to say that subversive organizations or civil society groups don't at times employ distinctly nonparticipationist practices, such as illegal logistical and financial activities. But the main thrust of an effort to subvert is not characterizable by such practices. Moreover, this is not to say that persuasion is about laying a cause on the table for society to pass judgment on. In reality, in line with the emphasis on legitimacy and illegitimacy, it might be useful to think about the most common types of subversive effort in terms of clusters of popular preferences. A vast range of inclinations and positions, learned through habituation to sociopolitical norms and normalized under particular structures, constitute the worldview of a given population. Counterculture rarely involves radical transformation of every element of a people's worldview; rather, it is most often an exercise in replacing critical parts of a population's clustered preference set in such a way as to produce transformation of the broader status quo.[33] National Socialism in Germany in the interwar years, for instance, succeeded in bringing previously taboo subjects into the mainstream by subverting the nature of discussion about Greater Germany and the interests of German culture.

Though generally nonspecific about what subversive or counterculture actors look like in terms of modes of operation, the neo-Gramscian body of work on counterhegemony in world politics does well to adapt realism[34] to describe the broad shape of efforts to fight an ideational status quo.[35] The counterhegemony body of thought is premised on the notion that different political systems pivot on particular hegemonies of thought—a status quo perspective manifested in the normative and structural outlook of the consensus that is deemed, to the exclusion of others, to be "legitimate."[36] Counterhegemony presents as an alternative normative perspective—often labeled in terms of prevailing ethical, moral, or ideological tendencies—that challenges the prevailing hegemony directly (i.e., there is an implied contest because the counterhegemonic perspective cannot coexist with the status quo).[37] Unfortunately for the purposes of this analysis, much scholarship in this vein is concerned with where such counterhegemonic movements come from and does not describe operations beyond basic terminology—propaganda, activism, persuasion, and so on.[38] Indeed, much neo-Gramscian work abandons the idea that subversion is a unique phenomenon past early efforts to persuade, with a consistent theme in the counterhegemonic narrative being the transition from basic persuasion to political extremism aimed at overthrow once enough support is available. There are clearly elements of accurate historical representation in such perspectives. But, as a body of work, counterhegemonic scholarship does not perform well as a mechanically effective framework for understanding the manifestation of subversion across the universe of cases.

Work on subversion in the context of terrorism, insurgency, and militant activism does better in this regard in describing some manifestations of the subversive effort. Though the focus of such efforts usually includes transformation of normative ventures to violent ones, such as is the case with Kitson's famous treatise on irregular and information warfare, Rosenau's discussion of modern sedition,[39] and Rid's summation of modern hacktivism,[40] the literature does well in describing the various modes of activities undertaken by subversive campaigns in propagandizing, persuading, and corroding the legitimacy of status quo symbols and institutions. Rosenau, in particular, takes cues from a range of past works in summarizing three different kinds of subversive activity in line with distinct categories of strategic function.[41]

First, the subversive enterprise is commonly composed of front operations.[42] Subversion is countercultural and naturally originates from a position set apart from mainstream norms and expectations of political behavior. Subversive groups often require arms that appear unattached to the countercultural core in order to achieve both logistical and activist goals. This is most particularly true of movements that practice "leaderless resistance," a form of resistant struggle characterized by the existence of public-facing and ostensibly disconnected clandestine cell groups within a broader movement. In the modern context, leaderless resistance was pioneered by Louis Beam, a Grand Dragon of the Texas Ku Klux Klan that borrowed the concept from its origins describing asymmetric military resistance to motivate a continued push for racial inequality in an era, the 1960s–1970s, when such a cause was increasingly taboo. The strategy emphasized that "phantom cells" would antagonize the forces of the status quo while a public set of corrolaries would frame the cause in palatable terms. The idea was to encourage thinking of the cause as something that was both mainstream enough for inclusion in public discourse and motivational enough that some nontrivial fraction of the population was willing to act to push the agenda, even if criminally. Given such a setup, the countercultural cause would seep into or remain in social thought over time.

Of course, not all movements that employ front organizations can be said to be observing a strategy of leaderless resistance. In general, there are two types of front organization: (1) those knowingly linked to the subversive cause and (2) those unwittingly or only informally operating as an agent of counterculture. The redirection of resources by pro-LGBTQ groups to religious organizations and education programs in countries like Chad, Burkino Faso, Iran, and Sudan serves as good example of the latter type of front group, where broad advocacy for one position is masked in the charitable operations of other, more permissible activities. By contrast, the function of entities like the Holy Land Foundation for Relief and Development, Union of Good, and North American Islamic Trust by affiliated members of branch elements of the Muslim Brotherhood movement—which, in some countries, might be characterized as subversive—provides a good example of the former type of group, in which representation of more extreme perspectives is knowingly maintained through informal and interpersonal connections.[43] In many cases, in other words, front organizations are a necessary cover for those needing to organize out of public or governmental sight. In some cases, the differentiation between public and clandestine elements of a cause are more significantly tied to the intended act of subversive transformation.

Second, subversion often involves infiltration and espionage-like activities to place sources of influence within the institutions of the prevailing status quo position.[44] This means the placement of individuals either belonging to or sympathetic to the cause of a subversive organization in either government, opposition, or civil society institutions. The role of such agents is twofold. First, it is often the responsibility of such an operative to sabotage or divert organizational processes that would otherwise hamper the subversive cause. Second, it is occasionally the role of the agent to affect institutional subversion in changing the shape and nature of an organization such that conflict with the subversive cause is reduced. For situations where the organization or community is not directly opposed to the function of the subversive enterprise, infiltration is often about persuasion and recruitment. This type of activity is not unique to subversion, of course, insofar as violent and legitimate political actors place operatives in locations of opportunity as a commonplace practice. There exists an extensive set of cases where Al Qaeda and affiliate groups have placed operatives in Muslim communities, organizations, and mosques across the West in an effort to either mobilize support or target specific recruitment needs,[45] as did the IRA, Nepal's Maoist insurgency, Aum Shinrikyo, and more in decades past. Islamic State agents likewise entered the ranks of Iraqi security forces in limited numbers prior to the initial push against Baghdad in 2014–2016,[46] much as had happened in 2003–2004[47] and much as did the Viet Cong in the 1960s and 1970s in South Vietnam (137–152).[48] Quite naturally, this idea of subversive agents amid the sheep is relevant for this book because the internet has dramatically expanded the opportunities for infiltration while at the same time reducing the barriers involved.

Finally, subversive groups functionally act to frame the contentious issue or broader normative conflict that motivates their campaign through active efforts to generate public upheaval.[49] In other words, subversive movements advocate and contend much as do other participationist sociopolitical forces;

the primary difference is the underlying strategic intention. Here, civil unrest provides an important role for subversive organizations in setting the stage for normative contention in the public limelight and not entirely because civil incidents accurately reflect a tension between the mainstream and counterculture. Indeed, civil protests and unrest largely pivot on secondary issues bound up in the construction of the current status quo rather than on the main platform advocated by the subversive movement. Causing civil unrest can be beneficial for subversive organizations for a number of reasons. First of all, large-scale disruptions can consume valuable state and nonstate opposition resources.[50] Second, the side effects of upheaval can exacerbate the exact society-government relations that subversive groups necessarily need to weaken in order to bring about a sea change in perspective on a given issue. Third, civil unrest is a source of new allies valuable to the subversive enterprise. Though often uncompromising in the integrity of the subversive cause, countercultural organizations have regularly benefited from the patronage or partnership of sympathetic actors motivated by related concerns (such as the alliance between elements linked to Hamas and branch organizations of the Muslim Brotherhood in Europe). Public upheaval and disruption produce a crucible from which such relationships can emerge. Finally, encouragement of civil unrest is one way to shut down a national system that does not revert to violence as a tool for structural transformation.[51] Much as might be the case with an old computer system, disruption to key functional processes can cause a national system to freeze up. This creates temporary political space in which subversive transformation of fundamental policy, process, or system norms might be affected.

As Figure 2.1 shows, of course, all of this boils down to an imperative for subversive organizations to influence societal discourse generally via the manipulation of sociopolitical conditions. Given that fringe actors are, by definition, on the outside looking in, this generally forces subversive activities toward engaging the population at large rather than direct intercession in elite discourse or media reporting. Due to the difficulties involved in spreading fringe influence in society absent support from either media or elites, it is perhaps easy to see why subversion is rarely successful in the maximalist sense of the term. As was described in the preface and introduction, however, strategies like leaderless resistance attempt to bypass such limitations by separating elements of a fringe movement.

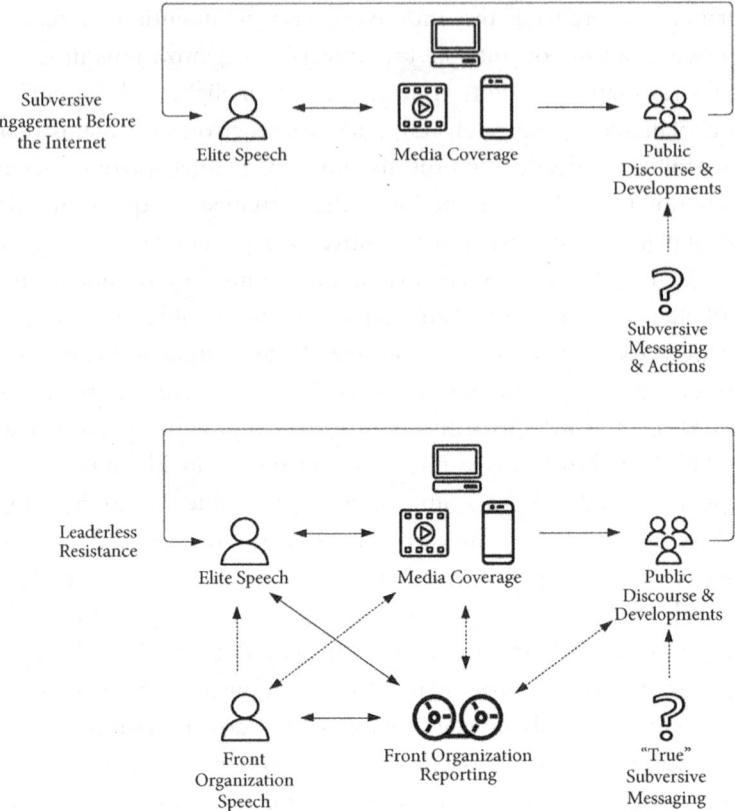

Figure 2.1 Fringe advocacy and the information environment before the internet.

Bringing the Internet Back In: Digital Antagonism and Subversion

It has been the goal of this chapter to make the case that subversion can be described in distinct analytic terms amenable to the task of drawing a common line around the otherwise diverse and fragmented fringes of global society. As a strategy for resisting status quo dynamics and relationships, subversion is a noncoercive approach that attempts to remove the legitimacy of prevailing power conditions. In doing so, subversion attempts not to contest or degrade power; rather it aims to vacate the capacity of status quo forces to accumulate and employ their power by detaching a given population's loyalties to the symbols and institutions of an establishment before transferring them elsewhere. In this way, subversion is not an exercise in material contestation at all but rather a normative contestation of what constitutes material power via a range of normative and material actions.

In practice, subversive causes, social movements, and their affiliated organizations start off life in the shadows; they, by definition, exist initially at the "fringes" of global society, not as part of the mainstream but inevitably defined by normative connections thereto. From this emerges the book's most basic proposition: that this societal positioning incentivizes subversion as a strategy of choice for those interested in sociopolitical change and that subversion itself conditions fringe elements toward information manipulation, social engineering, and attempts to covertly control the narrative. The incentive toward subversion itself holds for all fringe actors—individuals, social groupings, organizations—that desire change regardless of their feelings about violence. The next three chapters explore this proposition, delineating a tendency toward information manipulation across different kinds of subversive actors, including those actors that began life as something else and those elements—online communities, general users of the internet—that are not prompted toward such tendencies by leaders of any kind so much as by the trappings of their environment and the actions of their peers.

Why 1.0, 2.0, and Beyond?

Specifically, the next three chapters explore how different subversive elements have turned to the web across time. I delineate a different character of social subversion across the Web 1.0 and Web 2.0 eras, referred to in the next chapter as the Fringe 1.0 and Fringe 2.0. Both manifestations are characterized by the turn to using the internet in shady, manipulative ways over and above what is seen with conventional digital activists or issue-specific interest groups (e.g., fandoms, sports communities) spread across far-flung virtual spaces. The Fringe 1.0 experience undergirds the Fringe 2.0 experience, but Fringe 2.0 must be understood in the context of the web's social turn under the banner of rampant commercialization around user-generated content.

Herein lies the primary reason that the designation 1.0, 2.0, and so on is adopted over alternative schema for thinking about social movements and the internet, such as Karatzogianni's "firebrand waves."[52] It is a focus on how the agency of subversive societal elements interacts with the developments of Web 2.0 that permits a unique view of fringe activity and, specifically, antagonism in recent years. That is, the tendency toward social construction has meshed with the hyperconnectivity of modern social media platforms—themselves shaped by parochial developer and business interests—to create a distinct activation effect around elite rhetoric that does not require any degree of command and control on the part of said elite. Indeed, the effect appears so distinct as to exist even where subversive intent is not formalized in the tactical choices of key moderators, publishers, or other actors. The mechanisms for this are laid out across the next few chapters.

However, it's also worth noting again that the social evolution of web technologies is not the entirety of the story being told. Far from it, the agency of subversive societal elements itself dictates the effect observed and should be a guiding framework for thinking about the question of technological accountability. True, that certain Web 2.0 developments play a big role in the story being told in this book and in other works cannot be understated. They also indicate in broad terms that effective policy and advocacy might be able to walk back the severity of effects described. But efforts to better safeguard democratic process inevitably require a strategic approach based on understanding of how that process is being threatened. In this regard, the arguments put forward in the chapters to come about the tendencies and tactics of fringe social elements provide such a strategic framework.

The Empirical Strategy

This book's major empirical analysis focuses on *digital antagonism* at the fringes of global society in lieu of emphasis on the sporadic violence or the hard-to-parse rhetorical noise that is so much more often the focus of pundits and researchers studying extremist, countercultural voices. But what is meant here by "digital antagonism"? Methodologically, digital-age subversion is diverse and provides for ways to enhance a fringe movement's operational prospects, to forward favorable narratives, and to disrupt the activities of societal opponents. Prior to Germany's 2005 federal elections, for instance, hackers loosely associated with the far-right National Democratic Party launched a series of basic scripting attacks on government websites. These kinds of attacks are remarkably unsophisticated, involving the manipulation of syntax errors—meaning flaws in the design and implementation of an information system, in this case a website—in order to access data that is private but (usually) otherwise unprotected. Here, hackers stole voter roll and related demographic information, which they distributed online to a range of supporters and used to coordinate both outreach and harassment prior to election day. In a similar episode, American hackers linked with the "alt right" movement were recently tied to efforts to spread leaked and misleading information in an attempt to manipulate the information environment surrounding the 2016 presidential election. One individual in particular—a well-known neo-Nazi hacker called Andrew "weev" Auernheimer—by some accounts played a significant role in strategically distributing information that was published by WikiLeaks, promulgated by Russia-linked bot accounts, and that ultimately served as the basis for various popular conspiracy theories centered on the Democratic candidate Hillary Clinton.

It's easy to see the potential value in such shady and controversial actions, particularly for members of fringe social movements that typically operate detached from mainstream social and political spheres. Where, say, election infrastructure and political organizations outside of government might have weak cyber-security procedures in place, attempts to retrieve private information or to introduce new ideas into popular discourse often come with few risks. Even where hackers are deflected, attribution for failed information attacks is difficult. And the promulgation of false facts and misleading narratives is hard for governments to police, even where such activities are *not* legally protected as they are in democratic systems. Given the potential gains to be had in pushing alternative narratives and facts to shape public discourse, such actions are—at least on the surface—obviously attractive.

Likewise, it's easy to see the prospective value in more assertive forms of antagonism that aim to more visibly "hacktivize" by actively interfering with the work of those a social movement deems to be objectionable or to build disruptive narratives useful to a broader subversive cause. For subversive causes, disruption of societal opponents is valuable even where attribution is possible, particularly where a claim to disobedience—not criminality or aggression—is feasible. Organized trolling, for instance, is a mainstay of far-right digital activism in both Europe and North America, and occasionally emerges at scale to mimic the sophistication of effective grassroots advocacy campaigns. Paralleling such harassment techniques, far-right hackers in 2015 took control of a billboard in Kansas and displayed racially charged

WHITE MAN
ARE YOU SICK AND TIRED OF
THE JEWS
DESTROYING YOUR COUNTRY THROUGH
MASS IMMIGRATION AND **DEGENERACY?**

卐 JOIN US IN THE STRUGGLE FOR **GLOBAL WHITE** SUPREMACY AT 卐

THE DAILY STORMER
www.dailystormer.com

Figure 2.2 White supremacist fliers such as this were printed on hundreds of unsecured printers across university campuses in the United States in 2016.

hate speech for those driving on a nearby highway to see. Some months later, Auernheimer and other dissident hackers hijacked printers on more than a dozen college campuses in the United States and printed hundreds of fliers sporting racist, anti-Semitic material (see Figure 2.2). And the following year, compatriots of Auernheimer's launched denial-of-service attacks against Black Lives Matter organizers and vandalized several of the group's websites. These attacks—which mirror attacks undertaken by a diverse set of nonstate actors around the world over the past decade, from pro-nationalist collectives like China's Green Army and other American neo-Nazis to organizations like the Muslim Brotherhood that are regularly linked with extremist elements[53]—took little planning, gained media attention, and, because they largely targeted civil society organizations and small businesses, were difficult to investigate.

A Methodological Note on State-Sponsored Subversion, Hacktivism, and Cyberterrorism

In discussing digital antagonism and information manipulation at the fringes of global society, this book inevitably abuts evolving research on state-sponsored information warfare, cyberterrorism, hacktivism, and, as has already been broached, the pedestrian digital advocacy of participationist social movements. Given the confusion to be had in studying phenomena that share so many empirical traits, a clarification on how I view subversion vis-à-vis these others seems appropriate before moving forward. Broadly, *Subversion 2.0* argues that two interacting factors dictate the shape of subversives' use of the internet: (1) the nature of the subversive enterprise itself and (2) the sociotechnical context of evolving web technologies. The goal of disempowering status quo forces instead of challenging them by either participation or force has meant that fringe interest in splashy demonstration or violent action is limited by—and thus secondary to—the need to reach and activate dispersed elements of the broader population, the multiform points of resistance of Louis Beam's thinking. The initial rise of novel internet tools and the subsequent social turn in web usage since the 2000s have produced a common focus on social construction within fringe virtual spaces aimed at triggering support for antimainstream positions.

The distinction between those communities, persons, and organizations that this book labels as subversive and the broader universe of hacktivists, digital activists, and even so-called cyberterrorists is a murky one. In my view, this lack of a clean distinction is nearly inevitable. After all, these nonstate elements of global society call upon the same elements of the general-purpose "repertoire of dissent" presented by the internet, a toolkit that involves opportunities for engagement as distinct as basic use of web communications services and the employment of malicious code. Thus, in thinking directly about social movements and nonstate organizations using the web, the distinction between a hacktivist that is tied to a broader subversive cause and, for instance, one who hacks for the "lulz" can feel virtually meaningless.

And yet, while I fully acknowledge that these distinctions might never feel entirely clean, as seen in direct empirical analyses of nonstate uses of the internet, the broader logics underlying different forms of sociopolitical engagement *do* matter. As many researchers have noted, given that cyber operations tend not to produce physical destruction or even permanent disruption, the logic of terrorism has dictated far less terroristic interest in malicious code than popular imagining would typically have it. Here, subversion shapes internet usage into something distinct from that practiced by conventional protest movements or civic interest groups. Thus, while the empirical substance of *Subversion 2.0* might often seem indistinguishable in the details from that found in existing examinations of nonstate digital advocacy, it is my contention that the character of ideas underlying sociopolitical forces does present a sufficient case for thinking about hacktivists as defined by more than their choice to transgress, about digital activists as defined by their selection of messaging medium, and so on. This chapter has unpacked what differentiates the subversive enterprise from other forms of sociopolitical engagement and shown that while subversion is often tied to terrorism, sedition, and transgression, the particular focus on legitimacy both defines subversion and sets elements of society—the so-called fringe—apart from terrorists, protesters, and others.

Subversion 2.0 likewise overlaps in its analyses of influence campaigns and social manipulation with a growing body of work on state-sponsored political warfare and information operations. While this chapter has differentiated the book's focus on internal subversion (i.e., not directed by a state actor) from the strategy of external subversion (often used as a synonym for state-sponsored political interference tactics, hybrid warfare, etc.), the distinction here is also quite artificial. Particularly in later chapters' study of fringe attempts to sensationalize information, rapidly grow social network connections, and drive certain countercultural narratives, the actions of subversive communities and of states like the Russian Federation often parallel one another or even overlap. In this vein, this book does not consider the focus on internal subversion as a statement that some forms of information warfare, social advocacy, or cyber actions pertain *only* to nonstate actors. In actuality, the argument put forward in these pages resonates with much research on the patterns and logics of engagement among state sponsors of information warfare. Foremost among these is the assertion that social media manipulation often relies on the social construction of events or elite rhetoric to bypass a key obstacle for foreign actors, namely their inability to organically engage in sociopolitical discourse in target countries. Indeed, such dynamics substantially validate *Subversion 2.0*'s argument, not least insofar as intelligence operations launched by Russia, China, Iran, and other adversarial powers have regularly targeted figures linked with fringe advocacy to either harass or support in efforts to activate antagonistic elements of society and sow domestic division. Given this relationship, it is perhaps the case that the most significant value in this book's differentiation between internal and external forms of subversion is the relative lack of focus on the former at this time. The research in chapters to come thus adds substantially to the broader ecosystem of work on information manipulation and political warfare rather than artificially framing itself as entirely distinct.

The Subversive Enterprise and the Internet

This chapter has built a framework for understanding fringe behavior in common terms. Cutting across diverse ideologies, social movement structures, and national contexts, subversion is a distinct strategic posture for affecting societal transformation. Just as researchers often liken diverse terrorist actors to one another due to their common view of coercion as an approach for affecting societal change, so too can we generalize about the conditions and motivations of fringe actors. The next chapters illustrate several such common tendencies and perspectives among diverse subversive actors via examination of how the fringe has encountered evolving web technologies. Chapter 3 draws a technosocial line around the experience of those using the internet in what we now call the Web 1.0 era and highlights the shared strategic and operational emphasis placed by fringe actors on digital methods for socially controlling existing extremist communities, for building the ability to coordinate such communities, and for drawing in new members.

3
Fringe 1.0
Information Control and the Early Web

It is broadly accepted by scholars and national security practitioners that the internet is both a medium and a set of mechanisms around which entire cultures, economic classes, and sociopolitical movements have been—and are continually—socialized. This chapter takes the first step in extending this proposition by demonstrating that the socialization of the basic use of web functions is often purposive and is generally the rule rather than the exception for subversive actors. It does so by introducing the notion of the "Fringe 1.0." Here, that term is used to describe the manner in which subversive actors using the internet leaned in toward social engineering and information control practices *prior* to the era of broad-scope commercial socialization of web technology beginning in the mid-2000s. In recent years, information operations and manipulative political messaging campaigns have been empowered by the development and widespread adoption of mobile devices, social media platforms, and more. *Subversion 2.0* addresses these developments in subsequent chapters. Prior to those developments, however, the web was still a medium and a host for tools around which information manipulation strategies could be geared. Subversive societal elements embraced these opportunities systematically, albeit in diverse fashion, in their attempts to build and extend influence from a position of functional ostracization. This common behavior is a key underpinning of leaderlessness at the fringes of global society today.

In before the Lock

In the early days of the internet, much fringe advocacy and countercultural gathering could be quite readily found amid a broader landscape of diverse commercial, political, and social activity, both conventional and alternative. Whereas the web of the 1970s and 1980s was enthusiastically adopted by academic communities, technologist aficionados, and information technology developers, the global network of the following decade took on a different form. This was in no small part due to its growing user base, as well as to steps to privatize web ownership and functions in the mid-1990s. The internet in this decade was characterized by both rampant, speculative commercialization and widespread experimentation with new interconnectedness across different strata of global society. Authors of internet history and digital politics in the era often talk a great deal about the former trend and less about the latter. This isn't necessarily surprising because of the significant role of e-commerce in shaping the business, physical, and logical architecture of the internet to the present day as a unique sociotechnical global assemblage.[1] But the fact that so many everyday citizens turned to the internet in this period is also worthy of our attention, not least because the period cemented the idea of new information technologies as influence multipliers for many of society's peripheral elements.

In large part, this realization and the experimentation with new web technologies that produced it came from a basic economic reality. It was apparent to most from the start that much of the value in the internet was to be found in services and products that emphasized user-generated content. (The focus on networks with which to spread such content would generally come later.) Usership of the platforms and spaces constructed by a plethora of dot-com-era enterprises was the golden egg of success in the years following privatization. This prompted several different developments, the most commonly cited of which include the emergence of a complex market for the domain names and subsequent conversations about global internet governance.[2] Another noteworthy new condition, however, was the rise of relatively permissive norms of use among internet service providers and web developers. Particularly motivated by the protections afforded to the great number of American-based companies by Section 230 of the Communications Decency Act as of 1996,[3] the years of the dot-com boom saw widespread tolerance of extreme and unusual content in what amounted to relatively accessible parts of the web. Certainly, prime commercial spaces were shielded from the spread of such content, and a variety of early court cases—such as *Zeran v. America Onlines, Inc.*[4]—made companies wary of anything that rose to the level of inciteful hate speech. But anybody with basic web access could take relatively few steps and find themselves in the company of members of one part or another of society's fringe. And once there, a not-insubstantial number of people found themselves drawn into something at once uncomfortable, intriguing, and eye-opening.

Delineating the Fringe 1.0

Between the late 1990s and early 2000s, several years of full-fledged commercialization of the internet as a nascent, privatized global construct led to the appearance and rapid growth of what was quickly called "Web 2.0."[5] The term was coined to imply several interrelated characteristics of web technologies. It described a landscape of digital content that was fundamentally user-oriented, distinguished specifically from what came before by the interactivity of that content. It could be generated by users and modified, packaged, and reparceled for a range of purposes.[6] In this way, Web 2.0 was participatory and implied a networked understanding of the informational layer of cyberspace. The term also described more than just the websites that were the most common features of the web's informational terrain at the end of the 1990s. It encapsulated an interoperable web of systems, applications, and even devices enabled by various protocols, user actions, and offline development decisions. Web 2.0 was, in other words, an all-encompassing socialization of the internet presaged by the rampant commercialization of different socioeconomic services and by a series of novel protocols—such as the Hypertext Transfer Protocol[7]—that themselves took advantage of recent jumps forward in the power of computers to solve storage and processing problems endemic to what came before. The boom in global mobile device sales and the rise of multiple robust social media platforms just a few years later would then cement this "social turn"[8] of the internet.

The socialization of web technologies since the mid-2000s has played no small part in shaping a diverse landscape of social advocacy, political contestation, and fringe activity in the years since. In many ways, a subset of commercial innovations, emergent market realities, and corporate attitudes toward content management throughout the 2000s and 2010s have constituted a sort of short-term "lock" on the shape and potential of so much social activity online (much in the way that threads on forum sites are often locked to further postings, thus freezing the themes and shape of discourse at a specific moment). This dynamic is the subject of later chapters, particularly Chapters 5 and 8. Sufficed to say, however, there was an era of web usage prior to Web 2.0—the Web 1.0 era that stretched roughly from the outset of the 1990s to the early 2000s—that was substantially less socialized in terms of the standard systems, architecture, and norms of practical network behavior that characterized the digital world.[9]

This chapter discusses several instances of what I term "the Fringe 1.0." Much as with the phrase "Web 1.0," "Fringe 1.0" is meant to reflect the comparative characteristics of that which preceded the conditions of the Web 2.0 era. Specifically, later chapters delineate the Fringe 2.0 as an evolution of the subversive enterprise in the digital age that is substantially fitted to the contours of novel Web 2.0 commerce and network architecture. The idea of such a dynamic is not particularly controversial. Researchers of cybercrime have for some years described the degree to which the digital platform capitalism of the 21st century has shaped criminal strategy. What is valuable for criminal operators is, quite simply, dictated by the contours of the modern global e-economy. As a practical implication of Metcalfe's Law, the value of data and access connected to more widely adopted systems of design and user engagement is greater than the value of that linked to those with a lesser footprint. The Fringe 2.0 reflects a similar logic, whereby the natural tendency of subversive social movements and groups toward social engineering and information control is tactically easy to understand given the construction of several core styles of social communication platforms.

The Fringe 1.0, by contrast, constituted a diverse range of subversive societal elements whose efforts to organize, obfuscate, and disempower the status quo were largely not shaped by sophisticated socially oriented web technologies. The Web 1.0 era was, for fringe elements, a time of figuring out the network in terms of both the tools proffered by the increasingly accessibly internet and the user footprint of the thing. These efforts have been described, at least in part, in other research works. Fringe activists and dissidents as distinct as racial supremacists, left-wing artist "nomadic" resistance fighters, and Marxist-Leninist hacktivist forum-dwellers were each influenced by the need to encapsulate meaningful social connectivity in their use of the internet. Much as was true of pedestrian hacktivists and would-be cyberterrorists, automation was quickly deemed to be of paramount importance to any successful effort by the fringe to colonize the web. And yet automation was valued for the social stickiness it brought to intra- and intercommunity interactions rather than principally for its functional amplification effects. Likewise, diverse fringe actors rapidly evolved contrasting methods for funneling adherents and newcomers alike toward inclusion and inculcation in virtual fringe spaces. And in constructing such approaches, the Fringe 1.0 experience broadly entailed learning around the idea that tailored curation and framing of information mattered a great deal to the health of the enterprise. The result of this was a focus on close coordination between back-end moderation, information curation tactics, and the social construction of different symbols prior to the era in which Web 2.0 platforms standardized opportunities for the management of proprietary virtual spaces.

The Fringe 1.0 experience stands apart from the Web 1.0 experience of other kinds of sociopolitical actors. On the one hand, it's certainly the case that researchers of hacktivism or digital activism—among others—will see common themes in the experience of fringe social elements across the 1990s. Several of these are delineated in the next section as a starting point for thinking more clearly about the Fringe 1.0. Clearly, concepts like convergence culture and collective intelligence have as clear applicability to the fringe during the pre–Web 2.0 years as they do to communities defined by shared interest in entertainment topics or mainstream political issues. And yet, on the other hand, there exists a continuity of purpose around building the mechanisms of social engineering and control that is demonstrably linked to the unique perspective of those who exist—either by choice or by default—at society's fringes.

The Web and the Fringe: The Lessons of Far-Right Social Movement Research

The study of civil society actors in the context of the internet—from political parties and protest movements to hate groups and terrorists—is an enterprise that remains, at least at the time of writing this book, a surprisingly young one. Most early major analytic works on the dynamics of social forces in the digital age are barely two decades old, and the count of such research publications has risen exponentially in just the past several years. Looking to other internet-oriented fields of study, of course, this might be unsurprising. The cyber conflict studies field, for instance, traces back to the work of scholars like Arquilla, Ronfeldt,[10] and Diebert[11] in the final years of the 20th century—roughly the same timeframe as with early work on the digitization of civil society, in other words. Clearly, even given as much as has been written about human behavior in the age of the internet, researchers have been somewhat slow to the task in their discussion of web technologies as general-purpose information systems,[12] not only impactful for most sociopolitical phenomena but transformative.

What *is* surprising about trends in scholarship in recent years, however, is the prevailing lack of broad conceptualization and theorizing on social phenomena impacted by the internet beyond the mainstays of national security (terrorists, state militaries, etc.) and politics (e.g., political campaigns) discourse. As many scholars have noted—some quite recently—the broad array of works on what this book thinks of as the "fringes" of global society is generally guilty of tunnel vision on individual organizations, time periods, ideas, or even incidents. The reasons for this are legion, but perhaps foremost among them is the difficulty—highlighted in the first two chapters of this book—in developing and applying theoretical frameworks that effectively encapsulate the universe of relevant empirical data. A handful of works over the past few years have bypassed this oft-found limitation on the study of society's fringes, including Perliger's *American Zealots*[13] and Miller-Idriss's *Hate in the Homeland*.[14] As the titles of these books likely make apparent, of course, these books have the somewhat less than singular distinction of being focused on manifestations of far-right politics and hate actors, particularly in the American context. This focus is common enough that, while the focus of this book is on the societal fringe as something recognizable beyond the ideology and grievances of a single social movement, it is worthwhile for the empirical exploration in *Subversion 2.0* to begin by considering perspectives on and the experiences of far-right nonstate actors over the past few decades. After all, a robust starting point for our exploration of fringe experiences is needed, and the more narrow work of scholars on hate online fits the bill better than any other particular body of work and study. However, as the subsequent sections suggest, there exist recurrent patterns of preference across subversive actors sufficient to insinuate a further need to generalize beyond even the broadest possible definitions of ideologically linked political movements.

The Far Right and White Supremacy Online

A range of studies have explored the contours of far-right (often labeled "extreme right") social advocacy in the context of the internet. As Caiani and Parenti point out, the preponderance of these studies have focused on the North American context.[15] A lesser, though still substantial body of work has detailed the experiences of far-right extremism online as based in Western and Eastern Europe[16] and South America.[17] Taken together, the movements and organizations represented in such research have had and have presently an immense web presence. The Southern Poverty Law Center has cataloged several thousand distinct websites through 2020 linked to different manifestations of right-wing extremism,[18] from neo-Nazism and skinhead hate music content to Christian Identity conspiracy theories and various forms of paganistic dogma. These websites and their associated mailing lists, blogs, podcasts, and e-clubs go through cycles of activity and shutdown, many moving between hosting services or splintering into alternative versions of themselves as both commercial firms and law enforcement force movement from one virtual space to another. In spite of this constant migratory activity, however, the number of spaces linked to far-right advocacy continues to grow at an accelerating rate each year.

Caiani and Parenti describe the internet's impact on the global far right in much the same way scholars of cyber conflict or digital politics generally do, which is to say quite functionally.[19] Specifically, the authors argue that the far right's use of the web has centered on evolutions in six key thematic areas: (1) discourse and information aggregation, (2) propaganda, (3) recruitment, (4) outreach, (5) network-building, and (6) collective identity.[20] This final area is perhaps the most relevant to the research in this book, but each is relevant to the broader question of the role of the internet in upgrading the subversive enterprise.

Enhanced discourse and information aggregation is perhaps the simplest thematic outcome to understand. Simply put, far-right organizations and social networks have benefited—much in the same way that conventional social and protest movements have—from enhanced means of sustaining debate. Here, the minimally geographic footprint of much interaction over the internet comes into play in substantial fashion, as far-right supporters spread across nations, regions, and the globe are able to come together in a range of spaces to simply debate issues that are of significance to their cause.[21] While fringe spaces are often made to be restrictive and insular by their very nature,[22] the inevitable interconnection of so many like-minded individuals across distinct spaces means that openness inevitably brings at least some amount of value to the fringe cause(s). Debate is key to reconciling ideological issues inherent in the fragmented nature of many fringe ecosystems, as dogmatic adherents to "traditional" perspectives on White nationalism, for instance, come into close contact with those motivated by specific conspiracy theories or the heritage of alternative racial supremacy platforms (such as National Socialism). Likewise, debate is desirable even for the most insular of communities as a means of staying abreast of advances in tactics, technologies, and talking points.[23] Relevance is the lifeblood of any fringe organization, if not always in terms of society writ large, certainly in terms of the individuals targeted by the movement for persuasion, radicalization, and mobilization.

Similarly, the web has naturally enhanced opportunities for the generation and dissemination of propaganda. Collaboration and mobilization are functional outcomes of robust web usage that must inevitably give way to several tactical activities.[24] The construction and presentation of propaganda are perhaps the most obvious of these. Beyond just the greater ease of access to information and audiences brought about by web technologies, however, the internet has made the tailoring of content easier than ever before. Not only does diverse discourse and the sharing of information improve opportunities for remaining relevant; they also allow extreme actors to map the contours of the fringe beyond their immediate virtual surroundings and, in doing so, simplify the process of constructing content that generalizes and frames arguments in accessible terms.

The internet also generates new affordances for extreme actors in much the same way it does for status quo social forces.[25] Affordances are essentially new possibilities for action brought about by a particular technological development. The set of affordances brought about by some new technology constitutes an expanded space for sociopolitical engagement and contestation. In the case of the global far right, the web offers new methods for recruitment, network-building, and audience outreach. Caiani and Parenti distinguish these from the aforementioned capacities—for debate and propaganda—because they are not solely about communication. Rather, information technologies are increasingly used to shape and supplement relationships and cognition in the physical world.[26] In the aggregate, the internet enables outreach to potential sympathizers and longtime adherents alike. But the use of the internet to secure new contacts and obfuscate via a range of low-cost methods is shaped around real-world needs and desires, often to hide from prying government eyes. This implies no small degree of reflexive control of the virtual environment, with far-right entities shaping their digital habitat only to have their ideologies, group structures, and political touchpoints shaped by the technology (and the way that others use the same technologies) itself.[27]

Taken together, these reflexively developed capacities for new recruitment, network-building, and audience outreach constitute the socially determined substrate within which the collective identity of elements of the global far right is often found.[28] Different groups and collections of individuals are socialized across a range of interconnected spaces. The result is that informal rules of behavior and understandings of the costs/benefits of action are standardized. Some research shows that the greatest contributors to this development of collective identity are most often the secondary cultural and social context of fringe spaces, where shared experience with pastimes, literature, music, and more build an idea of community relationships that is then escalated into real-world relationships.[29] This, in turn, furthers the social evolution of online spaces around changing cyber-physical engagements between societal fringe elements.

Finally, and perhaps most important, these new dynamics of web-aided extremism amount to dramatically changed processes of mobilization, making it possible for otherwise dispersed and fragmented fringe elements to take to the streets or undertake acts of political violence. It is here that the combinatorial value of the aforementioned opportunities, affordances, and shared social reference points is the clearest. While reference to the decentralized, interconnecting architecture of the internet itself is extremely common among pundits and policymakers who seek to explain social advocacy in the 21st century, it is actually the second- and third-order socio-organizational effects of new capabilities that have produced so much extremist activity in recent years. New functional space for interaction creates new manifestations of a cause among individuals and collections of individuals. This, in turn, gives the cause new practical meaning and perspective as cyber-physical activities proliferate, resulting in the reflexive shaping and reshaping of the priors of those who—in the most basic fashion—again seek to leverage new spaces for interaction. This perspective does not, of course, offer an explanation of how and when such activity occurs in the moment and particularly does not address the source of so much novel political violence at the fringes—what Perliger calls the "spontaneous violence" that is such a feature of far-right extremism in the 21st century in contrast with eras past.[30] But it does effectively illustrate the social context and the informational substrate of so much fringe activity in recent years as something not only receptive and responsive to new media systems but ultimately circumscribed by their use.

Information and Intention: From Social Pariahs to Social Engineers

In this section, we consider the specific experiences of three ideologically and environmentally distinct kinds of fringe actors as they have used the web in different ways. In each case, there are elements in common linking the strategic perspective of each as causes "othered" by the status quo and the tactical use of ICT. It is important to note from the outset that there is no argument here regarding specific methods being the "methods of digital-age subversion" but not others. While there are certainly particular activities online that are more associated with subversive enterprise than others—astroturfing, for instance—this book in no way makes a deterministic argument about a specific technique as being characteristically subversive (or participationist, terrorist, etc.). As was stated in the first chapter, technology—and particularly general-purpose technologies like web systems—is not neutral and therefore not fundamentally characterizable in such a manner. Just as disruptive cyberattacks are increasingly seen as less the vehicle of new military activities originally envisioned by Western defense thinkers in the 1990s and 2000s, the toolkit of subversion online is defined principally by the utility of technology *in social, political, and technical context* for addressing the imperatives of subversion as a strategy of approach.

Automation and Funneling Effects in White Supremacy Networks

White supremacy is a diverse sub-ecosystem within the broader fringe ecosystem of the Western world. Though elements of the landscape of White supremacy can naturally be found in dozens of countries around the world, many of the most long-lived and widely dispersed elements are found in North America, particularly in the United States. White supremacy is often best understood in terms of a series of subcultures. Generally speaking, however, at the risk of too much simplification, one might land on conversation with any "type" of White supremacist and find a deep-seated belief in one of four interrelated propositions: (1) that White people should be dominant over people of other backgrounds, (2) that White people should live by themselves in a Whites-only or Whites-in-charge society, (3) that White people have a distinct culture that is superior somehow to other cultures, and (4) that White people are genetically superior to people of other backgrounds.[31] White supremacy is also commonly characterized by rampant anti-Semitism, regional sentiments (e.g., that the American South should be "kept White"), and Holocaust denial, though these are not universal sentiments.[32]

Of the specific ideologies or related organizations and social movements referenced in this book, White supremacy is perhaps the most clearly and distinctly subversive in its constitution. This becomes even more obvious when one considers the variegated subcultures that dominate White supremacy—often referred to as White nationalism, an intentional gentling of the "supremacy" term by certain far-right activists for the purpose of making elements of the cause more accessible to the public at large—across the West. Organizations like the Anti-Defamation League and Southern Poverty Law Center, as well as a host of scholars, describe several main branches of White supremacist subgroupings. Most obvious are the "traditionalist" White supremacists of the United States that are historically defined by the progressive enfranchisement of African Americans from the earliest manifestations of abolitionism as a political platform in the early 1800s through the present day.[33] Though it seems important to note off the bat that many racists are entirely unaffiliated with a formal group or collective, it is also the case that the landscape of "traditionalism" is dominated by arguably the most well-defined of all White supremacist organizations: the Ku Klux Klan.[34] The Klan is a post–Civil War set of affiliated organizations. Originally founded in Tennessee a year after the end of the war, the Klan seeks the social and political domination of non-White persons and the ascendancy of cultural practices tied to the Old American South. Over its lifespan, the KKK has risen thrice and fallen twice. The first iteration dominated Southern society and engaged in acts of terror—often at the direction of members who held official office of one kind or another—such as lynching and lethal arson. It eventually suffered in the public eye and declined due to the criminal trial and charging of prominent Klan members for acts including murder. The Klan gained some popularity again in the 1920s, however, rising to heights of influence even greater than before. This second iteration was geared toward social inclusion in the tradition of orders like the Freemasons and was particularly spurred on by increasing numbers of non-Protestant, non–Northern European immigrants on the East Coast, notably Italians, Irish, and Greeks.[35] A third iteration gained steam following the civil rights movement of the 1960s, never entirely diminishing and manifesting in a more decentralized fashion than the Klan of the early 20th century. This iteration is the one that continues in various forms today as a loose-knit web of "traditionalist" racist organizations, as well as several affiliated groups—such as the League of the South[36]—that espouse similar views but eschew the fraternal pomp of the Klan.

Other White supremacist subcultures are as varied in their symbolic and historical inspirations as they are uniform in their race-based beliefs. Neo-Nazis and racist skinheads are perhaps the next most populous set of semi-organized White supremacist movements after those linked to the Klan.[37] Neo-Nazis ascribe to many of the tenets of National Socialism, the ideology of the Nazi Party that was picked up and perpetuated in the United States by George Lincoln Rockwell. Though the formal political party of the neo-Nazis broke apart after Rockwell's assassination in the late 1960s, there remain a great number of neo-Nazis in North America.[38] This is in part because of the success of several literary portrayals of the neo-Nazi cause in the 1980s and 1990s by "intellectual" racists like William Pierce. At the same time, sympathy for fascist talking points has been shown to be unusually common among extremely conservative populations even where neo-Nazi party membership is low (perhaps 2,000 at the time of writing), often particularly tied to major events like the end of the Cold War or the election of Barack Obama. By contrast with neo-Nazis, racist skinheads embrace hate-filled music and particular formats of social gathering and garb as an outlet for their desire for race-based violence.[39] In reality, racist skinheads—to be clear, not all skinheads are racist—tend to espouse a rudimentary version of neo-Nazism when prompted for political statements.[40] But beyond a basic reference to emblems like the swastika, the symbols and meaningful traditions differ quite dramatically.

Beyond these three core branches of White supremacy are a range of parochial and often quite bizarre alternative perspectives on the superiority of the White race. Gang and prison communities often latch onto the broad tenets of White supremacy as a referent for setting social expectations or membership parameters. Much White supremacy is also packaged in the language of Christian Identity thinking, a peculiar belief system with ties to British Israelism that holds that only White people are the descendants of Adam and Eve.[41] Non-White people are thought to be the "beasts of the field" and the "mud people" referenced in the Bible, while Jews are considered the product of Satan emerging from an unholy union between Eve and the snake in the Garden of Eden. Yet other racists couch their beliefs in reference to a range of traditional European cultures, most notably pre-Nazi German heritage and Norse mythology.[42]

As Caiani and Parenti note in their 2016 review of far-right online activity, White supremacist websites have numbered in the low thousands between the late 1980s and the mid-2010s.[43] In the 1990s, however, White supremacists were taking initial steps in the digital world. Specifically, digital White supremacy during the Web 1.0 era was focused on, first, establishing an online presence of some kind and, thereafter, expanding the influence of the cause. In the course of writing this book, I interviewed 23 individuals affiliated with a variety of racist websites and web forums between 1993 and 2000. Of these individuals, nine had some degree of administrator privileges. Fourteen (including seven of the nine) were involved in moderating content, and the remainder worked—exclusively on a volunteer basis—placing graphic images, creating accounts on fledgling social media platforms (such as Six Degrees), and so on. At the time of the interview, most were rehabilitated—though several remain embedded in online conservative communities—and the average age was 46 (meaning an average age of 22 at the midpoint of the period they cover).

A study by Burris, Smith, and Stahm published in 2000 identified 80 White supremacist websites that covered a diverse range of perspectives and functional designs.[44] Many of these sites are still available today via the use of tools like Wayback Machine and cache databases made available by antiracist groups. Most were typical Web 1.0 constructions. They were largely text-based and offered limited options for formatting contributions.[45] Several either included or linked to sizable libraries of racist materials, from graphic imagery and member writings to Eurocentric literature and even pirated rips of well-known multimedia like the film *Birth of a Nation*. Some sites, particularly those run by racist skinheads, prominently featured music download areas.[46] Others had substantial merchandise sections, typically filled with numerous instances of member-made products and memorabilia of apparently antique (and usually symbolic) provenance rather than mass-produced items.[47] And, of course, most sites featured some version of a member conversation forum.

The early landscape of White supremacist websites reflected the subcultural diversity of the cause described above. From the sites of the Knights of the KKK and Stormfront to those of Aryan Nations and the White Aryan Resistance, traditionalist White supremacy could be found in a number of places online, often playing on themes of cultural patriotism and religious purism. Related websites, like that of the neo-Confederate Southern League, softened racist messaging by instead focusing on the heritage and political validity of past racist societal institutions. By contrast, a sizable number of sites took racist ideology in the opposite direction, preaching the inaccuracies of historical accounts of the Holocaust and denying the oppression of Jewish peoples. The Institute for Historical Review was one such group whose website attempted to couch racist sentiments in an "objective" tone of academic analysis. Various sites were published as well around the more bizarre or outlandish inspirations for White supremacist beliefs, including quite prominently those Christian Identity sites—like Scriptures for America World Wide and God's Order Affirmed in Love—that partially attempted to masquerade as generic Christian nondenominational portals. And, of course, many websites existed that were directly tied to White supremacist media organizations, from publishing houses like Fourteen Word Press to bands like Midtown Bootboys and RAHOWA (Racial Holy War).

As many researchers have asserted, there was a clear desire among those White supremacists with the wherewithal to build a website for collective identity. Of the individuals interviewed for this study, almost three-quarters were explicitly aware of the tenets of leaderless resistance as articulated by Beam in the previous decade (though only one claims to have been aware of the idea before getting involved in racist web culture).[48] All but two individuals interviewed spoke of collective identity (or the "meta–White nationalist" idea) as a distinct motivation for design decisions made in the running of different websites.[49] A former moderator-cum-webmaster for a White power music label stated, "[W]e wanted to inspire the little guys, yeah. The loners who felt what we felt but didn't have brothers."[50] This led to a range of practices intended to extend the social reach of website membership, including the use of symbols linked to alternative racist traditions and the softening of terms to make specific communities more accessible. Two interviewees with substantial time on Holocaust denial sites recalled oddly contrarian examples of this, as moderation decisions were clearly made at some juncture to give some more benefit of the doubt to posts that didn't deny the Holocaust so much as they justified it (often in line with Christian Identity interpretations of interracial origins).[51] A longtime lurker-turned-moderator on a forum site frequented by Aryan Nations, Watchmen, and other traditionalist racists likewise recounted a flurry of conversations about the use of the Iron Cross and the swastika on site banners as a recurrent event over the first year of site operation in 1995.[52] Another recalled an effort to build a softcore version of a popular Klan site with overt Christian and patriotic themes and minimal text on the landing page[53]—something unusual in the Web 1.0 era—that sympathetic site visitors could recirculate in other spaces. Its monthly traffic never rose above a thousand main page views.[54]

These actions show forethought about the challenges of both building collective identity within a fragmented fringe environment and enticing newcomers to spaces filled with imagery and rhetoric deemed taboo by most. As various network analyses of White supremacist websites has shown over the past two decades, however, such efforts achieved success only along narrow lines. Thematically similar sites, such as those centered on Holocaust revisionism, clearly enjoyed the mutual patronage of numerous members. Likewise, network analyses have shown clear linkages between different national iterations of similar sites, particularly those tied to hate music and neo-Nazism. But the broader coalescence of a meta–White supremacy ecosystem was pervasive, something that by 1998 had become obvious to various persons interviewed for this study.

The response to this reality was varied. At least half of those interviewed aligned with the characterization of these spaces found in various pieces of research since the early 2000s in stating that insular focus on the issues and subcultures of the sites in question produced a stagnant set of spaces, at least viewed via the lens of social advocacy.[55] Many websites acted as pressure valves for members, safe spaces within which to air grievances and regurgitate talking points without fear of social repercussion. In some cases, however, interviewees cited a set of attempts to overcome ongoing difficulties with building a metacommunity of White supremacists. Two developments bear particular mention.

First, there is clear evidence that various site designers and webmasters sought to expand their ability to network their community to others by referring to infrastructure beyond their control. Specifically, two interviewed moderators of a skinhead forum recall persistently linking members to antiracist websites. After all, they point out, counterhate organizations tend to be substantially better than fringe communities in producing holistic maps of hate spaces.[56] These resources, intended to bring publicity to hate groups, thus served as a cartographic resource for site users attempting to connect with more local manifestations of the cause or to better explore the traditions of racists elsewhere in the world. All site administrators and moderators had to do was encourage users to explore these resources, something that one interviewee noted had the added "effect of getting folk really riled up about the shit being said about them."[57] In fact, visiting these sites became a source of glee and revelry for many racist site users, as it reflected a clear opportunity to be disruptive and antagonistic beyond what was possibly normal.[58] And any time petty acts of vandalism or trolling were either planned or boasted about on White supremacist forums, of course, the user-generated funnel from one fringe space to others grew.

Second, as a kind of tactical addendum to this use of nonfringe rallying points, site users were also encouraged to be wary of how they communicated with one another.[59] As a number of other studies have reported, racist community leaders recognized that, even in the digital age, offline social dynamics were still key to creating a meaningful networked version of the camaraderie and coordination seen among (mostly) anonymous users on single websites or in small site clusters. Though none recalled the source of such prompting, more than half of those interviewed for this study reported trying to determine the best clandestine methods of communication.[60] While email and IM were in common use, interpersonal means of contacting those you knew in the offline world were pervasive. It seems likely that most saw this as a way of avoiding government scrutiny or masking the presence of the "racist among us" in other spaces online. As one recalcitrant webmaster of a blogging site with links to Stormfront recounted, however, this focus on staying beneath the radar served a double purpose, namely that "Mr. Johnny-come-lately won't be too keyed in to how f***ing alone he is."[61] Indeed, this reality illustrates the manifestation of subversive intent in the operational behavior of a dispersed social movement better than perhaps any other—quintessentially contrarian in terms of its functional, narrative impacts.

Disruption and Disempowerment among Resisting Nomads

Quite distinct from the context and position of White supremacists is the experience of a range of radical resistance individuals, collectives and groups operating in the two decades before the turn of the 21st century. Though there exists a broad category of what most would label as different forms of the "far left" given their advocacy for a range of progressive positions, a number of groups more clearly than most meet the criteria of "subversive" laid out in the previous chapter. In particular, descendants of the New Left of the 1970s and 1980s who were disillusioned by the experience of extreme left-wing operations-turned-violent-campaigns[62]—like that of the Weathermen[63]—reframed their quest for utopian transformation around the unraveling of the status quo rather than its forcible overthrow. A well-known early book on electronic civil disobedience[64] acknowledges this divergence from so much left-wing advocacy in the days before the internet (and indeed, from much left-wing advocacy since), stating that the choice of "strategy was unusual because the contestational groups decided they did not need to act violently toward those who occupied the bunkers of power, and chose instead to use various tactics to disrupt the institutions to such an extent that the occupants became disempowered."[65] These various individuals and groups saw themselves as "nomadic" resistors, a reference to the idea that the monolithic power of the capitalist status quo had been increasingly embedded into society such that it might crop up anywhere one turned.[66] They, in essence, saw no safe space to which it was possible to flee to escape capitalistic oppression, and so they embraced nomadic resistance as a strategic perspective for bringing about radical sociopolitical change via the degradation of what was already there.

As one might expect given the thesis of this chapter, of course, the distinct parochial sociopolitical perspective of these nomadic resistance fighters was married to a practical point of view mirroring the functional experiences of individuals among the far right. Too, these perspectives on the methods required to advance a social cause from a position of mainstream exclusion stand apart from what is often ascribed to early digital activism or, as Grindal notes, from the conventions of nascent hacker culture as of the 1990s.[67] Generally, "acts of civil disobedience" from progress-seeking activists "are generally intended to hasten institutional reform rather than bring about national collapse, since this style of resistance allows the possibility for negotiation."[68] Nomadic resistance on the early web, on the other hand, merely maintained the pretext of being a "moral force" akin to so many digital activists then and since. In reality, they saw "economic disruption" and "symbolic disturbance"[69] as the necessary means to combat the influence of nomadic power. Though this view of subversion implies the need for public acts in a manner that others do not—because the assumption is that the citizenry would, by default, favor the fringe perspective if only they could be detached from prevailing sources of binding power—the emphasis on degradation rather than participatory contestation is clear. And because such acts would require the complicity of points of resistance across a country or around the globe, the technical methods of subversion would—in stark contrast with the highly individualistic outlook of hacker communities and collectives—need to be "inherently social."[70]

Of those persons and actors being broadly described, perhaps the most well-known—relatively—are those often tied to the development of the distributed denial of service (DDoS) method of disruption, in particular the Strano Network, the Anonymous Digital Coalition, and Electronic Disturbance Network.[71] Denial of service attacks involve purposive efforts by some attacker to prevent the legitimate use of a service of some kind.[72] As far back as 1974,[73] such attacks had been the occasional purview of dissident hackers and mischievous script kiddies. Most often, such attacks were network layer disruptions, taking advantage of particular design characteristics of a target network or—occasionally—an application in order to disrupt. The DDoS envisioned and initially brought into being by these dissident nomads was distinct from what came before, however, insofar as immense social network buy-in was required both to coordinate an attack and to achieve the desired disruption.[74] Today immense botnets are regularly leveraged to achieve a disruption for some social, political, or economic purpose,[75] and indeed exist in such ubiquitous fashion that children with basic internet access have been able to find the relevant tools and direct them toward disruptive ends. But in the mid-1990s, DDoS was generally intended as a statement by many within a network of like-minded disruptors. In this way, it was conceived that evidence of latent resistance could be presented to the public at large, and resultantly, the power of prevailing neoliberal authorities could gradually be disentangled from targeted symbols.

The Strano Network was a semi–ad hoc group of artists and thinkers founded in Florence in the early 1990s.[76] It was intended as a "[s]eminari permanenti di comunicaione multimediale antagonista"—a "permanent seminar on adversarial multimedia communications."[77] The founders of the Network, which in English simply means the Strange Network, were obsessed with the opportunities born of the internet for organization of those at the periphery of mainstream society. As Grindal writes, one member, Tomasso Tozzi, was particularly responsible for conceptualizing DDoS as what he labeled a "net strike."[78] Tozzi, who had been involved in setting up bulletin boards and gathering places online for other like-minded persons, envisioned net strike as a way to use the web for targeted and "peaceful" protest with maximum effects (the quotation marks were used by Tozzi himself).[79] To accomplish this, Tozzi and others recognized that a network of users was required and that some method of triggering widespread visitation of a targeted website—to include specification of the target itself—would be needed.[80]

Strano members, relying largely on offline coordination, attacked sites linked to the French government[81] and, later, those of the United States[82] and Mexico.[83] The result was limited disruption.[84] Indeed, what's most interesting about the actions of Strano members was not the innovative method, though that is what most histories of hactivism focus on, but rather the manner in which the use of political targets contrasted with the accessible artist-oriented front portals of the group. Tozzi notes the significance of this in his book *Net Strike, No Copyright*,[85] indicating that the divergent imagery presented in Strano Network actions was critical to convincing citizens that counterhegemonic alternatives were within reach. And there is evidence to suggest that this dichotomy was emphasized in such substantial fashion that it prompted structural evolutions of the nomadic resistance concept by Tozzi and other Strano members in the form of the Anonymous Digital Coalition (ADC).[86] The ADC was yet another Italian resistance organization that publicized efforts to disrupt Mexican government sites in response to the repression of Zapatista forces in 1996 from behind a veil of anonymity.[87] Either composed of Strano members or directly aided by the materials produced by Tozzi and others, ADC evolved the net strike concept of asking users to refresh a webpage en masse primarily via publicization of the intended act in the days before it was scheduled.

The much better known collective Electronic Disturbance Theater (EDT)[88] advanced the accessibility of DDoS for counternomadic power activities by building software that would automate the actions required to limit legitimate traffic to a targeted site.[89] EDT was the brainchild of several individuals, including Ricardo Dominguez, an activist involved in the writing of two prominent books by the Critical Art Ensemble,[90] from which the conceptualization of nomadic power and resistance had emerged among these peripheral artist-oriented communities. Alongside Brett Stalbaum, Stefan Wray, and others,[91] Dominguez worked to make DDoS a realistic tool by which to accomplish acts of nomadic resistance, culminating in an applet called FloodNet[92] that built upon the basic principles of net strike introduced by Tozzi and other Strano members.[93]

EDT was explicit in stating the need to combat global neoliberalism by disempowering it wherever possible. The key to doing so was the disintegration of the narrative shields generated by media intransigence of key violators of core moral values. Thus, over several years, EDT targeted sites as distinct as those owned by the Mexican government, the Pentagon, and the Frankfurt Stock Exchange.[94] Indeed, those three targets were hit simultaneously as part of Operation SWARM, an effort to test-drive the new applet's automation of Tozzi's envisioned tactic.[95] Ironically, the attack failed, largely because it was seen by Pentagon systems as a hostile piece of software.[96] The applet, in short, would overcome barriers to persistent webpage refreshing by simply opening new browsers one after the other.[97] As Grindal explains, "[u]nless users were quick with their mice, the number of windows open on the desktop would continue to grow until the computer crashed."[98] EDT understood what had happened within hours and, quite ironically, proceeded to take legal advice on suing the U.S. government over what they saw as a government attack on civilians engaged in legal protest activity.[99]

The tactical evolution of web usage by the Strano Network, ADC, and EDT represents another clear effort by subversive actors using the internet in the days before Web 2.0 to socialize their enterprise.[100] Grindal claims that these efforts are directly linked to one another based on the consistency of backward-referencing from EDT to ADC concepts to Tozzi's original idea and tools.[101] Certainly, he notes, communication between key figures amid the different communities involved is not apparent. But the overlap between the fringe communities involved is clear, as is the motivating effect it had on bettering the design of methods of digital engagement. Specifically, here the key focus was on automation of two distinct processes: (1) the network development that was necessary for undergirding a successful "net strike" and (2) the actual execution of DDoS involving thousands of users. Given the right network aids, nomadic resistance could be funneled meaningfully toward a target. Later iterations of DDoS as the tool of hactivists, hackers, and more would, of course, automate yet further and rely on immense botnets to maximize disruption potential.[102] But these later manifestations of the thing strayed from the original intended use as a *social* denial of service action that would, beyond simply annoying and bringing momentary attention to a target, communicate nuanced grievances about the virulence of capitalistic power. For the nomadic resistance of the post–New Left world of the 1990s, the functional imperative that emerged was a need to socially engineer the conditions under which a sufficiently potent signal could be transmitted. The functional need for greater ease of access to distributed attack resources was secondary, not least because other forms of denial of service attack were possible for nearly 20 years prior to these efforts.

RedHack: Hacking for Change, Hacking with Conscience

Though the Web 1.0 experiences of both far-right and far-left subversive societal elements present strong descriptions of the Fringe 1.0 experience in leaning heavily toward methods of social control and information manipulation, it's worth considering another kind of fringe antagonist driven by the desire for sociopolitical transformation. RedHack, a Marxist-Leninist hacking group based in Turkey since at least 1997, is considered by many to be one of the oldest and most prolific politically oriented hactivist outfits.[103] The Turkish government itself, which is the target of many intrusions and data lifts over the past two decades, considers RedHack a hacker group (i.e., not merely a group of dissident hactivists) and a terrorist threat.[104]

Why cast a group like RedHack in the same breath as the fringe elements so far considered in this chapter?[105] First, it's worth repeating a caution previewed in the introduction to *Subversion 2.0*, namely that specific tools and tactics do not necessarily characterize the strategic outlook of an organization, movement, or other social group. An individual or group is not necessarily subversive simply because they utilize disinformation. Likewise, a hactivist may not be an activist in the traditional sense simply because they hack for a purpose other than for economic gain or in line with state interests.[106] Context, in short, matters. RedHack represents a fringe case among the universe of hactivist entities in world affairs. They have a core code of conduct premised on stringent ideologically defined political views. They also act with the goal of creating the conditions for a favorable transformation of society away from the status quo—which they see as fundamentally illegitimate. This has meant that they do not simply name-and-shame, as is the common tactic of hacktivism;[107] instead they curate their intrusions and their data releases so as to reconcile their dissidence with recognizable sociopolitically defined rules of conduct.[108] And, of course, the group's technique of hactivism and their highly precise approach to public engagement emerges from yet another condition that makes RedHack worthy of note here: they exist in a national context that is much further along the curve toward transformation than is typically the case, by default, at the outset of most fringe causes. RedHack represents a countercultural perspective on what Turkish society should look like and speaks, the group believes, to a nontrivial subcurrent of potential sympathizers spread around the country and in diaspora Turkish communities elsewhere in the world. And, of course, the group holds itself apart from other hacking groups and hactivists as a matter of definition. When asked if pro-government hacking or the hactivism of others was legitimate, RedHack members responded, "While these acts [of other hacking groups] would be considered political, they are never legitimate. The groups you mentioned have switched sides; even their friends question their legitimacy now."[109]

RedHack is composed of a small in-group of around a dozen members that, as previously mentioned, have been active since the late 1990s.[110] Over the years, they have researched and targeted corrupt institutions in Turkey, sometimes focusing on systems belonging to organizations that are—they believe—systematically amoral and at other times placing emphasis on specific scandals. Targets have included the Turkish Commando Brigade, the Turkish National Police, a national power company accused of cheating customers, and "milk companies that delivered tainted milk to schools."[111] Attacks have typically taken one of two forms: there have been regular, straightforward defacement incidents in which websites would be taken over and reseeded with RedHack messaging, and the group has proven adept at gaining access to secure files of political officials and institutions, many of which are then dumped on public media for public consumption.

The group's understanding of web technologies as a set of tools that fundamentally contain the potential for social manipulation and propaganda is clear. From the earliest point of their operation, including several incidents in the early 1990s involving members that would form the hacktivist group by 1997, two tactical choices speak to the tendency of fringe movements to gear available tools and spaces toward social engineering. First, RedHack's data dumps and takeovers are highly curated. The organization goes to substantial lengths to delineate innocent bystanders in the data they steal and then remove a great amount of imagery, personal communications, and more before they dump their scandalous findings. In one interview conducted via an intermediary, RedHack members described their decision along these lines as follows:

> We are Socialists, and our acts can only serve as the tools of a political struggle. Sometimes we hear so many people saying "Release it all! Are you bargaining with them? Why don't you release all the information?" We have seen all of the immoral and crooked relations that these people in power have built upon. But we are not paparazzi. We are Marxists who put up a struggle in a Leninist organizational structure. In the emails, there could be content of [a] private sort, but we cannot release those for the tabloids.

> When we filter out all such material, we will release the whole archive to the public for our strong belief in the freedom of information, and public's right to know.[112]

Second, RedHack's dissemination of data has almost unfailingly been geared toward the consumption of specific opposition communities within Turkey and in the Turkish diaspora community. Members of the group have variously referenced the fact that they seek to serve as a coordinating force for opposition to the society undergirded by the government of President Erdoğan and those who preceded him. In the same interview, a group spokesperson stated:

> The founding philosophy of The RedHack is opening a digital propaganda space to the opposition groups. Therefore, RedHack is an online "self-defence movement" of the oppressed. While our action capabilities seem to popularize us, as a significant power of self-defence, we will never get spoiled by our popularity.[113]

In short, RedHack's operational philosophy is centered on degradation and the promotion of conditions amenable to societal transformation rather than on the direct contestation that tends to characterize so many other hactivist, activist, and even terroristic elements of global society. And much as is true of the experiences of White supremacists and nomadic resistance fighters in the early days of the modern web, RedHack's tactical inclination has unfailingly trended toward the careful treatment of information altered, stolen, and leaked premised entirely on its perceived social value.

Automate, Funnel, Frame, Converge

The experience of fringe societal elements in using ICT during the Web 1.0 era was remarkably similar, at least when one considers their perspective as fundamentally set apart from the prevailing forces of the status quo. Across the cases considered here and many others, a range of common tendencies and lessons learned exist in common. The Fringe 1.0 was a period when many organizations, social groups, and individuals realized the potential value of using new ICT to automate many of the coordinative aspects of the subversive enterprise. Coordination, for subversive elements, is an inherently more difficult task than it is for other political actors, as fringe causes are beset by the dual challenges of separation from civil society and an often conflictual, even violent relationship with other parts of the fringe. Web technologies produce a unique affordance for the fringe in the opportunity to present a generic presentation and invitation to engage that can be found via the internet in juxtaposition to the need for active outreach in eras past. New systems, from software to web portals and digital publications, can be geared to maximize the funneling of persons toward information, activities, or spaces in line with the general subversive objective of inspiring points of resistance across a dispersed and diverse populace. But, of course, taking advantage of these tools still requires a degree of social control and deft manipulation of information presentation, generation, and dissemination. The Fringe 1.0 was characterized, first and foremost, by the realization of different subversive elements that framing matters a great deal, whether one's goals are coordinative, persuasive, or otherwise. With information technologies centered on the internet, this meant a close coordination between back-end design and moderation, information curation, and the symbolic presentation of the cause to different web denizens. Without this constellation of efforts, fringe causes generally failed to build convergence cultures—interlocking communities that demonstrate a degree of collective identity and intelligence—to mimic that seen in more mainstream areas of the internet, even in the mid- to late 1990s. With White supremacy, in particular, active attempts to improve interfactional community ties tended to do poorly in those instances where racists simply attempted to mimic outreach tactics seen elsewhere online. Intention and forethought, in short, mattered a great deal beyond just the perceived value of the new technology itself.

This chapter has described how the internet has presented as a unique affordance for those interested in societal transformation outside the conventional bounds of either participatory or coercive approaches. These case explorations reflect many of the themes and findings common across work on electronic civil disobedience, digital extremism, and cyberterrorism, particularly with regard to the novel toolkit of contestation constituted by web technologies. But the common tendency of fringe actors to emphasize the coordinative and information control affordance of the internet supports the idea that technology is not a neutral game-changer. Rather, it is the interaction of subversive preferences with the novelty of the emergent internet environment that seems to best explain why otherwise juxtaposed, diverse actors turn to similar modes of advocacy, self-organization, and outward engagement. Chapter 4 strengthens this argument by focusing on the curious case of Falun Gong, an amorphous social movement and directing set of leadership entities whose turn toward true subversive objectives over time is reflected in a parallel shift to use the internet for social engineering and information manipulation.

4
Subversion Found

The Curious Case of Falun Gong

Juxtaposed to the neo-Nazi, neo-Marxist, or subversive hacktivist denizens of what the previous chapter dubbed the "Fringe 1.0," the experience of certain social movements and organizations that today sit at the fringes of global society don't always reflect initial extremism. In other words, not all fringe elements begin from a position of "otherness" in ideational terms, where the driving beliefs or objectives of the cause are generally seen as external to the prevailing values, beliefs, and behavioral expectations of mainstream society. And yet, even in those cases, the functional circumstance of being othered by the status quo produces the same emphases seen among those nonstate elements more recognizable—at least, in recent decades—as extreme or subversive. Deft control of the social contours of cause adherence and outward messaging is a critical component of the successful campaign to reenter the mainstream. And where the goal of such a movement is to force the status quo to more closely resemble the values of the cause as it has evolved at the margins, emphasis on social control inevitably moves to encompass the capacity to manipulate the information environment.

This chapter focuses on a single case that represents the experience of so many societal elements that are "othered" or "canceled" by some sociopolitical development and thus represent an alternative perspective on the status quo to the actors considered in Chapter 3. Specifically, organizations like Falun Gong consider themselves—at least initially—to be a part of the status quo, even if some drive to bring about progress or change exists in the social, economic, or (in this case) spiritual outlook of the cause involved. They are then forced by circumstance to the fringes of national (and often global) society. This chapter explores the effect this had on Falun Gong, a spiritualistic organization-cum-social-movement from China that was banned and persecuted by the Chinese Communist Party (CCP) in the late 1990s, most arguably because its popularity was so great as to represent a potential source of social unrest within the People's Republic.

What's perhaps most interesting about the case of Falun Gong—the thing that makes this a "curious" case—is the manner in which the organization's tactics vis-à-vis web usage have evolved in two phases. First, the early years of the movement's exile and global diaspora produced a series of innovative attempts to bypass the oppression and censorship of the Chinese government. Adherents and practitioners built software to enable their membership to access information online even given the growing capabilities of the CCP to control its national cyberspace. Other than these circumvention tools, however, the web usage of Falun Gong has generally paralleled that of other groups repressed by the Chinese government and other authoritarian regimes. That is to say the internet has provided an opening for activism and funding, with web publications, blogs, and forums set up to make the voice of the oppressed heard. A second evolution of Falun Gong's web usage is apparent since about 2016 or 2017, however, specifically a turn to methods of social engineering, information manipulation, and shady media practices that are strongly reminiscent of the Fringe 1.0 experience described in Chapter 3.

The goal of this chapter is simple. Through narrative exploration of the Falun Gong experience, I bring to the surface the likely determinants of the shift from outright protest of the CCP and the focus on alternative activism—that is, circumvention and cultural outreach—to a strategy much more fitting to subversive objectives. This shift is odd given the early activities and experience of Falun Gong. After all, the group has globally accrued an immense amount of social capital in the rise of its image as a pro-democracy, anti-authoritarian voice. Though considered odd and even cult-like in its spiritual practices, the organization has undoubtedly benefited from its reputation as a peaceful human rights agitator and activist outfit. And yet, a post-2016 alignment with far-right political communities and the turn to shady digital tactics have already degraded this reputation. Moreover, numerous practitioners have publicly left the movement, stating that such methods run against the imperative toward moral improvement espoused by Falun Gong teachings. So what explains the shift and the commitment to a dramatic new approach to fighting the power of Beijing?

Resistance to the Forbidden City

Across the more than seven decades in which the CCP has held power, a sizable number of dissident organizations and social movements have emerged to contest the authority of Beijing. Particularly since the years immediately preceding the turn of the 21st century, no fewer than a dozen groups have been labeled "evil cults" by the government in addition to the repression of thousands of individuals tied in some way to counter–status quo advocacy. These elements of Chinese society are diverse but are probably best divvied up between region-specific resistance movements and sociospiritualistic protest fronts. In the former category, the immense protest movements linked to Hong Kong's ongoing battle against the encroachment of Chinese authorities and the sometimes violent resistance to apparent government atrocities against non-Han ethnic minorities in provinces like Xinjiang are the most visible examples. In the latter category, though a number of strange cultish groups like Eastern Lightning and more secular movements like the Tuìdǎng yùndòng occasionally make headlines (and are worth considering as a point of comparison later in this chapter), the most visible example of resistance to the power of the Forbidden City is, unequivocally, Falun Gong.

From Mainstream to Exiled: The Origins of the Falun Gong Movement

Falun Gong is a spiritualistic movement that was founded in 1992 by Li Hongzhi.[1] Variously called a loose-knit movement and a discrete group, Falun Gong is remarkably similar to a range of spiritual organizations across China that practice variations of *qigong*. *Qigong* is a form of exercise that encourages deep spiritual connection with one's body and a range of activities that divert human energies toward healing purposes. In practice, *qigong* is remarkably like exercise forms found elsewhere in the world that, regardless of how explicitly spiritual practitioners are, emphasize meditative physical exercise as a means of achieving highly specific health benefits. (Yoga is one such practice, as are a range of martial arts traditions.) What sets Falun Gong apart and what has qualified the organization for special investigation and prosecution by the Chinese state has at least in part to do—ostensibly— with supernatural elements added by Li in the initial years of his operation.[2]

In the early 1990s, Li—then a government clerk—began teaching *qigong* in the context of supernatural wisdom and lessons he had apparently received from a series of masters who trained him throughout his childhood. His story, elements of which would not be entirely unfamiliar to students of the life of Buddha or (to a lesser degree) Jesus Christ, involved an education at the hands of various masters of the spiritual practice who came to him at key junctures in his early life.[3] The result was a mystical philosophy that is today adhered to by tens of millions of Chinese citizens (most recent estimates range from 10 million up to 40 million, with as many as 100 million adherents worldwide)[4] and organized into thousands of local and regional cells. In essence, spiritual exercise can alter human energies to achieve what the PRC labels "supernatural" abilities. In many cases, this allegedly goes far beyond bodily healing and can include the capacity to fly, teleport, cure terminal disease, or achieve higher states of awareness.[5] Li's ideas gained popularity throughout the 1990s as he spread his message through pamphlets, magazines, and word of mouth, to the point that 10,000 or more Falun Gong members and devotees marched on government centers in Beijing and around the country after Li was quietly made to leave the country in 1999. Though initial protest was muted, these marches led to police clashes and began a spiral of dissident interactions with authorities that saw Falun Gong outlawed in China as a cult.

The protests following Li's exile—in which large numbers of Falun Gong protesters appeared in Beijing and other cities across China in protest of the action—bear particular mention in any history of the movement. Perhaps surprisingly, their presence was not expected by government agencies at either the local or national levels, largely because there had been no public call to action and because Falun Gong protests—which were overwhelmingly peaceful—were not precipitated by riots or violent clashes with authorities.[6] Remarkably, the organization of tens of thousands of Chinese citizens across the country in support of what official mouthpieces called a cult movement was almost entirely achieved by telephone, email, and internet chat.[7] More than 10,000 members and adherents responded to the call for mobilization that came through electronic and digital means— Li famously responded to questions about the protest's organization by saying that members "learned it from the Internet"[8]—a fact perhaps most incredible given the limited level of access most Chinese citizens still had to the internet and even landline telephones in the 1990s. Even more noteworthy, Falun Gong's activities in the following months and years relied almost exclusively on digital technologies—an unusually intense adoption of ICT even in the late 1990s—to avoid government interdiction and achieve a number of PR coups in spite of CCP efforts. In October 1999, for instance, Falun Gong succeeded in arranging and holding a clandestine press conference with a range of foreign journalists in Beijing.[9] The tools of their coordination were basic Instant Messaging, internet chat rooms, and email, which would evolve in the coming months and years into a constellation of websites and message boards that, even to this day, are regularly reconstructed and moved to new hosting locations in the face of pro-government harassment or direct Chinese government interference. Many such websites, of course, focus on *qigong* practices or community-building. Others, more particularly in the early 2000s than in recent years, have included clearer antigovernment messaging or are thinly veiled support forums for Falun Gong's political symbolism as a persecuted element of Chinese civil society. These web spaces have been constant targets of state-sponsored disruption, particularly where coordination of public protest occurs. The incidence of this style of public-facing coordination and the advocacy events they produce has dropped precipitously since the mid-2000s, however, as Falun Gong membership has embraced various publicly available methods for safeguarding intramovement communications, including, most notably, social messaging applications like WhatsApp, Snapchat, RenRen, Weibo, and WeChat.[10]

The Changing Tides of Acceptance

Falun Gong's relationship with both the Chinese government and mainstream society has existed across two distinct phases. Prior to Li's exile and subsequent protests in 1999, Falun Gong was generally accepted as a spiritual—but not religious—social organization whose core precepts, regardless of how supernatural they appeared, had understandable roots in the traditional exercise routines practiced by millions of Chinese citizens every day.[11] During the seven-year stretch from Li's founding of the group until 1999's crackdown, Falun Gong enjoyed broad acceptance and rapid expansion in the form of millions of adherents across the country.[12]

During that period, opposition to the group was minimal. In terms of social opposition, government polling itself demonstrates minimal concern among the Chinese population that Falun Gong was a unique source of societal disturbance.[13] Indeed, the operation of the organization in line with other social interest groups—with regular branch practice stations, open to the public, distributed about China's cities and towns—departs from the image of spiritual cultism that the government has since attempted to cultivate in that there is little in the way of money collection or secrecy. Even

Falun Gong's doctrine presented (and continues to present) as unorganized and unfocused beyond specific individualistic goals.

Following the government's crackdown on Falun Gong and various actions taken to censor members in the years after 1999, social opposition to the group increased. There is evidence that Falun Gong adherents are ostracized from society in meaningful ways beyond forums that link communities with the national government. For instance, there is significant evidence of bias against suspected members on entry examinations for high schools, universities, and the civil service.[14] Likewise, concerned members of the public have betrayed Falun Gong stations to local authorities on a number of occasions.[15] Curiously, however, almost no protest activity against Falun Gong has ever been recorded in China, nor is there evidence to suggest that the Chinese government itself has suppressed opposition to Falun Gong,[16] as it often has in situations where pro-government efforts would themselves bring about social unrest.

As with social opposition, government opposition can be thought of as taking on different forms before and after 1999. Prior to Li's quiet exile and subsequent actions against the broader organization that year, Falun Gong's relationship with the Chinese government transitioned from broad acceptance and official sponsorship to suspicion focused on the group's supernatural teachings.[17] Li's initial move to publicly teach his version of *qigong* in 1992 was met with widespread popular adoption of the practice, and Falun Gong was officially sponsored by a range of government agencies, including the state-run Qigong Association.[18] A turning point in China's interaction with the organization was in 1996–1997. Three years in, Falun Gong had successfully attracted members in the tens of millions and Beijing feared the social power of such an organization as a potential destabilizer of the status quo.[19] Beijing was faced with something of a dilemma, however, in that the organization and practice of Falun Gong was widely popular, with as many as 70 million "students" in China;[20] the practice of *qigong* more broadly was even more popular, with as many as 300 million practitioners across the country. Thus, the main step taken by Beijing to reel in Falun Gong and take some control was in many ways minor: the government decreed that all *qigong* groups establish official branch ties to the CCP.[21] Falun Gong leadership, however, refused this attempt to formalize the relationship between state and nonstate actors and attempted to withdraw from connections to all state-run associations and affiliations.[22]

In the period between 1996 and 1999, the Chinese government undertook a propaganda campaign against Falun Gong. The supernatural elements of the group's practices, which previously had been dismissed as clearly irreligious in nature, were the subject of many publications claiming the organization was theistic, superstitious, and anathema to communist precepts.[23] In 1999, tensions between the group and the government culminated in violence against peaceful Falun Gong protesters.[24] The Ministry of Public Security directly authorized these violent arrests.[25] Three days later, many thousands of adherents marched on Beijing in a civilized and nonviolent protest of their treatment at the hands of the state. At first, it seemed as though a civilized reconciliation might be possible, and meetings with the CCP premier were conciliatory.[26] However, Jiang Zemin, the Party chairman, explicitly expressed a desire that the group be disbanded and defeated as a threat to societal peace.[27]

Government opposition since 1999 has ebbed and risen with administrations. However, arguably in response to massive preemptive demonstrations held across more than 30 cities in protest of a perceived crackdown on Falun Gong practice and assembly, Beijing quickly transformed a propaganda campaign against the group into active suppression. In July 1999, hundreds of senior members and public faces of the organization were seized from branch stations and private residences across the country.[28] Beijing ordered active suppression of Falun Gong, though it took steps to single the group out from nontheistic versions of *qigong*, and mandated that any support of the group was a violation of the atheism demanded by communist doctrine.[29] In short, Beijing quickly and unequivocally banned Falun Gong and actively sought "group disintegration."

An Evolving Movement: Early Objectives, Outlook, and Organization

Across most of the history of the movement, Falun Gong has maintained a generally minimalist portfolio of grievances or objectives. At least throughout the 2000s, this manifested as a general criticism of and objection to the Chinese government without explicitly stated goals of structural revision (i.e., political overthrow) by the membership at large.[30] Indeed, Falun Gong, a movement that is remarkably peaceful and at least partially lacks some key features of cultism, is often characterized first and foremost by its explicit rules regarding doctrinal development.[31] In short, members are discouraged (forbidden, in many instances) from articulating social or political objectives beyond the practice of Falun Dafa. The prohibition is so ubiquitously observed that, in the context of the movement's presence in Western countries, one would be hard-pressed to credibly label Falun Gong a revisionist social movement. Rather, the main objections of both movement leaders and the broader diaspora community of practitioners have conventionally had to do with freedom of action in the authoritarian PRC.[32]

A number of features of Falun Gong stand in stark contrast to the actions and experiences of Eastern Lightning, mentioned at this chapter's outset, and other organizations that the Chinese government has attempted to repress over the past three decades. Foremost among these is the fact that Falun Gong has an unusually limited history of adherent involvement in criminal enterprise.[33] There were several instances of members assaulting police officers and civilians during protests in the late 1990s, all of which took the form of unorganized brawling in busy streets. Likewise, more than 500 members (though some estimates put arrests from direct protest in the thousands)[34] have been arrested for unauthorized protest over the years.[35] However, prior to state campaigns to identify and detain members, Falun Gong adherents were reasonably well known for their cooperation with police and for acting responsibly (by removing trash, escorting elderly members, etc.) in attempting to maintain peace around protest events.[36] In the wake of various police brutality episodes from 1999 to at least the mid-2010s, member responses have rarely been violent and tend toward pacifist (if illegal) protest.

Likewise, Falun Gong's spiritualism does not manifest in prophetic vision (beyond the spiritual) or conventional political advocacy, and so for much of the movement's history there have been no stated objectives that impact the political system in China (beyond a desire to practice and interact with all Chinese communities). Members' objection to the structure of Chinese society has typically, in fact, contextually focused on the existence of the PRC campaign to remove the group as a source of social discontent.[37] And, of course, the preponderance of critical elements of Falun Gong advocacy—including movement leadership—exists abroad. Though group membership within China is still estimated at between 10 million and 40 million, important membership clusters that perform specialized functions largely operate abroad and mostly in either the United States or Canada.[38] Thus, while group activity under the radar continues to plague the domestic countersedition activities of the PRC, it is those functional arms of the movement beyond China's borders that play a significant role in determining the movement's policy (such as it formally exists) and the nature of any efforts to resist Beijing's ongoing persecution.

Close analysis of Falun Gong in scholarly work and the reporting of different governments suggests that the movement is not perfectly decentralized. Rather, the movement appears to be possessed of something akin to a hub-and-spoke structure, though it should be noted that the organizational structure of Falun Gong advocacy is difficult to perceive as a matter of both circumstance and intentional design. On one hand, the movement has relied on no small amount of secrecy to protect itself from persecution, and this intentional opacity has become the ubiquitous characteristic of entities linked to Falun Gong. On the other hand, as James Tong notes, the difficulty in determining group structure in the case of Falun Gong can largely be attributed to the fact that the movement is represented differently by the Chinese government and by members of the group itself.[39] Specifically, two competing narratives exist about the nature of the movement's leadership, the shape of intra-organizational communications, the degree of functional specialization across elements of the movement, and the basis of Falun Gong's finances. The PRC claims Falun Gong is a highly hierarchical organization with clear lines of communication, direction, and funding. Falun Gong, by contrast, claims few organizational trappings. The truth almost certainly lies in between these competing claims. Though study of movements like Falun Gong is naturally difficult, historical analysis of documents of various kinds suggests that the formal organization—such as it exists—might best be described as a web of functional parts coordinated, though likely not commanded in the conventional sense, by a core in-group.

In part, this functional setup is more likely than alternatives because it would represent only a basic evolution of the early structure of the Falun Gong movement, which was characterized more than anything else by a decoupling of directional links between upper echelons and local stations that was enacted in 1996. Falun Gong leaders themselves have variously described the organization as a distributed spiritualistic movement focused on *qigong* instruction and practice at the individual level. To this end, there exist a broad number of "stations" across China, both formally and, later, clandestinely.[40] From the perspective of the organization, these stations function as guidance bureaus for facilitating learning of *qigong* techniques.[41] Throughout the 1990s, teaching stations operated under the jurisdiction of society organizations officially registered with authorities in different regions of the country. Local stations had no set infrastructure—phones, business equipment, staff, or office space requisitioned at the national level—and were often found in residential buildings. Tong suggests that organizationally Falun Gong in its earliest iterations looked much more like a hobby movement or an interest group than it did a religious or political entity. This is by design following 1996's decision to reorganize the group in preparation for a future without official patronage and continues in practice to the present day.[42] Following that decision, Falun Gong leaders hold that the organization, beyond being a social group, doesn't officially exist.[43] In line with this, group doctrine—officially, in any case—prohibits cash contributions, and there are no fees for *qigong* instruction.[44]

The PRC's description of Falun Gong's organizational structure is strikingly different. In essence, authorities claim that the group has replicated the administrative shape of the Chinese state itself in providing for effective coordination of the national mission.[45] Directive and communicative power is centralized in group leaders (originally Li Hongzhi), who practice direct control over the Falun Dafa[46] Research Society based in Beijing. The Research Society is an administrative mechanism for supporting a broad bureaucratic base for Falun Gong. Within and beneath the Research Society is a central station whose oversight includes main stations in different regions, a range of committees with oversight of specialized functions (propaganda, financing, etc.), and a hierarchy of practice-oriented states (branch, guidance, and practice).[47] This structure is similar to the committee-based structure of China's administrative state, with the leadership positions and the Research Society paralleling the functional power of the Standing Committee and Secretariat. The question is: To what degree is one narrative about Falun Gong's organizational structure more accurate than the other?

Naturally, any attempt to unpack Falun Gong in this vein must recognize the competing, antagonistic polemics that clearly drive public assessments of group operations. Falun Gong maintains its assertion that the group has no objectives other than to function as a social organization popular with large tracts of the domestic population. The PRC, by contrast, maintains a campaign that labels the group an "evil cult." The possible explanations for PRC policy toward Falun Gong are many. However, persecution of the group is far too ingrained in state policy to retreat at this time, and official rhetoric is inevitably guilty of exaggeration on several fronts.

In 1999, when the Chinese government first suppressed the group, official reports claimed that Falun Gong maintained 39 main stations, 1,900 guidance stations, and 28,263 practice sites around the country.[48] According to Tong, the hierarchical narrative of Falun Gong's neat organization and extensive distribution at various functional levels suffers from a number of irregularities. First among these is the fact that various subdivisions of the organization do not map perfectly onto different regional and local boundaries.[49] There is duplication in the main stations, branch stations, and practice sites servicing different locales, and this duplication is extreme in some areas. This implies a great amount of inefficiency in coordination. Likewise, Falun Gong designated the Wuhan main station as controller of other main stations in the late 1990s,[50] introducing new layers of administrative control, prompting enduring confusion about the jurisdiction of different main stations and causing a gradual devolution in planning authority to lower levels.[51] And finally, changing standards set by Chinese authorities across different regions on the standards for organization format—mostly becoming stricter over time—created massive variation in station local structure, further loosening the coordinative and directive abilities of group leaders.[52]

Overall, the image that emerges from any examination of the different elements of Falun Gong's organizational structure is one of diminished hierarchy. The group certainly began as a highly bureaucratic organization in 1992. However, by 1996 it started to suffer from a lack of mechanical resiliency. Some of this was intended,[53] and some appears to be subsequent bureaucratic blunder. Though there is clear and strong leadership from Li Chang, Wang Zhiwen, Yu Changxin, and Li Hongzhi—and while Falun Gong was for a brief time quite well organized—the enduring regime narrative about an authoritarian organization fails on several fronts. First, as noted, the various subdivisions of Falun Gong suffered from duplication and unclear links to higher levels of the group. Though Falun Gong maintained a number of committees with specialized focus, these have increasingly been disbanded, re-formed, or brought under the direct control of group leadership.[54] As a result, the early arms of the wing cannot be said to have specific functional value so much as the Research Society itself did increasingly centralize the organization of publications, irregular forums, and more. Likewise, group funding, though certainly benefiting from sales of merchandise and teachings counter to the claims of Li Hongzhi, suffered across the 1990s and into the 2000s from the need to keep prices for such services low and appears to be minimal.[55] Finally, Falun Gong's doctrinal evolution, despite the centralization of most functions beyond basic instruction to group leadership, was clearly fragmented as of 1999. Though messaging became clearer with the gradual removal of administrative strata to enable better communication with group members, there has increasingly been limited control over a large number of branch stations that advocate locally specific solutions to state repression, including violent protest. In many ways, it is this dynamic that has driven more recent evolutions of the movement, which have built on the functional successes of singular elements of the diaspora movement to create a viable subversive enterprise aimed at dissolving the cultural, political, and social authority of the CCP.

The Evolution toward True Subversive Objectives

To say that Falun Gong represents a clear case of countercultural, fringe perspective on either mainstream Chinese society or global society might at first feel like something conditioned as assumption by the government of the PRC. After all, Beijing has persistently labeled the movement and organization an "evil cult" and accused countless members from top to bottom of being seditious, subversive, and treasonous. This book does not make that case. Rather, it would be far more accurate to say that Falun Gong has transitioned over the more than two decades since its outlaw moment toward subversion as a strategy of approach to broad sociopolitical transformation. At the outset, Falun Gong's protest of the CCP and of the state's hold on Chinese society tactically mimicked that of any number of traditional advocacy movements around the world. Ardent condemnation of the CCP was found in peaceful protests across the West and in the explicit writings of anti-CCP advocates in publications sponsored by (or sympathetic to) Falun Gong, many of which had a greater online than in-person footprint. Perhaps of most interest in the movement's use of the internet, the first decade of Falun Gong life as an exiled community of communities saw the development of political rewiring tools by a few diaspora member groups. These tools were aimed at undermining the functional power of the Chinese state to censor and spy on Falun Gong practitioners, and, via their use by other dissidents and pro-democracy groups around the world, earned the movement no small amount of capital as a strident—if quirky—champion of anti-authoritarian principles.

However, these narratives around Falun Gong, which have earned the movement much goodwill in the West, can be misleading. While there is much to defend about the movement's efforts throughout the 2000s to protest the practices of the CCP and buttress the cause of oppressed organizations, to equate Falun Gong's advocacy with pro-democracy or even anti-authoritarian principles would be to misrepresent the quite narrow grievances and driving objectives of the group. In much private information uncovered by researchers and journalists over the past two decades, Falun Gong leadership and the more organized elements of the movement have emphasized the goal of disintegrating the power of the CCP and transforming Chinese society by shifting prevailing global views on Beijing's influence, ideologies, and mentalities of rule. It is this mission statement that has dictated the transition of the movement away from a somewhat unusual, secretive grassroots organization in the first decade of the 21st century to a more genuinely subversive social movement in the second.

As this section recounts, the most significant functional manifestations of Falun Gong today have been retooled in the mold of those state-sponsored influence campaigns that have plagued the West since at least 2014. Specifically, organizations like the *Epoch Times* news outlet and the Sound of Hope radio station have undergone major strategic reconditioning as sprawling news media operations that utilize techniques both legitimate and shady to grow outreach around often unrelated issues and build agenda-setting power. In doing so, Falun Gong has rapidly built an influence machine of surprising proportions, increasingly trading much of the accrued progressive capital of years past for such capacity. The cost of growth has meant alignment with far-right ideas, voices, and ideologies. Indeed, it is this rising tide of diminished goodwill that perhaps most strongly makes the case that this turn toward tactics that emphasize social construction and manipulation organically results from Falun Gong commitment to a subversive victory. After all, not only have other grassroots advocacy movements not reacted to the social turn in web technologies over the past decade by turning toward misinformation, but the leadership of Falun Gong has demonstrably accepted the loss of social capital built since 1999 in the most entrenched arenas of pro-democracy outlook in the West as a necessary cost to the furtherment of their subversive ambitions.

Toward Political Rewiring

As discussed in earlier sections, the exile of Falun Gong's leader and the subsequent crackdowns by the PRC government led to a diaspora of adherents. On the one hand, many adherents moved their practice of *qigong* and their support of the movement underground, operating only in clandestine settings to avoid government scrutiny in much the same way that China's many religious sects do. On the other hand, an already growing network of communities of practitioners—both expatriates and local converts—in other Asian nations and Western countries were joined by those forced into exile either by circumstance or by the actions of Chinese state security measures.

Both sets of diaspora communities—at home and abroad—rapidly set about opposing the oppression of the PRC. Through 2001, Falun Gong protesters organized in-person displays in Tiananmen Square and in several other cities across China. Though protests were largely peaceful, government response resulted in nearly 30,000 arrests in just the year following Li's exile in 1999. Hundreds of arrests in 2001 across just a few events were the final gasps of Falun Gong's on-street attempts to advocate for the acceptance of the movement and its practices. In the several years that followed, adherents were pushed almost entirely underground, with only a handful of hardline protesters remaining out of state custody who yet refused to accept the necessity of clandestine operation. This number dwindled quickly. For those underground, activism mimicked that seen in authoritarian countries in North Africa and the Middle East, both before and since. Central sites for producing and distributing protest materials were organized as a shadow iteration of the network of guidance stations that, by that point, had been closed by state security actions. These materials, from booklets and pamphlets to DVDs, were then distributed door-to-door or at small group meetings. In many cases, these efforts benefited from the sympathy of citizens with an interest in other underground practices, such as of Christianity. In many other cases, however, these attempts to spread material led to further arrests. In a few cases, practitioners caught distributing Falun Gong content were killed on site.

Interviews with adherents (many of whom are former practitioners) in China and abroad between 2000 and 2010 suggest that the movement's doctrine was centered on building social opposition to the restriction of Falun Gong among the mainstream of PRC citizenry such that popular backlash would provoke reform in one way or another. The result of this was only partially underground advocacy. It was also efforts to "radicalize" foreign populations against the CCP's campaign against Falun Gong and, as a necessary corollary to advocacy, to circumvent the power of the Chinese state. On the former point, two distinctions are clear and critical to note. Through at least 2006, efforts to set the agenda on the CCP abroad emphasized the crackdowns as an undesirable feature of the status quo in China but did not, aside from the overarching narrative that suppression was the result of corrupt politicking and nepotistic institutions within the broader state, levy the need for replacement of the PRC itself. At the same time, Falun Gong advocacy in this vein was, at times, curiously mute on the legitimacy of *all* such efforts to suppress certain social or political groups in China. Most notably, some early material for distribution door-to-door made a case against thinking about Falun Gong alongside the other social elements that the PRC had also labeled "evil cults," such as Eastern Lightning. These early signs of nuance in the style of protest advocacy favored by Falun Gong practitioners and communities were further strong evidence that the movement's subversive bona fides matured both as the techniques of the activist proved largely ineffectual and the methods and reach of the Chinese state gained sophistication.

With regard to the group's early attempts to circumvent CCP authority, members of movement have been implicated in the use of a range of off-the-shelf email spamming applications[56] and have advised practitioners to utilize encryption software over the years,[57] the use of which is outlawed in China. Falun Gong arrestees have used TOR (The Onion Router, which is used to anonymously access different kinds of websites on the internet, Deep Web, and Dark Web)[58] and have allegedly purchased malware.[59] Adherents of Falun Gong have certainly violated Chinese law, which they consider illegitimate in any case, numerous times by setting up websites that proselytize against the CCP. A specifically noteworthy feature of such efforts is the manner in which Falun Gong websites have persistently emphasized the creation of communities around *qigong* and group beliefs.[60] Emails retrieved by journalists in 2007 included instructions for website design for Falun Gong practitioners that argue that social features should be prioritized over the basic provision of information, for example, "Mind-Body Cultivation Requires Spiritual Experience" and "Benevolence Requires Connection."

This prioritization of social mobilization and construction is also seen in what is perhaps the most notable effort undertaken by affiliates of the movement to circumvent Chinese state censorship (in the form of the

Golden Shield system).⁶¹ Through the mid-2000s, a series of foreign-based practitioners and volunteers were the enabling mechanism for the development of Falun Gong's most well-known contribution to the circumventive abilities of protest groups around the world: a piece of software that allows users to access the internet free from censorship.⁶² Important to the functioning of this program is a series of proxy servers maintained around the world by individuals and groups supportive of Falun Gong. Versions of the software have variously pointed users to home webpages chosen, unsurprisingly, to advertise Falun Gong messaging or imagery. Interviews with five such hosts through 2016 also indicate that the prime directive of this web of involved persons and institutions is a social one around the growth of the network itself given that, as one individual puts it, "[the] Communists [are] relentless in takedowns because they know the threat of transparency."

The embrace of political rewiring as a core tactic of resistance against the Chinese state gained Falun Gong much social capital in the West through the early 2010s. Software like Ultrasurf and Freegate has become popular in Iran, Syria, Vietnam, and elsewhere among dissident groups and supporters of web freedom, and these secondary users have been the source of various modifications made to Falun Gong–sourced program design over the past decade.⁶³ The move toward developing such capabilities has also been the cause of authoritarian governments' attempts to build more sophisticated censorship tools, which were themselves a response to stepped-up attempts at digital interdiction. As early as the yearlong period between October 1999 and October 2000, the Chinese government engaged a number of companies to help them make their internet censorship campaign against Falun Gong more effective.⁶⁴ The PRC's Public Security Bureau stipulated a desire to effectively track Falun Gong adherents, monitor activities, and, where possible, retrieve information on the organization.⁶⁵ A number of companies, some like Nortel and Cisco based in the West, responded and provided the PRC with a range of tools for tracking down Falun Gong members using the web. By early 2000, more than four dozen Falun Gong members had been arrested based exclusively on their web-based activities.⁶⁶ Perhaps more significant, hundreds of thousands of adherents were increasingly denied access to Falun Gong websites and information repositories through the enhanced countersubversive efforts of the state in denying access.⁶⁷ Search terms linked with Falun Gong became the most stringently censored on Chinese social media sites, a trend that continues today.⁶⁸ In response to this suppression, Falun Gong volunteers led the development of DynaWeb, a system designed to allow members to circumvent state-imposed restrictions via rotating access to proxy servers located around the world. Practitioner-developed tools like Ultrareach and FreeGate quickly followed, forming a web of mechanisms with which a staff of sympathizers—calling themselves the Global Internet Freedom Consortium—could reroute traffic to allow for unfettered access to the web.[69]

In the months and several years after these developments, Falun Gong became the first target of denial of service attacks sponsored by the government.[70] Falun Gong's main web portal, Clearwisdom.net, was repeatedly attacked for a period of months in 2001 by hackers based in Beijing and Shenzhen.[71] It was in response to these attacks, in particular, that movement members noted in 2002, 2004, and 2005 the need to diversify the sources of Falun Gong teachings and the need to build a multifaceted community.[72] The result was the proliferation of Falun Gong teachings across the internet referenced above, aided by the decentralization of the organization that came with the international diaspora and the move by adherents to establish instruction and outreach portals in spaces as diverse as darknet sites, personal blogs, and social media. The grassroots character of the movement would be emphasized and embellished both by Falun Gong advocates and in media representations through the early 2010s. However, belief among the group's leadership that a movement so organized could succeed in toppling the influence of the CCP and the Chinese state never solidified as much as public representations often suggest. The result was a shift in focus after the midpoint of the 2010s toward an alternative set of methods for resisting the Middle Kingdom, rooted in the widespread socialization of the global information environment underwritten by the internet and functionally more compatible with the movement's evolving ambitions for subversive success.

Resisting the Reach of Beijing: Social Construction, Disinformation, and the *Epoch Times*

For years, the public arms of the Falun Gong organization-cum-social-movement in the West have been, principally, a cash-cow dance troupe called Shen Yun and two media outlets broadly geared toward presenting generic news coverage of a range of issues with a clear anti-CCP angle. Throughout the 2000s and into the 2010s, these two outlets—the television broadcaster New Tang Dynasty (NTD) and the newspaper *Epoch Times*—became synonymous with low-quality interest journalism. Ask anybody who lived and worked in a major East Coast urban center in the United States in that time if they recall the *Epoch Times*, and it is highly probable that, perhaps after some prompting, they will recall the street-corner newspaper vending boxes or the piles of fresh, unopened newspapers with an odd name plastered on the header being delivered to myriad businesses. Of course, it's also not unlikely the typical respondent will remember not ever picking up a copy or perhaps using the publication only for one of the secondary tasks assigned to all newspapers—as box padding, perhaps. Such was the relatively low readership of a paper whose claimed circulation was, even in the mid-2000s, in the tens of millions.

This was the long-standing experience of Falun Gong's affiliated media services. That is, until 2016. That year, the *Epoch Times* made the decision to lean hard into a new media strategy, one that mirrored a range of efforts undertaken by foreign affiliates, domestic supporters of then-candidate Donald Trump, and foreign information warfare campaigns alike. Indeed, perhaps it would be fairer to say that Falun Gong and not just *Epoch Times* made the decision to lean into new strategy and tactics, as the intervening five years—up until the writing of this book—have seen a range of new media transformations and new initiatives linked to the movement. But it was the *Epoch Times* that led the way, opting in 2016–2017 to anchor their style of reporting to the right-wing ecosystem that was attempting to elect a highly protectionist—and thus anti-China—Trump and betting big financially on the outreach power of Facebook.

The publication outlet and its leadership within the Falun Gong movement looked to several individuals who for some years had operated *Epoch Times* and affiliated media operations in non-Western markets, particularly the executive—Trung Vu—responsible for *Dai Ky Nguyen*, the edition of *Epoch Times* published in Vietnam. Under Vu, the *Times* focused on building a funneling machine of sorts, a pipeline of influence that would begin on Facebook by capturing the attention of millions of users across an immense diversity of circumstances and then lead them back toward the more directly controlled elements of Falun Gong's media empire. The *New York Times* reported in 2017 that the *Epoch Times* spent around $1.8 million on ads on Facebook in just one year, eclipsing similar purchases by more conventional news organizations and even many political campaigns.[73] They also heavily leaned into less-than-kosher methods for driving page viewership and building influence, which people many attributed directly to the lessons learned by Vu's team in the less-regulated and more congested information environment of Vietnam. This kind of activity ultimately led to the banning of much *Epoch Times* and related content from Facebook.[74] By 2019, *Epoch Times* was spending over half a million dollars per annum on what are called "sock puppet" accounts and spaces. These are misleading fronts for *Epoch Times*'s (and thus Falun Gong's) influence and included fake accounts parroting links to group-sponsored content alongside pages for hard-to-define advocacy fronts like the Patriots for America. A partner enterprise started by Vu several years earlier called TheBL.com, in which "BL" stands for "Beauty of Life," was particularly prolific in its use of fake accounts, so much so that Facebook banned the organization in late 2019 and publicly commented on *Epoch Times*'s own activities.[75] Shockingly, Facebook claimed that the organization's outlays on advertising had surpassed $9.5 million over four years by late 2019 and had resulted in immense popularity, with about 55 million followers of related content.[76] This figure does not count followers or visibility of content linked to organizations that have appeared since 2016 as clear doppelgängers of the *Epoch Times*, such as *America Daily* or *Vision Times*, and so this influence figure is likely somewhat higher still.

Falun Gong's dramatic shift in focus toward alternative media usage parallels much of what this book argues was the experience—driven by subversive positioning and objectives—of the Fringe 1.0. Specifically, the past several years have seen a clear embrace of tactics inspired by foreign influence campaigns and shady far-right advocacy groups. *Epoch Times* and parallel extensions of Falun Gong have particularly embraced the idea that subterfuge, clandestine influence, and social engineering are far more useful to the movement than the generally unremarkable focus on outspoken criticism and the generic pursuit of ratings to increase the readership of such criticism that characterized the pre-2016 period.

This is clear not only in the shifting practices of *Epoch Times* and the diversification of similar entities that have turned to less than legitimate methods for attracting followers and funneling them toward core content. In the wake of the January 6 attempted insurrection, a host of technology companies in the United States and Europe took action to ban accounts and content tied to far-right agitators perceived to have had some role in the digital preamble to the events of that day. In addition to high-profile bans of Trump himself and others, this included the deplatforming of far-right mouthpieces from Facebook and Twitter followed by the *voluntary* self-deplatforming of followers unwilling to continue in spaces that did not support their right to speech. The result was a diaspora to more accepting virtual spaces, from Parler to new services that popped up seemingly overnight. One such service that has gained a substantial following is SafeChat, a previously unremarkable Falun Gong–linked social media service that boomed in popularity in 2021. Month on month, the site's traffic quadrupled following January 6, and developer activity for the platform intensified by an order of magnitude. New landing pages set up to entice right-wing users appeared over a series of weeks in early 2021, many parroting conspiracy theories tied to QAnon. The site began a campaign of talking up its security over alternative right-wing platforms, enlisting conservative mouthpieces to advertise its "military-grade" encryption in spite of lacking evidence thereof, even given prompting by numerous journalists. And, as a cursory examination of activity since the start of 2021 shows, moderator activity has boomed with clear application of content curation and banning—ironically, given the "free speech" pitch made in advertising—in what appears to be an attempt to keep discourse focused and avoid the social fragmentation that has spelled the decline of so many alternative fringe spaces since January 6.

Falun Gong and the Lessons of Ideational Oppression

What explains Falun Gong's tactical shift as of 2016–2017 toward methods in line with the Fringe 1.0 experience described in Chapter 3? Several explanations seem possible. The first is simple functional opportunism. For almost the entire lifespan of the movement, Falun Gong's media strategy has been premised on the idea that publicity gained is influence gained. Generic reporting on celebrities and lifestyle trends in *Epoch Times* has always been undertaken in aid of the broader cause, specifically the critique of China and the spiritual salvation of "sentient beings" (i.e., nonpractitioners of Falun Gong). In 2016–2017, a series of emergent social realities about the use of web technologies by fringe social movements and communities, populist political parties, and even foreign influence operators came to a head. The problem of broad-scope interference in the 2016 presidential election is often underspecified by a singular focus on the tactics and intention of the Russian Federation and its agent, the Internet Research Agency. And yet, as the next chapter in particular explores, the basis of such successful interference—whether or not an actual impact on the eventual electoral result occurred—was the reflexive evolution of both social web architecture and the political interests of those embedded in different spheres of the digital world. The lessons for any actor interested in extending influence without regard for the perceived legitimacy of the tactics to be leveraged were obvious.

Another possibility is that Falun Gong leadership perceived that the past approach to engagement and media instrumentation was fundamentally doomed to failure. This explanation provides a reasonably robust basic rationale for the desire to alter approaches but is insufficient by itself for explaining the exact manner and timing of the tactical shift in the mid-2010s. In particular, while it may seem fair to say that a decade and a half of operating NTD, *Epoch Times*, and other wings of the broader Falun Gong ecosystem as a web for capturing attention and funneling it toward the group's preferred topics of advocacy, it's also the case that the group suffered almost no reputational or regulatory costs as a result of its activities. While pamphlet canvassing and protest activities aimed at CCP-linked issues certainly gained Falun Gong the reputation of a quirky, alternative, and perhaps cult-like entity, the group also garnered the benefits of their activism in support of human rights and against authoritarian oppression. In this way, it's quite arguable that they resembled something like the Church of Latter Day Saints or Scientology, but plus the benefits of the anti-oppression reputation and absent any particularly sinister cult-like associations. And so while the lack of substantial progress for the cause might motivate a change in approach, there is also a clear cost to having made such a commitment. The question then remains: What would incentivize such cost acceptance?

A range of other circumstantial explanations might also be considered. First, did the reach of Beijing's power play a role in prompting what amounts to something of an escalation—or at least a rise in the assertiveness—of methods favored? Little evidence exists that persecution of Falun Gong has worsened in recent years. While adherents in China are still often arrested and held without cause, censorship and repression have not surged in any observable fashion since the 2000s. Second, did something change in the worldview of those involved in pulling the strings of the broader organization-cum-movement? Specifically, might the example of Trumpism's rise as an apparently viable political force that saw Chinese power as fundamentally illegitimate have prompted the desire for an alignment with the political right in the West? It seems possible that this argument holds some weight. However, the nature of the tactics turned to by *Epoch Times* and other arms of Falun Gong influence suggests that the rightward shift is opportunistic more than a true political alignment. On the one hand, *Epoch Times* has been seen to take funding from conservative magnates and donors since at least 2019. On the other, the strategic character of the post-2016 shift has centered on social manipulation and tight control of information. Rather than underwrite conservative political interests directly, patterns of content promotion on Facebook, on SafeChat, and in more conventional news publications still seems to focus on the potential for attention over the salience of a topic.

Finally, it is possible that Falun Gong's tactical reorientation was premised on the decline of certain membership and practitioner demographics. If the adherent base was gradually becoming less diverse across generational, socioeconomic, and geographic lines, the shift could represent a somewhat desperate effort to evolve the way new members could be "captured." This explanation is appealing because it helps to explain the persistence of tactics like the use of fake accounts or the purposive spread of misinformation in the wake of objections by adherents that—in what seems to be a fairly robust argument—such shady activities fundamentally compromise the spiritual quest for moral betterment that Falun Gong encourages. It is also predicted by sociological work on New Religious Movements (NRMs), a label that at least partly applies to Falun Gong. Rodney Stark theorizes, for instance, that NRMs will succeed if success across eight criteria can be maintained:

> cultural continuity with the conventional faiths of the society in which it appears or originates; maintaining a medium level of tension with its surrounding environment; achieving effective mobilization with strong governance and a high level of individual commitment; attracting and maintaining a normal age and sex structure; occurring within a favourable ecology which exists as a relatively unregulated religious economy and weakened conventional faiths; maintaining dense internal network relations; resisting secularization; and socializing the young.[77]

The issue for this potential argument, alas, is simply that Falun Gong has been quite successful across each of these categories. While there has reportedly been a larger than normal exodus of second-generation practitioners in recent years, the movement as a whole has been enormously successful in onboarding young professionals from across the vocational spectrum. Moreover, the group never requires rejection of everyday occupations or social experiences, even if those circumstances often change as people become more committed to the practice of Falun Gong. If anything, the immense labor force that Falun Gong has persistently been able to call upon for protest and activism *in addition to* staffing the various media-oriented elements of its operations speaks to the commitment of those associated. And given that the group's main areas of operation are now outside of China, even a lack of freedom of religion does not stand as a likely pillar of dramatic behavioral change.

Toward Disempowerment

There is clearly a time-and-place opportunism to many of the specific recent actions taken by Falun Gong in its use of web technologies for subversive advocacy. Likewise, the long-term failure of the preceding tactical emphasis on participationist advocacy from a position of relative "otherness" in global society to do much more than sustain a minor voice on issues of interest seems likely to have made Li and other leaders open to the idea of change. Both conditions are only sufficient explanations of the post-2016 tactical shift, however. Neither explains the basis for suffering (1) the costs of lost progressive capital in the West or (2) the potential for membership fragmentation due to the conflicting moral bases of Falun Gong beliefs and new tactics.

What would explain the specific shape of the turn toward such tactics is a more full-throated embrace of subversion as the necessary strategy for achieving eventual success. This argument, of course, would suggest that Falun Gong was not a subversive enterprise after its ouster to the fringes of global society in the 1990s and 2000s. Based on this chapter's historical recounting of the movement—in particular, the manner in which it turned to the internet in the early Web 2.0 era—such a proposition seems reasonable. When the movement was forcibly ejected from mainstream Chinese society, its leadership and growth communities spread across the Western world. Though the base presumption of CCP illegitimacy has tinged perceptions of Falun Gong from an early point, the belief system espoused by the movement has little to do with the function of material systems, political, social, or otherwise. And of course, the group's tactics, online and off-, in no way smack of an attempt to create conditions favorable for a normative seachange prior to 2016. Like Eastern Lightning or nativist Hong Kong elements tied to the Umbrella movement, Falun Gong used the internet as a tool for coordination and basic proselytizing rather than for spreading the influence of a politically motivated cause.

So what factor provided the impetus for accepting certain costs and shifting toward a strategy of subversion? The most likely single factor is the meteoric rise of Trump, though the emergence of a global pandemic with initial infections in China may have played a reinforcing role. Trump's populist, protectionist approach to voter appeals from the start of his campaign in 2015 played off the idea that various social forces were giving Americans a bad deal. While this idea of a nomadic power dynamic tilted so as to disadvantage certain citizens is not dissimilar to generic critiques of CCP power made by Falun Gong adherents, it is (1) the tying of such a perspective to potential political power and (2) being successfully pitched to unusual and diverse populations both in the United States and elsewhere that seem most likely to have convinced Li—as with other conservative-leaning entities—to believe that a lateral approach to disempowering China was possible. Then, as with the Fringe 1.0, a subversive perspective begot a need for tactics that would simultaneously achieve several interrelated goals: (1) social control within both core and peripheral fringe spaces, (2) an ability to manipulate information conditions, and (3) a capacity for funneling mainstream audiences toward fringe ideas. The digital environment into which Falun Gong stepped, however, was inevitably quite different from that of the days of the Web 1.0. Rather, Falun Gong's new methods of approach have increasingly had to be geared toward a social environment as much defined by a subversive perspective as by the interaction of virtual spaces' architecture, management, and offline correlates—that of the Fringe 2.0.

5
Fringe 2.0
Cyber Cultism and the Effects of Networked Subversion

The previous two chapters established the case that subversion breeds a tactical focus on social engineering and information control. In particular, the Fringe 1.0 enterprise was one fundamentally defined by attempts to figure out the network and socialize the tools of new interconnectivity afforded by web technologies. And yet the experiences and groups referenced in Chapter 3—and in the case of Falun Gong, in its immediate postexile days, for that matter—are quite different from the landscape of fringe advocacy and antagonism seen at the outset of the 2020s. Today the landscape of fringe activity is fragmented and split across an immensely varied set of cyberspaces, at the same time more potent *and* less cohesive than in years past. This chapter describes the counters of the Fringe 2.0, a phenomenon not only framed around common subversive preferences regarding the use of media and information technologies but also given specific shape by structural developments in the architecture of the Web 2.0 era.

In particular, I look for the agency of subversive communities and social movements as it shapes and is shaped by the contours of online environments and various offline corollaries. The thesis of this chapter is simple: it is not possible to understand recent evolutions of fringe advocacy and antagonism without considering the agency of technology firms and sociopolitical actors that—due to the manner in which cyberspace has been socialized and automated in recent years—is present as a metaphorical ghost in the code, something that shapes users' actions by the simple fact of certain design and management choices. And yet fringe agency still has meaning, with the entrenched tendency toward disinformation and social control helping to shape a modern manifestation of subversion that thrives on network affordances.

Radicalization and Information Flows in the Era of Social Media

As previously described, the mid-2000s saw the rise of what would be called Web 2.0. This second "version" of the web would not fundamentally change the physical or logical landscape of the internet a great deal, that is, beyond seeing an expansion of the real-world footprint of telecommunications networks, the upgrading of protocols, the addition of redundancies to accommodate booming web usage, and so on. What *would* be entirely new would be the shift toward user-generated content by private firms that were driven to commoditize the tools and spaces they developed. More specifically, the rise of the Web 2.0 era—which the world remains within as of the writing of this book—would be premised on three sets of revolutions in web technologies. The first, as has been described, was the rise of socially oriented market capitalist internet products and services. The second was the emergence and then the swift boom of the mobile web, an industrial-informational revolution that succeeded in moving processing power, applications, and personal web experiences from the desktop to in-pocket devices in only a few years. And the third was the cloud. Cloud computing is, in essence, the provision of processing power and storage capacity from immense data centers to users on an on-demand basis but without any requirement for the user to manage those capacities. The cloud as a service freed up capital for a boom in the development industry—development of applications, hardware, web services, and more—as companies no longer had to buy their own infrastructure.

Much literature on the impact of the internet on social movements, extremism and terrorism, civil society, and more centers on basic web characteristics like the relatively borderless, gatekeeperless nature of the thing or on the constitution of the global internet as a massive repository of information around which social interactions can occur. While these attributes are worth initial consideration in any conversation about the impact of the internet on social engagement, the reality is that the Web 2.0 era is better understood in terms of several alternative characteristics, namely (1) dynamic content experiences, (2) rich user participation, (3) software as a service, (4) self-classification, (5) the essentiality of the web, and (6) commercialization of architecture. The first two quite simply refer to the way in which Web 2.0 spaces are characterized by extensive, alluring structured content—whether multimedia or otherwise—and by an ability on the part of the user to customize and shape the content of their environment. Countless applications can be restructured by user inputs to present different layouts, color schemes, functional options, and more in much the way a gamer might customize a video game character look or loadout. Social media platforms that emphasize user-built communities offer tools for guiding the experience of members of those communities. And social aggregation spaces often delineate clear rules for how content will be recirculated and viewed by other users, allowing for adaptive information production strategizing. "Software as a service" refers to the way cloud resources are leveraged to centralize application functionality and allow web users to access novel tools via their browser or through simple local interfaces. And self-classification—what is often called "folksonomy"—simply describes the manner in which users are empowered not only to create content in dynamic fashion but also to take an active role in defining the attributes (via tagging or otherwise interacting with data) of the content discovered online.

While these characteristics of the Web 2.0 experience are sociotechnical in nature, the final two listed above refer more to offline, nontechnical characteristics of the web experience that nevertheless have an immense impact on the development of internet services, tools, and spaces. Web essentiality is the recognition of the fact that internet usage has for many years not been an option for most elements of civil society in developed (and many developing) industrial economies. From e-services to job applications, many necessities for operation in modern society require access or management via the use of some internet-connected or -enabled system. The natural implication of this in the Web 2.0 era is, of course, that the demographics of web usage have rapidly come to mirror the demographics of societies writ large rather than the narrow slices of society that found purpose, entertainment, or connection in earlier times. The final characteristic of the Web 2.0 experience, the commercialization of architecture, is in many ways both the cause and the effect of such mass participation in internet usage. The years after the dot-com boom saw the commercialization of ideas implemented in fragmented parts during the 1990s, leading to the foundations of the rich user experience described above. But widespread adoption—forced adoption in some ways—of the services and platforms these efforts produced continues to spur yet further attempts to shape the online experience for billions of people in line with commercial interests. Indeed, this effect is so obvious that the accusation leveled against firms like Facebook or Apple or Google that their users are more the product than the actual hardware or software their company builds seems fairly uncontroversial. Commercial improvement of novel web technologies led to the hyperadoption of internet-connected systems, which has subsequently crafted commercial interests around the value that users themselves generate by their use of the network.

For our discussion of subversion in the digital age, the implications of Web 2.0 characteristics—both online and offline—are a unique set of expectations around fringe advocacy and engagement. While the agency of subversively motivated actors clearly produced certain tactical tendencies that were realized in early web exploration as attempts to build social and informational control, the same fringe agency in recent years has been both initially and reflexively shaped by the contours of an environment that itself produces distinct social effects. This means that attempts to radicalize, to persuade, and to organize activities that might disempower the status quo have been fundamentally augmented by the functionality of the environment itself. The remaining sections of this chapter explore what this has looked like, tracking the agency of subversive societal elements at work amid such environmental determinants. I then present a theory to explain why fringe narratives and activities seem to be so much more present in the mainstream of global society now than in the past.

Paranoia and the Cultish Character of Fringe Spaces

The spaces of the Fringe 2.0 are a strange beast, at least to the casual observer. In studying the communities, collectives, and free-for-all discussion forums of many alternative perspectives, one could be forgiven for feeling that the fringe is at once disorganized and highly coordinated. Whether the community in question is populated with White supremacist rhetoric, flat-earther theorizing, or misogynistic hate, it can be difficult to look at what notionally presents as a free, open space for social engagement and not think that there may somewhere be a wizard hiding behind a curtain. After all, Web 2.0 spaces—especially restrictive community spaces—are often defined by collective intelligence and a surprisingly rich personal experience for even transient visitors. In part, of course, this is the architecture of Web 2.0 at work. In part, however, collective and connective effects appear because of the cumulative social actions of users, user groups, and those who run distinct virtual spaces.

The best way to describe how a nuanced and robust fabric of fringe advocacy emerges online is by noting the manner in which their virtual operation mimics the paranoid mindset of cults. While such spaces are generally discoverable for the casual internet browser, the pathways to engaging with community content and members are quite narrow. Content is sometimes behind invitation-based or other types of access wall. Even where that is not the case, communities on social news aggregation sites like Reddit are indexed only such that threads are likely to reach a casual searcher if they are tagged as popular in some way. It is far more likely that users find their way to such spaces by pursuing a chain of issue-specific links or information requests than by general consumption of news or mainstream social media.

Such spaces also tend to exhibit social dynamics comparable to the self-policing subcultures often found in conspiratorial groups and cults.[1] On the one hand, communities often cultivate norms about initial contact with new members that, alongside the narrow pathway outsiders must take to engage in such spaces, emphasize "capturing" naïve or interested parties. Often, such contact involves a deluge of information on topics of interest to the new member and a sales pitch that emphasizes the exclusive nature of information and camaraderie to be found in the community. On the other hand, communities encourage content absolutism, wherein a set of prevailing perspectives drives acceptance of new content, members, and symbols. Such a system acts to reinforce members' buy-in to a group by tacitly—and occasionally explicitly—threatening members' position. After all, greater social value within the group becomes attached to the most conformist postings, and the development of deep trust relationships emerging from reasonably insular social processes provides a clear basis for potential coercion (e.g., the doxing of a member) should trust be violated.

As noted, the unique social fabric of conspiratorial communities generally leads to the framing of community knowledge as sacred, even if it is not factual or distinct. Cultivation of such a dynamic is particularly possible because of the regularity of lateral introduction of new information from mouthpieces where there is clear symbolic value being grafted onto discourse. The result is a tendency toward the legitimation of extreme rhetoric and views that, regardless of any other attributes, embody the "otherness" of the community's perspective vis-à-vis a mainstream system that is deemed to be rigged or dishonest.[2]

Of course, the context of conspiratorial communities hosted on various social media and social news aggregation platforms—or, for that matter, on darknet sites—is dramatically different from that of most cult organizations.³ On such platforms, owned by private companies or run by individuals paying for hosting services, there is no such thing as protections for free speech. As such, there is likewise no prohibition against the moderation or manipulation of discourse. Indeed, the operators of platforms like Facebook, X (Twitter), Reddit, Instagram, and YouTube provide their users with a large number of tools via which such shaping might occur. In part, these are by design. Facebook allows ad purchasers to target users based on keyword search, geographical information, and more. Reddit has at various points in time allowed moderators to delete content and promote via a system of pinning posts to the top of a subreddit's main board.

In part, of course, the existence of potential avenues for shaping content simply emerges from the observable design of such platforms. Reddit, X (Twitter), and other services whose content-promotion systems work based on likes, clicks, retweets, or upvotes are invariably sensitive to click fraud that sees bot accounts employed to artificially inflate the popularity rating of a given post.⁴ Optimization of keyword usage in titles, semantic tag (e.g., hashtag) usage, and so on make it more likely that ads will reach particular demographics or that certain video content will be monetized. Moderator privileges can often be used to augment such inflation by cross-listing across site sections. And both deft use of parallel reposting of content and narrative softening can allow communities to sidestep censorship restrictions set up by the administrators of broader content ecosystems. The result is an environment where the development of cultish communities is normal, but also where a range of covert channels exists via which content can be framed and broadcast beyond the traditionally insular boundaries of conspiratorial collectives.

Finally, an important element of conspiratorial communities' abilities to repackage and rebroadcast their messaging that bears retelling lies with the enduring problem of attribution of online action.⁵ Throwaway and bot accounts provide innumerable opportunities for such communities to amplify their apparent presence within and across social platforms. Perhaps more important, these opportunities for easy pseudonymous activity by one force across multiple fronts allows for added nuance to narrative messaging. Where throwaway accounts are employed by established users of platforms, debate not only seems more diverse than is reality; it can also seem more multifaceted. Softening of tone and rhetoric in order to sell new communities and members on a given perspective is an important capability, particularly where different platforms' norms and culture demand less dogmatic approaches to persuasion than might emerge from the relatively strict discourse of an insular community.

The Case of r/The_Donald

On Reddit, the subreddit "The_Donald"[6] has developed (at the time of writing) into a hub of questionable discourse and information dissemination that is by far the most well-known online space on a major platform devoted to alternative conservative and right-wing dissidence.

In this section, I discuss the cultivation dynamics of the space.[7] I then describe dynamics of thread conversations and private messaging within the community via reference to 34 interviews with members of the space, both former and current (though all current members have purposefully become inactive), including one moderator. This set of interviews was part of a broader study of cultural dynamics of conspiratorial and hacker spaces conducted between January 2017 and January 2019. These interviews were conducted via Skype and FaceTime over a five-month period starting in July 2018. Each interviewee provided identification and demonstration of access to account activity that was verifiable via the public-facing interface so as to ensure credibility of their identity and statements (which is often a barrier to such ethnographic work). The statements of these individuals embellish and add meat to the description of such communities as having cultish tendencies. I then describe the successes experienced by r/The_Donald in projecting its narrative messaging.

Cultivation in r/The_Donald

r/The_Donald was created in mid-2015 with the goal of hosting all discussions and media related to the support of Donald J. Trump as he sought the presidency. The community boasted hundreds of thousands of users before its banning and was one of the more active spaces on Reddit.[8] The space is well known for being a hotbed of competing attempts to cultivate fringe narratives along various lines. This cultivation might be thought of as occurring in two phases.[9] In the first, the main injectors of content constituting a trickle-up approach to community cultivation took the form of prominent bot/troll accounts posting news stories and opinion pieces to r/The_Donald as part of a multifaceted effort to gain attention. Accounts that were primarily active on Twitter up to and beyond the 2016 election were also found to have active presences on Facebook,[10] Tumblr,[11] Telegram,[12] LinkedIn,[13] WhatsApp,[14] TamTam,[15] SoundCloud,[16] LiveJournal,[17] and ok.ru.[18] On Reddit, posts that eventually made a splash and gained accounts a degree of intracommunity elite status were also posted on sister subreddits like r/HillaryforPrison.

Prior to the 2016 election, r/The_Donald was one of the biggest hotbeds of Russian propaganda efforts. Though the efforts of prominent Russian bot operators were broad in scope, particular intention appears to have been placed on the subreddit. The reasons for this could be numerous, but the obvious ones are simply that the community boasts a large population and was reportedly monitored by the Trump campaign so as to regularly have a "finger on the pulse" of the hardcore conservative elements of the base.[19] Moreover, Reddit regularly pushed back against calls from other communities on the platform to ban r/The_Donald. In part, the rationale was that, so long as appropriate steps are taken to ensure the community's content is not unduly favored over other content, members should have the right to their speech. In testimony offered to Congress since the 2016 election, the leadership of Reddit has further stated that banning the subreddit is unlikely to solve perceived issues of interference or of extremism cultivated on the site.

Russian cultivation of r/The_Donald appears to have largely followed the trickle-up approach of circulating content framed as potentially juicy, with two goals: to spread fake and inflammatory content to embed narratives in the culture of digital communities and enhance prospects for spoofing the countervailing tendencies of the broader population; to create where possible elite voices within conspiratorial communities that might pursue the first goal via a trickle-down strategy.

Through early 2018, a series of Russian-controlled propaganda accounts posted in r/The_Donald in tandem with promotional efforts taken on Twitter, Instagram, and elsewhere. Almost 3,000 posts have at the time of writing been linked to accounts clearly paralleling the actions of Russian trolls on Twitter.[20] Two in particular were until 2018 extremely active on the subreddit, posting about 2,000 times and garnering tens of thousands of upvotes. Those two accounts, @ten_gop and @pamela_moore13, over the course of mid-2017 specifically commanded community attention in the form of 10 of the top 20 most upvoted posts. This is quite a remarkable statistic given that estimates of Russian-backed postings on the subreddit are thought to stand at only about 3% of the total amount. These posts included quotes defending the Trump campaign from accusations of racism, as well as falsified and sensationalized reports of leftist extremism. In one post, for instance, Al Sharpton was reported to have urged supporters, "Kill Police."[21] In others, calls to lock up Hillary Clinton were promoted, and a Swedish official was misreported as advising women simply not to go out at night if they didn't want to worry about being raped by Muslim refugees.[22] Each post received at least 10,000 upvotes and at least one of the two accounts was remembered as trusted sources by 27 of the 34 interview respondents.

Following a crackdown on fake personas linked to foreign influence operations that included Reddit's removing 944 accounts, clandestine influence on r/The_Donald has shifted toward an emphasis on back-end content promotion at the cost of abandoning the tactic of building up elite troll voices. During the course of 2018, a series of websites appeared for the first time as repeat hosts of content promoted by accounts (and upvoted hundreds and thousands of times) on the subreddit that had many of the hallmarks of a Russian setup. Two of the most prominent (geotus.army[23] and geotus.band;[24] "geotus" is a common acronym trafficked in right-wing discourse referring to Trump as the "God Emperor of the United States") have indisputable links to Russian oligarchy and the Internet Research Agency (IRA). When clicked on, all links to both sites redirect to a secondary site hosted in Russia called "USA Really." Aside from the attribution of major U.S. cybersecurity firm FireEye that USA Really is a front for the IRA,[25] that site's "About Us" section[26] links to a LinkedIn profile[27] that reveals site ownership belonging to a man named Alexander Malkevich. Malkevich works directly for Yevgeny Prigozhin, a Russian oligarch under indictment by the United States for his role in financing, operating, and directing the IRA (and spinoff operations) in their efforts to interfere with American democratic processes.[28] Alongside other websites that share clear Russian connections and the informational hallmarks of IRA efforts, thousands of posts have been made up to the time of writing.

Narrative Building, Reinforcement, and Conspiratorial Features of Discourse on r/The_Donald

Both as a fringe environ distinct from direct outside intervention and including those posts made by IRA or affiliated operators, user activity on r/

The_Donald and in posts linked to the subreddit are demonstrative of the cultish nature of social dynamics of conspiratorial communities in several distinct ways. First, thread activity invariably trends toward repetition, with deft moderator deletion of deliberative comments and (often moderator-encouraged) community punishment (via the downvoting feature) of objecting voices ensuring the monotone nature thereof. In essence, there is significant evidence of astroturfing[29] by those running community processes. Such activity is present across community content, not only in instances where Russian influence might be suspected. Interestingly, particularly given the community's stated rule of maintaining a safe space for their advocacy, mockery of individuals buying too deeply into one or another conspiracy is not infrequent. Rather, the clear target of moderation is attempts to promote counterrationales.

Former and current (inactive) members of the community interviewed offered various recollections and records that illustrate the dynamic of censorship by repetition within the community. Almost half of all interviewees described private messaging from moderators or (more often) handles that would be seen in most threads that aimed to build camaraderie around an errant post or line of thinking evident on a post. In most cases, respondents described a pointed effort to clarify the exact defensive or counteroffensive argument that errant discourse should be met with. Almost all respondents, even beyond those who regularly received such messaging, felt pressure in how their responses to errant voices should be crafted. Interestingly, in 29 of 34 cases, members of the community described this pressure as being about form rather than substance. Argument and divergent perspectives on a situation are encouraged to some degree, but straying from the premise of the topic (i.e., expanding a conversation to something beyond "them versus us") was punished by moderator deletion or mass downvoting. One particularly interesting practice reported by 11 members is the act of massively piling onto threads wherein the initial comment or countercomment has been deleted. Those situations, one member said, "made it easy to make the thread an us versus them clusterf***." Another noted about the same behavior:

> Its not uncommon for the longest thread reponses to not [be] related to the original post but you have to be on the thread early to kno that. Ive seen a few where someone was pointing out that it could be wrong about hillarys pneumonia seizures being something more serious and the next comment

was just agreement that she was clearly hiding something more. then the original comment was removed and others piled on.

Yet another reported that such threads were used as an opportunity to spam thread participants with private messages linking to several information sources that "disproved" the original poster's position and encouraged further new posting against that position.

INTERVIEWEE: Yeah, it sometimes feels like as much talk goes on in DMs [direct messages] as on the thread.
CW: Under what circumstances would you say you were most likely to get thread-specific DMs like that?
INTERVIEWEE: idk.
I guess when I commented on the megathreads about big issues.

The one I remember getting most stuff in my messages about was when I asked a quesiotn [sic] about a source of a source that Rush Limbaugh had referenced that had been posted about the DNC sabotaging Bernie and I got called a hater and an idiot and stuff. Made me not ask questions like that again.

Some such rebukes occurred on the public-facing threads also. For instance, one set of messages read, "[A poster]needs to gtfo . . . hed should have kpt to the libtarders in [other subreddit.]."

Second, language on the subreddit tends toward the use of distinct phrases and the invocation of common memes to reiterate a sentiment. Beyond the clear tendency in most threads toward greater simplicity in language usage as more comments are appended to a topic, a common example of this is the use of the word "cuck," which appears and reappears across settings applied to different challenges to the community's principles. As McMillen points out, the term is clearly used to signify an opponent of the shared perspective held by the community, which he describes as one of "masculine hegemony." And it has spawned a variety of offshoot and related terms that dot the landscape of nearly all postings in spaces like r/The_Donald. When given the prompt "Would you say there is a common language of r/The_Donald that separates it from more mainstream subreddits?," various interviewees reported this common lexicon:

> Absolutely, everyone not bought into the movement is a cuck and everyone in the know is all lord pepe and the army of kek.

> hahah... for sure everythings trumpified... the lingo is actually a hard sell for newcomers, especially when they're note [sic] challenged on the facts but just called a chad and told to go back to r/politics.

> there's more posting of GEOTUS memes here than anywhere else but theres a lot of crossover mostly with subs like MGTOW[30] and a lot of incels[31] from SRS[32] talking about how pilled[33] everyone is.

But according to those interviewed, terminology like "cuck" is far less often the content of "meme-ification" than are emergent terms and logics that appear in threads clustered around artifacts of current affairs (whether factual or otherwise). Two-thirds of all respondents described the popularity of memes as highly temporal, with specific memes (beyond a few mainstays like original versions of the "Pepe" meme) widely circulated for less than a week before being ousted by another. In most cases, stated one interviewee, the most popular memes were reactive, "pounc[ing] on major criticisms of Trump or Hannity and so on" and recycled one of several jokes about supposedly "liberal" logics of social and political operation. Much of the time, interviewees reported seeing popular memes in private locations or messages first, a particular image's popularity coming from publication in a Discord server or group chat before being blasted to lists of users that at least 13 of the 34 members interviewed suspected they belonged to.

Third, newcomers to the space, when not directly hostile from the outset, are bombarded with information and invited to explore the community in a highly supervised setting. This behavior is not unusual for conspiratorial and more mainstream communities alike in that newcomers to a space often find it difficult to grasp norms of operation. Supervision in one form or another amounts to the formalization of rules of the road where those rules may be minimally apparent in written form. With conspiratorial communities, however, the significant difference lies with the manner in which newcomers are groomed toward behaviors that are reinforcing of the restrictive community patterns described above.

With r/The_Donald, 17 of the individuals interviewed got involved in posting via users known from other online spaces, while the remainder found the community on their own, bar one who was introduced by a coworker. A common theme in interviews focused on the manner in which messaging from other members of r/The_Donald changed over time in private settings. Aside from the occasional abusive or apparently genuine attempts at conversation (usually centered on particular threads), private communications shifted in tone from informational (i.e., including links and focusing on outlining the logic of a position/piece of content) to something akin to identity appeals. Posts on the subreddit that either stated newcomer status or were actively aggressive toward the alternative positions not favored by moderators gradually earned, for most respondents, reinforcing messages from other users (and, in two instances, moderators) replete with hyperlinked sources of information that apparently supported a given view and/or were additionally relevant. Of interest, when asked what those messages looked like in format (seven of which were reviewed directly in the course of the interview process), interviewees described in-text linked text blocks where the argument being made was rarely supported by the information on the site linked. Rather, the site was simply topic-adjacent.

Finally, members of the community invade other spaces when directly provoked. One user noted, "It was like some kind of raid on enemy territory. There was so much ra ra ra go get them feeling and I remember getting way more involved with other posters in DMs after that for a while." Most important, such invasions showcase extreme rhetoric and occasional threats that are less clearly present in the meme-heavy environment of intracommunity discussion threads. Cumulatively, these characteristics of the community have contributed enormously to the successful narrative development of themes thereafter projected to other settings. With the case of r/The_Donald specifically, according to those interviewed who identified such a phenomenon (19 of 34), the most common "invasions" followed three trends: (1) the "pursuit" of deviant accounts to other spaces on Reddit, (2) various forms of attack on users and content in spaces that specifically target r/The_Donald (such as the subreddit "r/Trumpgret"), and (3) accompaniment of meme content to non-Reddit spaces.

Of those interviewed who either formerly or currently had accounts subscribed to r/The_Donald, one was at one juncture a moderator. My interview of that individual focused only partially on the content-deletion practices of the community's moderators and instead largely focused on moderator messaging to other members. Aside from coercive messages sent to keep deviant users away from particular positions (not usually directly aimed at anti-Trump accounts, which would instead be quickly banned from the space), much of the respondent's nonpersonal private conversations revolved around r/The_Donald's content as it appeared elsewhere on Reddit. A common practice among some moderators, according to this individual, was alerting trusted user accounts that a deviant user or some subreddit content was receiving significant attention elsewhere on the platform. The main concern, the respondent stated, was that such content would be captured by Reddit's algorithms for recirculation to the front page (the landing page of the main site, where the highest rated content appears on a shifting basis): "[Y]ou've got to move quickly when that happens. I'd have maybe a dozen people browsing by new on a couple of other subs each late at night. The idea was that something bad getting attention would happen overnight when the US was asleep and then be at the front page by the morning so you had to jump on it before then." Indeed, the individual reported that as much as a quarter of their time was spent on a series of subreddits they thought most resistant to r/The_Donald, including r/politics, r/PoliticalHumor, r/EnoughTrumpSpam, r/TrumpCriticizesTrump, r/esist, and r/MarchAgainstTrump. More than half of all respondents reported that they maintained "throwaway" accounts to engage in conversation elsewhere, and about half of those (9 of 34) reported that they regularly created accounts so as to engage in political content without being linked by their post history to r/The_Donald. (The rest used throwaway accounts for more innocuous reasons.)

Likewise, respondents reported spending significant time (~10–25% on average) on related subreddits and spaces commonly linked from r/The_Donald, including r/MGTOW, r/incel, r/Conspiracy, and r/4chan4Trump. On Reddit, where company actions to de-emphasize right-wing rhetoric decimated the popularity and visibility of some communities, this meant a shifting array of possible venues. However, 21 of the 34 members interviewed reported posting on sites where they found republished memes or source information originally seen on r/The_Donald. In most cases, they navigated to those external sites via links in comments posted on the subreddit or on an aligned space on Reddit.

Fringe 2.0: At the Intersection of Information Warfare and Constructed Symbolism

Conspiratorial communities and more conventional advocacy spaces are often characterized as echo chambers in which insular thinking and rhetoric is amplified to produce discourse that does anything but resemble the ideal marketplace of ideas described by advocates of democratic process like John Stuart Mill and Alexis de Tocqueville. These echo chambers are produced in large part by the mechanisms described so far in this chapter. And yet, as so much research and commentary has noted, it is the way content and behaviors produced within such insular information environments are increasingly found in mainstream digital settings that is of particular interest and concern. Specifically, in some cases, fringe spaces on sites like Gab or 4chan end up influencing the growth of parallel echo chambers on mainstream social media platforms, like X (Twitter). In other cases, particular rhetorical styles and techniques of user response/engagement are cloned across account networks linked by an immense diversity of topical overlap. Some scholarship has studied the mechanisms and pipeline of information transmission from fringe spaces to the mainstream, delineating a key feature of the Fringe 2.0 phenomenon brought about by the trappings of Web 2.0 social web technology architecture and management. The next two sections discuss this dynamic. However, what matters most for us here—given the attempt *Subversion 2.0* makes to better understand how the agency of fringe elements produces unique forms of sociopolitical engagement—is how the pipeline of such information transmission influences fringe behaviors. And content analysis of the textual substance of two fringe communities *does* provide strong evidence that there is such an effect, specifically that narratives which make their way to mainstream spaces and are then tied to specific persons (such as experts and politicians linked to the emerging discussion) are then reborn in fringe spaces centered on those persons as symbols of the issues in action. In this way, fringe communities clearly appear to frame issues around persons presented to them by means of mainstream context as narrative anchors, moving discourse in their space from general deliberation toward calls for action.

Trends in Projection from r/The_Donald

Given our examination of the subreddit r/The_Donald thus far, it seems appropriate that it now stand as one of the better examples of how alternative content has been cultivated and projected into mainstream settings. According to Zannettou et al.,[34] mainstream social media platforms like X (Twitter) are influenced far more by fringe communities like r/The_Donald than they are by open versions of the community like Reddit's r/worldnews or r/politics. The community specifically is responsible for "around 6% of mainstream news URLs and over 4.5% of alternative news URLs posted to Twitter that appear on all three platforms."[35] The authors note that, given the scale of Twitter as a social media platform whose usership is in the hundreds of millions and is represented across virtually every layer of Western society, r/The_Donald's impact is immense.

In particular, recent research has demonstrated that the influence of the subreddit on broader systems of information presentation is clearly a function of cyclical processes of content reproduction that utilizes knowledge of social media platforms' algorithmic design to make narrative proliferation seem organic. Zannettou et al. show that r/The_Donald is far more likely to amplify fringe content found on other platforms, like Twitter, than are other subreddits or communities on other platforms.[36] r/The_Donald also has strong weights attached to it when it comes to the influence of mainstream Twitter content on the content of the community.[37] This interesting contrast to what is commonly the case across other community studies implies that r/The_Donald is as susceptible to discussing mainstream reported events as others, but that the community recirculates far more fringe content than the average *that must have come from non-mainstream sources*. In other words, r/The_Donald actively features efforts to balance mainstream discourse and content with extreme or alternative content that is not found on other platforms. Then this content is reintroduced to Twitter and other services at higher rates than is the case with other communities, dramatically increasing the likelihood that those platforms' algorithms will suggestively present alternative narratives to otherwise disconnected elements of the conservative ecosystem operating thereon.

This fact was supported by statements made by about a third of those interviewed in support of the case study analysis. When asked what they thought made the content of r/The_Donald so amenable to being picked up in other settings, respondents rarely pointed to the directed actions of community members and moderators (despite the great deal of evidence they produced that cult-like manipulation of the information environment within the space takes place). Rather, they identified the character of the content as being primarily responsible. r/The_Donald's content is often thought of as fringe, but the space's memes and threads are tinged far more with humor and masked appeals to racist or otherwise bigoted positions than are more private or alternative spaces found on Discord channels and on sites like Gab.[38]

This fact is also particularly interesting given the degree to which community threads are then rebroadcast to other parts of Reddit and, from there, both on mainstream social media platforms and by conservative social media presences. Specifically, in addition to being popular within the community, r/The_Donald is responsible for almost 10% of all alternative content that is cross-linked with staple news subreddits like r/pol and r/news.[39] In these cases, Twitter acts as a go-between. At the same time, certain Reddit design considerations have consistently aided community leaders' attempts to repackage and broadcast content beyond the closed subreddits' boundaries. The most significant of these was a feature, which has since been reworked, that allowed moderators of subreddits to dramatically improve the likelihood of content appearing on r/all (the site's top overall content listings) by "pinning" a thread to the top of the community page.[40] Taken in context, these control opportunities manifest a fascinating dual-face environment that allows for deep cultivation of conspiratorial narratives alongside lateral projection thereof into other informational settings.

From Echo Chambers to the Mainstream

What the case study of r/The_Donald illustrates is what a great number of researchers call an echo chamber.[41] Echo chambers dot the landscape of both fringe spaces and more mainstream areas of the social internet. The term is a reference to an acoustically controlled space, often purpose-built for music recording and similar activities, that reverberates sound only within the space itself.[42] The most common use of the term plays to the general idea that an echo chamber is a place or circumstance in which individuals hear only opinions and information that confirm their own perspective. A great amount of research has been done on echo chambers in the era of the internet. Some scholars have suggested that echo chambers naturally tend toward extremism,[43] whether the topical area is a sociopolitical issue or something more benign (such as a video game or the fandom of a book series). Several empirical analyses, however, have demonstrated that this may not always be the case.[44] A distinction emerges that divides the internet between true echo chambers and the far more common closed epistemic spaces.[45] Epistemic spaces are those defined by shared knowledge and understanding about a given issue. They may be generated by particular habits of user social engagement or by algorithms. However, most spaces with the basic characteristic of a narrow focus come about the condition of absent alternative perspectives naturally. Gaming communities, for instance, often form their own subreddits or Discord servers that simply happen to not attract users who aren't already interested in the topic. The insularity of the thing is, in short, quite natural.

Echo chambers contain intentional mechanisms for social control and social engineering. These manifest in a range of forms, but generally constitute either direct attempts to leverage the architecture of a given platform space or more conventional social strategies. Epistemic communities may certainly become echo chambers of a sort. After all, as some research has suggested, isolation may breed self-confidence and produce a trust-disparate relationship between the insular space and other spaces/users that may be tied somehow to the knowledge in question.[46] But the condition of purposive manipulation does make the line between the two phenomena relatively distinct.

Echo chambers have now relatively consistently been linked to the mainstream, specifically to the manifestation of conspiratorial perspectives and fringe ideas reported in traditional newspaper, internet, and television reporting. One prominent study demonstrated that a number of communities on Reddit and 4chan were responsible for significant volumes of external news URLs posted to Twitter.[47] The authors of the study noted that, while news stories posted to Twitter by organizations like Reuters or the *New York Times* are often quickly reposted to alternative spaces, it is clear that original content posted in those spaces is, in turn, rapidly recirculated to Twitter. Indeed, testing suggests that nearly 3% of all alternative content injected into Twitter discourse in 2016–2017 came from r/The_Donald.[48] The subreddit also influenced other major mainstream sections of Reddit, including around 8% of content on the more general-issue space r/pol, which itself was clearly responsible for the recirculation of around 2% of all alternative content posted to Twitter.[49] And, of course, both of these subreddits were influenced by a series of smaller, even more restrictive and insular spaces that contribute to the diffusion of fringe content upward to the mainstream via what amounts to a grassroots cross-pollination of ideas supported by small user and moderator cluster linkages.[50]

The relationship between social media platforms is arguably unsurprising given that, while different services offer different mechanisms and parameters for information transmission and user engagement, the topology of each is entirely social in nature. In essence, platform dynamics are allowing for unique formats of information presentation and recirculation, but it is networked communities that are engaging with one another. Research on the messaging habits of antivaccine ("antivaxxer") communities backs this up, showing that most response activity—meaning any time where the accounts of antivaxxers associated with specific Facebook groups, subreddits, and so on responded to others' tweets—was cluster to cluster.[51] Outreach targeted social networks rather than simply users either (1) beyond the community space in question or (2) generically on other social media platforms. Moreover, there is demonstrable variation in outreach behavior depending on the nature of the community being addressed. With research on antivaxxer behaviors online, the emotionality of content varied dramatically depending on whether or not the network targeted was deemed to be adversarial, politically prominent, neutral, or sympathetic.[52] More important, the nature of efficacy messaging differed across the same set of potential social clusters. Efficacy messaging is any form of communication that tries to convey the target's ability to take action,[53] meaning that neutral audiences were targeted with positive emotional appeals absent an efficacy component while prominent political users and sympathetic communities received efficacy appeals blended with either extreme negative or positive emotional pleas. This tactical variation in messaging is shockingly similar to that practiced by foreign state-sponsored influence operators, like the IRA that was so centrally involved in Russian efforts to interfere in Western democratic processes through the 2010s.[54] In short, Fringe 2.0 spaces are not only incubators of extreme discourse and narratives; they are also (1) clearly linked to nonfringe communities via a series of social and algorithmic mechanisms and (2) tactically motivated by the broader connective attributes of social media spaces.

Finding the Trigger: The Constructivist Tactics of Fringe Spaces

Research on variation in messaging in fringe spaces demonstrates a degree of tactical awareness of the contours not only of the echo chamber itself but of the nature of linkages between such spaces and the broader information environment. Indeed, it is this dynamic condition that has made fringe spaces so open to elite co-optation. As Rietdijk reports, the Italian antivax community has in recent years been characterized by the co-optation of Facebook groups and dedicated medical skepticism websites by populist voices within the country's far-right political landscape.[55] Lega Nord, for instance, is a right-wing nationalistic political party that has increasingly dipped into such communities to stoke fears of vaccine-linked autism, the health threats of 5G wireless technologies, and more to drive users toward favorable discussion of anti-immigration positions and anticommunist rhetoric.[56] The limited success of Lega Nord and other populist actors around the world in this endeavor, however, is generally best explained by the need to be opportunistic. Driving conversation in particular narrative directions within fringe spaces is difficult when the issue in question diverges from the conventional substantive focus of the community involved. Whether looking at domestic political operators or foreign elements seeking to inspire greater divisiveness in Western societies, the clear reality is that nonfringe actors are forced to play off triggers for fringe activity that appear organically in the conduct of social discourse.[57] A range of research has demonstrated that seeding new, extreme narratives in social media settings is remarkably difficult without clear anchoring events or developments with which to "capture" a substantial enough cross-section of networks that constitute the fringe-mainstream pipeline.[58] And, of course, this reality pertains to fringe communities and groups themselves. Simply put, broad-scope subversion requires a substantial degree of engagement with the natural tendencies of the broader information environment as much as it does the conditions necessary for cultivated rich alternative rhetoric. The remainder of this section demonstrates the simple way in which fringe spaces often accomplish this.

From No Pills to Black Pills: The Rhetoric of Medical Skepticism and Male Misogyny

To consider how the internetwork connectedness of the modern information environment impacts the tendencies of fringe communities and their insular virtual spaces, I draw upon a large amount of social media data that can be broken down along two lines. First, I use data archived from two now-banned subreddits frequented by adherents to two fringe belief systems: vaccination skepticism (specifically, COVID-19-linked skepticism) and male misogyny. Second, in addition to this data detailing the substance of so much posting in fringe spaces, I also draw on Twitter data from time periods curated to reflect the narrow interests of the aforementioned subreddits. By using a topic modeling approach,[59] I illustrate not only that the general narrative seems to flow from alternative spaces to mainstream settings but also that alternative spaces appear to undergo a process of topical focusing following surges in issue-specific Twitter discussion. This suggests a unique recursive relationship wherein the actions and statements of public figures, experts, and others might take on meaning—positive or negative—in fringe communities absent any intentional effort to garner such influence.

The two communities studied here—the subreddits r/NoNewNormal and r/incels—represent two perspectives holding that society is functionally rigged to the detriment of the everyday citizen (the majority of male citizens, in the latter case). r/NoNewNormal was created in June 2020 and was a specific manifestation of vaccine-denial subcultures focused on the threat of the COVID-19 pandemic.[60] Antivaccination beliefs have been present in modern society for nearly two centuries.[61] Early experimentation with the use of cowpox blisters to inoculate children against smallpox infection resulted in substantial outrage on the part of certain people in Victorian England, particularly clergymen and rural parishioners. The earliest organizations built around vaccine denial, the Anti-Vaccination League and the Anti–Compulsory Vaccination League, organized vaccine protests throughout the 1800s, at one time commanding the support of several hundred thousand English citizens and inspiring the development of several cousin organizations in the United States at the outset of the 20th century.[62] In more recent years, most vaccination safety discussions in the mainstream have developed around concerns for specific inoculation effects. Pertussis vaccination was claimed to be linked to neurological conditions in some children in the 1970s, and in the late 1990s a paper was published under unethical conditions that claimed a potential link between the MMR vaccination and autism development in children.[63] That paper, published and then retracted by the *Lancet* medical journal, was produced by a man hired by a law board to find any evidence to support litigation alleging such a side effect of the vaccination. The man, Andrew Wakefield, was later found to have falsified data, and an enormous amount of follow-on research has shown no relationship between inoculation and autism.[64] Nevertheless, the incident has served as a sort of narrative ground zero for vaccine skepticism and denial in the modern era and, in recent years, has been framed as part of the common foundation from which most antivax thinking emerges. And while vaccine hesitancy has been politicized over the past decade and can be found among the general population, r/NoNewNormal represents the more organized formation of medical denial ideology that exists at society's fringes and believes, among other things, that vaccinations are mechanisms of elite control. Today, in some settings, this ideology pervades intercommunity discourse and rivals the perspective of organized White supremacy in its complex description of society as being shaped by sadistic and evil forces.

By contrast, at least in terms of ideological substance, the incel movement refers to online subcultures that believe they are unable to have sex or other romantic contact despite desiring it and, in most cases, pursuing it.[65] The term "incel" is a portmanteau of "involuntary celibate" and was taken from a website in the late 1990s entitled Alana's Involuntary Celibate Project, an effort by an undergraduate at a Canadian university to give frustrated youths a space in which to vent their feelings.[66] For a few years, incels were simply those who had not had sex despite trying. However, in the 2000s, incel communities evolved to reflect numerous subcultural trends on emerging Web 2.0 sites and platforms, including Reddit, 4chan, and, later, 8chan (or 8kun).[67] This created a hard fork in content online that invited and supported incel perspectives. On the one hand was an ever-shrinking core of sites that were essentially support groups for individuals attempting to date but without the social skills required.[68] On the other was a set of forums and sites that embraced hateful language, representations of forced sexual encounters, and, eventually, regular reference to violence as a natural outcome of the "unavoidable" frustrations of all but a few men in modern society.[69] The subreddit r/incels reflected this militant turn and existed for several years—before being banned by Reddit—alongside other incel communities to support the conversations of tens of thousands of members. And, like the case with extreme vaccine denialism, the beliefs represented in r/incels and in subsequent virtual settings are as ideologically complex as those purported by more conventional fringe elements, such as racial supremacy or militant anarchist advocates. In this case, incels believe that the world is a hierarchy constituted of a small group of attractive persons at the top and the rest beneath. This dynamic, they additionally believe, makes women reflexively shallow and biologically inclined toward men with only a specific set of bodily features, creating an imbalanced biological gene pool that cannot be overcome by anything so simple as better manners, charisma, or a good personality.[70]

To examine these communities and their relationship to discourse on mainstream virtual platforms, I draw upon two different data sets cataloging

FRINGE 2.0   139

activity on both subreddits across two yearlong periods. I use topic modeling as an approach to examine the narrative content on both spaces and their connection with what can be found on Twitter during the same period. Topic models are statistical models that look at a library of documents—a corpus, in which documents can be anything from newspaper articles or even books to social media posts or comments—and consider thematic trends across the entire library regardless of the current breakdown of the documents themselves.[71] These models assume that the library is a fixed vocabulary of sorts from which distinct topics—combinations of words—emerge.[72] Term collocations and frequencies are used to determine what cohesive topics look like and how those topics are ultimately distributed across the documents in the corpus. The approach does not ask anything from the researcher beyond basic values on how granular and how various the topics produced by the model should be. In this way, topic models are a probabilistic way of finding latent themes that run through an unstructured corpus of documents, bypassing issues of researcher bias and providing a novel way of viewing large amounts of data in text form.

Figure 5.1 shows interesting results from topic models obtained for the r/NoNewNormal and r/incels data sets over their one-year periods (June 2020 to June 2021 and January 2013 to January 2014, respectively). I combine the sets and used a latent dirichlet allocation[73] tool to detect 25 latent topics characterizing the text related to all subreddit posts and the top 10 (where relevant) posted comments on posts by site popularity metrics (or "upvotes"). Importantly, I set parameters for topic selection from content that corresponded to a range of terms common to male misogyny rhetoric. In Figure 5.1, I utilize eight of the topics that resulted.

Figure 5.1 arrays these topics against the same results for Twitter data pulled for the same two yearlong periods. This data, previously made available by other researchers working on issues of conspiracy theory pervasiveness and alternative content circulation, includes tweets and retweets that contain certain keywords to make them relevant to these fringe spaces. In the case of vaccine hesitancy, the data was drawn using search terms in the Twitter API such as "COVID19" and "wuhanpneumonia." It was then curated further by looking solely to tweets containing the words "vaccination," "vax," and "vaccine." With male misogyny, a similar but broader approach was taken, focusing on a range of terms that relate to incel ideology and social habits, including "Chads," "Stacys," "neckbeard," "Beckys," "rapeglish," "gendered," and "ebile." Figure 5.1 shows similarity coefficients for

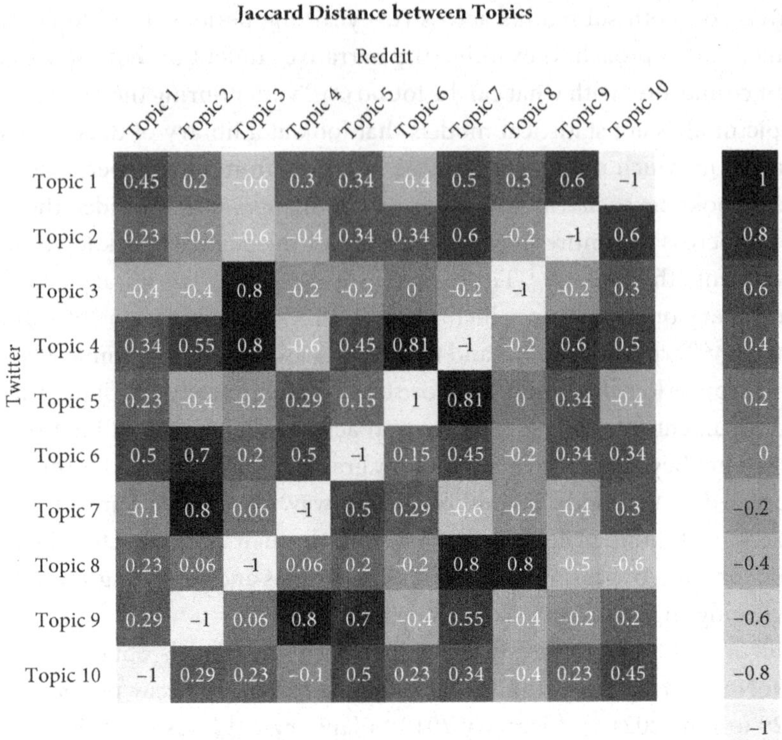

Jaccard Distance between Topics

Reddit

	Topic 1	Topic 2	Topic 3	Topic 4	Topic 5	Topic 6	Topic 7	Topic 8	Topic 9	Topic 10
Topic 1	0.45	0.2	–0.6	0.3	0.34	–0.4	0.5	0.3	0.6	–1
Topic 2	0.23	–0.2	–0.6	–0.4	0.34	0.34	0.6	–0.2	–1	0.6
Topic 3	–0.4	–0.4	0.8	–0.2	–0.2	0	–0.2	–1	–0.2	0.3
Topic 4	0.34	0.55	0.8	–0.6	0.45	0.81	–1	–0.2	0.6	0.5
Topic 5	0.23	–0.4	–0.2	0.29	0.15	1	0.81	0	0.34	–0.4
Topic 6	0.5	0.7	0.2	0.5	–1	0.15	0.45	–0.2	0.34	0.34
Topic 7	–0.1	0.8	0.06	–1	0.5	0.29	–0.6	–0.2	–0.4	0.3
Topic 8	0.23	0.06	–1	0.06	0.2	–0.2	0.8	0.8	–0.5	–0.6
Topic 9	0.29	–1	0.06	0.8	0.7	–0.4	0.55	–0.4	–0.2	0.2
Topic 10	–1	0.29	0.23	–0.1	0.5	0.23	0.34	–0.4	0.23	0.45

(Twitter, row axis)

Figure 5.1 Jaccard similarity coefficients for topic models obtained from Reddit fringe communities and Twitter using keyword search.

topics that appear to align with one another, demonstrating immediately the strong relationships that exist between topics and themes in both restrictive and mainstream settings.

Basic visual comparison of the topics produced sees clear relationships between themes on Twitter and those in subreddit spaces. Figure 5.2 adds further information to the broad trend patterns across these divergent mainstream and fringe spaces along two lines. The figure shows a measure of topic coherence output from a skipgram Word2Vec model across the months of the yearlong period under study. Topic coherence is, in essence, short-form identifiable, semantically meaningful topic areas in the corpus. Figure 5.2 shows, on the left, that topic coherence improved for the r/NoNewNormal subreddit community across the period quite substantially. On the right, topic coherence improved on Twitter much more dramatically, starting at a

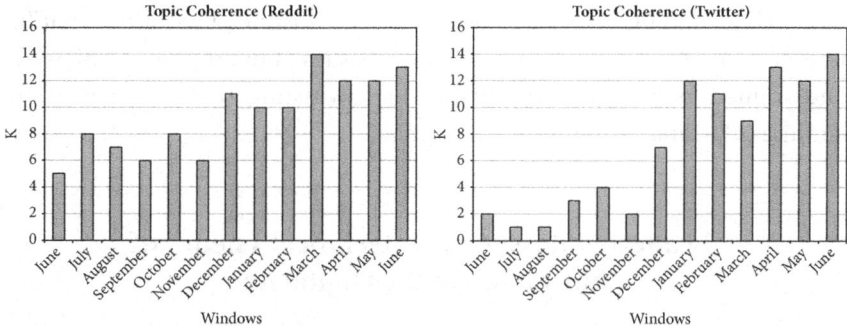

Figure 5.2 Topic coherence for themes drawn from r/NoNewNormal and Twitter using keyword search.

relatively low measure and spiking several times across the year. This implies, at the very least, a linkage between conversations in the separate spaces in line with what other researchers have found. Of particular interest, however, is the pattern of change on Twitter in which coherence rose in periods prior to a similar increase on the subreddits. This notionally suggests that a recursive effect wherein fringe spaces, having spread narrative beyond their borders, learn and react from mainstream discourse.

Clearly, the redefinition of topics on Twitter around specific persons and events has a subsequent impact on the coherence of topics on fringe spaces. From incel murderer Elliot Rodgers to vaccine skeptics like Trump advisor Scott Atlas, a range of specific identifiers appear first in mainstream Twitter discourse before rising as significant elements of the thematic substance of fringe discourse. In most cases, the individuals referenced are those who might otherwise be ignored by fringe spaces prior to their mention by mainstream media outlets. After all, mass murderers or new expert entrants to prominent public policy conversations often have little to no public visibility prior to something like a violent act or a promotion. And yet their actions and voice are clearly often placed in the topical context of discourse exported to Twitter, Facebook, and other popular platforms by alternative communities. The data illustrated here as a basic exploration of any recursive relationship between such a pipeline effect and the ongoing activities of alternative spaces suggests, quite simply, that these mentions are seized upon by those at the fringes. And while it might be tempting to think that fringe conversation simply reflects developments in mainstream treatments of relevant subject matter, the broad history of subversive socialization of new web technologies and environs suggests a distinct alternative: that figures and events tied in the mainstream to issues of interest are emphasized and framed as a means for further narrowcasting rhetoric beyond the confines of insular, fringe spaces.

Leaderlessness: A Sociotechnical Theory of Subversion in the Digital Age

From the outset, this book has attempted to build knowledge and understanding of empirical trends linked to strategic intention in aid of answering a simple question: What explains the meteoric rise in the visibility of fringe elements in mainstream sociopolitical discourse? In particular, how might we explain the rising tide of extreme fringe acts in recent years—from incel-inspired acts of violence to the attempted insurrection on January 6, 2021, in the United States—connected in distinct and diverse ways to web technologies? This book began with the assumption that the internet has played some part in bringing fringe advocacy into closer contact with mainstream sociopolitical discourse in the 21st century. The exact role of the internet in doing so remains broadly underspecified in a range of scholarly and popular works, however.

The evidence and analysis presented in the previous three chapters have laid clear foundations for a sociotechnical theory of subversion in the digital age, one that simply states that fringe behavior is shaped by the interaction of subversive preferences with the sociotechnical architecture of the information environment in which subversive actors must operate. This proposition offers a dynamic view of subversion as it harnesses and is shaped by emerging information technologies, not least because novel information technologies change society at the same time they expand the toolkit for all kinds of sociopolitical contestation.

Off the bat, the preceding chapters have aligned with so much existing scholarship in demonstrating that the internet has clearly produced new affordances for subversive nonstate actors, organizations, and social movements. Likewise, it is clear that the character of sociopolitical engagement and worldview dictate exactly how such affordances are perceived and harnessed. Those interested in subversion, either by intention or due to circumstance, have prioritized the use of web technologies as tools of social engineering, propaganda, community control, and automation. This finding, which underwrites scholarly thought in areas of focus like cyberterrorism and digital extremism, is a significant contribution in its own right.

But recognizing that sociopolitical perspective and circumstance shape how new technology is used is only part of the picture. This chapter has shown that the internet is more than a series of technical advances and associated information systems. It is a complex sociotechnical global assemblage. It is purposive, providing sense and meaning to society and citizens. That said, this purposiveness is not purposeful but rather emerges from the evolving arrangement of its complex parts, including the logical, social, economic, and political architectures of the digital world. It is the interaction of our new understanding of subversive motivations and tendencies with this assemblage that explains the meteoric rise in visibility of fringe narratives and activities in the mainstream areas of global society.

Leaderlessness. Evidence presented thus far suggests that subversives use the internet in a unique fashion, and that the emergence of Web 2.0 platforms, tools, and information ecosystems around the turn of the 21st century has flipped the directionality of the relationship between the fringe and the mainstream. Whereas subversive social movements have traditionally followed the mainstream and relied on emergent trends and media conditions to craft persuasive messaging, the shifting sociotechnological basis of internet usage away from that centered on large-scale user consumption of static information (i.e., Web 1.0) has weakened traditional barriers to the spread of fringe influence. The rise of a global paradigm of web usage characterized by user-created content, dynamic media, and mass audience participation (i.e., Web 2.0) has underwritten the potency and virulence of fringe perspectives that are increasingly visible in those areas of the global information environment where mainstream internet users engage today. As this book reports, this situation is driven by a range of factors, including the ubiquity of user-side media controls and moderator capabilities, visibility algorithms that favor extreme information, profit-oriented platform management decision-making, and the general porousness of conventional social media spaces such as Facebook and X (Twitter).

I call the emergent condition that produces so much fringe interaction with mainstream information environs "leaderlessness" because of the way it mimics the intended circumstances of leaderless resistance, albeit not by design or intent. Instead, subversive narratives emerge from fringe spaces where a series of controls ensure that information is filtered, shaped, and manipulated to reflect extreme perspectives. These controls are numerous, but most notably include the ubiquity of user-side controls for content moderation and media customization. These controls are often aided by platform algorithms that—on top of favoring extreme content as a default strategy for driving user engagement—are often predictable and, thus, manipulable.

Algorithms and social interconnection then interact these narratives with mainstream web spaces, which are inherently porous relative to a range of business interests and overlapping population effects. In this way, fringe narratives and information interact with social media discourse, which lays the foundation for media coverage and elite response as fragments thereof are filtered, reframed, and adopted by everyday web users and communities. Elite speech, influenced by media dynamics and public discourse, is then reflected back in fringe spaces and communities as the most critical representation of how the mainstream responds to subversive ideas.

Much like leaderless resistance, the leaderlessness phenomenon is characterized by a clear separation between the levels of subversive causes. On one level, public-facing elements of advocacy, such as political parties or celebrity commentators, reflect the agency of fringe ideologies in a format and framing that is palatable—or, at least, digestible—to the mainstream. The other level, by contrast, contains the raw substance of fringe causes in the discourse and actions of elements beyond the mainstream. The contrast with leaderless resistance is that, for most subversive movements or campaigns in the 21st century, this separation between levels is generally not something engineered by the leaders and planners of a fringe cause, despite clear evidence that the two nonetheless influence one another. Instead, leaderlessness has emerged as a distinct output of how the internet, as a sociotechnical assemblage with unprecedented utility for social control and engineering in the Web 2.0 era, now interacts with subversive behavioral preferences and perspectives. Of course, as the concluding chapter will discuss, this argument intrinsically assumes that such a phenomenon will change to reflect future transformations of the global information environment. Nevertheless, the ubiquitous character of user-driven web usage in the Web 2.0 era has persisted for years at the time of this book's writing, thanks to the retrenchment of business and technical architectures that value conflictual, extreme engagement as a key pillar of profit. Thus, the leaderlessness phenomenon (Figure 5.3)—what the title of this book references as the 2.0 form of subversion—seems likely to persist for some time also.

While the chapters thus far have illustrated the distinct tendencies of subversive elements of global society toward information technologies and built

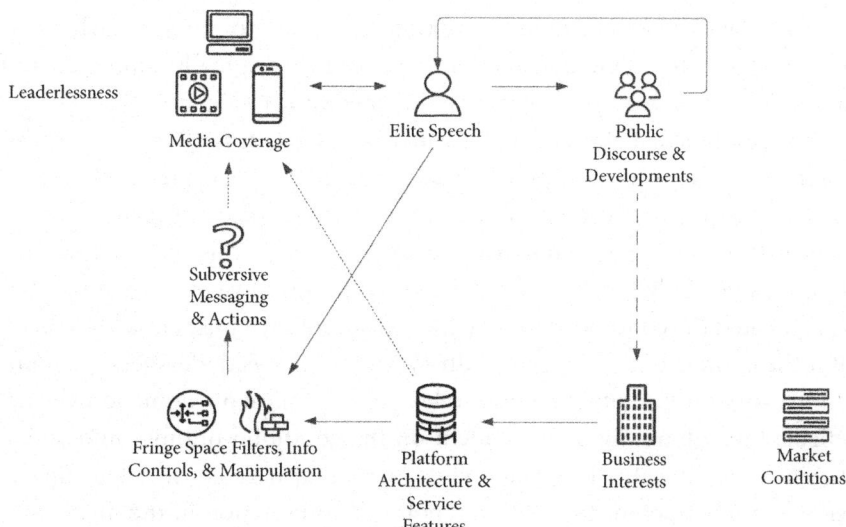

Figure 5.3 The dynamic of leaderless subversive interaction with mainstream information environment in the Web 2.0 era.

the logical basis for the leaderlessness argument, the implications of the feedback loop being described require further specification. This chapter, in particular, has demonstrated that there is a resonant feedback between fringe communities and mainstream web spaces. But what exactly is the shape of this relationship, and what can it tell us to expect about subversive engagement—messaging, disruption, violence—going forward?

Leaderless Antagonism in Sociotechnical Context. Chapters 6 and 7 marshal a great amount of data about the use of information technologies over the past four decades and illustrate the selective reaction effect that the leaderlessness argument implies about fringe advocacy and the rhetoric of elites in the societal mainstream. Specifically, the leaderlessness condition describes an uneven interaction between fringe and mainstream information environments. Statistical testing in Chapter 7 shows that the rhetoric of elites significant to a subversive cause are often associated with disruptive, escalatory actions by representatives thereof. This provides further robust support for the leaderlessness hypothesis and fits with the dynamics of case evidence surveyed thus far wherein elites—either supportive of or opposed to a given cause—are socially constructed in fringe spaces as figureheads and common points of reference. However, the effect is not universal. Clearly, many of the factors already specified regarding the normative construction of fringe spaces factor into the conditions necessary to produce such an effect. For one, the same information controls that originally simplified and amplified extreme outgoing content filter incoming influences.

The result is that elites who associate with fringe ideas often find their influence fragile in hard-to-predict ways. Certainly, as Chapter 7 illustrates, their influence is occasionally more potent than intended, triggering extreme acts by those indoctrinated in fringe environments. In this way, the feedback loop has not only heightened public exposure to subversive narratives but also created the conditions for heightened acts of extremism linked to them. But the context of the uneven feedback loop of the leaderlessness phenomenon cannot be forgotten. As a complex sociotechnical phenomenon, the felt effects thereof are highly dependent on the condition of those underlying business, technical, and social architectures that have constructed subversion as such a potent form of sociopolitical contestation in the digital age. After the explorations of the next two chapters, Chapter 8 returns to this reality and considers the implications of leaderlessness for national security, democracy, and the future of the networked world.

6
The Landscape of Subversion in the Digital Age

In line with the empirical strategy previewed in Chapter 2, this chapter lays out the landscape of antagonistic digital activities by subversive societal elements over more than three and a half decades. It begins by generalizing about nonstate actors and the new tools that the internet has presented them in the context of social and political engagement. To date, there exists a considerable body of research and thought on the way in which the information revolution centered on the internet has upgraded the toolkit of contestation for numerous kinds of nonstate actors. However, subversion is understudied to such a degree that it would be shortsighted to simply appraise such work and therefrom generate expectations. Instead, this discussion is simply a starting point. Because subversion differs in its strategic logic from coercion, so too must our expectations about how *subversive* nonstate actors might turn to the web for antagonism and activism.

The chapter lays out a framework for the analysis and prediction of incidence of digital antagonism by social movements and organizations operating at the fringes of global society. To briefly recount the theory proposed in Chapter 5, I argue that the internet has made "leaderlessness" the natural formation of such activity among subversive causes spread around the world. Though leaderless resistance has often been a favored approach to subversion, today the sociotechnical architecture of the Web 2.0 era organically predisposes fringe movements to leaderlessness as a form of engagement. This dynamic carries with it distinct implications for the prediction of subversive antagonism, not least the idea that activity among fringe societal elements are triggered by rhetorical signaling from significant figures.

To build the empirical foundations that support the leaderlessness theory, this chapter first largely puts aside the idea in order to marshal raw data about how subversives use the internet. I describe a first-of-its-kind data collection effort aimed at identifying the incidence of activist and antagonistic digital action linked to the phenomenon of subversion. Rather than simply catalog subversive causes or actors based on a broad definition, this book bases its data-gathering approach on preexisting data collected to illustrate the landscape of activism in the age of the internet. Doing so provides a robust, replicable foundation for analysis that offers unique insight into subversives' use of the web.

Specifically, the initial illustration of trends provided in this chapter demonstrates that digital antagonism among subversives is remarkably unsophisticated. Though there is a clear increase in emphasis on more sophisticated hacking techniques in recent years, by far the preponderance of activity involves simple methods of engagement—including DDoS attacks, website vandalism, and theft of private data from poorly protected systems—that lend themselves to harassment and obfuscation. Further, exploration of the data collected shows that digital subversion is increasingly a common feature of world affairs, with almost 500 incidents—most of which occurred in just the past five years—in 69 countries perpetrated by 113 named or anonymous affiliated persons or entities of subversive movements since 1982. And while left/right forces in democratic countries are responsible for the output of much digital antagonism, a significant number of incidents emerge from movements motivated toward religious, spiritual, or civic transformation of all manner of national circumstances.

Though most of the evidence presented in this chapter is descriptive and meant to support quantitative testing of the leaderlessness theory discussed in Chapter 7, I nevertheless find initial support for the theory's underlying assumptions. Subversives clearly seem to favor information enrichment and manipulation uses of web technologies. And more subversive entities and movements use the web to engage others during the Web 2.0 era. While the number of incidents recorded in the data set built for this study may seem small at first glance, it is still substantially greater than the number of major cyber campaigns recorded by international security scholars over the past several decades. It seems initially fair to suggest that the subversive enterprise has been substantially impacted by the opportunities and affordances of the internet.

Nonstate Actors and the Toolkit of Digital Engagement

Though prior studies of the effects of the information revolution on nonstate actors rarely, if ever, address subversion as a strategic motivator of digital actions, they do provide a baseline from which we might contextualize digital-age subversive activities. Generically, this diverse literature describes new digital technologies as affording nonstate actors unique opportunities in three categories. I discuss these before considering the specific case of societal fringe elements.

First, nonstate actors, from lobbying organizations and protest groups to terrorist cells, can use new information and communication techniques to persuade, organize, and perform outreach of different kinds.[1] The internet is a vast repository and a communications game-changer for those elements of global society that might traditionally have lacked the informational tools necessary to coordinate social change. Added to this, new information environment dynamics mean that digital platforms for information framing and dissemination—like X (Twitter), Facebook, Weibo, Reddit, and 4chan—are the new gateways to the kingdom of public opinion and sentiment.[2] These platforms generally allow for the bypassing of traditional agenda-setting gatekeepers (newspapers, television networks, etc.). Moreover, they are often predictable in how they disseminate content—particularly in terms of the algorithms that dictate visibility of information—resulting in opportunities for manipulation of news cycles and broader sociopolitical narratives.

Second, information and communications technologies allow for direct interaction with information in terms of the design and contents of digital systems. Nonstate actors and state entities alike can steal or manipulate information stored on servers and, through a variety of network or media actions, can disrupt systems that undergird a multitude of social, economic, and governmental functions.[3]

Finally, ICT allow nonstate actors the opportunity to accomplish noninformational disruption through the manipulation of computer systems.[4] Though the incidence of such disruption is not common in the relatively short history of conflict and contentious politics online, it is not impossible that a nonstate actor might cause kinetic disruption through actions like cyberattacks on state-operated utilities.

Naturally, the spectrum of new tools available to nonstate actors—both from the adoption of new technologies and in the context of massive changes to the information environment of the modern global system—describes abilities that are as potentially benign as they are dangerous to civil society and governments. Moreover, the "ICT" label describes a diverse set of technologies that range from the primitive to the futuristic in terms of sophistication.[5] On the low end of the complexity scale, useful ICT might simply include small and more readily concealable media devices for storing and transporting sensitive information than have previously been available. At the midpoint of the scale, nonstate actor use of ICT might entail basic syntactic techniques employed in efforts to infiltrate, intrude into, or vandalize opponents' websites and computer systems.[6] These might include denial of service attacks or site scripting attacks. And at the high end, this might include the employment of more sophisticated malware against targets or multistage operations aimed at influencing a target audience.

New abilities in the "low-intensity" category of opportunity for nonstate actors particularly tend to be among the simplest, and it is in this category that we find most legitimate actors: interest groups, lobbying organizations, and so on. Indeed, for the purposes of operating in the new and expanded information environment of the digital age, the utility of different methods derives almost entirely from the sociopolitical context of nonstate actors' circumstances.[7] Depending on the precise context of technology adoption and common practices, organizations and individuals interested in influencing public sentiment and opinion might choose to employ email for spreading a message, social media for mobilizing an audience, or web ads for criticizing specific opponents.[8] Methods of approach here are far less about the context of complex technical systems than about how civil society and other actors use ICT for sociopolitical purposes. The use of invasive techniques to embarrass or challenge political opponents—through, for example, vandalism of websites or the theft of sensitive data for the specific purpose of gaining advantage in activist efforts—also reflects the low end of the sophistication spectrum when it comes to using ICT to better operate in modern information environs.[9]

By contrast, new nonstate actor abilities to disrupt computer systems to achieve either informational or kinetic effects can range from the simple to the highly sophisticated. Such attacks temporarily disable or diminish the functions of information systems to allow the antagonist some specific advantage.[10] At the low end of the spectrum, this might include the use of botnets to overwhelm server traffic abilities and temporarily shut down specific websites.[11] At the high end, this might entail the manipulation of security design flaws to infiltrate a network or the use of sophisticated combinations of gambits and malicious code to force entry into a guarded system. High-intensity operations, it should be noted, are not always more expensive, and the knowledge of code and systems design needed for implementation is not always difficult to access.[12] Information disruption always has temporary effects, at least in terms of the functionality of the systems involved, and can be undertaken for a variety of reasons. Common outcomes include the theft of sensitive data about, for instance, commercial products or an organization's members/customers and the defacement of websites for political reasons.[13]

Finally, nonstate actor abilities to cause actual destruction or kinetic disruption through the use of ICT are almost always sophisticated, expensive, and time-consuming in that such capabilities reflect the extreme difficulty involved in translating digital action into physical results.[14] While disruption of information systems can lead to the destruction of data or the temporary loss of control over specific organizational functions, the use of ICT for destruction describes information actions taken to maliciously pervert digital systems that actively control physical systems. Though the global adoption and integration of ICT across most global societal functions have entailed a massive transformation of infrastructure worldwide over the past three decades, examples of systems controlled by computers vulnerable to intrusion that could be used for actual violence are hard to come by. The most commonly cited possible targets that fit the bill include power grids and utilities systems,[15] the widespread disruption of which could cause loss of life through, for instance, the disruption of emergency services or the failure of certain control systems. Meaningful disruption of such systems, which are highly distributed, well-protected, and redundant in their design, necessarily implies the design of advanced and adaptable abilities. The expense and broad functional knowledge needed to produce such capabilities, as well as the risk involved in designing a weapon with so many potential opportunities for failure in its employment, make them uncommon.[16] As such, we might expect few, if any, nonstate actors to be able to produce such disruptive effects, even under circumstances where they may be strategically desirable.

Studying Subversive Nonstate Actors' Digital Engagement

Studying subversion has historically been difficult for scholars of world politics, in no small part because of the difficulty in linking strategic intent to the phenomenon in practice. In developing this book, I aimed to provide an empirical picture of subversion in action in the 21st century that overcame the two issues bound up in that enduring research challenge: defining subversion itself in an analytically useful fashion and thereafter identifying the outputs of subversive enterprise. Specifically, there were three tasks involved in measuring variation in the use of ICT by actors at the fringes of global society sufficient to engage in research on the determinants of digital subversion. First, of course, it was necessary to identify a population sample of subversive groups operating in world politics. Second, proper identification of different techniques and uses of ICT was required. Third, data collected needed to be contextually framed; in other words, a data set of digital antagonism not anchored on broader understanding of the shape or agency of a given subversive cause lacks the utility of one that is so anchored. Though the problem of attribution of cyber incidents is to some degree as present with subversive nonstate actors as it is with state security apparatuses, the dichotomous existence of subversive movements between shadows and the public eye dictates a clear criterion for selection of cases based on involvement in digital activism. Thus, in order to accomplish each of the above tasks, I turned to the Global Digital Activism Data Set as a basis for coding and testing.

The result of a collaborative project (the Digital Activism Research Project) founded in 2012, the GDADS is a large events database that describes incidents of and organizations involved in digital activist activities over more than thirty years. Based at the University of Washington, the project is an ongoing effort to apply rigorous coding and testing methods to identify instances of civic engagement, citizen activism, journalism, and more in world politics. The project is an increasingly useful resource for scholars seeking to reference or work with data that reflects the realities of political persuasion and activism in the digital age—largely linked to the shape of digital infrastructure and changing information environment dynamics. The project is financially supported by the U.S. Institution for Peace and has been the basis of a range of scholarly works designed to study, among other things, human rights organizations, citizen social movements, and American foreign policy and diplomacy centered on civic liberalism.

The database produced by the broader project itself consists of almost 2,000 observations—released in several tranches between 2012 and the present—of instances of digital activism. Each observation consists of a range of useful pieces of data, including information on the organization, individual, or movement involved in an activity and contextual information on the nature of the operational political environment. The GDADS also, naturally, contains source information and breaks down observations of digital activist activities via reference to a coding list of different types of actions. These actions are listed in this chapter's methodological appendix.

The GDADS product is defensibly comprehensive, and both source lists and raw coding outputs are made available publicly. This includes all narrative accounts that were used to verify digital activities and code for the variables provided in the data set. Overall, the database includes almost 1,800 instances of digital activism—1,180 in the initial tranche, 426 in the second, and more than 200 additional entries that include organization-level information based on a digital activity provided in supplementary materials. The data set covers activities in more than 150 countries and spans 30 years, from 1982 until 2012. As mentioned, the GDADS has been published in several tranches and is due to be updated further in the future. However, in the course of developing this project, I was able to provide a provisional extension to the database through early 2019 using the documented methods and sources outlined by the GDADS project. Between 2004 and 2012, I find an additional 239 episodes and incidents of digital activism, with another 1,407 between 2012 and 2019.

For the purposes of this book project, the GDADS is particularly useful because it provides a preexisting data resource and documented approach for describing organizations and movements undertaking digital activist activities. Not all groups described in the extended version of the GDADS I employ here are subversive, of course; the vast majority of groups, in fact, are not. Nevertheless, the data set provides an exceptional foundational opportunity to identify subversive organizations among the broader universe of digital activist cases and to perform testing on possible explanations for variations in activity.

A first step in building usable data was the identification of those groups that we might consider subversive. Working with the GDADS, my first step in preparing the data set so that it is useful for investigating the premise of the project was to code out organizations, movements, and informal groups identified within the original data set as not subversive. The aim was quite simply to be left with a data set that emerges from the same reliable original coding practices of the broader GDADS in which each observation describes the behavior of a subversive group. Initially, this task involves identifying subversive organizations broadly construed. More specifically, this task involves classifying activists by their relationship to the subversive organization. The links that exist between activist groups or movements and subversive causes can take a number of formats, from direct involvement in activism to frontground or surrogate operations.

To preliminarily identify subversive groups for the purposes of basic data set construction, I apply the definitional rubric described in Chapter 2. Subversion is most identifiable by the condition of contested legitimacy. Indeed, this condition is necessary in any effort to identify subversive actors. A successful subversive outcome, either actual or stated by the subversive actor, involves not only a replacement of one status quo set of conditions with another; subversion is, in fact, principally characterized by institution of a new status quo that the former manifestation would consider illegitimate. Subversive groups themselves may not necessarily consider the prevailing normative status quo entirely illegitimate, but the subversive enterprise is by definition characterized by the countercultural mantle of an unsanctioned idea (or platform of ideas). To be subversive, a group or organization must aim for transformation and eschew the notion of normative adaptation or addition. Using the definition above, groups like Greenpeace, the Republican Party of the United States, and Amnesty International were eliminated from the set, leaving only activist organizations like League of the South, Falun Gong, and Eastern Lightning alongside a range of lone wolves connected to fringe communities. The remaining set of subversive social movements and organizations that populate the data set, identified via specific reference to the normative legitimacy of prevailing versus suggested societal conditions in group statements, are far from uniform. Some actors taking part in digital activist efforts are clearly linked to core subversive causes; others appear to be front groups, "legitimate" sister organizations, and a host of self-affiliated acolytes. Coding issues on this front are discussed further in Chapter 7, as it most directly relates to explanations of subversive behavior based on organizational structure and group strategy.

Exploration of the landscape of subversion in the digital age further requires identification of the broad range of techniques and tactics involved in ICT usage for antagonistic purposes that the GDADS project alone generically labels "circumvention" techniques. A broad range of sources were used to catalog common types of actions or categories of activity that might characterize the efforts of groups trying to (1) organize (i.e., overcome logistical challenges), (2) mobilize already sympathetic supporters, or (3) mitigate the counterorganizational efforts of opposition interest groups and law enforcement. These included use of Factiva, Lexus Nexus, Google News, and Google Scholar, alongside a number of RSS feeds and publicly available social media databases to survey groups included in the GDADS. Source information is discussed further below.

These antagonistic actions and action categories are summarized in Table 6.1. Importantly, coding for these categories of actions is episodic in two senses. Data is episodic in a temporal sense, which is discussed further below. However, data on ICT employments is also episodic in that one observation of, for instance, a DDoS attack might include multiple disruptions against a target. Thinking of such incidents in the context of *campaigns* rather than in terms of individual actions is not uncommon in cyber conflict research, as prosecution of a particular technique may include a series of repeated actions for tactical purposes. The demarcation point is that of distinct episodes in the form of a significant period of time or a change in an organization-level target.

Table 6.1 Non-GDADS Variables Coded for Digital Techniques and Applications

	Digital Actions Captured
1	Use of website or social media for explicitly illegal purposes
2	Nonpublic, nonpermission source data collection (e.g., hacking into CCTV systems)
3	Non-DDoS, nonadministrative blocking of specific websites
4	Use of darknet sites specifically for the purpose of illegal data sharing
5	Use of darknet sites or other encryption protocols specifically for the purpose of hiding funding activities that would violate laws/regulations
6	Denial of service attack
7	Online publication of private information obtained illegally (bank account information, IDs, addresses, etc.)
8	Private data theft from web-based or hard media vulnerabilities
9	Illegal installation of hardware used to interfere with digital systems
10	Employment of malware (via email, website, hard media, etc.)
11	Use of illicit mass-communication spamming programs
12	Blocking of websites through administrative takedown requests
13	Use of peer-to-peer (P2P) or similar techniques specifically for the purpose of illegal data sharing
14	Spear-phishing emails
15	Reconnaissance intrusions (ping mapping, access probe attempt, etc.)
16	Explicit solicitation of funding online from groups blacklisted/outlawed in host country (non–Dark Web)
17	Website defacement and vandalism
18	Nonpermitted change of access point control

Beyond the identification of the range of activities listed in Table 6.1, coding the use of circumvention techniques by subversive actors occurred in several steps. First, I established appropriate guidelines for verification of technique employment by the individuals and groups in question. A clear challenge in undertaking any research on cyber conflict is the need to robustly attribute responsibility for particular actions to a specific actor. This challenge presents at two levels. First, actor attribution of cyberattacks or circumvention tools can be difficult because, though technical attribution is often easier than expected by the layman, the inherent anonymity and easy deniability of cyber actions presents challenges in connecting actions in the digital and physical realms. Responsibility, different from technical attribution, is the outcome of forensic investigation by law enforcement, intelligence actors, and, increasingly, media examiners. Naturally, the challenge in undertaking this kind of research is in setting an appropriate standard of verification and reliability for data collection in this regard. Second, and relatedly, research on cyber conflict faces the challenge of bias in reporting on responsibility for different usages of cyber techniques. Reporting agencies may have political incentives to over- or underreport the full scope of activities discovered, and, though this is increasingly less true at high levels, journalists may misreport cyber intrusions and actions insofar as they fail to differentiate between employments that appear similar in profile to the layman.

For the purpose of this project, I chose to attribute cyber technique usage to particular groups or movements in the data set via reference to (1) governmental and intergovernmental entity reporting, to (2) government-cited nonprofit reporting, to peer-reviewed scholarly work, and to (3) a standard of multiple independent media reports. This follows a series of authors in using the investigations of national agencies (such as the Federal Bureau of Investigation), intergovernmental organizations (such as Interpol), and nonprofit entities (such as Freedom House) wherein information is cited directly in government/intergovernmental reporting as the basis for robust inclusion of incidents in data collection. For scholarly works, source material must be peer-reviewed and the scholarly outlet cannot be state-owned or -funded. With media reporting, attribution must be corroborated in multiple independent reports. The nature of the collection approach as focused on a range of specific digital techniques itself compensates for bias in reporting, as statements regarding illicit activities without details are discounted as a basis for linking a group to an ICT application. Addressing the second challenge is actually bound up in the data collection approach described above, wherein distinct categories are bounded so as to allow the researcher to more easily group broadly described actions (such as common data theft as distinct from advanced persistent threat (APT) espionage or disruption campaigns).

As mentioned, the data collected are temporally episodic. For each subversive actor identified in the data set, I code for incidence of each particular type or category of activity for 18-month periods spanning either side of the incidence of digital activism coded in the original GDADS. The rationale for this is straightforward. First, the point here is to measure contemporaneous activities. Therefore, it makes sense that the data be bounded to capture actions within a short period of time. Moreover, much as occurs with terrorist and insurgent campaigns, subversive movements might have traction while operating in the public eye (and resultantly revert to actions typical to earlier, nonactivist phases) or even transition to other kinds of organization (including criminal, terrorist, or political party) over longer periods of time.[17] The case of the Egyptian Muslim Brotherhood, which rose to prominence in the wake of Hosni Mubarak's fall from power and was forced out of the public limelight following the fall of Mohamed Morsi, is an excellent example of such a progression of circumstances. Episodic data collection controls for this possibility in that observations are limited to short time periods unless extended by the continued incidence of digital activist efforts. In the data set, observations are set at a baseline of 18 months and considered to be one observation if extended due to continued incidence of such activist efforts. If there is a gap between activist efforts such that the baseline periods do not overlap, they are coded as separate organization observations.

In full, this produces a data set of a broad range of digital techniques employed by subversive groups. The remainder of this chapter explores this data in detail and offers perspective on the nature and practices of digital-age subversives.

The Global Landscape of Digital-Age Subversion

Between 1982 and 2019, at least 313 subversive social movements and organizations have used the web to engage the public. Be they cohesively organized under a centralized authority or completely lacking in any formal coordination, activists linked to these causes have used email newsletters to communicate with their constituent audiences, have performed outreach with acts of citizen journalism, and have employed e-petitions to generate interest in particular issues. One hundred four of those, representing just over a third of all causes studied, have also used web technologies antagonistically to harass and disrupt the activities of other societal actors, to manipulate the information environment, or to ensure operation out of sight of the public. This section explores the landscape of digital-age subversion in five parts, first reporting the nature and global context of antagonism at the fringes before considering the national backdrop and tactical characteristics of incidents over time.

What Antagonism at the Fringes Looks Like

In 1999, hackers claiming affiliation with the KKK launched DDoS attacks on the websites of three state officials in Kansas and Missouri. The attacks appear to have been linked directly to recent support by these officials to an early primary candidate for Kansas governor who advocated the integration of certain predominantly Black elementary and middle schools across the state with predominantly White counterparts as a means of overcoming education funding shortfalls. The result was a limited disruption of access to the sites in question. Indeed, when prompted, a local government spokesmen claimed no knowledge of the incidents. Though the attack was little more than a nuisance and was barely reported on in the week following the incident, the DDoS attack became a point of pride for local KKK members for some months, even though they were not formally claimed by the organization in any capacity. One member, interviewed on condition of anonymity, summed up the attacks as a demonstration of how "true" American society was "pushing back against the forces of Sodom and Gomorrah." Ironically, the brief local attention paid to the incident was enough to prompt an internet service provider to shut down a KKK-affiliated website run by individuals in several Midwestern states on the grounds that some displayeddirect incitation to violence against "race traitors," content not often encountered by the public to that point.

This episode parallels a great number of others over the past several decades. Acolytes of one subversive cause or another use the web to strike out against the symbols of the prevailing status quo in the hopes of achieving some delegitimizing effect. Often, attempts like the one just described are broad and imprecise in their technique, the equivalent of drive-by violence that takes aim at targets of chance rather than carefully selected opportunities for ideational impact. At other times, digital antagonism at the fringes is reasonably precise in its intended effects and clearly benefits from some degree of coordination by those responsible. In the mid-2000s, for instance, no fewer than nine far-left and progressive mainstream organizations in Germany and Austria were the targets of both disruptive and intrusive cyber assaults over a four-year period. In most cases, far-right hacker groups or forums were suspected as being responsible, though evidence was either lacking or minimal in most cases. In two cases, however, both of which resulted in the theft of membership information by leftist organizations, hackers claiming broad affiliation with the far-right National Democratic Party of Germany (NPD) took credit. They did so during the process of releasing data on right-wing forum sites. This release of private, stolen data—generally called "doxing"—was clearly intended to be strategic, as those and other righ-twing online persons urged NPD supporters to use the information to harass and libel leftist activists in the lead-up to local and federal elections.

Despite the heterogeneity of the subversive causes under study here, initial survey of the data reveals clear patterns of similarity in cases of digital antagonism at the fringes. Figure 6.1 shows the count of incidents of digital antagonism by category of method employed by subversive social movements and organizations across the 37-year period covered by *Subversion 2.0*'s data set. The three most common methods are the denial of service attack (either DDoS or more conventional DoS), doxing, and the use of encryption

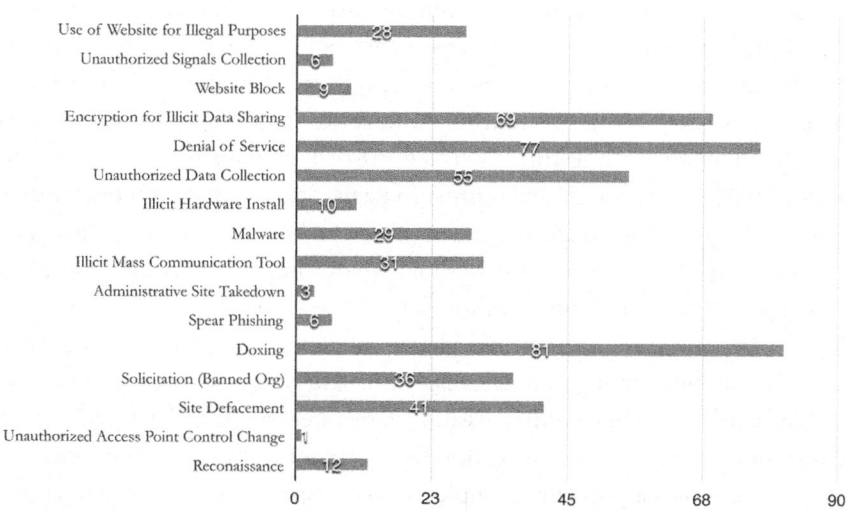

Figure 6.1 Digital antagonism events perpetrated by subversive actors.

technologies to mask illicit communications, such as the sharing of stolen information or the planning of illicit digital or physical disruption.[18] Also common are website vandalism, illegal solicitation, and unauthorized data collection, the latter two of which are natural corollaries of illegal website usage and doxing.

Without a doubt, the most notable feature of digital antagonism undertaken by subversive elements of global society is that it is organically unsophisticated. Cyber actions are almost exclusively focused on the informational value of systems and content rather than the functional nature of computers or web technologies. Even where there is emphasis on disruption—as is, by definition, the case with denial of service attacks – harassment by subversives rarely takes the more dramatic shape of those cyber events that are the focus of so much national security and industry preparedness efforts today, such as attacks on critical infrastructure or persistent intrusion targeting an organization's vital systems. In only 109 instances (i.e., just over 22% of all antagonistic incidents observed here) were cyber events of different categories observed in tandem with one another. In almost all cases (i.e., all but 29—or less than 4% of—cases) such co-occurrence was the doxing of individuals or organizations using data stolen during a preceding breach. Only in 11 cases was one antagonistic use of the web followed by an escalatory step. Three times between 2014 and 2017 in incidents spread across Central Europe, for instance, hardware was illegally planted so as to allow malware to enter a target system. In four cases—twice in the United States between 2009 and 2013 and twice in China between 2000 and 2002—websites constructed and published by affiliates of subversive causes were employed in watering-hole attacks wherein victims would be identified and routed to the sites in question so as to facilitate the clandestine downloading of Trojan horse malware. In the four remaining instances, spear phishing gave way to data theft. In all other cases, co-appearing antagonistic uses of web technologies reflected a duplication of effort, such as the use of email spamming software alongside the posting of illicit solicitations online.

In many ways, this trend toward low-intensity disruptive and intrusive digital activities among subversives is unsurprising. In much recent empirical work on cyber conflict issues, it has become standard practice to consider cyberattacks as fitting along a spectrum from low to high impact. Figure 6.2 shows a popular example of such a spectrum, the Brown-Tullos Cyber Action Response Spectrum, that has been variously used to align

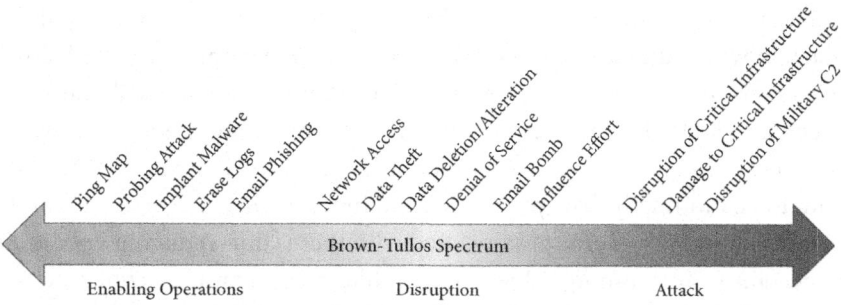

Figure 6.2 The Brown-Tullos Cyber Action Response Spectrum.

policy and technical responses with different forms of cyber actions and threats.[19] Given what we know about the goals of subversive organizations as interested in normative transformation and the conditions that allow for such an ideational inflection, it is unsurprising that we might find minimal evidence of high-level cyber assaults undertaken by subversive organizations. Aside from the fact that high-level attacks are inherently more expensive and time-consuming to prosecute, subversion is—at least according to what limited literature has covered the topic—far less focused on systematic chaos and disruption than on targeted acts of manipulation and mitigation of opponents.

On a spectrum like the Brown-Tullos Cyber Action Response Spectrum in Figure 6.2, the left-hand group of low-impact and low-intensity cyber interactions is labeled *enabling operations*. In other literature, analysts have labeled such techniques and methods of approach the natural substance of "grey zone tactics" and "twilight operations."[20] The idea is that such methods are themselves adjunct enhancement tools that enable attacks that are more meaningful in the context of an attacker's portfolio of objectives. For studies of hactivists, spies, or foreign militaries, such low-intensity techniques—if employed smartly and successfully—give way to greater abilities to prosecute highly disruptive cyberattacks, from sophisticated persistent information exfiltration to assaults on critical infrastructure. For subversive organizations, they are a doorway to rhetoric and acts that build or counter narrative in a number of ways. Indeed, for those at the fringe, the focus on low-intensity digital antagonism fits remarkably well within the growing literature linking cyber actions to conflict utility and corresponds with what we know about the payoffs involved with this group of cyber techniques across a range of characterizing categories.

Figure 6.3 breaks out the Brown-Tullos spectrum into a Schmitt Analysis Stack in which different characteristics of cyberattacks are estimated along the length of the impact scale.[21] Actions that fall along the left-hand side of the spectrum, including simple reconnaissance, data espionage, and information modification activities, are inherently low-risk/high-gain in that they tend to be minimally disruptive to system functionality and there are rarely delayed or unknown effects associated with them (thus reducing operation uncertainty in planning). Likewise, unlike more complex cyberattacks, there is little chance of "catching others in the blast" through unintended side effects, as is common with the employment of reasonably sophisticated cyber weaponry. Such activities (which are often combinations of different cyber actions leveraged to cumulative effect), though somewhat easy to measure and attribute in technical terms, are more relatively tricky to assess in terms of real-world criminal or political responsibility. And such activities are often difficult to legislate, particularly as jurisdictional standards for identifying intent and organizational involvement are highly variable. Given the desire to avoid overt scrutiny and the common lack of formal resources available for engaging in more complex digital activities, the attraction of such techniques to subversive organizations of such low-risk/high-gain options for antagonism is fairly clear. Moreover, the availability of such options for disruption and harassment that are not characterized by risks commonly associated with civil and criminal disobedience in eras past suggests that digital antagonism may be a new normal at the fringes of global society. Simply put, though there is certainly evidence that subversive groups occasionally undertake more disruptive actions and complex cyber actions than is the norm, it makes sense that new space for sociopolitical contestation beneath traditional thresholds of physically disruptive or violent disobedience has prompted greater incidence of antagonism by subversive social movements and organizations than has been true in eras past.

The Evolution of Digital Age Subversion over Time

The data under study covers the digital actions of subversive organizations and social movements over more than three decades. As Figure 6.4 shows, however, by far the greatest volume of events recorded are observed in just the past decade. Since 2010, just under two-thirds of all incidents (311 out of 494 distinct events) of digital antagonism have occurred. More than half of these incidents have

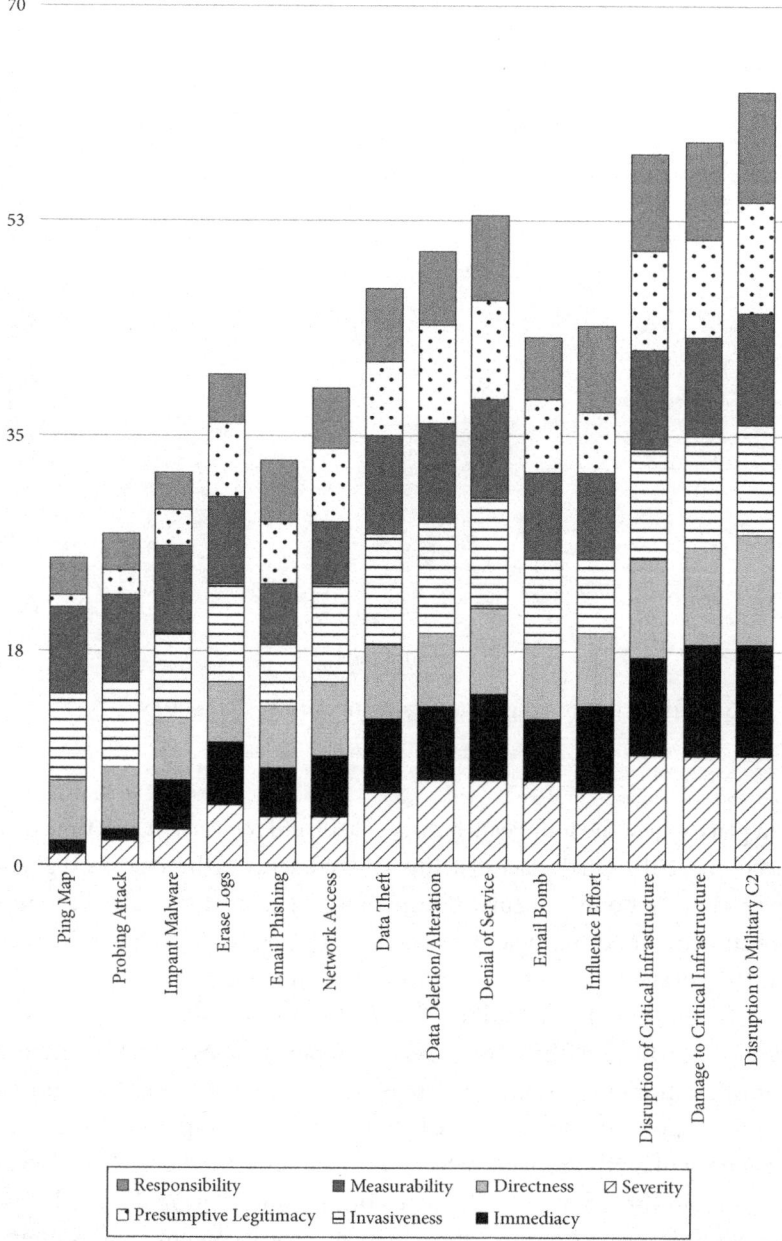

Figure 6.3 Schmitt analysis stack of the Brown-Tullos Cyber Action Response Spectrum.

164   SUBVERSION 2.0

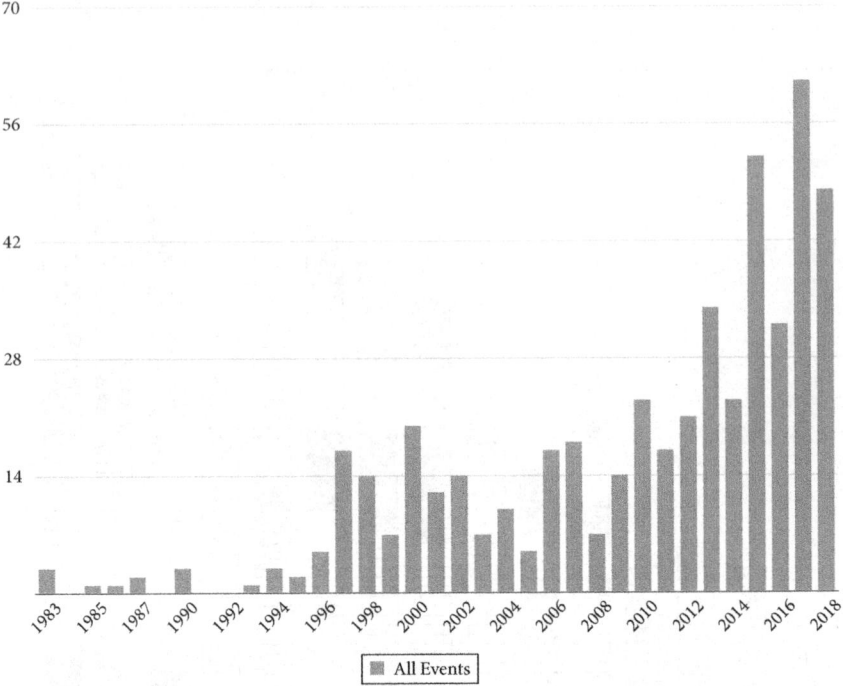

Figure 6.4 Total count of digital antagonism events, 1982–2019.

taken place in just the four years between 2015 and *Subversion 2.0*'s time of data collection in 2019. On the face of it, this lends credence to the idea that digital-age subversion is not only a regular feature of world affairs but is also becoming a more attractive mode of engagement at the fringes in line with expanding access to and the diversification of web services and technologies.

Moreover, though the toolkit of subversion in the digital age is remarkably unsophisticated, there are several notable changes in the nature of antagonistic actions undertaken by fringe elements over the past three decades. Figure 6.5 shows the temporal distribution of all events from 1982 to 2019 by category of action recorded. Several stories emerge therefrom. However, the common thread in all is the focus on the informational and ideational value of the internet over and above new disruptive potential, as is often the emphasized feature of traditional hactivism.

Early uses of the web by subversive actors primarily—and unsurprisingly—revolved around the basic manipulation of the website as an informational

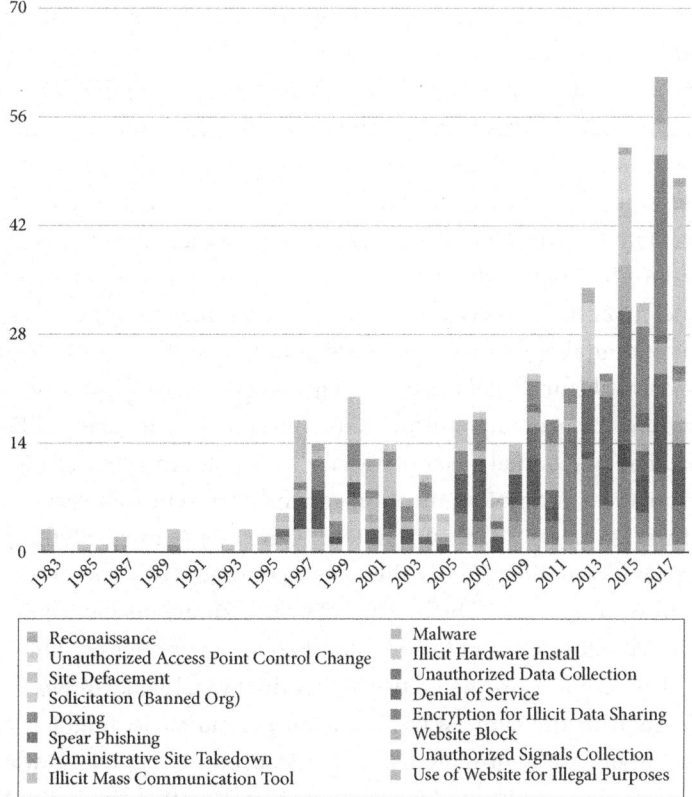

Figure 6.5 Digital antagonism events by event type, 1982–2019.

medium for communicating with civil society in line with the Fringe 1.0 experience explored in Chapter 3. By far the most common early hacking actions linked with subversive social movements were simple website defacements. In 1994, for instance, radical animal rights activists altered the home page of a British university research center to include pictures of animals killed by toxic waste leaks and messages that decried "global capital" as the antithesis of a "just moral society." Other antagonistic actions prior to the late 1990s involved the use of websites to illegally advocate violent protest, as was the case with an attempt to rally support for property destruction as a means of protest by persons self-affiliated with the Earth Liberation Front in 1996 or to denigrate national persons in violation of national law, as occurred in 1997 when acolytes of Hassan al-Banna—the populist Islamist founder of the Muslim Brotherhood—published doctored pictures of President Mubarak alongside accusations of apostasy.

Over time, the toolkit of digital-age subversion has diversified and become more sophisticated. This parallels the diversification and democratization of access to web technologies useful for a host of activist and antagonistic outcomes since the 1980s. Indeed, subversive flirtation with novel techniques is apparent in the data. Denial of service attacks, which present as the second most common antagonistic activity among subversives, is far more evenly distributed over the years covered in the data set than are other frontrunner methods of digital-age subversion, such as doxing or the use of off-the-shelf encryption tools for illegal purposes. This is unsurprising given the history of DDoS and the growing multiformity of web tools for sociopolitical contestation. The first denial of service attack took place in 1996, a SYN flood—in which a succession of connection requests are sent to a server without follow-through so as to tie up system resources—aimed at the internet service provider Panix.[22] Early the next year, the artist collective–turned–protest group Electronic Disturbance Theater launched Floodnet, a basic program that allowed users to consistently reload webpages.[23] The idea—to reiterate—was that coordinated use of Floodnet would take down a targeted website much in the same way that an in-person sit-in might practically deny customers the legitimate use of a restaurant. Early DDoS was, in essence, envisioned as a form of performance art, a virtual version of the civil disobedience that characterized civil rights movements throughout the 20th century.

The data—parsed apart in clearer terms in Figure 6.6's representation of (1) only "hacking" techniques among subversives over time and (2) only the most common events observed—shows that subversive elements of global society flocked to the use of DDoS in much the same way that less extreme protesters and activists did. In the decade between 1997 and 2007, no fewer than 35 denial of service attacks were prosecuted by subversive actors. In many cases, targets were mainstream political organizations, media outlets, or, most commonly, individuals clearly linked to positions antithetical to a given subversive cause. In Bangladesh over a two-month period in 2005, for instance, hackers linked to pro–gay rights groups operating underground consistently managed to take down the personal website of one particularly outspoken conservative government minister. In Brazil, a government-supported website aimed at providing language immersion and cross-cultural translation training for missionaries attempting to integrate

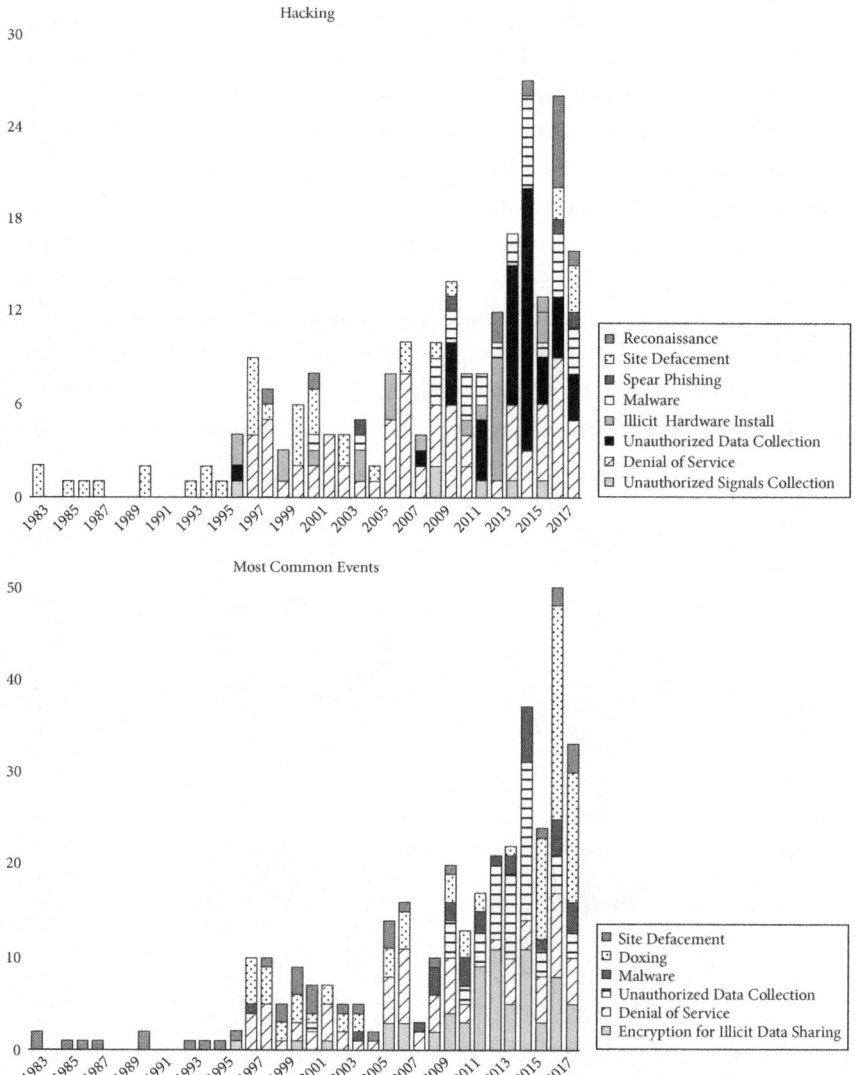

Figure 6.6 Digital antagonism events by event categories and popularity, 1982–2019.

native populations into developing urban workforces was hit several times by persons clearly—due to their prior vandalism of the same site with anti-government slogans and pornographic images of a politician having sex with a tree—in opposition to further violation of natural Amazonian habitats. In other cases, DDoS was used by subversive elements to disrupt the activities

168 SUBVERSION 2.0

of competitors at the fringe. In 2001, for instance, self-affiliated communist advocates in Italy employed denial of service attacks against forum sites popular among neofascist elements in the lead-up to regional elections.

Interestingly, this mode of usage of DDoS has persisted over time, even as DDoS employment has broadly declined (as Figure 6.7's summary of technique employment by decade shows). Since 2010, more than 85% of denial of service attacks by subversive elements have targeted ideological competitors. A notable example of this—one of the few subversive employments of the web antagonistically to receive widespread media coverage even in the past few years—was the six-month-long series of more than 100 denial of service attacks against Black Lives Matter websites in 2016. Though no attribution for the attacks was forthcoming in that case (and thus are not recorded in

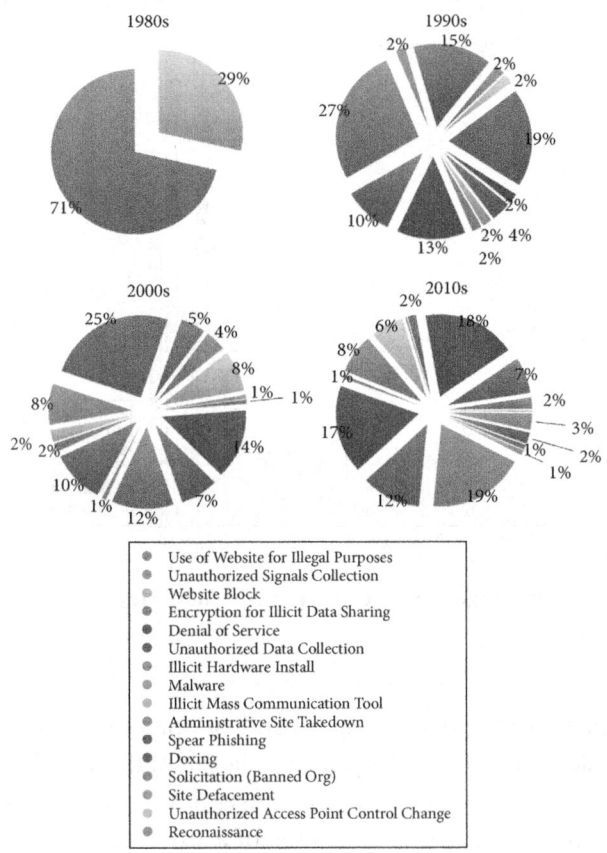

Figure 6.7 Digital antagonism events by event type by decade.

the data set), the attacks and the trend away from DDoS employed against mainstream targets since 2007 are representative of the apparent focus by subversive elements on the ideational value of antagonistic digital actions. Disruption is a useful counter to ideological opposition. As societal views coalesced on DDoS as less a mode of attention-drawing performance art and more a form of punctuated disturbance, however, its usage as an adjunct to strategies of narrative construction has faded and given way to new, alternative parts of the toolkit of digital engagement.

Since the 2000s, the most common illicit activities of subversive elements of global society online have been the theft, sharing, and publication of private data. It will not be surprising to any student of global cyber conflict that theft of intellectual property or data with prospective utility for creating sociopolitical scandal is a common activity among those interested in using the internet maliciously. Among subversives, however, theft of private data is rarely an innovative or particularly sophisticated activity. Most unauthorized collection of data is the result of either social engineering or basic scripting attacks on web platforms. The former consists of phishing or spear phishing designed to prompt a victim to give up credentials that might be used to access email accounts, administrator portals, or other private systems. The latter is a category of information attack constituted of methods for exploiting syntax errors or security lapses in the design of web systems. In neither case is advanced skill with information systems' design particularly necessary. As one prominent work on cyber conflict noted of techniques like SQL injection, in particular, a scripting attack is just about "the least . . . [a hacker] can do."[24] Thus, while the rising emphasis of a clear lifecycle of activities in the form of theft leading to the sharing and then publication of stolen data does suggest a coordinative sophistication of the subversive enterprise, the underlying skill level required to enable such actions has not itself appreciably changed.

Rather, the clear emphasis remains on normative outcomes over purely disruptive ones, a point which is perhaps clearest in the rising use of malware by subversive elements of global society. While the injection of malware *does* suggest a complexification of the subversive toolkit of digital antagonism, most employments thereof observed in the data set (just over 82%) were characterized by the focus on ideational outcomes. Malware employed by neo-Nazis in Hungary against progressive political donors in 2011, for instance, was simply designed to scrape information found within a contact and private file database. Likewise, far-right hackers in Western Europe targeted French-speaking social media users in an attempt to get them to download malicious software from a front website. While there is little evidence that many webizens downloaded the program, analysis of the code demonstrates a clear emphasis on messaging over disruption insofar as the program was designed to open browser windows unbeknownst to the victim, navigate to subversive content—including political memes and fabricated media reporting—and promote it.

This evolution of "click fraud"—a form of malicious online activity originally designed to fabricate clickthrough statistics so as to illegally generate ad revenue—to political purposes is increasingly common in recent years.[25] In particular, similar efforts have featured in the influence campaigns of the Russian Federation and Iran, a fact that suggests in no meaningless way that subversion in practice has more in common with state-sponsored information warfare than it does with performance hactivism or more pedestrian forms of digital protest activism. This is additionally borne out in the dynamics of agency and response to subversive antagonism online. More than 79% of all such incidents are the work of persons who self-affiliate with causes instead of being claimed by a formal organization, and fewer than 15% of incidents warrant an official response by state authorities at any level (most of which are simply website takedowns), suggesting that digital-age subversion remains a normative, largely nondisruptive enterprise that is the provenance of zealous devotees engaging in low-intensity efforts to harass, manipulate, and circumvent.

Digital-Age Subversion around the World

Though subversive uses of the web for antagonism in pursuit of the delegitimization of opposing social forces is found most commonly in the world's top economies, it would be disingenuous to say that subversion is a phenomenon constrained to the first world. Indeed, as Figure 6.8 shows, at first blush it almost seems fair to say that most countries in the world have hosted some form of fringe social movement of which elements have used the internet to harass, hide, or persuade. In reality, the 313 subversive movements or organizations cataloged in the data set are spread across 91 countries (though only 37 have more than one), while the 104 linked to incidence of digital antagonism are found spread across 69 countries (whose activities are represented in the heat map in Figure 6.8).

LANDSCAPE OF SUBVERSION IN THE DIGITAL AGE   171

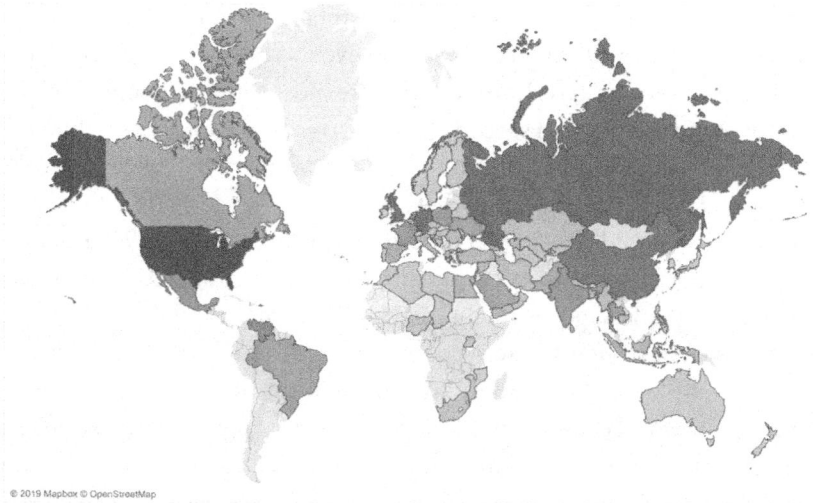

Figure 6.8 Digital age subversion around the world, 1982–2019.

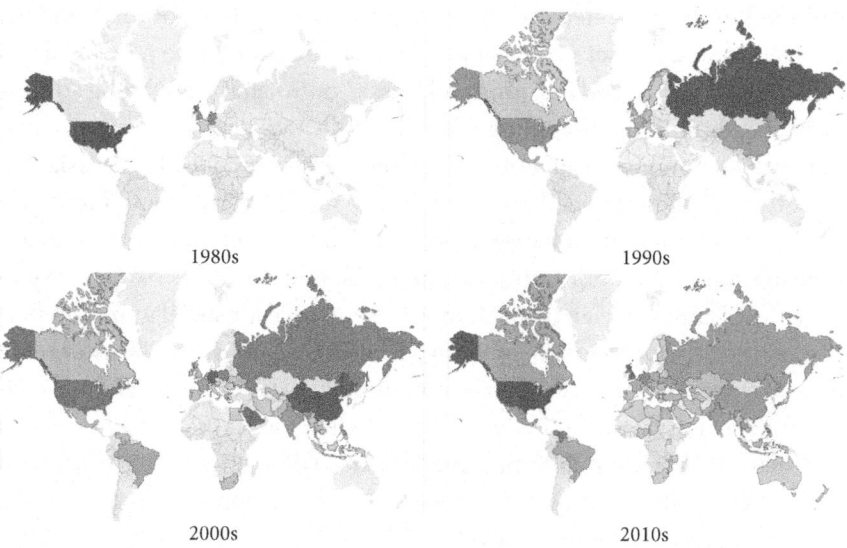

Figure 6.9 Digital age subversion around the world by decade.

As a distribution of incidents over the *entire* 37-year period covered in the data set, there is too little information in Figure 6.8 to intelligently infer the dynamics of digital-age subversion around the world. Figure 6.9's representation of the same data spread across four distinct decade-long periods, however, matches what one might expect of antagonistic uses of the internet by subversive causes. During the 1980s, all events recorded occurred in the United States or in Western Europe, a picture most simply explained by the limited evolution and global spread of the internet by the mid-1980s. Indeed, the internet—meaning the privatized version of the internetworked networks still operated by the U.S. government, National Science Foundation, and other entities—would not itself come into existence until 1994. Prior to this, interconnected networks employing packet-switching technology like ARPANET or the U.S. government's MILNET were centrally planned and concentrated in just a few Western countries.[26] During the 1990s, the privatization of what became the internet saw the rapid spread of web connectivity to other major world economies. Perhaps not surprisingly, in this period antagonism is most concentrated in major authoritarian and postauthoritarian states like Russia, China, and Mexico. With regard to Mexico, much subversive focus on national politics came in the form of externally supported advocacy for lingering antigovernment forces that held—and, in some cases, still hold to this day—territory in Chiapas and other parts of the country's southern states. A brief survey of incidents in the period also tells a story of civil society unshackled in China and Russia, both states with strong authoritarian traditions and grappling with the challenges of economic privatization amid a booming influx of new technological products. For Russia, the mid- to late 1990s heralded the storm before the calm that would ultimately become a reformation of national politics under the semi-authoritarian administration of Vladimir Putin. In China, the mid- to late 1990s saw several episodes of authoritarian realization of the potential for social unrest. In particular, the experience of Falun Gong's popularity and use of the internet to organize peaceful protests of government power, discussed at length previously, helped drive the rapid development of the means of digital repression within the People's Republic and several years of dramatic crackdown against societal elements—often labeled subversive or "evil cults" by Beijing—seen to be antithetical to communist rule.

Indeed, just as the spread of the internet beyond the West seems to explain the spiking incidence of digital antagonism from the fringes in countries like Russia and China, so too does the context of authoritarian upgrading and the rise of democratic populism in the West seem to offer a basis for making sense of trends across the 2000s and 2010s. During the 1990s and 2000s, digital technologies were often thought of as "liberation technologies" for seeming to enable all manner of democratization effects across global society.[27] From

Ukraine to Central Asia and the Middle East, the internet enervated civil society and enhanced the prospects of social movements taking aim at governmental corruption, religious intolerance, and more. From 2010 onward, the internet played a significant role in what would become the Arab Spring. In Tunisia, hacktivists both local and foreign aided protesters on the streets by launching DDoS attacks on government websites and leaking scandalous information about entrenched elites.[28] In Egypt and Libya, social media proved to be a great coordinating tool for both protesters and rebel forces, as Twitter was famously used to draw the attention of NATO military forces to an impending government assault on Benghazi.[29]

While the utility of the internet for cultivating antigovernment sentiment and new sources of social unrest had not escaped the eyes of authoritarian governments in the region to that point, the Arab Spring made concrete for the leaders of those governments the necessity of controlling the conduct of civil society online. Much in the same way that the experience of Falun Gong and other social movements in China had prompted the rapid shift toward elaborate methods of digital social control a decade earlier, the Arab Spring prompted a significant investment in the same as a key element of authoritarian upgrading. This "upgrading," according to Heydemann and others, has been broadly characterized by several interrelated efforts to (1) provide economic freedoms to national populations while at the same time (2) presenting a façade of a vibrant civil society and (3) extending the apparatuses of total population control (via actions such as enforcing registration for most societal activities and diluting the apparent value of actual democratic engagement).[30] With the internet specifically, the aims of many major authoritarian states have often been to strike a clear balance between restriction of civil society and the provision of a pressure valve that functions to prevent social frustration from slipping into civil or violent action. As such, governments from the Persian Gulf to Central and East Asia have enthusiastically invested in the infrastructure of digital repression, a broad strategic perspective on censorship that is often characterized more by focus on quashing attempts by social forces to assemble than it is (beyond a core set of topics) on the direct limitation of free speech.

With subversion, the normalization of the distribution of antagonistic episodes across countries from the 2000s to the 2010s makes significant sense in this context, and a case-by-case assessment of observed trends bears this out. In China, no fewer than eight episodes of subversive antagonism were undertaken between the 1990s and 2000s by movements that would either be pushed overseas or, due to state repression, would practically cease to exist in China by 2013. In parts of the Middle East and North Africa, pro–gay rights activists and Islamist advocates of societal transformation that had effectively staked out an online presence through the years of the Arab Spring have since suffered from the efforts of state security forces deployed to discredit, dishonor, or even kill individual affiliates. Particularly in the Gulf monarchies, such efforts have often revolved around repressive employments of web technologies, including the use of malware to track and monitor those seen by governments as subversive. At the same time, even just from this data it becomes clear that subversion has quite clearly been on the rise in the Western world, with populism born of economic disaffection in particular opening space for many countercultural causes to glom on to upstart political movements.

The National Context of Subversion

To this juncture, our exploration of the landscape of digital antagonism at the fringes of global society has focused more on the metadata of the phenomenon—that is, the methodological, temporal, and geographic disposition of subversive forces operating online—than the character of the causes in question and their targets. Figure 6.10 adds detail to the geographic representation of digital-age subversion discussed in the previous section. Here, we can clearly see the degree to which the digital activities of subversives correspond most closely to the world's major economies and largest internet-using societies: China, the United States, Russia, the United Kingdom, and Germany. To a lesser extent, digital-age subversion is not infrequently seen in India, Brazil, Indonesia, Mexico, Venezuela, Thailand, and France. Naturally, a great many factors tie these countries together. Digitally enabled subversive activities are seen in almost all G20 countries. Moreover, the countries of the G20 account for more than half of all episodes of antagonistic digital action by subversives over the 37-year period under study. As was suggested previously, there are obvious reasons why this might be the case. Countries in Western Europe and North America have "been online" longer than any others, and wealth obviously thereafter corresponds with internet accessibility and the rise of e-commerce in the 1990s and 2000s.

From the perspective of national governance, digital subversion is found most commonly in those countries ranked (by the Polity IV project) as either

LANDSCAPE OF SUBVERSION IN THE DIGITAL AGE 175

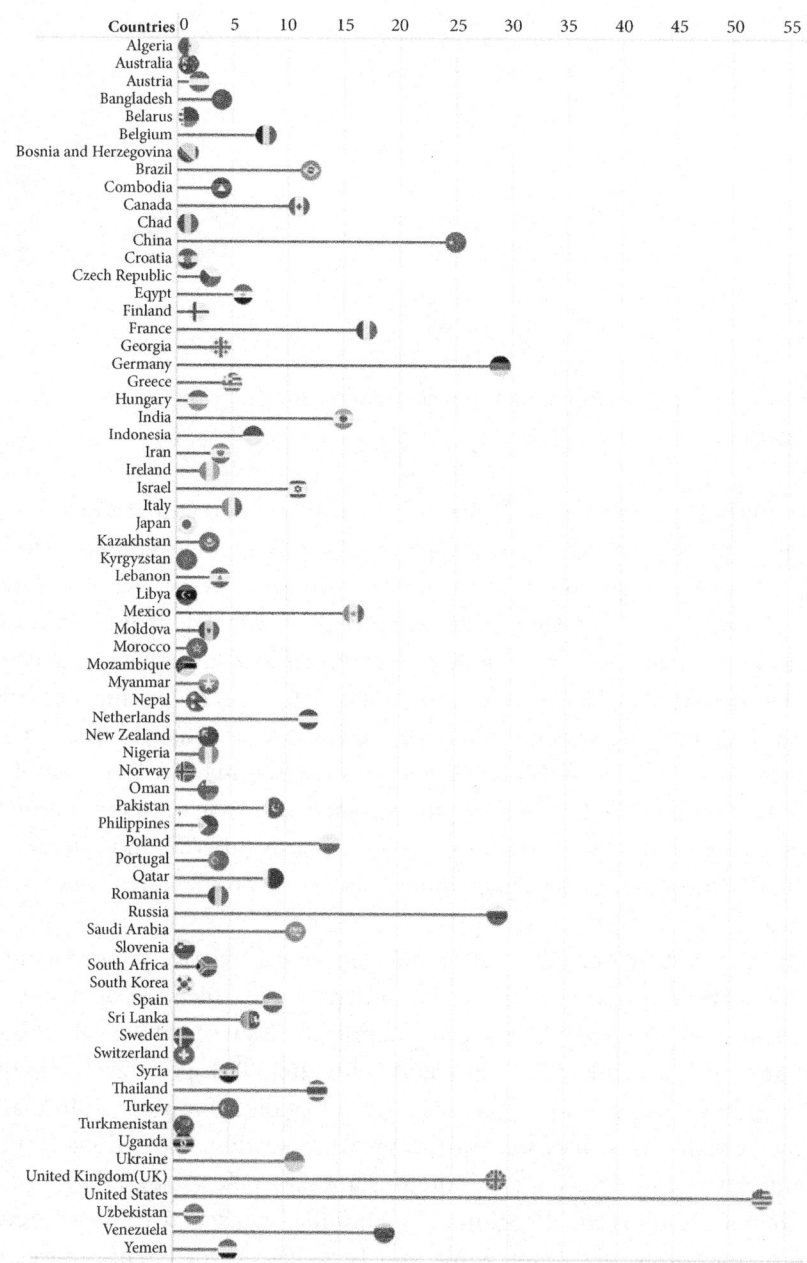

Figure 6.10 Incidence of digital age subversion by country.

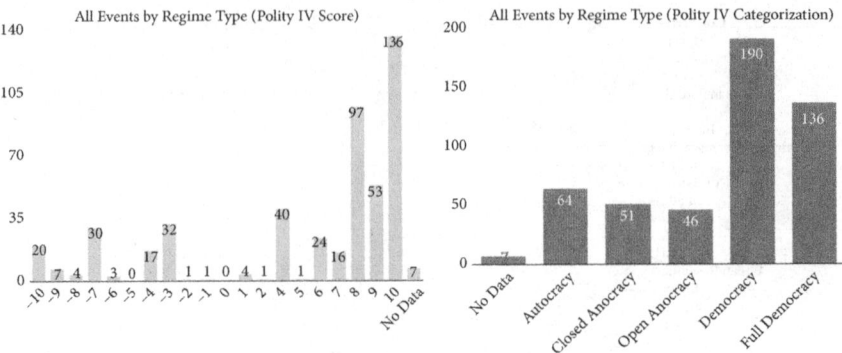

Figure 6.11 Incidence of digital subversion by regime type scores and categories (Polity IV).

partially or fully democratic. Figure 6.11 shows the raw count of antagonistic digital actions across countries by both the Polity IV regime-type score (from full authoritarianism to full democracy as −10 to 10, respectively) and the corresponding category labels, illustrating that more than half of all observed hacking or circumvention activities undertaken by subversive elements of global society take place in democratic states. This is unsurprising, not least because democratic societies offer the greatest protections and freedom of movement for social movements that consider the mainstream to be illegitimate. With limited exceptions, for instance, offensive or taboo speech is largely protected by law in countries across North America and Europe, as well as in the major advanced economies of Japan, South Korea, and South Africa.

By contrast, digital-age subversion is found relatively infrequently across states with authoritarian and anocratic (i.e., blended democratic-authoritarian systems) regimes. Most significant, a survey of the data shows remarkably few incidents in autocratic states after 2011, possibly due to the general move toward sophisticated programs of digital repression in many authoritarian states discussed in the previous section. Exceptions to this trend reflect numerous special circumstances—such as several recorded incidents in subnational regions with unique status and/or clear secessionist traditions, like Hong Kong and Balochistan—or circumstances in which governments score poorly on their ability to affect social control, such as Indonesia.

The commonplace nature of subversive enterprise in democratic societies is also evident in the ideological disposition of the social movements and

LANDSCAPE OF SUBVERSION IN THE DIGITAL AGE   177

groups under study. Figure 6.11 utilizes a modified version of the ideology coding scheme employed by the START initiative in its construction of the Global Terrorism Database.[31] By far the most common ideological classification appropriate for subversive groups is either right or left wing. In truth, with subversive elements of global society, this dichotomy somewhat misstates the character of most fringe elements. While some groups in the data set would be clearly recognizable as far right or far left, it is important to remember that subversion is categorically characterized by the focus on de-legitimization of the status quo via tactics that call for degradation of the symbols and prevailing norms thereof. Thus, while racial supremacy organizations may qualify as subversive, for instance, they do not automatically do so (and, indeed, often do not because they emphasize forcible overthrow or acts of racial violence).

Subversive elements that fall into the left- and right-wing categories (Figure 6.12) track closely the preponderance of digital subversion that occurs within democratic states. Subversion characterized by a focus on environmental conservation and transformation is also reasonably commonplace

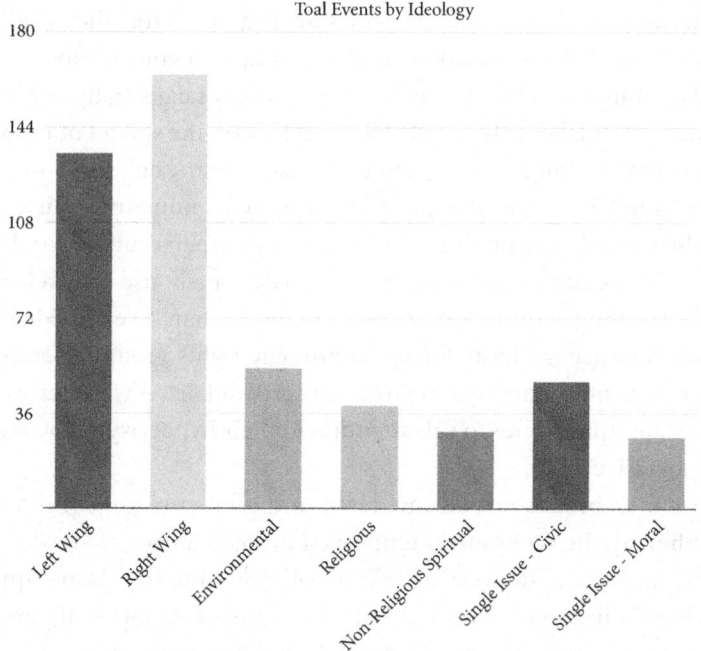

Figure 6.12 Incidence of digital subversion by group/movement ideology.

within democratic states, though there is an interesting spike in this category in anocratic states since 2015. One such episode bears particular note. In 2016, a pair of hackers stole data from several logging companies in China whose operations had significantly benefited from the patronage of several CCP officials for the better part of two decades. In many ways, this is an interesting case of subversive intent both clashing with the status quo and finding popular acceptance. The hackers cited numerous radical environmental causes in the course of publishing their actions, including the famous Earth Liberation Front, and demonized the CCP as intending the death of the planet. At the same time, the actions fit ongoing anticorruption narratives promoted by both civil society voices and CCP leadership. As such, the officials involved were detained even as the government attempted to crack down on the individuals involved.

As a descriptor of subversive enterprise, nonreligious spiritualism alone seems to be evenly distributed across different regime contexts, with cult-like organizations like China's Eastern Lightning mirroring Western cults like the Brethren. Aside from a few noteworthy recent incidents of environmentally motivated activities in relatively more autocratic societies, by contrast, subversion in authoritarian and closed anocratic states is most often characterized by a focus on single issues or religion. Across the Middle East, a range of Islamist organizations and social movements ascribe to the "Al Jihad Électronique," a broad-scope manifesto only tangentially linked to the direct actions of Islamic terrorists that emphasizes the spread of fundamentalist Muslim teachings as an approach to vacating the cultural power of the West. In countries across Africa and Central Asia, numerous causes aimed at producing relief from legal, state-sponsored persecution for LGBTQ individuals operate in the shadows and occasionally use the web to fight hateful prevailing cultural narratives. In no fewer than seven incidents since 2003, for instance, activists linked to pro–gay rights groups operating underground in nonpermissive regimes either vandalized websites or doxed leading status quo figures to call attention to their hypocrisy as gay members of an oppressive force.

Figure 6.13 breaks out all incidents of digital antagonism in the data set further by the techniques employed across categories of ideological persuasion. Several interesting, albeit unsurprising trends are apparent. First, there is limited focus on disruption across categories of persuasion *not* characterized by the right-versus-left dichotomy. Given how closely those categories track to incidents that take place within democratic

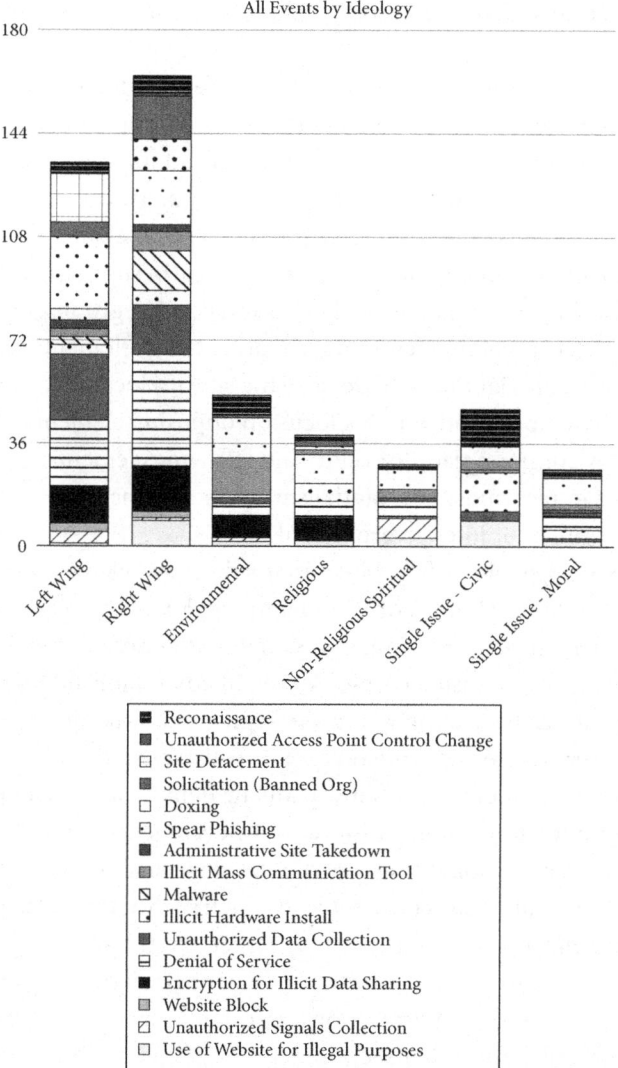

Figure 6.13 Incidence of digital subversion by group/movement ideology and event type.

states, this implies that disruption is simply not seen to be as useful a tool of subversive elements under circumstances of limited civil society discourse and participation. This, in turn, reinforces the notion that subversive use of the internet for antagonism emphasizes information outcomes, despite the assumptions often linked with hactivism more broadly that hold disruption to be valuable in itself as a means of sociopolitical protest.

Second, as a proportion of the actions undertaken across different categories, environmentally motivated movements appear to do the most to directly engage the public at large, with significant focus on the use of illicit mass communication tools (i.e., email spamming software). Even the limited number of incidents of website defacement by such elements suggests the same popular engagement focus that is not typical of subversive movements, at least according to the data. With left-and right-wing groups, nearly 80% of all website defacement incidents targeted other fringe elements (e.g., hackers linked with the alt-right in 2016 defaced the site of a local Black Lives Matter group in Mississippi). Indeed, this focus on opposing elements of the fringe is reasonably commonplace for right- and left-wing elements, as Figure 6.13 shows. By contrast, most site vandalism by environmentally linked groups target government or intergovernmental sites.

It seems reasonable at first blush that subversive elements operating in democratic states are both more willing to employ the web antagonistically and have more clearly determined a structured approach for doing so. To some degree, this is unsurprising. We've already established that left- and right-wing causes utilize the web more regularly for antagonistic purposes than all other categories, and there is a substantial correlation between left/right-wing elements and subversion in democratic societies. Greater freedom to operate leading to more well-developed repertoires of digital subversion seems reasonable as a sort of conventional wisdom. At the same time, Figure 6.14 illustrates the degree to which such actors regularly achieve more severe effects on the systems they target. On the surface, this suggests more well-fleshed-out capabilities for antagonistic digital engagement and matches the trend toward greater or lesser emphasis on certain techniques over time described in earlier sections.

Digital-Age Subversion, Not Protest, Hacktivism, or Conflict

Given a range of characteristics found in common among such causes' experience with hacking and digital circumvention, the dynamics of subversion in the digital age are clearly distinct from many of the nonstate actor and social movement activities online that beget the broad labels "cyber disobedience"

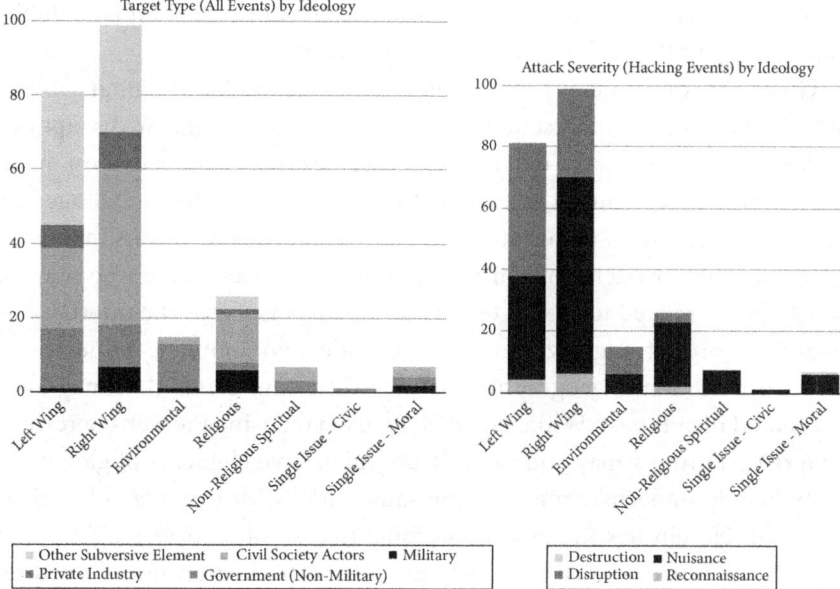

Figure 6.14 Incidence of digital subversion by ideology, target type, and attack severity (hacking events only).

or "hactivism." This seems to be true on a number of fronts. First, the methodological focus of subversive elements of global society differs from that of other nonstate actors that use or may want to use the web antagonistically, particularly that often associated with hactivists writ large. Hactivism is a phenomenon most closely linked with civil disobedience and an emphasis on transgression as the means of political or social change. Hactivists, mimicking the practical focus of transgressive activists in eras past on disruption and naming-and-shaming societal opponents, most often hack in order to make a splash. Subversives, by contrast, seem to hack in this way only when the informational value of an action is sufficient to call the legitimacy of their status quo target into question. Moreover, subversive digital actions infrequently appear aimed at engagement with popular discourse (e.g., via the use of email spamming software) but rather tend—at least when the target is not the disruption of fringe opponents—to emphasize impact on the popular narrative surrounding an issue or perspective. And even more severe attacks or harassments are moded toward the betterment of information conditions relevant to subversive causes. As noted in previous sections, recent employments of malware across several countries have invariably been part and parcel of attempts to either steal private information for later publication or boost the visibility of subversive content.

Given this dynamic, it is tempting to label the toolkit of digital subversion "information enhancement" rather than harassment or disruption. Indeed, this label and the dynamics it describes fit well the assertion made near this chapter's outset that nonstate subversion in the digital age has far more in common with state-sponsored influence operations than with cyber conflict or hactivism. In reality, subversive uses of the web may be most closely related to that of terrorists, at least insofar as the internet has enabled terrorist organizations to persuade and mobilize populations free from the many geographic and logistical constraints that may have presented in eras past. While not at all focused on using the web coercively, as terrorist groups may additionally be, subversive elements of global society clearly undertake many of the same tasks with the same objectives in mind. Herein lies the false dichotomy that so often drives differential analysis of nonstate actors; subversion is a phenomenon not defined by its tactical corollaries in the same way that terrorism is. Terrorist organizations might absolutely be characterized, at least in part, as subversive given a sufficient body of normative actions to detach popular loyalties from the symbols of one image of society and transfer them to another. When it comes to characterizing particular movements or organizations, of course, the "subversive" qualification must be determined by the scope of the study. Here, that scope is the digital actions undertaken in aid of subversive goals. Thus, this data set and the analysis of subversive elements of global society exclude actors that clearly use either digital or conventional means to coerce.

Second, digital-age subversion differs from other forms of digital contestation in the logistical form it takes. At first assessment of the data marshaled here, it appears as though subversive actors are opportunistic. They rarely attack government or military targets, except in a few cases. Along the same lines, official response to subversive acts of digital antagonism is infrequent, if not quite rare, bolstering the case that avoidance of the gaze of authority is desirable. And their choice of techniques has tracked closely their strategic focus on normative transformation rather than simply the opportunity to use new techniques as they become available. Added to all this, subversive antagonism on the web is less often the work of an organization or formal social movement that claims attribution for disruptive acts. Of the 494 episodes recorded in the data set, fewer than 120 are attributable directly to such an entity. The remainder are attributable to various causes, social movements, communities, and organizations by self-affiliation. To put it differently, nearly 76% (374 out of 494 incidents) of events recorded emerge from *peripheral* elements of subversive causes.

Finally, digital subversion differs from other forms of digital contestation in its setting in world politics. It is found far more often in open national societies than in closed or restrictive ones. Though there is clear evidence of digital subversion in closed societies, the distribution weighted so heavily toward democratic societies is novel in the context of existing scholarship on nonstate actors' uses of the internet. Indeed, this is particularly the case when one considers the character of digital engagement described previously (i.e., that subversion isn't activism in the traditional sense, but it is also not transgressive disobedience).

Keeping One Foot in the Shadows?

This chapter's exploration of the landscape of digital subversion offers a number of insights into the ways the web is used for antagonistic purposes by society's fringe elements. In particular, initial survey of data about subversives' online activities constructs digital subversion as something with unique methodological characteristics. Because of this, it is possible to construct and test the leaderlessness theory, specifically the assertion that we should expect the incidence of antagonistic engagement to correspond to the rhetoric of societal elites tied to a given cause.

To do this, however, requires consideration of the totality of digital activities undertaken by subversive social movements and organizations around the world. The data presented here reported on the 104 subversive causes that have been linked to antagonistic usages of web technologies since 1982. However, this is just a subset of the broader universe of subversive movements identified via reference to their digital public engagement—that is, to their digital activism. In reality, barely a third of all such movements engage in those antagonistic digital activities that are the focus of this book. As such, Chapter 7 primarily aims to answer the following question: What explains why some subversive actors and movements turn to the web for antagonism and some do not?

High-level analysis of the data offers no obvious, immediate explanation. As Figure 6.15 illustrates, there is no significant correlation between

184 SUBVERSION 2.0

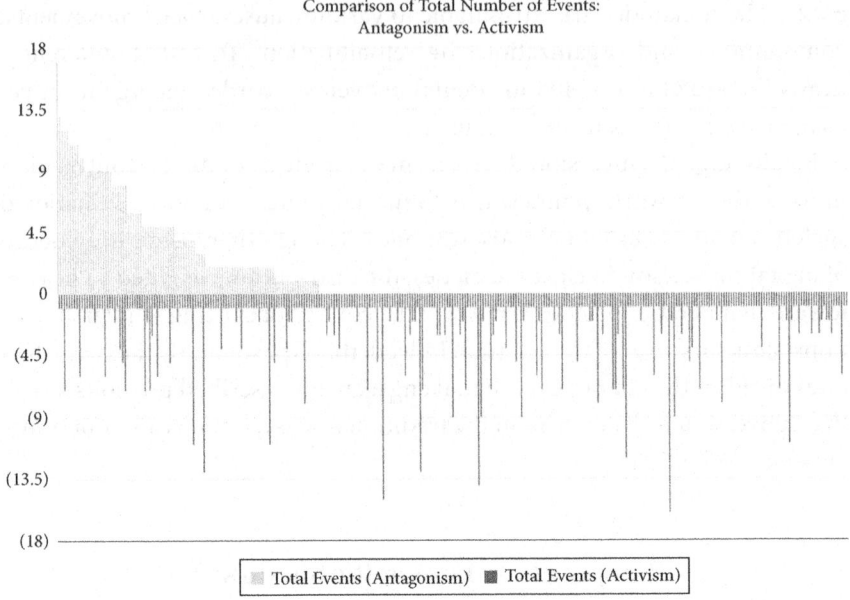

Figure 6.15 Digital engagment (activism and antagonism) across all subversive movements/groups.

the intensity of digital activism and digital antagonism among subversive nonstate actors. This strongly indicates that emphasis on both toolkits of digital engagement does not emerge from initial emphasis on just one of the two. In short, repeated web activism does not predict antagonism and vice versa. This is particularly vexing given that wholesale movement of the dispersed parts of subversive movements to the internet might, at first blush, be an obvious explanation for the otherwise unusual trend of some subversive causes being linked with *both* activism and antagonism. The social movement that attempts to engage the broader population and generally operate in the public eye must consider the potential costs of continued association with illegal or subjectively shady activities. Such association invites the scrutiny of authorities and risks harming the integrity of the cause—of the ideational platform of a given movement—in the eyes of everyday citizenry. The existence of a subversive cause as largely digital—in essence, the distancing of a normative movement from real-world context—might have acted to deconstruct such logical expectations. And yet, a greater online presence does not itself seem to predict digital antagonism. What, then, does?

Looking Forward

This chapter has established the scope of digital subversion as an increasingly frequent feature of world affairs. Understanding fringe digital activities is critical for a range of reasons, not least that the practical implications of the internet for subversive enterprise are significantly more opportunities for harassment, propagandizing, and circumvention of authority than existed in eras past. By understanding the dynamics of subversion augmented by the internet, we can more accurately make statements about the impact of fringe elements of global society on the mainstream and shape policy accordingly.

Having built a qualitative and descriptive quantitative understanding of the landscape of subversive agency and web usage in the modern era, I now turn to quantitatively test the implications of theory offered in *Subversion 2.0*, namely that there exists a feedback loop that links subversive activities to the rhetoric of elites. Chapter 7, specifically, marshals statistical evidence in support of the theory and provides the basis with which the final chapter, Chapter 8, returns to the case of January 6 and the implications of subversion enabled and emboldened in novel fashion by the internet's own evolution.

7
Leaderlessness at the Fringes
Explaining When Subversives Hack

Subversion is a complex enterprise. Whereas coercive action is so often focused on altering the material payoff structures involved in government or societal positioning on a given issue, subversion seeks the dissolution of something less tangible: the loyalties of a population to the symbols and institutions of the status quo. Subversive antagonism, as shown in Chapter 6, is most often geared toward informational gain. Particularly given that informational gain is a highly subjective outcome, this has traditionally made the prediction of such acts more difficult than might be the case with elements of global society—including terrorists, organized criminal interests, and more—that are more often the focus of social science investigations.

The theory presented in Chapter 5, however, holds that the sociotechnical architecture of the Web 2.0 era has produced a default formation of subversion in the practices of fringe elements that use the web (which is almost all) to engage the mainstream. The underlying arguments forwarded in this book about the transformation of global society in the age of the internet are not new, of course; indeed, they form the bedrock of a sprawling literature on digital politics that has sprung up over the past two decades.[1] What *is* new is the application of such arguments to a previously understudied phenomenon, as well as the contention that the practical manifestations of subversion—whose diverse format, often indistinguishable from the outputs of other sociopolitical approaches to engagement, has historically been the key obstacle to scholarly effectiveness—are predictably tied to emergent social movement dynamics in the digital age.

This chapter builds on the data collection effort described in Chapter 6 to provide evidence that subversion in the digital age is characterized by "leaderlessness," a dynamic of subversive operation defined by the organic development of engagement capacity at the peripheries of fringe movements. I use the puzzle of digital antagonism among a subset

Table 7.1 Breakdown of Observed Organizations by Evidence of Antagonistic ICT Usage

Subversive Activists	No Evidence of Digital Antagonism	Evidence of Digital Antagonism
All Observations	209	104
Top 10% Most Active	22	9
Top 25% Most Active	57	21

of fringe elements that use the web for activism to guide multivariate statistical exploration of the determinants of subversion. As was discussed in the previous chapter, it is certainly not the case that subversive activist users of ICT are guilty of explicitly transgressive digital antagonism (see Table 7.1). Of those organizations studied, 209 have no discernable affiliation with antagonistic utilizations of ICT.

But a nontrivial number of organizations studied *are* guilty of digital antagonism—that is, of employing ICT for disruptive or circumventive purposes. Of the groups studied, 104 social movements and organizations were linked to acts as diverse as website vandalism, the theft of private data, and the employment of malware. Table 7.1 shows two cuts of the data collected for this project. The table first shows the overall distribution of groups wherein there is basic evidence (in the form of a raw count) of activity across both categories of digital activity. Second, the table shows the same result for both categories for those most digitally active groups. It does so by assessing the top 10% and 25% most active groups for both categories (calculated by raw score, where each episodic employment of ICT is worth 1 and episodes are summed).

Not only are some subversive groups, persons, and communities guilty of employing ICT for illicit purposes; the information in Table 7.1 shows that such activity is not the exception to the rule. For both the top 10% and 25% categories, there is clear evidence of such actions by elements affiliated with a number of subversive causes. In other words, some of the most prolific users of ICT for activist purposes also use ICT for digital antagonism—for circumventive, illicit purposes. Figure 7.1 visually confirms this and more readily illustrates that digital antagonism is neither rare nor particularly less common among prolifically activist organizations.

The existence of this dynamic provides the basis for construction of dependent variables that directly address *Subversion 2.0*'s core interest in

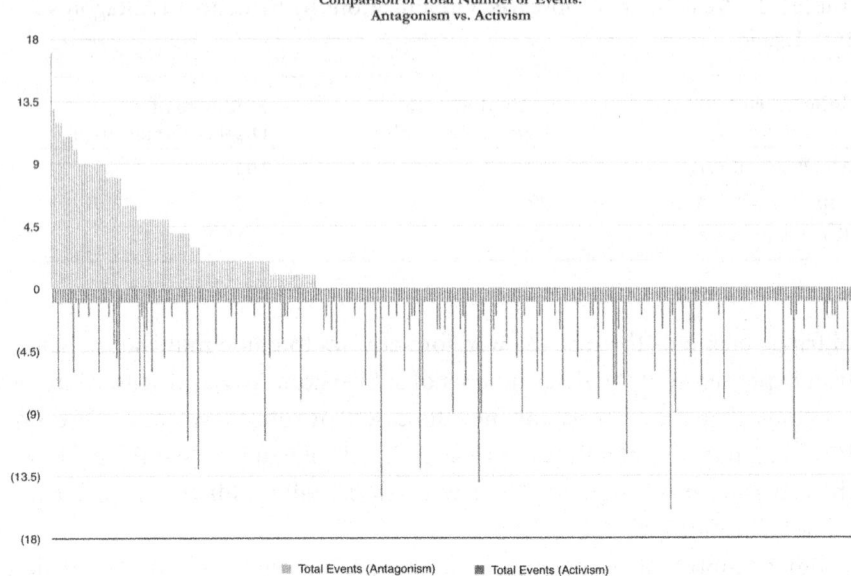

Figure 7.1 A raw count of total digital actions categorized as either activist or antagonistic in nature across 90 groups found to be linked with both.

the determinants of fringe engagement with the mainstream. Specifically, testing in this chapter addresses when society's fringe uses the internet for more than just activism (as opposed to simply not using the internet at all). I consider a diverse range of potential explanations for hacking and other shady activities common among subversive groups. Ultimately, however, I demonstrate that there is significant evidence to support the theory of leaderlessness as the common form of subversion in practice in the 21st century. Broadly, there exists a relationship between the nature of subversive grievances and apparent willingness to antagonize. This is not surprising in itself. However, antagonistic events are acutely predicted by greater incidence of revisionist statements—such as the claim that a cause is under attack by the mainstream, for instance—and is not infrequently tied directly to virtual communities. Likewise, while major events like elections and referenda do not clearly predict incidence of antagonism as a category of behavior—against the initial expectations articulated in this chapter—they do somewhat predict incidence of disruptive hacking, indicating again that subversive antagonists are sensitive to the dynamics of national information environments.

Digital Subversion: Expectations

The theory of leaderless subversion in the digital age presented in Chapter 6 describes a redistribution in the capacities of subversive social movements from the core to the peripheral elements of such movements. The core assumption of the theory is that this new formation of subversion lacks key mechanisms of command and control that would otherwise, in eras past, have allowed prominent figures within a movement to directly coordinate antagonism and the construction of narratives needed to translate fringe advocacy into something suitable for consumption in mainstream discourse. As such, multivariate statistical testing here emphasizes different possible alternative command-and-control mechanisms that might predict incidence of digital antagonism.

This chapter considers four such alternative mechanisms. First, much literature on the determinants of terrorist violence suggests that the underlying nature of a movement's grievances lays the foundation for greater incentive to use the web antagonistically. Simply put, if there are insoluble differences between the status quo and the fringe in terms of the prevailing structural setup, leaders and affiliates of a movement alike are going to be more willing to transgress than their counterparts. With subversion, revisionism takes on a particular form in that a given cause identifies the material manifestations of an ideology or set of norms as fundamentally tied to the illegitimacy of the status quo. In many instances, this is not the case. In the United States, for instance, many far-right organizations emphasize the significance of existing government structures and constitutional formations, claiming that they should exist even if some meaningful reinterpretation is required. Thus, the first hypothesis to be tested is:

H_1. *Revisionist grievances make it more likely that a fringe social movement will engage in digital antagonism.*

Departing from many of the conventional expectations of work in the terrorism studies field, *Subversion 2.0* suggests that the rhetoric articulated and gestures made by significant figures linked with a subversive cause can act as catalysts or tampers for antagonism. To clarify, scholars studying political violence have regularly linked the significant role of rhetoric to the function of movements employing the strategy of leaderless resistance.[2] However, it is rarely considered a direct control mechanism. Here, the assumption is not that broad ideological or functional priors prompt antagonism—and that rhetoric helps construct that broad basis—so much as it is that supporters of a cause interpret significant signals as an indication of willingness to condone it. The rhetoric of an important public leader of a cause or the direct denigration of an important symbol of the status quo, for instance, defines the context within which decision-making at the peripheries of fringe movements occurs. Though not a direct command, such gestures either amplify or mute incentives to antagonize depending on the tone. Thus, the second hypothesis to be tested is:

H_2. *Incidence of nonparticipatory rhetoric on the part of public figures significant to a given cause will vary in direct proportion to incidence of digital antagonism.*

In much the same vein, *Subversion 2.0* also adopts the assumption that antagonism breeds antagonism. Because so much of the capability and enthusiasm for digital antagonism exists apart from the formal manifestations of most subversive social movements today, acts of transgression may themselves operate as additional mechanisms that signal the acceptability of antagonistic behavior. As such, the third hypothesis to be tested is:

H_3. *Incidence of antagonism attributable to a subversive cause increases the likelihood of subsequent incidence of antagonism.*

Finally, the theory of digital-age subversion presented in Chapter 6 suggests a significant relationship between the emergent role of virtual communities as centers of subversive engagement and more punctuated acts of digital antagonism.[3] Expectations in this regard take two forms. First, and most simply, community processes should be clearly linked to such acts across the universe of cases, both in terms of action planning and in the use of such forums as opportunities to claim attribution, spread stolen information, and more. As such, a fourth hypothesis to be tested is:

H_4. *Incidence of antagonism is more likely to be linked with explicitly related activity in virtual community spaces than are activist efforts.*

Second, since I theorize that virtual community spaces play a significant role in the construction of subversive narratives and the encouragement of more punctuated acts of antagonism, it logically holds that periods of greater ideational dynamism should link to greater incidence of digital transgression. Such periods might include the lead-up to elections or referenda, as well as the duration of major protest incidents. Thus, a final hypothesis to be tested is:

H_5: *Major participatory events make it more likely a fringe movement will engage in digital antagonism.*

Taken together, these hypotheses represent the mechanical expectations of the theory described in Chapter 6. Evidence supporting these hypotheses will, if borne out in redundant testing, represent our first significant body of support for the existence of digital subversion as not only a newfound use of a toolkit of cyber contention but a dynamic of engagement premised on new relationships between elements of the fringe that operate in the public eye and those that remain in shadows.

Using Data to Test the Determinants of Digital Antagonism at the Fringe

The dependent variable (DV) for this chapter's quantitative assessment of digital antagonism at the fringes of global society is a dichotomous variable that operationalizes whether or not subversives involved in digital activism also look to the toolkit of digital antagonism. There were three tasks involved in measuring variation in the use of information and communication technologies for such purposes and constructing indicators useful to testing the hypotheses posed in the previous section. First, it was necessary to identify a population sample of subversive groups operating in world politics. Second, proper identification of different techniques and uses of ICT was required. Third, there needed to be a clear selection of cases for observation based on involvement in digital activism. As described in Chapter 6, the GDADS was used as a basis for coding and testing in order to accomplish these tasks.

The subversive social movements and organizations that populate the data set are not uniform. Some perpetrators of antagonistic and activist digital acts are linked to core subversive causes and organizations distantly. Some appear to be front groups, while others claim to be individual supporters.

Coding issues on this front are discussed below in the section on coding for independent variables, as it most directly relates to explanations of subversive behavior based on organizational structure and group strategy.

Based on the data set, I created a dichotomous index variable that operationalizes the DV by describing whether or not subversives involved in digital activism also employ the alternative techniques described in the data set. I also employ another DV reflecting a different categorization of the techniques described. Independent variables were constructed to consider a broad range of possible explanations for variation on subversive behavior. These might be grouped into three broad categories: (1) strategic perspective and subversive prospects, (2) group or social movement structure, and (3) environmental conditions. Pursuant to initial testing and theorization, I also include variables specifically geared toward assessing the credibility of leaderlessness as an explanation of subversive behavior in the digital age.

Operationalizing Strategic Perspective and Prospects

Operationalizing strategic goals and perspective is not an easy task. As a large group of political scientists engaged in research on actors from political parties to insurgent organizations have recognized, simply coding for the stated goal of particular subjects of study can provide data both imprecise and diverse to the point where it is inappropriate for use in a simple, robust testing regime. Coding needs to be adapted to fit the circumstances of a particular program of study. Here, that means coding for the most telling features of subversive organizations' strategic behaviors.

In Chapter 6, I used a coding practice common in studies of terrorism to ideologically define subversive actors linked to incidence of digital antagonism. Here, I drop that practice for two reasons. First, initial inclusion of ideology codes in testing resulted in no significant findings. Secondarily, ideology less clearly links to the logic of subversion than do other measures of nonstate actors' motivation. In particular, in line with past work—also common in studies of terrorist and insurgent transitions toward alternative forms of political participation—I adopt the assumption that operationalization of strategic perspective means constructing a typology of strategic inclinations based on common characteristics. Here, those common characteristics relate to two categories: (1) the nature of a group's or movement's strategy as aimed at accomplishing discrete outcomes and

(2) the commitment that group exhibits to that strategy, in terms of both responding to strategic imperatives and shaping tactics. I focus primarily on the first category in testing in this project.

Type of Agenda. I code in line with the work of Abrahms[4] and others on the nature of a group's portfolio of objectives.[5] Abrahms is well known for work outlining how variation in the nature of this portfolio among subversive groups effectively predicts target choices and eventual campaign outcomes. He codes the portfolio of objectives of a given terrorist group as belonging to one of four categories: maximalist, limited, idiosyncratic, or ambiguous. Maximalist objectives/policy portfolios cite a broad range of grievances held by a given organization. Following past work, I code a group as having a maximalist portfolio if there are five or more clearly identifiable and distinct goals (i.e., not incremental elements of a single desired process). Groups that do not fall into this category can then fall into one of the three other categories. Limited portfolios have clear goals but very few specific grievances or stated objectives. Groups with ambiguous portfolios state a broad grievance but do not outline clear operational or tactical objectives, while those with idiosyncratic portfolios have a variable range of campaign objectives that are unusually mixed with functions or goals not linked with the main stated objective. In many cases, "idiosyncratic" subversive entities take the form of niche advocacy groups with concentrated local support—and the accompanying need to provide community support services—but national opposition and macro objectives, such as elements of the Batasuna Basque separatist group. For the purposes of testing, I construct these categories as dummy variables, omitting the "ambiguous" category in different models.

The Nature of Grievances. Second, I code for the nature of the grievance held by the subversive group. Here, I follow a well-known schema for differentiating levels of perceived legitimacy of a given sociopolitical regime.[6] I code for objection to prevailing normative conditions on two fronts. First, I consider whether or not the objection of the subversive cause is structural in nature. Are there *specific* institutions or structures tied up in the claim a given cause makes about the illegitimacy of the status quo (as opposed to a general disavowal of current practices or policy)? In other words, are objections codified in the structures of the prevailing order? Second, I consider the grievance of the subversive element not as a foundational condition but something that varies over time given its sociopolitical context. Does the tone of the subversive cause itself emphasize nonparticipatory approaches to change? I capture this data across two dimensions: a count of participatory or nonparticipatory statements made by cause leaders (such as a directive toward electoral involvement or a claim that a cause is under existential attack) and a count of statements by prominent national figures that directly attack that cause. The period of time for which this data is captured is one year prior to incidents of digital antagonism, segmented by quarters.

In constructing my variables in this way, I aim to capture several possible dynamics of subversive strategic goals. Specifically, variables that describe the nature of organization grievances speak to the overarching desire of a subversive group to modify a policy regime or to replace underlying processes. It is important to note that I do not argue subversive groups are motivated *only* by policy objections or *only* by structural considerations. Indeed, for many countercultural movements, objections to the essential tenets of the prevailing order are echoed in the policy outputs of the system they face. Subversive organizations may object to policies only or may do so in the context of broader objectives to modify or replace. Likewise, subversive movements and organizations may disavow government practices without constructing a specific counterpolicy mission.

Leaderless Resistance. Though the research undertaken in the course of this project involved inductive testing of the determinants of hacking among subversive elements of global society, the resultant theory presented in Chapter 6 necessitated revisiting statistical testing in two distinct ways. One is discussed below. The other is the inclusion of a dummy variable to control for evidence of adherence to a strategy of leaderless resistance by a group or with a particular social movement historically. Simply put, if leaderless resistance has been the strategy of choice for a given subversive element, we might more readily expect to see evidence of the dynamics of leaderlessness in the digital age in those cases.

Operationalizing Structure

While the research presented in Chapters 3 through 6 offers case-specific evidence on the manner in which so many subversive movements are increasingly structured in the digital age, rigorous large-N exploration requires a more systematic approach to coding their formation. Along these lines, I follow a range of scholars in the literatures on terrorism and, more broadly, political violence in insurgencies, organized crime, and militant activism. In particular, I use the work of Arquilla and Ronfeldt[7]—adapted by a number of others, including Rowlands and Kilberg[8]—to operationalize structure based on a series of organizational characteristics that are common across group types.

Characteristics of Structure. The first of these characteristics is leadership. To what degree does the existence of a clearly defined leadership structure explain variation in group or social movement practices? Leadership can take a number of forms. Nonstate organizations, whether terrorist groups, subversive movements, or protest formations, can be run by a single person in a discrete position of authority. Likewise, organization leadership can take the form of an oligarchic or plutarchic governing body where key members—often core funders and supporters—deliberate on direction and implement pol[9]icy. Here, leadership is coded as a simple dichotomous variable[10] on whether or not there is a clear leader or leadership structure in place for the organization in question.

The second characteristic is that of command and control. Coding for leadership is not the same as coding for centralized authority or the ability for a particular leader to effectively direct his organization. Many terrorist and subversive groups maintain figureheads who are more or less in control of the functional direction and activities of their organization. Whereas Osama Bin Laden was a relatively effective leader for Al Qaeda and was involved in global operations of various arms of his organizations, groups like Shining Path have historically presented more of what might be called symbolic leadership institutions where a figurehead delegates functional operation of the organization to subordinates. To code command and control, evidence is required that demonstrates the involvement and direction of a central executive authority in the actions of the group or movement. I code dichotomously for such evidence (either command and control is evident, or it is not) and code an additional control variable for whether or not there is evidence of such direction for only digital activist activities (or for both activist and "shady" activities).

The final characteristic is that of functional differentiation (or specialization). This characteristic describes the political and/or logistical specialization of distinct suborganizations within a broader movement. Compartmentalization of functions within a group indicates several things about the ability of a group to both efficiently pursue objectives and effectively direct commands from an executive center. To code this effectively, evidence is required indicating the existence of specific arms of a group tasked with specialized functions. I code dichotomously for evidence of functional differentiation (whether it is apparent or not).

For each of these variables, I control in two ways for the reality that group information is often sparse or difficult to obtain with any measure of clarity. First, I limit data collection—as I do for the DV—to the 36-month period surrounding the incident of digital activism recorded in the GDADS and on which the data set selects. This helps control for structural changes that occur within an organization over time. Second, I record variables based on an ability to corroborate information about the group in question in one of two ways. First, I record information on leadership, functional differentiation, and command and control when described in the reporting of government and intergovernmental organizations, as well as by available public-facing scholarly databases. The Terrorism Organization Profile data set at the University of Maryland[11] and Jane's World Insurgency and Terrorism database[12] were the primary sources used for corroboration purposes in the latter instance. Second, I record information for the above structural variables when reported consistently in a large volume of media reporting on the activities of the subversive group in question (20+ stories that corroborate the detail was the standard used) and corroborate wherever possible. Insufficient evidence was in all cases coded as inconclusive.

Variation on these three variables describe—depending on the combination of values involved—a set of four organization structures with unique patterns of authority and command over group functions. A range of scholarly works in the literature on terrorism and political violence describe these alternative structures in detail,[13] but I will briefly summarize them here.

Negative values on all three variables described above indicate the existence of an organizational structure known as a *market structure*. As described in Figure 7.2, organizations with a market structure lack a central executive to direct the group, determine strategy, and implement policy. Naturally, with no executive, there is additionally no element of direction emanating from one specific section of an organization. Moreover, there is little in the way of functional differentiation. Members of an organization may have particular skills and can tend toward specific types of tasks as the norm of their involvement in a group's mission, but there is no formal specialization. Much as governments have departments dedicated to specific functions, politically extreme groups often have elements dedicated to the procurement of materiel, accounting, or strategic development. Subversive organizations might have subunits dedicated to the function of front groups, the mitigation of

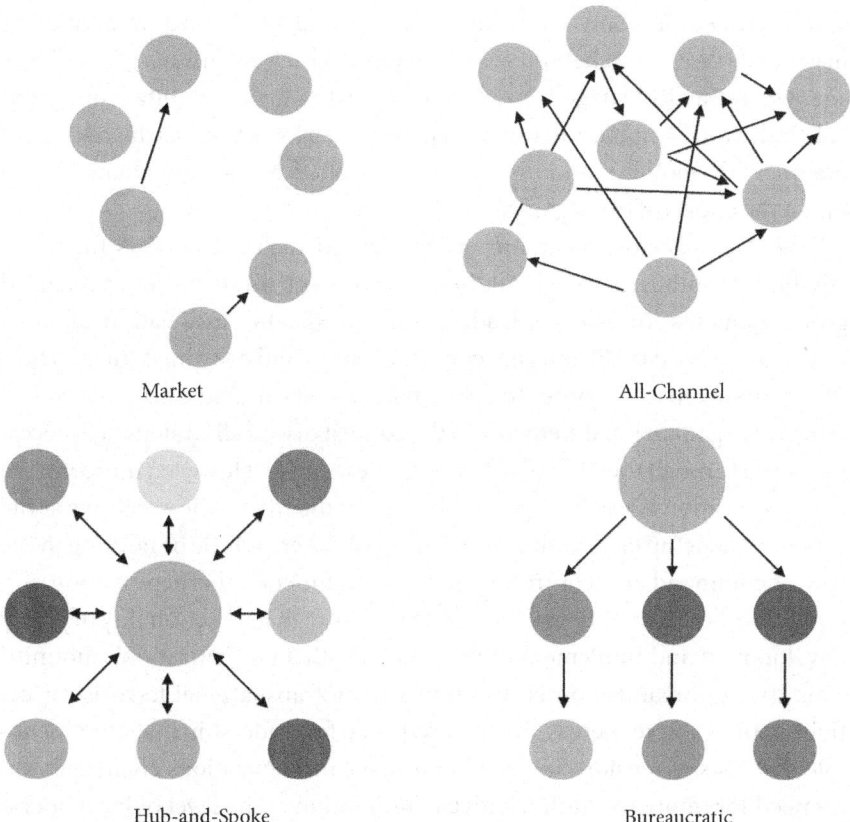

Figure 7.2 Structural patterns for organizational format.

political opponents, or the crafting of political messages. Organizations with market structures have none of this.

Not significantly different from market-structured organizations, *all-channel* organizations are network entities with central leadership. Despite clear leadership, however, all-channel organizations lack directionality and functional differentiation. There is no clear hierarchy of command and control. Likewise, there is no real degree of specialization between different elements of the group. A good example of this type of organization is the Anonymous hactivist collective.[14] Though there have at various points been clear leaders among the hackers of that organization, there is remarkably little power of authority that such a leadership holds. Likewise, operations are actually quite often not organized or planned in any centralized way, but rather a crowdsourced set of actions improvised by those who are available and interested. In many ways, Anonymous—and all-channel organizations in general—are the archetypical form of political activist groups in the digital age, where (as Rid suggests) information technologies simultaneously enable individual members to undertake diverse tasks, encourage high levels of membership mobility, and discourage symbolic leaders from attempting to direct the efforts of the organization.[15]

Hub-and-spoke organizations are structured such that leaders functionally, but not authoritatively, sit at the center of a web of competing specialized group elements. In essence, leaders—or a leadership association of some kind—are critical to the internal communication and coordination efforts of the group involved. In order to coordinate operations and clarify the role of different organizational elements in the context of overall strategy, it is necessary to go through the "office" of the central executive. However, the format of the organization is not hierarchical insofar as the role of the executive at the center of the setup ends with communication. There is little or nothing in the way of command and control. High levels of functional differentiation and limited authority on the part of leadership ensure that directionality of policy development and implementation remains with an organization's subunits. This style of organization is common among transnational terrorist or activist entities where there is an increased need for leadership that can ameliorate the costs or tensions involved in broad communications challenges but no need for improved authoritative coordination at the level of local operations. As Kilberg points out, Al Qaeda prior to the events of September 11 fits the description of a hub-and-spoke entity remarkably well.[16]

Finally, organizations can possess a *bureaucratic* structure, where there are positive values on all three structural variables described above. Bureaucratic organizations are highly hierarchical. Leaders or leadership bodies not only coordinate the function of specialized subunits; they also dictate strategy and policy and direct their implementation. By contrast with Al Qaeda, the Islamic State—both within the territorial boundaries of the proto-state and in the context of links to Libyan and some other affiliates—appears to be highly hierarchical, with a clearly defined set of leadership structures directing the organization across terrorist operations in Europe, black market trading, and traditional battlefield functions.[17]

Other Structural Descriptors. I also introduce dummy control variables for prior criminal activity of a social movement or group using the same selection criteria as was introduced for ICT employments in data collection (i.e., referenced in government, intergovernmental organization, cited nongovernmental organization reporting, or peer-reviewed scholarship). I do this because criminal enterprise can determine the value of different elements of a movement or organization beyond what hierarchy (or lack thereof) might tell us. In other words, criminality can indicate that a group won't fit expectations regarding organization structure. Groups engaged in the narcotics trade, for instance, might organically adopt an oligarchic form of bureaucracy to better control a distributed supply chain and minimize risk of interdiction. I code for prior criminal activity in three ways. First, I introduced a dichotomous dummy for involvement in economic crime prior to the episode observed in data collection on ICT employments. I then do the same for violent crime. Finally, to control for the longevity and format of subversive movements and their formal organizations over many years, I introduce a dichotomous dummy for any prior involvement in criminal activities that have taken place within three years prior to the observed episode.

Operationalizing Environmental Pressures

The operation of subversive elements, much as might be the case for terrorist organizations, insurgent movements, and activist formations, has variously been suggested to be sensitive to a range of environmental pressures. Here, it seems reasonable to split such environmental pressures into two categories: (1) the degree to which there exists direct government or popular opposition to a group's operation and (2) the degree to which there exist either prohibitive or enabling operational conditions that affect a movement's tactical function.

Official Opposition to Subversion. To operationalize opposition to a subversive campaign, I rely on three variables that describe both the potential for meaningful opposition and actual incidence of repression or opposition. First, I include a basic measure of GDP drawn from the most recent Polity IV data set.[18] Studies of terrorism, militant activism, and insurgency almost universally hold that states with higher GDP are better able to devote resources to either oppressive or security activities.[19] For terrorist groups, of course, this means better funding for counterterrorism forces and more support for efforts to mitigate the underlying causes of terrorist success, including poverty and border security. For subversive groups, though the emphasis is not on political violence and subversion can occur without the violation of state laws, the logic holds insofar as states with higher levels of economic growth and productivity have more resources to contribute to judicial and legal investigations of rule-of-law violations. Such states are better able to adjudicate on issues where the question is on a group's role as a protected voice or a seditious entity. Likewise, there is greater opportunity for broad-based funding of security and surveillance efforts aimed at not only core violent threats to state integrity but also dissidents across the spectrum of threat. Second, for each instance, I draw the most recent government approval rating and normalize to a 100-point scale for each case (adaptation required in only one case). These are provided by Gallup over time and across all countries.[20] Finally, I code dichotomously for specific evidence of government investigation, legal action, use of law enforcement, or military action against the subversive group. Evidence is drawn in line with coding for activities used to operationalize the DV in the section above. For inclusion, evidence has to present as more than simple reporting of an activity, though that action can qualify a group's case if the observation is made explicitly as the result of state investigation. In many cases, measurement of government opposition specifically pertains to the group, individuals linked to the organization, or affiliated organizations being placed on blacklists.

Permissiveness of the Environment. I code for the permissiveness of national environments as more or less amenable to the types of activities subversive groups undertake to effect normative transformation. Following a range of scholars working on democratization and dissent politics, I assume that more liberal national regimes will incentivize subversive groups away from risky tactics because of greater expectations of viable tactical options related to nonviolent political advocacy. Thus, I include variables for regime type (in the form of the ordinal Polity score provided by the Polity IV data set that describes a spectrum from full autocracy to full democracy) and a contestation (drawn from Polity IV as an ordinal score of competitiveness of political participation in a given country). Collectively, these provide controls for the degree to which protest and persuasion are ceteris paribus viable options for effecting transformation, for the degree to which a group may discount openness as being temporary, and for the nature of a group's national audience as monolithic and more or less susceptible to opposition perspectives.

Popular Opposition to Subversion. There is a degree to which the competitiveness of participation variable described above and drawn from the Polity IV data set is also useful in measuring popular opposition to a given countercultural movement or organization. Measuring contestation, according to some scholars, indicates the degree to which groups considered to be countercultural and opposed to the prevailing normative status quo are opposed on grounds of contested legitimacy. Reasonably high contestation, in other words, dictates strong opposition to any group that opposes prevailing tolerant conditions, even if only on single issues. Thus, the comparative participation variable is relevant as a control for popular opposition as well as for structural constraints and pressures.

Constructing variables for the degree to which there exist prohibitive or enabling environmental conditions that affect group operation beyond specific opposition or support demands thinking about the environment in two distinct ways: (1) as including actors able to enhance an organization's capabilities and (2) as more broadly permissive in terms of group access to relevant capabilities. Thus, I employ two sets of indicator variables. The first is a set of dummy variables coded to reflect either financial or capabilities sponsorship of a group (attribution of the relationship assessed in the same manner described above for data collection on ICT employment). One variable assesses sponsorship from any domestic source, while a second assesses the same from foreign sources.

Access to Capabilities. The second set of variables is drawn from the World Bank's Digital Dividends project and database (the Digital Adoption Index) and includes indicators describing the degree of media freedoms in a country, the extent to which the internet is regulated and/or censored, the national protection of civil liberties, internet access statistics, and more.[21] Specifically, the Digital Dividends project constructs three indicator variables for the degree to which a given country has access to digital technologies (drawing on data regarding broadband internet usage, mobile-cellular access, etc.), the degree to which a national population is able to use digital technologies (drawn from data regarding national literacy and education), and the degree to which a national population is ready to adopt new technologies (drawn from data regarding use of e-governance services). These indicators are constructed of sixteen macro indicators and proxy for the degree to which a country is online and to which a nonstate organization (1) is likely to have easy access to digital opportunities and (2) is able to effect desirable campaign outcomes through digital means.

Complex Opposition. Finally, in order to capture the degree to which an organization is affected by a permissive environment in the context of opposition, I introduce a dichotomous control variable drawn from data on adoption of digital technologies across society, business, and government in the Digital Adoption Index. For society, adoption is measured as an index variable in reference to the purchase of computers, mobile-cellular devices, subscriptions to broadband or above internet, and more. For government, adoption is measured as an index variable in reference to spending on cybersecurity initiatives, e-government program usage, and more. In line with work that suggests radical nonstate actors are sensitive to government abilities to investigate and interdict their operations, I am most interested in operationalizing a mismatch in digital adoption in the national environment. Therefore, the introduced control variable holds that adoption trends are mismatched when the ratio of state to government adoption is greater than 2 (i.e.,

$$\frac{societal\ adoption}{goverment\ adoption} > 2$$

where original adoption index values are on a scale from 0 to 1).

Anonymous Involvement and Virtual Communities

Additionally, I consider corollaries of digital antagonism often considered in scholarship on hactivism and digital activism. First, I operationalize the actions of the Anonymous hactivist collective in either direct or indirect support of a subversive cause. The intercession of Anonymous agents has been a notable feature of the experience of a handful of subversive movements and a broader number of more conventional activist efforts over the past decade. The assumption here is that the inclusion of a control variable for either evidence of direct sponsorship of or assistance by Anonymous agents will proxy for the significance of developing transnational *ICT-capable* support networks for dissentious nonstate actors attempting to enhance their operations via the use of ICT. I argue that this differs somewhat from controlling for foreign sponsorship writ large in that the intervening significance of Anonymous connections would indicate a more nuanced link between global access to useful ICT platforms and knowledge—essentially, access to cyber arms—than is implied in simply accounting for the specific sponsorship of a foreign actor. Thus, I introduce a dichotomous control variable for evidence of

Anonymous support, either direct or as an unsolicited aid to a particular subversive organization's cause.

Finally, I consider the role of distinct virtual spaces in direct relation to antagonistic digital acts. This is the second control added to better determine the validity of Chapter 3's theory of leaderless subversion in the 21st century. Specifically, I include a dichotomous control variable to denote such a role within the episodic time frame of a given incident. In coding this variable, I take great pains to link virtual spaces to events only where there is a direct connection between perpetrator and community. Virtual spaces may serve as a place within which discourse about antagonism and subversive platforms may occur, but this rarely indicates any direct role in facilitating such activity. Instead, I code a positive linkage only where such a space is used by a perpetrator to either (1) plan an action that then takes place, (2) claim attribution for an action, or (3) directly undertake illicit activities (such as publishing stolen information).

The Determinants of Digital Antagonism at the Fringes of Global Society

Naturally, much support for the theory presented in Chapter 6 emerges in the descriptive analysis of the landscape of digital subversion. Most antagonism of the kind described in this book's data set is the work of virtual persons and supporters that self-align with a given cause. Likewise, while subversive utilization of the internet for antagonism differs little from that of other non-state actors in its lacking sophistication, there is a clear emphasis on the ICT employed for informational gain. And while ICT usage at the fringe appears to have gotten somewhat more sophisticated over time, temporal and geographic mapping of incidents suggests that subversive elements of society are adaptive in their choice of techniques more than they are inclined toward particular forms of disruptive capability. However, clearer elucidation of the dynamics of digital subversion is needed for a theory of subversive leaderlessness to be judged effectively.

Off the bat, it is necessary to eliminate explanations for subversive ICT usage as premised on web presence. And indeed, basic bivariate analysis of the data presented in both Table 7.1 and Figure 7.1 does exactly this, particularly when separately performed on (1) the whole set of 313 groups and (2) the set of just 104 social movements linked to hacking. Results show that greater involvement in digital activist efforts weakly predicts antagonistic web usage for the entire set of subversive elements described in the data set ($r = 0.089$). By contrast, correlation analysis of *only* the set of 104 movements with hacking linkages indicates a relatively stronger correlation between greater involvement in both types of ICT employment ($r = 0.2023$). One clear interpretation of this result is that an expanded online presence during the activist phase of a subversive campaign does not itself incentivize deviant tactical choices, but prior use of the web does predict a larger overall digital footprint. This suggests a potentially interesting link between organization capabilities and the incentives for the leaders of social movements to greenlight the use of ICT for antagonistic purposes.

Statistical testing for purposes of shedding light on the puzzle takes the form of regression analysis. Figure 7.3 presents the results of three logit models in the form of forest plots. Variation across the models comes in the form of alternative omission and inclusion of different theoretical and technical control variables. These are described below and the results are robust

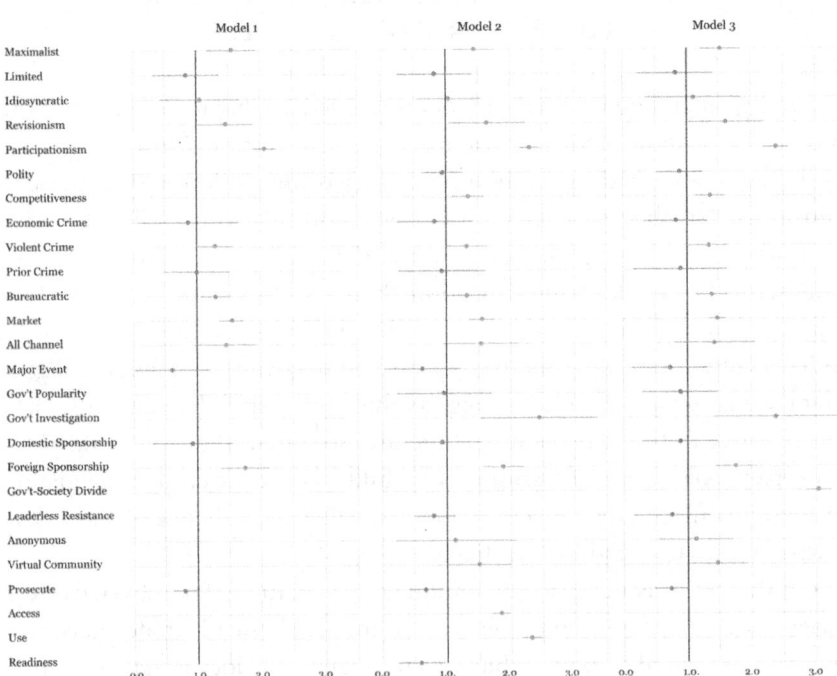

Figure 7.3 Binomial logit model results predicting antagonistic ICT usage. Psuedo R^2 scores are: Model (1) = 0.055; Model (2) = 0.074; Model (3) = 0.076.

across modeling choices, principally the use of Ordinary Least Squares (OLS) regression to consider factors that can predict frequency of deviant ICT usage across cases (discussed at the end of this section). Again, the time frame for this study is 37 years, from 1982 to 2019. For the models in Figure 7.3, the break point of positive and negative impact on the appropriate DV is 1.0, reported in the form of odds ratios.

The results show positive and significant values for a number of explanatory variables. The three models presented in Figure 7.3 are constructed to test the different intervening effects of group-specific and environmental variables. Specifically, Model 1 contains all actor-specific variables, including those that control for group perspective, structure, and sponsorship linkages. Model 2 introduces relevant environmental controls. Model 3 is discussed further below and robustness checks (in the form of OLS modeling) are provided in Appendix A.

With regard to the strategic perspective of subversive organizations, the most prominent results have to do with the nature and expression of group grievances. First, social movements with a structural grievance are more likely to employ ICT for antagonistic purposes at the same time they attempt to digitally engage the public as are ones whose grievance relates to prevailing sentiment or specific policies. Specifically, the odds of antagonistic action linked to activism being found in the revisionist case group are almost 50% greater than the odds of finding such activity in the alternative category. This result is significant at 95% confidence. By contrast, digital antagonism is more than twice as likely to be predicted by incidence of nonparticipatory speech than a lack thereof, significant at 99% confidence. Figure 7.4 presents this finding in more detailed fashion, using predicted probabilities drawn from a model that breaks out incidence of nonparticipatory speech by length of time before an antagonistic event. Here, we can see the manner in which such rhetoric predicts antagonistic uses of the web by subversives in the periods just before incidence. Given the presence of nonparticipatory speech in the year before an incident, the probability of antagonism from some element of a given subversive cause is 37%. This predicted probability jumps dramatically to 58% when such statements occur in the three-month period preceding acts of antagonism.

Further controlling for the influence of group objectives outputs only one significant positive result for measurement of maximalist group objectives. Here, groups whose grievances are both numerous and diverse are more likely to employ ICT for shady and antagonistic purposes while at the same

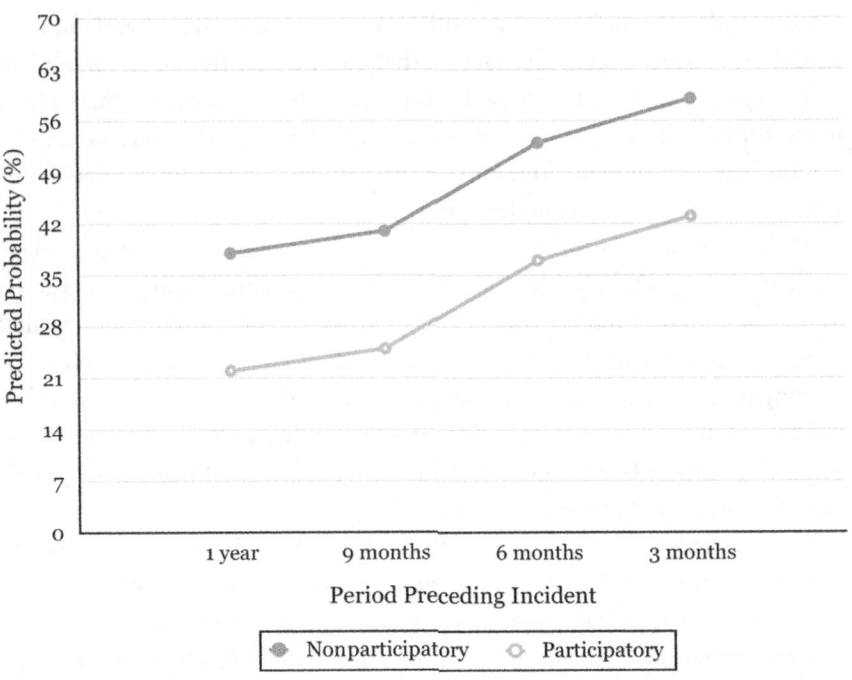

Figure 7.4 Predicted probabilities of antagonism by rhetoric type and length of period preceding incident.

time attempting to digitally engage the public. However, the result is minimally significant and, as Model 2 demonstrates, not affected by the inclusion of additional controls. This implies that among those groups with maximalist objectives portfolios, the articulation of a revisionist agenda in both broad and punctuated fashion is of greater importance in predicting variation on the DV.

Finally, testing on those variables that describe the systemic prospects of subversive groups presents significant values on only one front. While there appears to be no meaningful relationship between regime type and variation on the DV, there is a significant and slightly positive relationship between the competitiveness of political systems and the likelihood a group will deviate from expectations. Specifically, the more competitive a political system, the less likely a group will be to employ ICT for antagonistic purposes while trying to digitally engage the public (significant at 95%). As will be discussed below, these results lend some credence to the notion that uncompetitive political systems, regardless of regime type, predict the willingness of a social movement to employ ICT for shady purposes.

Turning to structural explanations of variation on the DV, it appears that both highly centralized and decentralized social movements are more likely (at different confidence levels) to employ ICT for antagonistic purposes than are other types of organization. This result is somewhat perplexing on the surface in that past theory on terrorist and insurgent campaigns suggests a clear link between the spectrum of group centralization and the ability of a group to centrally drive policy on tactics and prevent free-agent issues (i.e., issues of loose-cannon deviation from group doctrine by individual members). This link appears to exist, but so too does it appear to be the case that highly centralized movements are guilty of employing ICT for subterfuge and circumvention. Here, an obvious initial conclusion might be that group structure does not significantly factor in to the propensity for digital antagonism, a finding that would broadly fit the overarching contours of the theory. However, further data manipulation is clearly needed.

Control variables for incidence of past involvement in criminal enterprise—which to some degree, of course, secondarily proxies for the characterization of particular movements as less willing to adhere to participatory approaches to sociopolitical change—present a clear, if minimal, result for violent crime. Specifically, there is a slightly positive and significant relationship between past involvement in specifically violent crime and incidence of antagonistic ICT usage that does not exist for past incidence of nonviolent crime.

In considering environment pressures that might impact group decision-making, three separate significant results bear mention. The first is the marginal evidence that direct government investigation predicts variation on the DV. While the government popularity control produces insignificant results, there is clear evidence (at 90% confidence) that such a government-organization relationship appears to make it less likely a group will employ ICT for antagonistic purposes while attempting to digitally engage the public. Likewise, the sponsorship of foreign actors of organizations linked to a cause appears to make it *more* likely that a movement will employ ICT antagonistically. Finally, though there is marginal evidence that ICT "readiness" in a given country predicts variation on the DV, both the "use" and "access" metrics drawn from the World Bank's Digital Adoption Index present as positive at 99% confidence.

This last result is particularly interesting, as it suggests there is a relationship between the capabilities environment (i.e., those environmental considerations that ultimately affect nonstate actor abilities to employ ICT in an effective manner) and events captured in the data set. As the obvious question leading on from such a result has to do with whether or not it is a sufficiently technically permissive environment or the condition of countersubversive forces within such an environment that matter, of course, Model 3 takes the step described earlier of omitting the three Digital Adoption Index indicators in favor of a dichotomous dummy variable that describes a digital technology adoption imbalance between government and society (or not). The result is positive and significant at 99% confidence. This suggests not only that greater potential for digital antagonism in the form of technology availability and literacy improves the chances for variation on the DV, but specifically that antagonistic ICT employments are likely when government adoption of digital technologies lag behind broader societal trends.

Perhaps even more interesting, the inclusion of such an alternative measure of national adoption of digital technologies produced a nontrivial change in results for group structure. Though the trends remain the same, additional comparison of results between a model that does not include such environmental controls (Model 1) and those that do shows that highly centralized groups only marginally, all else equal, appear more likely to predict variation on the DV than do less centralized ones. Indeed, if we consider the statistical strength of the different results, Model 1 shows that decentralized movements, in line with expectations, are more likely to employ ICT for antagonistic purposes than are centralized organizations. The decentralized result then holds with the inclusion of digital adoption environmental variables. Where digital technologies are nationally widely available and in intense use, but where there is relatively limited government adoption of the same in the form of (1) spending on cybersecurity initiatives, (2) provision of digital services, or (3) the adoption of digital technologies by law enforcement, more highly decentralized social movements do appear to have significant difficulty in preventing members from employing ICT for circumventive purposes. Here, however, highly bureaucratic organizations show a similar, significant result. This strongly suggests that while decentralization of structure does lead to free-agent issues, fringe movements are characterized by the use of ICT for subterfuge and disruption *particularly* when there is a relative mismatch between the opportunities for digital gain and the capacity of governments to prevent, investigate, or legislate such actions.

Adding Nuance: Subversive Movements and Information Enrichment Operations

The dichotomous categorization of ICT employments as either activist or antagonistic is, of course, arguably less appropriate for our analysis than might be a measurement scheme that reflected the particular formation of *subversive* uses of the internet. With the fringe elements under study, as the exploration of the compiled data set in Chapter 3 illustrated, it would be disingenuous to simply say that a great number of subversive actors regularly prosecute cyberattacks, intrude into governments systems, and undertake all other manner of disruptive digital activity while engaged in activist efforts. When the data is broken out, a reasonably clear trend appears. By far the most common antagonistic web activities are those that have clear utility for influence operations or other informational gain, including website vandalism, basic information theft, the use of encryption to share illicitly obtained information, and doxing.

Though common practice among scholars interested in cyber conflict dynamics is to label low-intensity cyber activities as "enabling operations,"[22] a different categorization seems appropriate here given that subversive actors do not appear to employ the web in such a fashion to enable future disruption. As such, I hereafter label the range of common techniques employed by subversives for informational gain "information enrichment operations" (IEOs). Naturally, this more nuanced understanding of subversive campaign employments of ICT for circumvention and disruption lends itself to greater nuance in testing. Specifically, by grouping observations of those low-intensity employments into an information enrichment category, it is possible to undertake testing to answer two questions: Do different factors predict digital antagonism wherein only low-intensity information enrichment techniques are employed? And across the observed incidents, what factors predict the move from low-intensity ICT employments to more disruptive and risky choices of technique? Figures 7.5 and 7.6 rerun binomial logit analysis with two new DVs in an effort to answer these questions. A positive value on the first DV denotes observation of *only* information enrichment techniques alongside activist efforts, while a negative value denotes

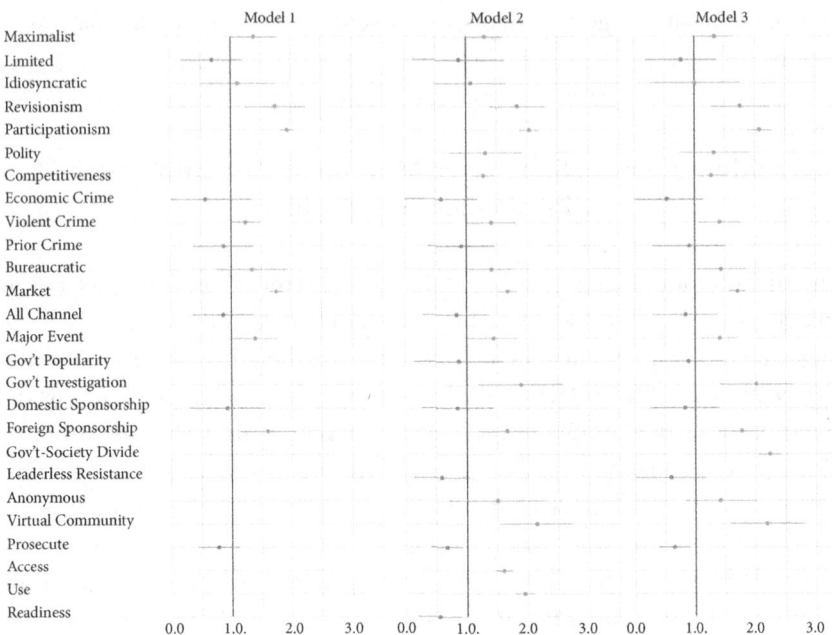

Figure 7.5 Binomial logit model results predicting variation on the use of information enrichment techniques for the entire set of observed organizations. Psuedo R^2 scores are: Model (1) = 0.033; Model (2) = 0.059; Model (3) = 0.057.

either no deviant behavior or more severe actions alongside activism. For the second DV, testing covers only the group of 104 fringe movements observed in the broader set to engage in digital antagonism. A negative value denotes *only* observation of information enrichment techniques, while a positive value denotes more severe forms of cyber antagonism.

The results for the first DV are reasonably similar to previous sections' findings. Much as was true in previous models, there are variably significant results for competitiveness of a political system, decentralized organization structure, and the condition of prior involvement in violent (though not necessarily organized) criminal enterprise. The finding for centralized movement structure is weaker here and significant only in Models 2 and 3. This indicates, in line with what one might expect given the theory presented in Chapter 3, that relatively unstructured movements and organizations are the mainstay of subversive antagonism in the digital age. Arguably the most interesting change in the results between Figure 7.5 and the prior model, however, lies with the result for major events. In Figure 7.5, there is a positive and

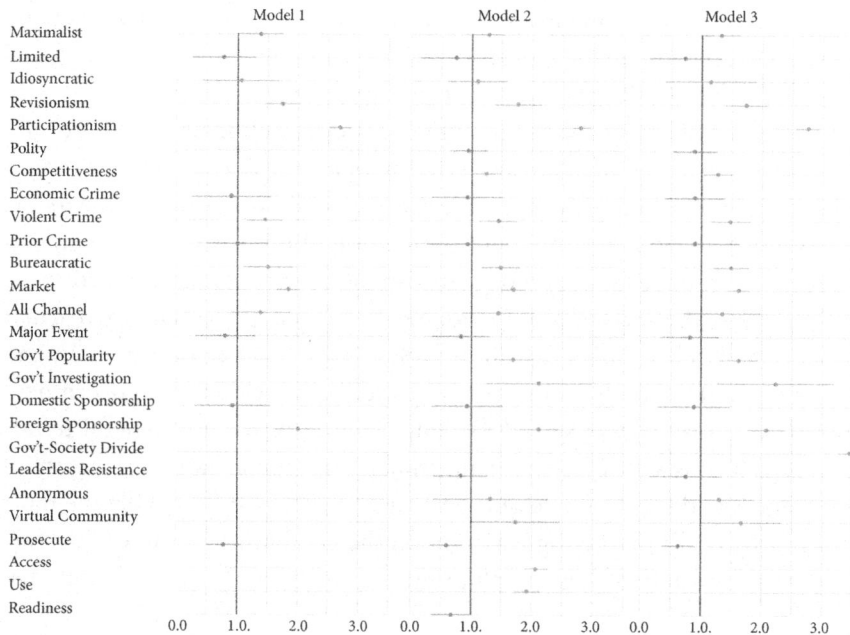

Figure 7.6 Binomial logit model results predicting variation on the use of information enrichment techniques for the entire set of observed cases *minus* groups that do not move beyond the use of ICT for activism. Psuedo R^2 scores are: Model (1) = 0.061; Model (2) = 0.083; Model (3) = 0.084.

significant (at 95% confidence) finding that proximity to national elections or referenda predicts variation on the DV.

Of additional interest, there is an enduringly strong finding in terms of the nature of organization grievances, the signaling of nonparticipatory preferences by significant figures, and the government-society adoption divide (in the form of both the adoption control variable and the original adoption indicators). Where a group holds a structural grievance, they are more likely—though the result *is* weaker than in the models presented above—to solely select to use IEOs. This result holds true—at 99% confidence—for evidence of statement-based signaling. Likewise, where there exists an adoption imbalance in the form of high societal digital adoption against low government buy-in, groups are more likely to select only the same. Indeed, in this model, these two findings are the only ones significant at 99% confidence.

The natural question that emerges from the results of Figure 7.5 has to do with the differentiation that can be made between digital antagonism that takes the form of low-intensity cyber actions and that which moves beyond to riskier employments, such as unauthorized hardware alterations or denial of service attacks. Models 4–6 address this issue with an alternative measurement of the DV as denoting observation of *only* enrichment behavior or not among the set of 104 antagonism cases (thus ignoring movements and organizations not affiliated with engagement in digital antagonism). As the model shows, there is actually remarkably limited variation in results from models that use alternative DVs. Certainly, the strength of results changes across the board. Here, the inclusion of the foreign sponsorship control in particular predicts a much stronger, significant relationship than in past models, and measurements of both group structure and direct evidence of government investigation remain linked, if variably significant. But the general trends involved in this set of tests remain similar. Of singular note, the nature of grievances and the presence of triggering statements are arguably the most interesting result predicting variation on the DV, both in terms of the scale of the findings and the high p-value significance. Figure 7.7 shows additional

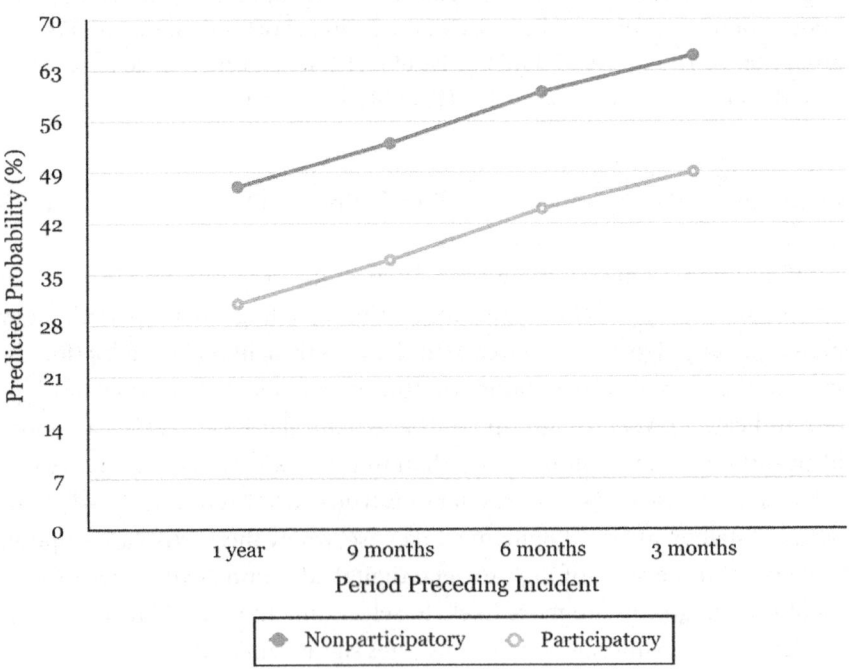

Figure 7.7 Predicted probabilities of antagonism by rhetoric type and length of period preceding incident.

predicted probability values that illustrate the greater predictive strength of nonparticipatory context for incidence of IEO antagonism. Given the presence of nonparticipatory speech in the year before an incident, the probability of antagonism from some element of a given subversive cause is 47%. This predicted probability jumps dramatically to 64% when such statements occur in the three-month period preceding acts of antagonism.

Clearly, there are a number of stories that might be told about subversive activism in the digital age based on the results of testing presented here. In the next section, I use the guiding puzzle of dual focus on activism and antagonism to describe the apparent empirical contours of digital antagonism

What Quantitative Testing Tells Us about Subversion in the Digital Age

In broad strokes, it seems clear from the evidence presented in this chapter that subversive social movements tend toward antagonism (1) where the underlying grievances of a cause necessitate replacement of an extant political system, (2) where environmental signals prime movements toward nonparticipatory modes of advocacy, and (3) where success via such advocacy seems achievable. In the results presented above, no other variables so consistently predicted strong and significant variation on the DV. Where the grievances are structural—that is, explicitly focused on affecting structural revision (not simply policy modification) alongside ideational transformation—and where additional statements emphasizing friction between the fringe and the mainstream occur, groups are far more likely to employ ICT for antagonistic purposes while also trying to digitally engage the public. Indeed, in the evidence presented, it seems clear that subversives in such circumstances are far less sensitive to the costs and risks of antagonistic ICT usage than are their counterparts. Under those conditions, fringe elements are clearly more likely to escalate their use of cyberspace to more disruptive formats of interaction—including malware employments, tailored DDoS attacks, and direct, unauthorized tampering with hardware—as well as to employ ICT disruptively even where there is a clear precedent of prosecution of such actions. And though no subversive elements studied in this chapter directly sponsor criminally violent acts, revisionist movements primed toward nonparticipation *are* more likely to be linked to political violence in the form of sponsorship of or collaboration with more explicitly violent organizations, unsanctioned violent activity by members, and links to past incidents of criminal violence.

Over and above this relationship between the nature of a group's grievance and online activities, there is a positive relationship between maximalist portfolios of grievances and digital action. In essence, where a cause's aims are stated broadly, there is a greater likelihood that digital antagonism will occur. At first glance, one might be forgiven for developing a straightforward theory of self-assessment and decision-making among subversive groups from this quantitative analysis. From such a perspective, where there exists an assumption that subversion of national social and political conditions will entail a move to operate as a legitimate political force under current (or slightly modified) structural conditions, subversive groups appear highly sensitive to the risks involved in what might be seen as disreputable or illicit activities. Where this is not the case—that is, where operation as a legitimate political force is not assumed to be premised on acceptance into extant processes—subversive groups adopt relatively risk-dominant strategies. And yet such an explanation for digital antagonism at the fringes flies in the face of the empirical reality of subversive social movement form and activity seen in data breakdown across Chapter 6 and in this chapter. Perhaps most significant, most antagonism occurs at the peripheries of subversive social movements. As a result, while it seems fair to see support for the observation made in Chapter 5 that subversives in world politics adapt their use of the web to fit contemporary trends, a theory that emphasizes centralized decision-making seems inappropriate.

The Dynamics of Leaderless Subversion in the Digital Age

These results describe distinct patterns of web usage by those at the fringes of global society. In terms of the hypotheses posed at this chapter's outset, I find robust support on most fronts, albeit with some interesting variation in the directionality of some findings. H_1, in which it was proposed that the underlying grievances of a cause feed into the propensity for a social movement's acolytes to consider antagonism a necessary part of the effort to transform society, is borne out in broad terms. Across all models, subversive causes characterized by a focus on structural revisionism rather than contemporary modification were between 24% and 33% more likely to engage in antagonism than their counterparts.

And yet it is not immediately clear in a review of the universe of cases under study how such revisionism translates into direct action. Rather, differential analysis of the data and survey of different episodes suggest that underlying sentiment is a priming condition only and is not the trigger most acutely linked to incidence of antagonism. For instance, while a number of far-right organizations in Europe that fit the revisionist mold have been associated with basic disruptive digital attacks on left-wing opponents or against mainstream political celebrities, a great diversity of other such nonstate social movements have shown no such tendency. Deeply spiritual religious movements in Turkey and the Caucasus region, among others, have no perceptive link to digital antagonism in spite of a reasonable web presence geared toward conventional activism and existential grievances levied at prevailing social forces. Likewise, many of the causes linked to multiple instances of digital antagonism—indeed, 7 of the top 10 movements by volume of hacking incidents—hold policy-specific grievances, suggesting that revisionism may be a corollary of antagonistic engagement broadly writ but performs poorly as a predictor of individual incidence thereof. This is borne out in robustness testing of the data, where removing the variable for nonparticipatory rhetoric from the primary regression model (see Appendix A) leads to drops in terms of the magnitude both of positive predictive relationship and of significance (to 90%) for the finding for causes' revisionist underpinnings. Clearly, the significance of revisionist foundations emerges in interaction with the presence of rhetorical statements made by either subversive leaders or opponents that shape contemporary motivations for some forms of sociopolitical engagement and against others.

Over all other explanatory factors, the proximity of statements encouraging nonparticipatory action or the adoption of a nonparticipatory perspective on engagement is most clearly linked to incidence of not only digital antagonism but also of more severe forms of ICT usage such as malware injection or DDoS attack. Differentiation in results between Figures 7.5 and 7.6 demonstrates a dramatically more pronounced tendency for subversive causes to feature antagonism via the web when preceded by such statements. This relationship becomes more particularly acute when the data is controlled for different categorizations of ICT usage (i.e., IEOs vs. more severe hacking) and the proximity of such statements. These results provide strong initial validity for the theory proposed in Chapter 5.

The theory at the heart of this book is also supported by the employment of control variables for past adherence of a movement to strategies of leaderless resistance, major participatory events, and the relationship between acts of antagonism and virtual communities. Controlling for leaderless resistance allows for a clear demonstration that the dynamics being explored in this study do not simply emerge from past emphasis on two-level advocacy characterized by separation of activism and militancy. With the presence of national elections, referenda, or other participatory events within months of an incidence of antagonism, however, there is a more nuanced story to be told. Presence of such events actually has a negative and insignificant effect in the models of both Figures 7.3 and 7.6. Figure 7.5, on the other hand, illustrates that subversive IEOs—uses of the web that are primarily aimed at influence efforts—are positively linked to the proximity of such events at 95% confidence. This suggests that while there is no relationship to speak of between antagonism and election-like events, there is some incentive to use the web illegally where the outcomes of antagonism are ideational. Given that bivariate correlation analysis shows a negative relationship ($r = 0.384$) between such events and nonparticipatory rhetoric—suggesting that leaders of subversive movements often tamp down rhetoric that is revisionist or otherwise inflammatory in the lead-up to important discursive inflection points—this dynamic is, to some degree, unexpected. And finally, there is a positive and significant relation (though only at 90% confidence) between antagonism and the use of virtual communities as a supporting element thereof. This suggests a clear relationship between subversive transgression online and such spaces, specifically where IEOs are involved. Though significance of the results does not vary, greater predictive value can be assigned to the link between such spaces and antagonism when attempting to predict *only* those incidents more clearly linked to operation for ideational purposes.

Looking Ahead

It is important to be clear about what has been done in this chapter. This chapter has produced large-N evidence to support the notion that rhetorical signaling primes peripheral elements of fringe social movements toward digital antagonism. Moreover, there is a clear association between such activities, revisionist intent baked into the ideational perspective of subversive causes, and virtual spaces. Again, in this data we see clear and repeated uses of the web by subversive elements of global society characterized by (1) the self-affiliation of culprits with the cause in question, (2) obvious proximity of rhetorical signaling, and (3) the not infrequent involvement of virtual community spaces as hubs for antagonistic activity. This means that external stimuli proxy for the direct command and control of antagonism we might have expected of subversive movements in eras past; it also suggests strong support for the idea that such stimuli are important because of a ubiquitous dynamic of leaderlessness at the fringe. Clearly, the rise of the internet has not only created new space for contestation below the threshold of violence; it has also created new mechanisms for the inculcation of diverse audiences and provided the means of rapid analysis of societal dynamics for interested parties. As a result, the median subversive social movement is far more dispersed than in eras past, with formal representations thereof playing more of a hub-like role in directing sociopolitical engagement via rhetoric rather than by directive.

Ultimately, the key takeaway from this chapter is that subversive elements of global society exhibit radically different tendencies when it comes to the use of ICT than do other, more commonly studied nonstate actors. Indeed, if pressed to identify a secondary theme emerging from the evidence presented in this chapter, subversive opportunism wouldn't be a bad one. Notably, digital antagonism as a tool is substantially more likely to appear under conditions of a dramatic government-society digital divide (i.e., where government adoption of digital technologies flags far behind that of civil society). This supports much of the descriptive evidence discussed in Chapter 6, particularly that fringe uses of the web ebb and flow less in reference to the emergence of new techniques and more in terms of those techniques' utility for subversion's ideational approach to activist and antagonistic engagement.

The data produced and utilized in this chapter and the preceding one is an interesting contribution in its own right. However, it is the contextualization offered in previous explorations of fringe use of web technologies over time that makes the idea of leaderlessness in the current era of the internet so compelling. Taken together, the findings of different elements of this study highlight the unique nature of the threat posed to status quo institutions and cultures by subversion upgraded by the internet. In contrast with that of eras past, the sociopolitical phenomenon of subversion in the 21st century is no longer singularly associated with clearly definable organizations nor the purview of countercultural perspectives tightly delineated by a select few fringe figureheads. Rather, it is something far more prone to natural occurrence, more dangerous specifically because it organically injects meaning into the broader information environment rather than trailing the mainstream.

8
Leaderlessness, Subversion, and the Fringe 3.0

On a cloudy day in early January, supporters of a defeated candidate for the office of president invaded the offices and meeting spaces of members of Congress. Thousands of protestors-turned-insurrectionists bypassed barricades set up to contain their movement, advancing across hallowed democratic grounds to smash windows and storm government buildings. In the hours that followed, police forces struggled to contain rioters and to regain control of hallways, offices, and entrances from those the newly inaugurated president quickly labeled "fascist fanatics."

This was January 8, 2023. The country was Brazil and the electoral loser in question was Jair Bolsonaro, the former president who lost to Luiz Inácio Lula de Silva by more than two million votes. The details surrounding the January 8 attempt by Bolsonaro supporters are eerily similar to those of the January 6, 2021, attempted insurrection in the United States. In particular, the digital dimensions of the event closely parallel the surging vitriol, misinformation, and narrative coordination seen across web spaces in the weeks following Joe Biden's 2020 election win. For weeks prior to the attack in Rio de Janeiro, far-right community spaces and conspiracy theory accounts pushed incredible volumes of misinformation about the results of the election. Influencers tied to these narratives called for attacks of every kind against national critical infrastructure and political institutions. And plans for the events of the day coalesced around common slogans that proliferated widely across social media spaces and private messaging networks, inviting "patriots" to a Festa da Selma or "War Cry Party."

Amid this outpouring of so much extremism in the weeks leading to January 8, there was also elite rhetoric that—on the surface—appears to mirror that emerging from Trumpworld two years earlier. Bolsonaro's statements and accusations through January railed against a supposed fraud perpetrated against the Brazilian people. Key supporting voices and associates suggested the need for repeated elections and, as Lula's inauguration loomed, the necessity for a national political rebirth to save the Brazilian democracy. Even the counternarratives from the Bolsonaro camp—which operated from Florida, where the losing candidate had fled, supposedly on vacation, at the start of January—mirror those from the Trump campaign as they reeled from the tumult of January 6. Nonpeaceful demonstration was denounced in broad terms while, at the same time, it was implied that a left-wing subversion of normal, patriotic protests may have taken place.

The déjà vu of the January 8, 2023, attacks in Rio de Janeiro underscores a call to action for those who might otherwise be willing to call the events of January 6, 2021, a rare event. Subversion shaped by the internet is a pervasive and disruptive phenomenon in the 21st century. Its evolution around the proliferation of web technologies over the past several decades has pushed the fringes of global society into greater contact with the mainstream. This has taken the form of invasive narratives and assumptions. But it also manifests as a heightened propensity for disruption and tumult operationalized by a transformed series of mechanisms that link events and elite rhetoric to fringe advocacy as triggers. In this view, these attempts at insurrection and antidemocratic progress should not be seen as aberrations but rather as high-water marks in a world where the sea level, thanks to changing environmental conditions, is on the rise.

In this concluding chapter, I contextualize the leaderlessness theory I have proposed in this book. I consider the events of January 6 in the context of the arguments made in this book and consider the future—what should be studied from here on out, what can be done to combat fringe extremism, and how to make the information environment of modern democracies healthier.

The Leaderlessness of January 6

The context and events of the insurrection attempt on January 6, 2021, are the result of a set of informational processes made real by several interacting factors going back at least two and a half decades. Other scholarship, journalism, and overt public investigation have surfaced the shape and significance of many of these factors, from the practices of technology companies to the willfully antagonistic rhetoric of populist political leaders. The theory, framing, and evidence presented in the chapters of this book, however, have attempted to shed light on a set of processes that, while certainly not entirely ignored by researchers, tend to be underconceptualized and underappreciated in so much discourse about domestic and foreign policy: the tendencies and the agency of fringe, subversive societal elements.

This book has argued that the meteoric rise in visibility of fringe elements in mainstream societal discourse stems in large part from the manner in which the internet has enhanced the linkages between social movements and leaders whose rhetoric persistently acts to shape and activate fringe advocacy for parochial gain. Subversive causes tend toward the social construction of narratives that ingratiate fringe ideas without inviting outrage and the building of symbols—figureheads, rallying phrases, and so on—that can be used to activate dispersed and disaggregated populations. They do so because their fringe status affords them few other avenues toward broad sociopolitical change. In the age of the internet—and especially in the Web 2.0 era—this has increasingly manifested as a ubiquitous proclivity toward social control and disinformation in the use of web technologies. The irony in this argument, of course, is that this novel condition of leaderlessness emerging from subversives' use of the internet was never some inevitable outcome. Rather, it is a moment-in-time condition when the changing character of web technologies through the early years of the 21st century has synergized with the trappings of the subversive enterprise. I return to this theme below. First, however, it is first necessary to return to the story of attempted insurrection on January 6 and highlight the manner in which elite prompting produced the events of the day even without extensive methods of command and control.

Returning to the opening pages of this book, it seems likely that the events of January 6, 2021, will live in infamy in the minds of many Americans for years and decades to come. The storming of the Capitol Building was an incident like almost no other in American history, an event in which citizens urged on by a wayward politician gathered to forcefully throw out the legitimate results of a national election in which nearly 160 million people participated. But what explains the willingness of the crowd to enter the Capitol? What prompted certain members of the assembled crowd to bring restraints and methods for harming those they hoped to find inside the lawmaking heart of the American republic? Certainly there appears to be a degree to which certain conservative political insiders actively planned for the disruption of the day, not least a set of lawmakers who at time of writing this book stand accused of holding meetings to scheme on the best approach for stopping the process of congressional vote certification. And yet, even if a handful of parties were in contact about the course the day might take, there is minimal evidence that high-level officials in the government were directly involved in bringing the most common elements of the insurrectionist crowd to Washington that day. What, then, explains why a diverse crowd of Trump supporters and other right-wing citizens converged on Washington?

"Be There. Will Be Wild."

The crowd that marched on the Capitol numbered in the thousands, as did the crowd that gathered for the Rally to Save America event hosted just the night before. Many showed up on the day; however, clearly a great many more voices were involved in conversations about the planned event across the right-wing digital ecosystem in the preceding weeks. Beyond singular calls to action like Trump's infamous "Be There. Will Be Wild" tweet in days prior, the *New York Times* reported following the event that the term "Storm the Capitol" was mentioned over 100,000 in the month before January 6. Much of this volume was concentrated in forum threads dedicated to discussing the possibility of just such an action. Countless thousands of subconversations in such threads were also dedicated to the logistics of the day, including what blunt instruments should be brought along for the purpose of breaking into the building and, the implication seems clear, committing acts of both property damage and violence. However, as many scholars and commentators have persistently pointed out about the digital trends preceding January 6, it is hard to see a cohesive plan or any substantial amount of organization amid the morass of incitements to action and general conspiracy-filled discourse about an election stolen and a corrupt establishment that should be overthrown. Unless law enforcement and journalistic investigation turn up some major effort to coordinate the travel, assembly, and actions of the crowd on the day beyond the actions of a violent minority, it seems reasonable to assume that the events of January 6 emerged from something other than the mere rhetoric of an elite voice or the outrage of a genuinely aggrieved citizenry.

Given this, developments on the ground on that Wednesday morning suggest that the mob reacted to symbolic speech and to the words of those specifically tied to the cause of the crowds gathered by weeks of online agitation around the results of the election. Many of the people assembled were active users of fringe social media platforms, ranging from Gab to Parler and more traditional alternative spaces like 4chan, 8kun, and the reconstituted The_Donald.win (now officially banned by Reddit). In interviews following January 6, several have referenced how they pushed others online by way of patriotic appeals. Others claim they were incentivized to attend because of the clear corruption of specific figures on the political left, from Joe Biden and Nancy Pelosi to the recently deceased Ruth Bader Ginsberg who were the subject of conspiracy theories tying their antidemocratic vices to electoral fraud. In Facebook groups, users were presented with polls about what weapons would work best if it was necessary to defend democracy. Forums on Telegram popped up linking users to old content about how best to sneak firearms into public events. And more than 367,000 posts on mainstream social media platforms referenced a possible "civil war" in the weeks prior to the event.

The January 6 crowd was radicalized online. More than just this fact of radicalization, which has naturally been reported and problematized by numerous experts and journalists in the months since, the crowd was empowered by a shared understanding of what signals and developments mattered for the effort to stop congressional certification. Robust evidence for this can be found in the fact that the crowd began its move toward the Capitol before Trump himself had finished speaking—in point of fact, the first barricades were overrun 19 minutes before then. Indeed, the moment when so many broke away from the words of the then-president was the moment when Vice President Mike Pence announced before Congress that he would not be complicit in Trump's ongoing attempts to throw out the results of the national election. The language of Pence's remarks was captured and rebroadcast rapidly by those in the crowd and participating remotely, with viewership of his specific usage of the term "complicit" reaching several tens of thousands in just under 15 minutes.

Pence's language has not been lost on investigators and experts interested in the events of January 6. In the wee hours of the morning that day, Ron Watkins, a prominent figure within the QAnon conspiracy movement, tweeted that Pence was implementing an attempted coup against Trump. Trump himself picked up on this theme by around 8 a.m., having seen the trending discussion about Pence—according to staff testimonials in the months since—and tweeting out a clearcut expectation about Pence's actions during the certification process. And so when Pence spoke in the early afternoon, those online and in the crowd saw a Rubicon, a moment beyond which deliberation was no longer the imperative of the day. One particular result of these remarks was the rapid promotion of messages that claimed Trump had ordered the storming of the Capitol, one widely seen post claiming "TRUMP GAVE YOU AN ORDER STORM THE CAPITOL NOW." Again, of particular note, this online activity and the on-the-ground move toward the Capitol began prior to the phrase in the latter parts of Trump's speech that many have since pointed to as evidence of his complicity in the events of the day: "And we fight. We fight like hell. And if you don't fight like hell, you're not going to have a country anymore." In short, the actions of the crowd were clearly responsive to the rhetoric of those important to the Stop the Steal cause—both allies and those perceived to be adversaries—but the nuance suggests that narrative context and the symbolism of certain speech mattered more than the direct command of those notionally in charge of the movement.

Of course, it seems impossible to speak of January 6 without bringing in the influence of the QAnon conspiracy. The belief system set up around Q, an anonymous internet poster that claims to be deep undercover in a position within the political establishment, holds that Trump is fighting a cabal of pedophilic, corrupt politicians who have rigged the world in their favor and are the predominant threat to freedom and national salvation. There are a great many forks and perspectives within the broader QAnon ecosystem on sites like 4chan and in member-only spaces (e.g., on Discord servers), including divergent views on what the poster is implying in a given post. Regardless of this diversity, however, the impact of the ideology is immense; one NPR poll found that the general idea of a "deep state" in America was held by nearly one in three respondents. With regard to January 6, interviews with those arrested and questioned in the aftermath have demonstrated the degree to which Q influenced turnout and willingness to transgress. Some, like Cleveland Meredith Jr., attested that his desire to shoot Nancy Pelosi in the head "on Live TV" stemmed from his belief in Q's revelations. Others interpret Trump through the lens of Q. Quite apart from using QAnon arguments to interpret Trump's words, however, a great many of those interviewed cited QAnon in their belief that Trump agrees with them despite a lack of explicit support from the then-president or others in his close circle. One QAnon supporter stated of Trump that he says "a whole lot by not saying a whole lot at all. For a lot of us supporters, we knew that he really [can't] come out and say, 'Oh yes, I support it.'" And indeed, while some rioters on the day claimed to be acting on the orders of

Trump, the mood of the crowd turned on Trump when he made a reserved video request that people return to their homes. Disbelief that the president was appearing to give up surfaced immediately in the ranks of those near the Capitol Building, and online conversations quickly turned to the question of continued disruption.

It is in this spirit of confusion and disbelief pertaining to the political actions of the Trump-oriented far-right ecosystem at the highest levels that perhaps the most interesting demonstration of the "leaderlessness" of the Stop the Steal movement and its subsequent evolution is visible. Efforts to de-platform significant voices within the far right by banning their posts or accounts from services like Facebook—a response to fringe antagonism that is discussed further in the next section—has naturally been followed by the re-platforming of rhetoric and the influence of prominent far-right community members in alternative spaces. As Innes and Innes note, this behavior usually follows one of four strategies, which are essentially efforts to reestablish presence by either (1) moderating antagonistic rhetoric, (2) delegating voice to "minion" accounts, (3) moving entirely to another virtual setting, or (4) "mingling" with entirely new communities or ideas.[1] This final tactic is particularly widespread and of substantial interest given this book's hypothesis. In short, much of the digital ecosystem invested in the Stop the Steal campaign and the events of January 6 have been dramatically reoriented in the almost year since. On the one hand, many pro-militia spaces have seen rhetorical shifts away from favorability of Trump-linked figures and toward antagonistic criticism of Biden and others. Pandemic-concerned conspiracy theorists have likewise reoriented on a set of conspiratorial celebrities like David Icke. On the other hand, Q-focused communities that hold up Trump as the leader of the rebellion have nevertheless persistently seconded the former president to the sideline, preferring John F. Kennedy Jr., suggesting that the momentary relevance of mainstream voices matters for fringe advocacy more substantially than any particular recognition of ultimate authority. After all, while Trump may be a figurehead above all to many on the fringe, it's certainly not the case that his voice or his role in defining various issues has informational value. Quite the contrary, the former president's ban from various social media and traditional media has broadly coincided with new diversification in fringe activities in 2021 as his informational value as a leader for subversive elements has diminished relative to the need for more potent rhetorical anchors.

Leaderlessness, for Now

This book has made an original contribution in conceptualizing subversion and describing the manner in which such a strategic outlook incentivizes particular kinds of tactics and tool usage. But the leaderlessness that explains so much antagonism and increasingly visible acts by elements of the societal fringe is a time-and-place condition, a manifestation of digital-age subversion that has been amplified by the technological and commercial-political externalities of the Web 2.0 era. Going forward, those interested in mitigating the potential sociopolitical instability—which can clearly include threats to national security—emanating from subversive advocacy would do well to consider that the problems of the past decade have resulted from specific developments in the landscape and architecture of web technologies as much as it has the agency of fringe elements. This section considers challenges facing those interested in countersubversion.

The Dangers of Pushing the Fringe Back to the Fringe

As mentioned, government agencies and private companies across the United States were forced in the wake of January 6 to grapple—indeed, at the time of writing of this book are still grappling—with the realities of deep-seated subversion in the nation's information environment and the potential for further acts of seditious violence. This effort is likely to persist for months and years to come. At present, the prevailing theme for many both inside the Beltway and in security communities beyond is to liken these efforts to challenges inherent in the mission of counterterrorism forces, as well as in actions taken to restructure the politics of nations emerging from conflict.[2] In other words, debate on the paranoia of American politics[3] rapidly shifted to envisage fringe elements less as countercultural advocates and more as the unsophisticated, alternately capable force often found in America's small wars.

Countless months on, analogies to major terrorist threats continue to play a particularly significant role in setting the tone of security policy discourse around America's domestic extremism problem.[4] One not unpopular analog to the events leading to January 6, for instance, likens key Republican figures to the leadership of Al Qaeda—that is, as the mouthpieces of a dispersed extremist movement that set the agenda but don't directly command anyone.

Another equivalency that has received some attention is the idea that the Republican Party needs to undergo a process of de-Ba'athification to strip the decades-old influences of far-right political interests from the core conservative platform.[5] And this narrative has only gained popularity as elements of the party continue to characterize themselves as agents of a Trumpian political revolution.[6]

As the content of this book might suggest, however—and, in fairness, as some experts have written or taken to social media to argue in reply—there are issues with these parallels, among them the politically charged context in which they're often made and the unique context of a vibrant democracy in America that has nevertheless produced extremism. Simply put, the United States isn't Iraq, Pakistan, or any of the other authoritarian states from which historical examples are most commonly drawn. And the shape of what both government and private stakeholders are now trying to wrangle isn't as neat a fit with so many of the parallels to state-sponsored counterterror operations that are commonly made. The broader backdrop of the events of the Capitol insurrection certainly involves radicalized persons, diverse militia organizations, and explicit intent to force change through violence. But it also involves regular Americans, a congested and fragmented media environment, and a culture of paranoid narratives normalized by the political right going back beyond Reagan.[7] Very few terrorism analogies are likely, in short, to hold up beyond a first glance.

This being said, one parallel that might be worth considering is the experience of states that have attempted to fight terror, insurgency, and sedition by simply suppressing those most apparently responsible. The Russian experience in Chechnya provides a good example. After some years of de facto independence from the Russian Federation, rebel activities in neighboring Dagestan drove the government in Moscow toward war and a concerted counterterrorism campaign in Ichkeria, the Chechen republic. This turn toward coercion represents an obvious recourse of any government faced with insurrection: to directly neutralize key players and create disincentives for others to turn toward extremism via direct acts of repression. A number of terrorist organizations, from Peru's Shining Path to Russia's Narodnaya Volya, have been effectively dismantled or outright destroyed in this way over the past century.[8]

Russia's opening of the Second Chechen War did not lead to the end of insurrection, however.[9] Though the intended result was a disruption of the rebels' abilities to operate and a quelling of popular support in Ichkeria,

Russian engagement ultimately widened the conflict. Not only did military operations not create disincentives toward radicalization and rebel support; they actually created incentives for Chechen forces to redefine the scope of their grievance. In the decade after Russian occupation, Chechen attacks across Russia and political operations in neighboring republics like Ingushetia dramatically increased.[10] It's arguable that Russian actions also directly drove Chechens toward Al Qaeda and, eventually, the Islamic State. In short, suppression tactics so often don't work because terrorists reconsider the scope of the struggle and scatter across borders, making them much harder to pin down.[11]

Policymakers and practitioners would do well to consider the experiences of state efforts to suppress and repress terrorist movements at this moment. To be clear, this is not because the United States or Western countries in general are dealing with something altogether similar to even those significant terrorist threats in decades past that enjoyed great popular support—the Irish Republican Army or the Palestinian Liberation Organization, for instance. Rather, it's relevant because the people, communities, and organizations now in the sights of status quo forces are defined by common access to the web and because the immediate recourse of government and private companies—already substantially underway—is to shut down sedition online.[12]

In this vein, the preponderance of the focus in major media outlets in the days following January 6 was on Trump's permanent ouster from services like Twitter and Instagram,[13] as well as the effective shutdown of right-leaning social media forum Parler after Amazon's refusal to continue hosting the platform.[14] But numerous other conspiratorial accounts and hate-tolerant virtual communities have also felt the ban hammer or have been dropped by hosting companies. Major platforms like Facebook have banned QAnon-linked accounts, and pressure has built for small sites like CloutHub and MeWe to follow suit. In truth, these kinds of crackdowns aren't a particularly major development. Yes, this is a weightier and more widespread cluster of ousters than has typically occurred in the past. But at various points in the past few years, spaces like r/The_Donald have been quarantined to prevent sensationalist speech from leaking into other sections of the site,[15] and hosting companies have booted clearly hateful publications like the neo-Nazi Daily Stormer, which subsequently found a new home on the dark web.[16] This recent suppression of subversive spaces and voices is just the most notable iteration of backlash following an incident involving individuals who've been radicalized in such spaces.

Perhaps what's most unique about these crackdowns is the targeting of so much speech that might previously have been considered merely risqué or sensational by social media platforms and hosting services. After January 6, so much speech is being removed beyond the clear-cut incitements to hate and violence that would previously have got someone banned. The QAnon conspiracy, in particular, has being targeted,[17] as have groups like the Proud Boys and the Three Percenters that played some visible role in the insurrection at the Capitol.[18] How widespread yet also targeted these crackdowns are makes for a uniquely dangerous period of flux and reformation in the far-right fringe ecosystem, much of which might be credibly thought of as subversive in constitution.

Though any parallel illustration can be taken too far, of course, the situation of canceling fringe voices across a range of mainstream formats in many ways mirrors the manner in which terrorist organizations are often forced to change how they operate as they move to occupy new physical and societal spaces. As digital crackdowns occur, users in the United States and elsewhere are being forced into alternative spaces and media. On the surface, it's easy to imagine how such moves will inevitably be correlated with an intensification of those features that make extreme social movements dangerous. Indeed, initial research illustrates that this is the case.[19] Individuals with a political agenda who are forced out of public spaces will gather in more private spaces where the incentive to mask more extreme ideas, ideologies, and intentions is much reduced.[20] In eras past, this process has taken the form of extremists forced by police crackdown or bad publicity to retreat to rural locales or insular communities. With forced migration between spaces in the age of the internet, the situation is likely even more worrisome. The cult-like dynamics of fringe spaces described in this book amplify beyond mainstream social media platforms and hosting services.[21] With the move to smaller services, business interest is often less willing to reject even extreme content as each user is more valuable, and back-end design, being generally weaker, makes it easier to restrict and shape speech. These constraints become even less relevant or entirely irrelevant if extreme communities move to utilize technological protections like peer-to-peer encryption or migrate to a darknet location, given that such tools can shield companies or even provide an entirely independent ability to operate.[22]

One good thing about crackdowns and forced migration of extreme voices from mainstream digital spaces, of course, is the reduction of potential audiences for extremism. In particular, banning certain prolific accounts and continuing to pursue particular individuals across platforms is arguably akin to killing the leadership of a terrorist organization. With the postinsurrection situation, however, things are likely to be at least somewhat different. The broad appeal and long exposure of the sociopolitical messaging that led to January 6 are already producing greater incentives to go looking for new spaces to discuss right-wing positions on national events, as well as guaranteeing greater than normal receptivity to any messaging that invites such migration.[23] It also seems likely that large numbers of individuals inculcated in the far-right media ecosystem will adopt an even greater distrust of mainstream media than previously as a result of crackdowns across the web and willingly turn to novel methods of creating new "spaces" for rhetoric and discourse more reflective of the fringe than the mainstream. QAnon believers have already turned to cascading text message networks to spread word about the evolving nature of the struggle against mainstream leftist forces along these lines.

The result of this dynamic is a diverse and rapidly diversifying far-right information ecosystem dispersed by ongoing internet crackdowns, but not necessarily substantially reduced in scope or fervor. While many conservatives caught up in the frauds perpetuated by certain high-ranking Republican officials and right-leaning news organizations were sobered by the assault on the Capitol to a degree, many more have failed so far to come around to the dangers of the insular narratives emerging in right-wing media spaces. To those individuals, the options for information consumption will be harder to see but still more readily available than one might imagine. And perhaps most significant, within the context of these developments even rhetorical leaders—from Ted Cruz and Donald Trump Jr. to Charlie Kirk and former Proud Boy leader Enrique Tarrio—aren't as individually significant as the spaces that provide succor to the deep-seated anxieties that fueled insurrection in Washington. In so many wars, as the chapters of this book have argued, this is the organic digital-age manifestation of leaderless resistance first envisioned by White supremacists in the 1980s.

Tangled Webs, the Web, and the Fringe 3.0

Much of the analysis in this book centered on the idea that the transition from Web 1.0 to Web 2.0 has been incredibly meaningful in shaping the exact dynamic of fringe leaderlessness that underwrites so much subversive engagement with the societal mainstream in recent years. In particular, fringe causes, narratives, and agency have been captured by the machinations of user-oriented social network platforms and have benefited from the specific way in which technology companies like X (Facebook), Twitter, and Google have implemented management of their services. Algorithms have been built that favor extreme or conspiratorial content because, among other things, it is linked to higher-than-average subsequent clickthrough behavior than is less inflammatory content. Companies like Reddit were, for a long time, reluctant to entirely jettison fringe accounts or spaces from their platform, fearing that the value of their service would be diminished by the action. And controversial voices have been allowed to tie activity on one social media platform automatically to outreach on others, amplifying misinformation and sensationalist content without a robust check on content validity.

Web 2.0 is itself, of course, likely to evolve with the development and implementation of new information technologies. Web 3.0 is already a concept broadly defined by technology developers as something distinct from today's norm along several lines. Specifically, Web 3.0—for which only a handful of sites already exist—is likely to be centered on the idea of intelligent web interfaces and back-end systems. Building on what is already possible given the proliferation of cloud infrastructure, Web 3.0 is likely to be defined by ubiquitous access to online content. No matter the type of interface being used—not just the mobile devices and computers that are standard today—the web experience will be accessible and full. Web 3.0 is also intended to be less "dumb"—for lack of a better way of putting it—than Web 2.0. Today rich content experiences still require manual user input and clarification of intention in order to function effectively. With the building of the semantic web, which will leverage advances in natural language processing and content recognition, the data put and found online by users will be organically more connected without the requirement of much user input. And, of course, functionality will also be improved by artificial intelligence (AI). Today, AI already permits rapid actions at scale to companies interested in interacting with users in dynamic fashion or managing the behavior of millions of users to correct for outlying perturbations in the way a service or system works. With Web 3.0, AI will likely continue to streamline an ability for the web to be presented as a more highly connective experience to the average user, specifically as new mediums for interacting with content—including virtual and augmented reality—become more accessible and powerful.

Given the further evolution of the web, what might we expect from subversion in the future—from the Fringe 3.0? One worrisome possibility is that the reflexive loop of user content, rhetoric, and socially constructed information described in past chapters might be captured in various efforts to further automate web services and imbue the connective internet experience with a degree of intelligence. The world of tomorrow will, inevitably, be built atop the world of today. In technology development terms, there is a sizable degree to which that means that data captured on the way network spaces function and interact today will be used to delineate the parameters for the function of new tools, applets, devices, and services in years to come. At the same time, the assumptions and the behavior of those who design and manage our many virtual spaces—technology companies, principally—will also be a part of this package of assumptions around which new tools and new modalities of engagement will be built. There are several potential implications of this. The first is that if the propensity for radicalization and the spread of extreme perspectives across networked social spaces is not addressed in the near term, enabling dynamics in the setup of those spaces' connections could be mirrored in future systems that are functionally intended to minimize the need for user input. Another is that the Fringe 3.0 may itself reflect a degrading moral basis for the conduct of democratic discourse. After all, even if extreme social behavior is effectively scrubbed from mainstream social media platforms, the normalization of assumptions and behaviors that led to their appearance initially might remain in effect. Those perspectives on where value exists in the operation of socially oriented web technologies dictated architectural decisions, technology investments, and management choices in the past. Without a civic recognition in the need to redress the issues identified here and elsewhere in the function of so much social web technology, even a nominal effort to reduce the worst excesses of fringe influence in mainstream spaces could still lead to future systems that offer opportunities for subversion and radicalization.

To pick up a thread from the previous section, it's also worth noting that many experts believe the next iteration of the internet will be much more significantly decentralized than what we have today. Specifically, peer-to-peer technologies like the blockchain are already promising to offer novel options for securing interactions and transactions without the need for trusting gatekeepers like big technology firms. While this likely development doesn't necessarily imply a substantially increased capability for fringe advocacy to interact with mainstream sociopolitical discourse, it does indicate that web affordances will continue to improve for actors interested in subversion. Given a substantial enough alternative network footprint, it is possible that the ability of law enforcement, researchers, and journalists to track fringe activities will be diminished during the Web 3.0 era. After all, while the hyperconnectivity of big technology platforms and social media services lies at the heart of many current challenges for democratic governance and national security, their openness also provides an ability to study widespread social activity and to—at the very least—problematize fringe extremism.

It's All about the Information

Subversion is a hallmark of human society, perhaps particularly of democratic societies. Where there exists a consensus on different social, moral, political, economic, or cultural issues, there will also likely always be a peripheral view that considers the status quo as fundamentally illegitimate. This is not necessarily problematic for democratic functionality. Just as political spin or extreme political contestation can actually make a democracy more vibrant—so long as safeguards exist to underwrite agreed-upon processes—fringe causes are a natural side effect of any society that fundamentally makes progress. What *is* problematic is the propensity for subversion to slip toward antagonism and the dissolution of those systems that prevent the disenfranchisement of some people. Given the degree to which subversion is an enterprise clearly enhanced by the development of novel, socially oriented web technologies, how might governments, citizens, and other responsible stakeholders (such as technology companies) act so as to mitigate these extreme externalities?

Quite arguably the best way to approach such a challenge is to think about democratic governance and national security in the same terms in which subversion has been cast in this book—that is, principally, in informational terms.[24] Social scientists regularly invoke the metaphor of a "marketplace of ideas" (MOI) to describe democratic discourse.[25] In doing so, they have often intended to describe how democracies are an idealized forum for public debate.[26] The MOI, much like its traditional economic parallel, embraces a "libertarian, laissez-faire approach to speech" where the "same 'invisible hand' that guides unregulated economic markets to maximum efficiency will guide unregulated markets in ideas to maximum discovery of truth."[27] In other settings, scholars have embraced the idea of the marketplace in variable formats as a functional set of processes that determine how democratic societies do politics, make policy, and prosecute conflict.[28]

The metaphor of the marketplace is, in reality, simply a description of an information system. Whether a marketplace of human interaction is concerned primarily with commodities or ideas, the underlying shape of the thing is that of a system designed to channel informational inputs toward particular outcomes. If one accepts that the metaphor of the MOI holds some basis in fact, that outcome is moderation via the representation and interaction of a democracy's citizenry.[29] Here, it is helpful to think of the MOI in Bayesian terms.[30] Social understanding of a particular issue begins at a baseline. Over time, with the introduction of new information and continued deliberation, society updates its beliefs. In this way, democratic societies tend to exhibit a prudence and a resilience to outlandish sensationalism, inflicted or otherwise, that others do not. In theory, given enough time and unfettered competition of arguments, "correct" ideas—or, at least, prudent ones with a basis in observable and verifiable facts—triumph over falsehood, and society's understanding comes to reflect an underlying reality.

Democratic functionality, however, actually depends on more than just the availability of information and a willingness to discuss the issues of the day. A generation of literature in political communication has argued that there may be systematic sociopolitical forces—natural "bugs in the system"—undermining the market.[31] In that literature, assessment of the significance of these "bugs" pivots on the shape of key stakeholders within the discursive system, including a free and vigilant media, diverse experts, loyal and disloyal opposition, and a responsible executive. Marketplace failure occurs when one or numerous of these stakeholders fail to do their jobs, either because they are motivated to shirk their duties or are denied the opportunity to do so. Given what has been covered in this book, it seems reasonable to add certain technology developers to this list of stakeholders.

Those discussing the idea of the MOI in democracies—which is more metaphor than theory—often stress four requirements that must be met in order for such a marketplace to function. At the most basic level, for discourse to be democratic there must exist methods by which it is reasonably easy to know where information comes from. This means two things. First, it means that social and political interlocutors should not be able to entirely hide their identity as it relates to public speech. While a degree of obfuscation of agency is to be expected in democratic systems in the form of corporations or interest groups "speaking" on behalf of individuals affiliated therewith, it should be the case that a reasonable investigation of any mouthpiece awards a robust understanding of where speech is coming from. Second, it means that the factual sources of information should be observable by a reasonable deconstruction of surveyed rhetoric, opinion, and reporting. Regardless of the "spin" offered in punditry or advocacy, democratic functionality requires that the average reasonable effort to unpack the facts and voices involved in any given conversation will be successful. Significantly, "spin" itself does not work against democracy *unless* the origination of information is difficult to ascertain. Opinion journalism and advocacy, even where it appears extreme, can be beneficial to the overall function of the democratic information system as it works to process and update priors so as to produce a moderating information effect.[32] Only when the underpinnings of such elements of discourse are obscured or manipulated does the marketplace suffer. In this way, the parallels to be drawn between information assurance of democratic functionality and computer systems break down in a single sense—to work, democracies do not require that information remains free of tampering. Rather, they require only that such tampering is reasonably discoverable.

More generally, democracies depend on a consensus view that discourse *is* discourse. Democratic populations must believe that—given an allowable amount of manipulation of national conversation by special interests—social and political discourse is not a façade. Here, the parallel to how many authoritarian states affect social control is highly relevant. In Russia, there are a series of well-documented steps that have been taken since the late 1990s by the governments of Vladimir Putin and Dimitri Medvedev to diminish the credibility of democratic processes as significant for ensuring good governance and stability in civil society.[33] The idea is that nonbelief in liberal democratic political mechanisms as guarantors of benefits to the citizenry leads to rising tolerance of, among other things, corruption and limitations on social freedoms.[34] Rigged elections are met with limited protest, and nepotistic promotion of political cronies is accepted because democratic process is not seen as a credible alternative,[35] particularly in the context of at least some degree of responsible stewardship of society on the part of the autocrat. In China, censorship has increasingly taken the form of targeted limitations on attempts to assemble with only special constraints set on speech itself.[36] The idea is that the appearance of a vibrant civil society debate wherein much criticism of authority is allowed produces a pressure valve that keeps a population away from the urge to protest.[37] In reality, the conversation is largely artificial, with astroturfing and disinformation being common features of the landscape.[38]

A third requirement of the effective function of democratic systems is information quality sufficient to allow a reasonable degree of parsing signal from noise via diverse, widespread discourse.[39] Though this requirement is in many ways secondary to the underlying imperatives of ensuring the attributable nature and credibility of information (because quality cannot be assessed unless that information is known), it is nevertheless critical to the realization of democracies' moderating processes. Even where limited information on a given issue is known, repetitive reporting from independent sources and contextualization in both media analyses and social settings help identify and define meaningful elements of the foci of debate. Inhibition of a reasonably complex ecosystem that enables such repetitive investigation and interpretation leads to the domination of few perspectives without a societal capacity for exploring issue nuance.

Finally, democratic systems' functionality requires a secondary belief in the credibility of information. As opposed to the need to ensure that discourse itself is seen to be credible, however, this final requirement concerns the relative freedom of information that can be brought to bear in discourse. Marketplace participants must not be conditioned to think that certain types of opinion or certain objects of empirical observation are off limits, at least beyond a small subset of extreme positions normatively juxtaposed to prevailing societal sentiment. Even in those instances, citizens must feel able to employ any fact or argument in discourse without incurring a predetermined penalty based, for instance, on a prevailing political or civic mood. The violation of this requirement of marketplace functionality sits alongside a broader argument about presidential threat inflation at the heart of Kaufmann's seminal description of marketplace failure in the lead-up to the 2003 U.S. invasion of Iraq.[40] Quieted by fear of backlash from an electorate highly mobilized in the aftermath of the September 11, 2001, terror attacks, countervailing forces of democratic discourse in the media, among opposition politicians in Congress, and in expert communities failed to effectively problematize and investigate claims of Iraqi WMD being forwarded by the administration of George W. Bush. Clearly, limitations of the freedom of relevant information can have dramatic effects on the functionality of democratic information systems.

Efforts to regulate technology firms, to encourage better moral standards for commercial practice, and to define rules of the road for political uses of social network infrastructure should be mindful of the informational implications of their recommendations. The reflexive process of fringe-to-mainstream rhetorical interaction that sits at the heart of the leaderlessness theory in this book degrades the functionality of the national marketplace of democratic discourse in a variety of ways. It makes the process of figuring out where ideas originate remarkably difficult. Even worse, it actively links issues and rhetoric to popular mouthpieces in the eyes of the median user regardless of the true origination of the ideas and symbolism involved. This dynamic also splits the discursive electorate of democracies into those plugged in to certain network-enabled echo chambers and those not. Quite naturally, this in a very real sense diminishes the case that could be made that citizen participation in conversation is citizen participation in some national conversation. It also encourages widespread disbelief in the credibility of information coming from alternative information environments among the citizenry. The implication of such a reality is quite simply that policymakers, activists, and regulators would do well to weigh the prospective value of solutions proposed in terms of these informational dynamics. Restrictions or requirements that might improve the quality of technology or political uses of technology in such a way that the informational functioning of democracy can be better assured should be favored over those that do not. Otherwise, we risk the continuation of sociotechnological interactions that, in a very real sense, have afforded subversive and extreme fringe actors in the 21st century the ability to influence mainstream discourse in unprecedented fashion.

Conclusion

This marks the end of my investigation into social subversion in the era of the internet. The main contention of this book is simple: that the internet has altered the functional elements of the subversive enterprise so completely that leaderlessness is, for now, the organic shape of so many fringe activities today. Both qualitative and quantitative evidence provided across several chapters seem to validate this notion. More than that, the large-N evidence brought to bear in Chapters 6 and 7 offer a truly unique look at the landscape of antagonistic digital acts undertaken by nonterroristic, nonstate elements operating at the fringes of global society. Optimistically, almost everything observed emanating from fringe elements—from attempts to build fringe collaborations to disruptive cyberattacks—was unsophisticated in the extreme. The idea that such communities and organizations as those with a hand in the events of January 6 could or would attempt the kinds of major digital disruption today associated with organized criminal activities or state-sponsored cyber operations is simply a nonstarter. Not only are such outcomes beyond the resources of so many fringe organizations; they also simply do not mesh well with the objectives of the subversive enterprise. As such, the challenge of social subversion in world affairs remains much as it ever was: a narrow and marginal area of concern for all but the most unstable of societies.

The difference in the digital age, of course, has been the manner in which so much power for social coordination and organization has simultaneously been placed in the hands of users and wielded by those interested in commercial gain by technology firms and the governments that have enabled them (i.e., have failed to effectively regulate them). The silver lining in what has been described here is that these issues are artificial, a manmade product of the very socioeconomic processes that must now be safeguarded. Now the steps we take to address subversion as a force in our modern, informationatized global society must reflect that realization.

APPENDIX A

Additional Evidence and Diagnostic Testing

This methodological appendix contains several supplementary data features and tests referenced in Chapter 7. Table A.1 controls for modeling choice by presenting the same set of models utilized in Figure 7.3 in OLS testing with a scale-dependent variable that measures the raw number of shady ICT employments by subversive activists (no deviation = 0). To be clear, this measure of the dependent variable both proxies for the dichotomous measure of deviation from expectations outlined earlier *and* additionally provides insight on the severity of that same deviation. As a result, this approach to testing is, in many ways, superior. As expected, it seems reasonably clear at first glance that the trends described by the results of the logit models presented in Figure 7.3 are borne out and reflected in these linear regression results. This is unsurprising and reflects a basic diagnostic check on the validity of the models presented. Naturally, however, there is variation in the scale and intensity of the trends described that reflects predictions of severity of deviation different from simply the fact of it.

Again, the use of a scale-dependent variable allows for some additional insight into factors that predict varying levels of intensity in antagonistic ICT usage. In particular, regardless of similarly positive trends across the range of independent variables with significant results in the previous set of tests, there are exceedingly strong relationships between intensity of antagonistic ICT employments and several variables. Subversive activist organizations are about twice as likely to employ ICT for circumvention and disruption when the cause's grievance is structural in nature than when it isn't, and more than three times as likely to do so when primed by rhetorical signals. Likewise, the existence of foreign-based sponsorship of a subversive movement predicts that such groups are, on balance, likely to use ICT for antagonism more than twice in a given 18-month episode than are those with either no sponsorship or solely domestic support. And where there exists a digital adoption gap between society and government, groups are likely to use ICT in a deviant fashion just more than four more times across the observed periods of engagement in digital activism than when there exists no gap. There are also strong results for group structure as reflected in initial testing. As with the original logit model results in Chapter 7, however, the strength of these relationships seems to be dependent on the inclusion of environmental control variables, with only the nature of group grievances and—to a lesser degree—the sponsorship of a foreign entity holding strong across models.

The use of a scale-dependent variable for linear regression analysis in addition to the primary logit analysis reduces the need for extensive robustness testing. In secondary testing, trends appeared to match those predicted in Chapter 7's logit models. Thus, there is limited concern that primary testing suffers from multicollinearity (i.e., variation based on the nature of different independent variable measurements). This is the case given the presentation of the several different basic binomial logit models in which independent variables are variably included to reflect different measures of significant potential intervening factors.

Nevertheless, primary analysis *was* performed using dichotomous measures of the dependent variable, and analysis was undertaken for a relatively small number of

Table A.1. Ordinary Least Squares (OLS) Regression Model Results Predicting Antagonistic ICT Usage

	Models		
	(1)	(2)	(3)
Maximalist	0.644*	0.791*	0.801*
Limited	−0-414	−0.452	−0.435
Idiosyncratic	0.203	0.243	0.249
Revisionism	1.212**	1.389**	1.394**
Participationism	3.201***	3.287***	3.299***
Polity	—	−0.191	−0.203
Competitiveness	—	0.544***	0.524***
Economic Crime	−0.130	−0.142	−0.141
Violent Crime	1.416*	1.492*	1.482*
Prior Crime	−0.020	−0.005	−0.051
Bureaucratic	0.923***	0.944***	0.942***
Market	1.465***	1.489***	1.492***
All Channel	0.327	0.332	0.331
Major Event	−0.401	−0.414	−0.417
Gov't Popularity	—	−0.233	−0.239
Gov't Investigation	2.391*	2.394*	2.399*
Domestic Sponsorship	−0.089	−0.092	−0.094
Foreign Sponsorship	2.012***	2.121***	2.157***
Gov't-Society Divide	—	—	4.012***
Leaderless Resistance	—	−0.424	−0.423
Anonymous	—	0.231	0.254
Virtual Community	—	0.745**	0.789**
Prosecute	−0.481**	−0.490***	−0.492***
Access	—	1.982***	—
Use	—	2.229***	—
Readiness	—	−0.340*	—

*$p < .05$; **$p < .01$; ***$p < .001$

observations over a reasonably limited time frame of 33 years. Therefore, I repeat my analysis in Figure A.1 using conditional log-link (Model 1), rare events (Model 2), and fixed effects (Model 3) regression analysis.

The results show no major variation in values across the odds ratios reported for any variable. Though there are various minor differences in the scale of results, new values do nothing to diminish the significance of earlier findings.

APPENDIX A 241

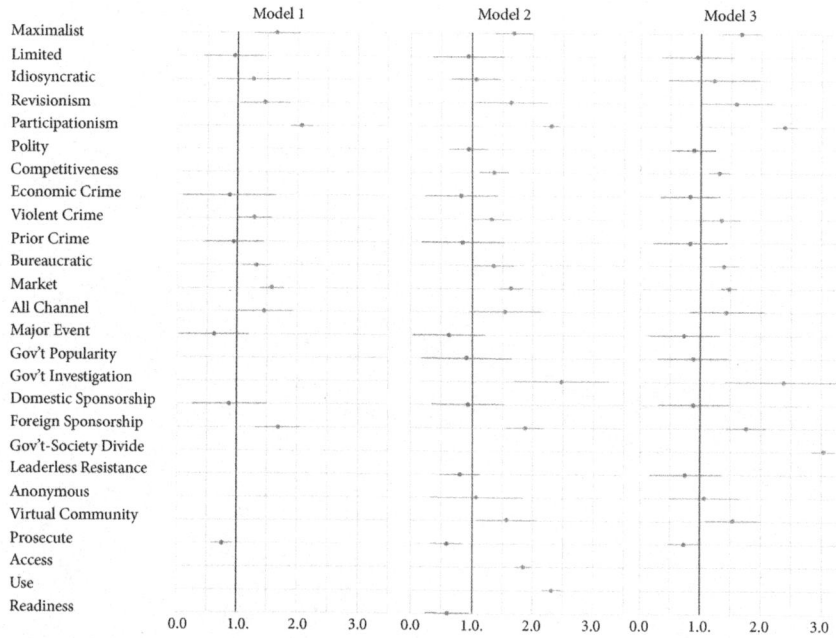

Figure A.1 Diagnostic models for results predicting antagonistic ICT usage using the conditional log-link function, rare events logit, and fixed effects.

Notes

Preface

1. Joosse argues that leaderless resistance is most useful to causes where there is a need to avoid major cleavages. This cuts two ways. First, it becomes the strategy of groups that feel the need to pay closest attention to the integrity of a broader idea in the eyes of the mainstream and so must carefully separate antagonism from the cause. Second, the strategy helps iron out differences that might otherwise be felt between supporting elements of a given cause that disagree on one or more points. See Paul Joosse, "Leaderless Resistance and Ideological Inclusion: The Case of the Earth Liberation Front," *Terrorism and Political Violence* 19, no. 3 (2007): 351–368.

Introduction

1. The most coherent reporting of which at the time of writing this book can be found in the documentation published by the Select Committee to Investigate the January 6th Attack on the United States Capitol. This report can be found at https://www.govinfo.gov/committee/house-january6th?path=/browsecommittee/chamber/house/committee/january6th/collection/CRPT.
2. Bruce Bimber, *Information and American Democracy: Technology in the Evolution of Political Power* (Cambridge: Cambridge University Press, 2003); Philip N. Howard, *The Digital Origins of Dictatorship and Democracy: Information Technology and Political Islam* (Oxford, UK: Oxford University Press, 2010); Jennifer Earl and Katrina Kimport, *Digitally Enabled Social Change: Activism in the Internet Age* (Cambridge, MA: MIT Press, 2011).
3. Joseph Pierce and Olivia R. Williams, "Against Power? Distinguishing between Acquisitive Resistance and Subversion," *Geografiska Annaler: Series B, Human Geography* 98, no. 3 (2016): 171–188.
4. Since Vidal's famous first utterance of the phrase, "fifth column" has entered common usage as a descriptor of forces that seek societal sabotage. Though occasionally used in discussions of state efforts to influence foreign cultures and political systems, the term is most often used to describe countercultural social movements and organizations, as well as front groups for violent and hate actors that seek to "betray" and erode the power of the forces of the status quo. This book is about such actors, though it uses the concept of subversion as a lens through which we might better analytically bound what is meant by fifth columns.
5. For more information, see https://www.icpsr.umich.edu/web/ICPSR/studies/34625.

Chapter 1

1. See, among others, Bruno Latour, *Reassembling the Social: An Introduction to Actor-Network Theory* (Oxford: Oxford University Press, 2007); Martin Müller, "Assemblages and Actor-Networks: Rethinking Socio-material Power, Politics and Space," *Geography Compass* 9, no. 1 (2015): 27–41; Rolland Munro, "Actor-Network Theory," *Sage Handbook of Power* (London, 2009): 125–139.
2. Jonathan Topaz, "Pew Head: Fringe 'Outsized Influence,'" *Politico*, June 12, 2014, https://www.politico.com/story/2014/06/pew-alan-murray-fringe-msnbc-107769.
3. Similar polling was completed by the Cato Institute. See Emily E. Ekins, "Poll: 62% of Americans Say They Have Political Views They're Afraid to Share," Survey Reports (Washington, D.C.: Cato Institute, 2020).
4. https://www.americansurveycenter.org/research/after-the-ballots-are-counted-conspiracies-political-violence-and-american-exceptionalism/; https://www.ipsos.com/sites/default/files/ct/news/documents/2021-05/Ipsos%20Reuters%20Topline%20Write%20up-%20The%20Big%20Lie%20-%2017%20May%20thru%2019%20May%202021.pdf.
5. Among others, Savvas Zannettou, Tristan Caulfield, Emiliano De Cristofaro, Nicolas Kourtelris, Ilias Leontiadis, Michael Sirivianos, Gianluca Stringhini, and Jeremy Blackburn, "The Web Centipede:

Understanding How Web Communities Influence Each Other through the Lens of Mainstream and Alternative News Sources," in *Proceedings of the 2017 Internet Measurement Conference* (London, 2017), 405–417; Manoel Horta Ribeiro, Raphael Ottoni, Robert West, Virgílio A. F. Almeida, and Wagner Meira Jr., "Auditing Radicalization Pathways on YouTube," in *Proceedings of the 2020 Conference on Fairness, Accountability, and Transparency* (Barcelona, Spain, 2020), 131–141; Srijan Kumar, William L. Hamilton, Jure Leskovec, and Dan Jurafsky, "Community Interaction and Conflict on the Web," in *Proceedings of the 2018 World Wide Web Conference* (Lyon, France, 2018), 933–943.
6. Castells, Manuel, and Manuel Castells. *City, class and power*. (London: Macmillan, 1978).
7. Felix Stalder, *Manuel Castells: The Theory of the Network Society* (Boston: Polity, 2006).
8. Manuel Castells, João Caraça, and Gustavo Cardoso, eds., *Aftermath: The Cultures of the Economic Crisis* (Oxford: Oxford University Press, 2012), 230.
9. P. N. Funke and T. Wolfson, "From Global Justice to Occupy and Podemos: Mapping Three Stages of Contemporary Activism," *TripleC: Communication, Capitalism, and Critique: Open Access Journal for a Global Sustainable Information Society* 15, no. 2 (2017): 393–403.
10. Jackson, Sarah J. "Progressive social movements and the internet." In *Oxford Research Encyclopedia of Communication*. (2018).
11. As does the attraction of conspiracy theory and counterculture generally to individuals with mental health conditions (Bloom and Moskalenko 2021).
12. W. L. Bennett and A. Segerberg, "Digital Media and the Personalization of Collective Action," *Information, Communication & Society* 14, no. 6 (2011): 770–799.
13. Z. Papacharissi, *Affective Publics: Sentiment, Technology, and Politics* (Oxford,New York: Oxford University Press, 2014). Also see Z. Papacharissi, *A Private Sphere: Democracy in a Digital Age* (Cambridge, Malden, MA: Polity Press, 2010).
14. Fenton, Natalie. *Digital, political, radical* (Hoboken, NJ: John Wiley, 2018).
15. See, among others, Larry Diamond, "Liberation Technology," *Journal of Democracy* 21, no. 3 (2010): 69–83; Larry Diamond and Marc F. Plattner, eds., *Liberation Technology: Social Media and the Struggle for Democracy* (Baltimore: JHU Press, 2012); Giovanni Ziccardi, *Resistance, Liberation Technology and Human Rights in the Digital Age*, vol. 7 (Springer Science & Business Media, 2012).
16. Also suggested in N. Fenton, "Mediating Hope: New Media, Politics and Resistance," *International Journal of Cultural Studies* 11, no. 2 (2008): 230–248.
17. Dana L. Cloud, "Progressive Social Movements and the Internet." In Dana L. Cloud, ed. *The Oxford Encyclopedia of Communication and Critical Cultural Studies* (Oxford: Oxford University Press, 2019).
18. Ibid.
19. Ibid.
20. Ibid.
21. Robert Prus, "Terrorism, Tyranny, and Religious Extremism as Collective Activity: Beyond the Deviant, Psychological, and Power Mystiques," *American Sociologist* 36, no. 1 (2005): 49.
22. Alex Schmid, *Violent and Non-Violent Extremism: Two Sides of the Same Coin?* (The Hague: International Centre for Counter-Terrorism, 2014).
23. Charlie Winter, Peter Neumann, Alexander Meleagrou-Hitchens, Magnus Ranstorp, Lorenzo Vidino, and Johanna Fürst, "Online Extremism: Research Trends in Internet Activism, Radicalization, and Counter-strategies," *International Journal of Conflict and Violence* 14 (2020): 1–20.
24. Ibid.
25. Luigi Bonanate, "Some Unanticipated Consequences of Terrorism," *Journal of Peace Research* 3, no. 16 (1979): 197–211; Floris Vermeulen and Frank Bovenkerk, *Engaging with Violent Islamic Extremism* (The Hague: Eleven International, 2012).
26. For example, Peter Neumann, "Options and Strategies for Countering Online Radicalization in the United States," *Studies in Conflict and Terrorism* 36, no. 6 (2013): 431–59.
27. Ronald Wibtrope, *Rational Extremism: The Political Economy of Radicalism* (Cambridge: Cambridge University Press, 2012).
28. Ibid., 79.
29. Ibid.
30. Ibid.
31. Winter et al., "Online Extremism."
32. Clark McCauley and Sophia Moskalenko, "Mechanisms of Political Radicalization: Pathways toward Terrorism," *Terrorism and Political Violence* 20, no. 3 (2008): 415–33.

33. For example, Peter Neumann and Brooke Rogers, *Recruitment and Mobilisation for the Islamist Militant Movement in Europe* (London: International Centre for the Study of Radicalisation, 2011).
34. Ibid.
35. For example, Bruce Hoffman, *Inside Terrorism* (New York: Columbia University Press, 2017); Peter Bergen, Bruce Hoffmann, Michael Hurley, and Erroll Suthers, *Jihadist Terrorism: A Threat Assessment* (Washington, D.C.: Bipartisan Policy Centre, 2013).
36. Marc Sageman, "Understanding Jihadi Networks," *Strategic Insights* 4, no. 4 (2005): n.p..
37. Marc Sageman, *Leaderless Jihad: Terror Networks in the Twenty-First Century* (Philadelphia: University of Pennsylvania Press, 2008).
38. Quintan Wiktorowicz, *Islamic Activism: A Social Movement Theory Approach* (Bloomington: Indiana University Press, 2003); Quintan Wiktorowicz, *Radical Islam Rising: Muslim Extremism in the West* (Oxford: Rowman and Littlefield, 2005).
39. Phyllis B. Gerstenfeld, Diana R. Grant, and Chau-Pu Chiang, "Hate Online: A Content Analysis of Extremist Internet Sites," *Analyses of Social Issues and Public Policy* 3, no. 1 (2003): 29–44.
40. Gabriel Weimann, *www.terror.net: How Modern Terrorism Uses the Internet* (Washington, D.C.: U.S. Institute of Peace, 2004).
41. Weimann expands these analyses in Gabriel Weimann, "Virtual Disputes: The Use of the Internet for Terrorist Debates," *Studies in Conflict and Terrorism* 29, no. 7 (2006): 623–39; Gabriel Weimann, "Terrorist Migration to the Dark Web," *Perspectives on Terrorism* 10, no. 3 (2016): 40–44; Gabriel Weimann and Katharina von Knop, "Applying the Notion of Noise to Countering Online Terrorism," *Studies in Conflict and Terrorism* 31, no. 10 (2008): 883–902.
42. Aaron Y. Zelin, "Picture or It Didn't Happen: A Snapshot of the Islamic State's Official Media Output," *Perspectives on Terrorism* 9, no. 4 (2015): 85–97; Charlie Winter "Documenting the Virtual 'Caliphate,'" Quilliam (2015); Charlie Winter *An Integrated Approach to Islamic State Recruitment* (Barton: Australian Strategic Policy Institute, 2016).
43. Sanne B. Geeraerts, "Digital Radicalization of Youth," *Social Cosmos* 3, no. 1 (2012): 25–32.
44. Neil D. Shortland, "'On the Internet, Nobody Knows You're a Dog': The Online Risk Assessment of Violent Extremists," in Violence and Society: Breakthroughs in Research and Practice. Hershey, PA: Information Science Reference, 2016), 591–615.
45. Andrew Hoskins and Ben O'Loughlin, "Media and the Myth of Radicalisation," *Media, War, and Conflict* 2, no. 2 (2009): 107–110.
46. Ibid.
47. Winter et al., "Online Extremism."
48. Tiana Gaudette, Ryan Scrivens, and Vivek Venkatesh, "The Role of the Internet in Facilitating Violent Extremism: Insights from Former Right-Wing Extremists," *Terrorism and Political Violence* 34, no. 7 (2022): 1339–1356.
49. Ibid.
50. Ibid.
51. Ibid.

Chapter 2

1. For a good description, see James Morton Smith, *Freedom's Fetters: The Alien and Sedition Laws and American Civil Liberties* (Ithaca, NY: Cornell University Press, 1956); Geoffrey R. Stone, *Perilous Times: Free Speech in Wartime from the Sedition Act of 1798 to the War on Terrorism* (New York: W. W. Norton, 2004).
2. Of note, Adams and his supporters held the two threats—the overthrow of the state and the subversive erosion of prevailing culture in favor of another—as separate challenges for the new American republic, even if the latter raised the prospects of the former.
3. See Kenneth O'Reilly, *Hoover and the Unamericans: The FBI, HUAC, and the Red Menace* (Philadelphia: Temple University Press, 1983).
4. See Paul W. Blackstock, *The Strategy of Subversion: Manipulating the Politics of Other Nations* (Chicago, IL: Quadrangle Books, 1964).
5. See José Ortega y Gasset, *Invertebrate Spain* (New York: Howard Fertig, , 1974).
6. For an excellent overview of great power political interactions in Europe across this period, see Talbot Imlay and Monica Duffy Toft, eds., *The Fog of Peace and War Planning: Military and Strategic Planning under Uncertainty* (New York: Routledge, 2006).
7. See T. E. Lawrence, Seven Pillars of Wisdom (1922).
8. See Audrey Kahin and George Kahin, *Subversion as Foreign Policy: The Secret Eisenhower and Dulles Debacle in Indonesia* (New York: New Press, 1995).

9. For discussion of subversion or forced ideational change in what we might call the mainstream IR literature, see inter alia K. J. Holsti, *Peace and War: Armed Conflicts and International Order 1648–1989* (New York: Cambridge University Press, 1991); Stephen M. Walt, *Revolution and War* (Ithaca, NY: Cornell University Press, 1996); Mark N. Katz, *Revolutions and Revolutionary Waves* (New York: Palgrave Macmillan, 1999); Mark L. Haas, *The Ideological Origins of Great Power Politics, 1789–1989* (Ithaca, NY: Cornell University Press, 2005); Barry Hashimoto Lo and Dan Reiter, "Ensuring Peace: Foreign-Imposed Regime Change and Postwar Peace Duration, 1914–2001," *International Organization* 62 (2008): 717–736; John Owen, *The Clash of Ideas in World Politics: Transnational Networks, States, and Regime Change, 1510–2010* (Princeton, NJ: Princeton University Press, 2010).
10. See Frank Kitson, *Low Intensity Operations: Subversion, Insurgency, Peacekeeping* (Harrisburg, PA: Stackpole Books, 1971).
11. Roger Trinquier, *Modern Warfare: A French View of Counterinsurgency* (Liverpool, UK: Pall Mall Press, 1964), 6–24. Also referenced in Kitson, *Low Intensity Operations*, 5.
12. See Yuri Bezmenov, "Soviet Subversion of Western Society," lecture, 1983, https://ghostarchive.org/varchive/youtube/20211117/5gnpCqsXE8g.
13. U.S. Department of Defense, Joint Education and Doctrine Division, November 2010.
14. See, for instance, R. J. Spjut, "Defining Subversion," *British Journal of Law and Society* 6, no. 2 (1979): 254–261.
15. Though his work lacks a strict attempt to define or bound the phenomenon, Beilenson's work is one of the few to consider the phenomenon of subversion entirely on its ideational merits. See Laurence Beilenson, *Power through Subversion* (Washington, D.C.: Public Affairs Press, 1972).
16. Blackstock, *The Strategy of Subversion*, 56.
17. See Beilenson, *Power through Subversion*, 5–6.
18. Ibid., 56.
19. See Owen, *Clash of Ideas in World Politics*.
20. Ibid., 48–52.
21. U.S. intelligence community reporting and analysis released to the public describes how, in summer 2015, a Russia-based entity labeled APT29 (Advanced Persistent Threat 29) prosecuted a spear-phishing campaign using directed emails that contained a malicious link to over 1,000 recipients, including multiple U.S. government victims. APT29 used legitimate domains, which included domains associated with U.S. organizations and educational institutions, to host malware and send the spear-phishing emails. In the course of that campaign, APT29 successfully compromised a U.S. political party. At least one targeted individual activated links to malware hosted on operational infrastructure of opened attachments containing malware. APT29 delivered malware to the political party's systems, established persistence, escalated privileges, enumerated active directory accounts, and exfiltrated email from several accounts through encrypted connections back through operational infrastructure. In spring 2016, another Russia-based entity (APT28) compromised the same political party, again via targeted spear phishing. This time, the spear-phishing email tricked recipients into changing their passwords through a fake webmail domain hosted on APT28 operational infrastructure. Using the harvested credentials, APT28 was able to gain access and steal content, likely leading to the exfiltration of information from multiple senior party members. The U.S. government concludes that information was leaked to the press and publicly disclosed in an effort to exert influence on the deliberative processes during the 2016 U.S. presidential election period. For the full publicly release report on Russia's actions during the 2015–2016 presidential election season, see Joint Analysis Report 16-20296A, *GRIZZLY STEPPE—Russian Malicious Cyber Activity*, December 29, 2016, https://www.cisa.gov/sites/default/files/publications/JAR_16-20296A_GRIZZLY%20STEPPE-2016-1229.pdf.
22. For further coverage and discussion of how Russia has employed cyber techniques, troll/bot armies, and traditional intelligence disinformation operations to achieve foreign political manipulation objectives, see Peter Pomerantsev and Michael Weiss, *The Menace of Unreality: How the Kremlin Weaponizes Information, Culture and Money* (New York: Institute of Modern Russia, 2014); "Russian Trolls Spread Government Propaganda," *Al Jazeera*, August 11, 2015, http://www.aljazeera.com/news/2015/08/russian-trolls-internet-government-propaganda-150811205218686.html; "This Is How Pro-Russia Trolls Manipulate Finns Online—Check the List of Forums Favored by Propagandists," Stopfake, July 13, 2015, http://www.stopfake.org/en/this-is-how-pro-russia-trolls-manipulate-finns-online-check-the-list-of-forums-favored-by-propagandists/; Michael McFaul, "What's It Like to Be Hated by the Russian Internet?"

Guardian, May 26, 2015, http://www.theguardian.com/world/2015/may/26/russia-internet-hated; Anton Butsenko, "Тролли из Ольгино переехали в новый четырехэтажный офис на Савушкина" [Trolls from Olgino Move to a New Four-Storey Office on Savushkina Street], *Delovoy* (Petersburg), October 28, 2014, http://www.dp.ru/103iph/; Jessikka Aro, "Yle Kioski Traces the Origins of Russian Social Media Propaganda—Never-before-Seen Material from the Troll Factory," *Yle*, February 20, 2015, http://kioski.yle.fi/omat/at-the-origins-of-russian-propaganda; Alec Luhn, "Game of Trolls: The Hip Digi-kids Helping Putin's Fight for Online Supremacy," *Guardian*, August 18, 2015, http://www.theguardian.com/world/2015/aug/18/trolls-putin-russia-savchuk.

23. See Blackstock, *Strategy of Subversion*.
24. See Mark R. Beissinger, *Nationalist Mobilization and the Collapse of the Soviet State* (Cambridge: Cambridge University Press, 2002).
25. See Douglas Pike, *Viet Cong: The Organization and Techniques of the National Liberation Front of South Vietnam* (Cambridge, MA: MIT Press, 1966).
26. See Jeremy Varon, *Bringing the War Home: The Weather Underground, the Red Army Faction, and Revolutionary Violence in the Sixties and Seventies* (Berkeley, Los Angeles, and London: University of California Press, 2004).
27. See Philip Selznick, *The Organizational Weapon: A Study of Bolshevik Strategy and Tactics* (New York: McGraw-Hill, 1952).
28. See, among others, Kenneth A. Schultz, *Democracy and Coercive Diplomacy*, vol. 76 (Cambridge: Cambridge University Press, 2001); Alexander L. George, William E. Simons, David Kent Hall, Bruce W. Jentleson, Scott D. Sagan, Richard Herrmann, Paul Gordon Lauren, and Tim Zimmermann, eds., *The Limits of Coercive Diplomacy*, vol. 296 (Boulder, CO: Westview Press, 1994); Alexander L. George, *Forceful Persuasion: Coercive Diplomacy as an Alternative to War* (Washington D.C.: U.S. Institute of Peace Press, 1991); Thomas C. Schelling, "The Diplomacy of Violence," in John Garnett, *Theories of Peace and Security* (London: Palgrave Macmillan, 1970), 64–84; Thomas C. Schelling, "Arms and Influence," in Thomas Mahnken, Joseph Maiolo, Joseph A. Maiolo, eds. *Strategic Studies* (New York: Routledge, 2008), 96–114.
29. Among others, see Christopher Whyte, "Ending Cyber Coercion: Computer Network Attack, Exploitation and the Case of North Korea," *Comparative Strategy* 35, no. 2 (2016): 93–102; Travis Sharp, "Theorizing Cyber Coercion: The 2014 North Korean Operation against Sony," *Journal of Strategic Studies* 40, no. 7 (2017): 898–926; Brandon Valeriano, Benjamin M. Jensen, and Ryan C. Maness, *Cyber Strategy: The Evolving Character of Power and Coercion* (Oxford: Oxford University Press, 2018); Erica D. Borghard and Shawn W. Lonergan, "The Logic of Coercion in Cyberspace," *Security Studies* 26, no. 3 (2017): 452–481.
30. Pierce, Joseph, and Olivia R. Williams. "Against power? Distinguishing between acquisitive resistance and subversion." Geografiska Annaler: Series B, Human Geography 98, no. 3 (2016): 171–188.
31. See Ian Hurd, "Legitimacy and Authority in International Politics," *International Organization* 53, no. 2 (1999): 381.
32. This argument finds support in recent efforts to better situate subversion as a unique phenomenon that requires more study in the digital age. Though they yet blur the line between the outputs and mechanisms of power emerging from legitimacy, Breitenbauch and Byrjalsen, for instance, argue that external subversion is best understood as a "state's purposive destabilization and undermining of the authority and functioning of other states in order to achieve significant political gains." Henrik Breitenbauch and Niels Byrjalsen, "Subversion, Statecraft and Liberal Democracy," *Survival* 61, no. 4 (2019): 31–41.
33. This is a common conceptualization of the worldview expressed in the literature on political communication and behavior. Generically, the idea is that a worldview is constituted of a range of different preferences and predispositions woven together to form a particular attitude and decision-making paradigm for the individual. Alteration of that worldview, thus, has to do with efforts to alter the significance of different predispositions to the individual, the nature of different perspectives, or the composition of the cluster as a whole. See, for instance, Jörg Matthes and Matthias Kohring, "The Content Analysis of Media Frames: Toward Improving Reliability and Validity," *Journal of Communication* 58, no. 2 (2008): 258–279.
34. With initial jump-off points being the works of hegemonic stability theorists and the literature on systems transformation. See, for instance, Duncan Snidal, "The Limits of Hegemonic Stability Theory," *International Organization* 39, no. 4 (1985): 579–614; Susan Strange, "The

Persistent Myth of Lost Hegemony," *International Organization* 41, no. 4 (1987): 551–574; Robert O. Keohane, *After Hegemony: Cooperation and Discord in the World Political Economy* (Princeton, NJ: Princeton University Press, 2005); Robert Gilpin, *The Political Economy of International Relations* (Princeton, NJ: Princeton University Press, 2016).

35. For a good overview of this vein of thought, see Robert W. Cox, *Production, Power, and World Order: Social Forces in the Making of History*, vol. 1 (New York: Columbia University Press, 1987); Robert W. Cox, "Social Forces, States and World Orders," in *Neorealism and Its Critics*, ed. Robert Owen Keohane (New York: Columbia University Press, 1986): 126–155..
36. See Robert W. Cox, "Gramsci, Hegemony and International Relations," *Millennium Journal of International Affairs* 12, no. 2 126–155 (1987); S. Gill and D. Law, "Global Hegemony and the Structural Power of Capital," *International Studies Quarterly* 33 (1989): 33–475.
37. Cox, *Production, Power, and World Order*, 43.
38. Works like Jessop's neo-Gramscian exploration of urban governance regimes do a good job outlining what is meant by propaganda and subversion in the abstract, but do remarkably little to describe techniques or offer example of parameters for implementation and success. Bob Jessop, "A Neo-Gramscian Approach to the Regulation of Urban Regimes: Accumulation Strategies, Hegemonic Projects, and Governance," *Reconstructing Urban Regime Theory: Regulating Urban Politics in a Global Economy* 5 (1997): 1–74.
39. See William Rosenau, "Subversion and Insurgency," RAND Counterinsurgency Study, Paper 2 (Santa Monica, CA: RAND, 2007).
40. See Thomas Rid, *Cyber War Will Not Take Place* (Oxford: Oxford University Press, 2013).
41. See Rosenau, "Subversion and Insurgency," 6.
42. Ibid. Also see John Thompson, *Other People's Wars: A Review of Overseas Terrorism in Canada* (Toronto, Ontario, Canada: Mackenzie Institute, 2003).
43. See Lorenzo Vidino, *The New Muslim Brotherhood in the West* (New York: Columbia University Press, 2010).
44. See Rosenau, "Subversion and Insurgency," 6–7.
45. See Niles Lathem, "Qaeda Claim: We 'Infiltrated' UAE Government," *New York Post*, February 25, 2006.
46. See, for instance, "Protesters Storm Baghdad's Green Zone Again, Dozens Hurt," Thompson Reuters, May 20, 2016.
47. See inter alia Inspectors General, *Interagency Assessment of Iraq Police Training* (Washington, D.C.: U.S. Department of State and U.S. Department of Defense, July 2005); BBC News, "Insurgents 'Inside Iraqi Police,'" September 21, 2005.
48. See Pike, *Viet Cong*. Also see John Prados, "Impatience, Illusion, and Asymmetry: Intelligence in Vietnam," in *Why the North Won the Vietnam War*, ed. Marc Jason Gilbert (New York: Palgrave, 2002); U.S. Information Service, Office of Policy and Research, "The Viet Cong: The United Front Technique," R-13-67, Record 128321, Douglas Pike Collection: Unit 06—Democratic Republic of Vietnam, April 20, 1967; U.S. Central Intelligence Agency, Directorate of Intelligence, "The Vulnerability of Non-Communist Groups in South Vietnam to Political Subversion," Record 31052, CIA Collection, May 27, 1966.
49. See Rosenau, "Subversion and Insurgency," 7–8.
50. See U.S. Marine Corps Intelligence Activity, *The Urban Threat: Guerrilla and Terrorist Organizations* (1999).
51. See Carlos Marighella, *Minimanual of the Urban Guerrilla* (1969); Andrew R. Molnar, *Undergrounds in Insurgent, Revolutionary, and Resistance Warfare* (Washington, D.C.: Special Operations Research Office, November 1963).
52. Athina Karatzogianni, *Firebrand Waves of Digital Activism 1994–2014: The Rise and Spread of Hacktivism and Cyberconflict* (New York: Springer, 2015).
53. Alanoud Al Sharekh, "Reform and Rebirth in the Middle East," *Survival* 53, no. 2 (2011): 51–60.

Chapter 3

1. For histories of this long developmental process, see inter alia Barry M. Leiner, Vinton G. Cerf, David D. Clark, Robert E. Kahn, Leonard Kleinrock, Daniel C. Lynch, Jon Postel, Larry G. Roberts, and Stephen Wolff, "A Brief History of the Internet," *ACM SIGCOMM Computer Communication Review* 39, no. 5 (2009): 22–31; Barry M., Leiner Vinton G. Cerf, David D. Clark, Robert E. Kahn, Leonard Kleinrock, Daniel C. Lynch, Jon Postel, Lawrence G. Roberts, and Stephen S. Wolff, "The Past and Future History of the Internet," *Communications of the ACM* 40, no. 2 (1997): 102–108; John Naughton, "The Evolution of

the Internet: From Military Experiment to General Purpose Technology," *Journal of Cyber Policy* 1, no. 1 (2016): 5–28.
2. Scott J. Shackelford, Enrique Oti, Jaclyn A. Kerr, Elaine Korzak, and Andreas Kuehn, "Back to the Future of Internet Governance," *Geo. J. Int'l Aff.* 16 (2015): 83.
3. Eric Goldman, "The Complicated Story of FOSTA and Section 230," *First Amend. L. Rev.* 17 (2018): 279.
4. See Annemarie Pantazis, "Zeran v. America Online, Inc.: Insulating Internet Service Providers from Defamation Liability," *Wake Forest Law Review* 34 (1999): 531; David R. Sheridan, "Zeran v. AOL and the Effect of Section 230 of the Communications Decency Act upon Liability for Defamation on the Internet," *Alb. L. Rev.* 61 (1997): 147.
5. For a primer on the history and functional differentiation of the Web 2.0 shift, see inter alia Matthew Allen, "What Was Web 2.0? Versions as the Dominant Mode of Internet History," *New Media & Society* 15, no. 2 (2013): 260–275; Payal Arora, *The Leisure Commons: A Spatial History of Web 2.0* (New York: Routledge, 2014); Maria Bakardjieva and Georgia Gaden, "Web 2.0 Technologies of the Self," *Philosophy & Technology* 25, no. 3 (2012): 399–413.
6. Hugo Adrián Delgado Rodríguez, "Web 2.0 History, Evolution and Characteristics." (2019).
7. Robert Cailliau and Helen Ashman, "Hypertext in the Web—A History," *ACM Computing Surveys (CSUR)* 31, no. 4es (1999): 35-es.
8. A phrase made popular in reference to the internet by researchers in psychology, sociology, and elsewhere attempting to effectively describe the impact of complex emergent information systems on human cognition and affect. See William Hirst, Dora M. Coman, and Alin I. Coman, "A Social Turn for the Internet: Commentary on Sparrow and Chatman," *Psychological Inquiry* 24, no. 4 (2013): 310–313; Betsy Sparrow and Ljubica Chatman, "Social Cognition in the Internet Age: Same as It Ever Was?," *Psychological Inquiry* 24, no. 4 (2013): 273–292; S. V. Tikhonova, "Social Networks: Problems of Internet Socialization," *Polis. Political Studies* 3, no. 3 (2016): 138–152.
9. See Nupur Choudhury, "World Wide Web and Its Journey from Web 1.0 to Web 4.0," *International Journal of Computer Science and Information Technologies* 5, no. 6 (2014): 8096–8100; Graham Cormode and Balachander Krishnamurthy, "Key Differences between Web 1.0 and Web 2.0," *First Monday* (2008); Sareh Aghaei, Mohammad Ali Nematbakhsh, and Hadi Khosravi Farsani, "Evolution of the World Wide Web: From WEB 1.0 TO WEB 4.0," *International Journal of Web & Semantic Technology* 3, no. 1 (2012): 1–10.
10. Famous for, among other works, John Arquilla and David Ronfeldt, "Cyberwar Is Coming!," *Comparative Strategy* 12, no. 2 (1993): 141–165; John Arquilla and David Ronfeldt, "The Advent of Netwar (Revisited)," *Networks and Netwars: The Future of Terror, Crime, and Militancy* (2001): 1–25.
11. For instance, Ronald Deibert, *Parchment, Printing, and Hypermedia: Communication and World Order Transformation* (New York: Columbia University Press, 2000).
12. A categorization of web technologies notably offered by Naughton, "The Evolution of the Internet."
13. Arie Perliger, *American Zealots* (New York: Columbia University Press, 2020).
14. Cynthia Miller-Idriss, *Hate in the Homeland* (Princeton, NJ: Princeton University Press, 2020).
15. Manuela Caiani and Linda Parenti, *European and American Extreme Right Groups and the Internet* (New York: Routledge, 2016).
16. Such as Peter J. Davies and Paul Jackson, *The Far Right in Europe: An Encyclopedia*, No. 10.133 (Westport, CT: Greenwood, 2008); Margit Feischmidt and Peter Hervik, "Mainstreaming the Extreme: Intersecting Challenges from the Far Right in Europe," *Intersections East European Journal of Society and Politics* 1, no. 1 (2015): 4–17.
17. For instance, to a small degree, Cas Mudde, *The Far Right Today* (London: John Wiley, 2019); Flávia Biroli and Mariana Caminotti, "The Conservative Backlash against Gender in Latin America," *Politics & Gender* 16, no. 1 (2020).
18. Aaron Winter, "Online Hate: From the Far-Right to the 'Alt-Right' and from the Margins to the Mainstream," in S. Woolley, *Online Othering* (Cham, Switzerland: Palgrave Macmillan, 2019), 39–63.
19. Caiani and Parenti, *European and American Extreme Right Groups and the Internet*.
20. Ibid.
21. This is, naturally, a movement-specific articulation of the web benefits generically detailed in so much literature on web activism and liberation technologies, such as Dorothy E. Denning, "Activism, Hacktivism, and Cyberterrorism: The Internet as a Tool for Influencing Foreign

Policy," *Networks and Netwars: The Future of Terror, Crime, and Militancy* 239 (2001): 288; Larry Diamond and Marc F. Plattner, eds.m *Liberation Technology: Social Media and the Struggle for Democracy* (Baltimore: JHU Press, 2012).
22. Various authors have written about the insularity and self-isolation of White supremacist communities in offline settings. See, for instance, Pete Simi and Robert Futrell, *American Swastika: Inside the White Power Movement's Hidden Spaces of Hate* (Lanham, MD: Rowman & Littlefield, 2015).
23. Caiani and Parenti, *European and American Extreme Right Groups and the Internet*.
24. Ibid.
25. As seminally described in Jennifer Earl and Katrina Kimport, *Digitally Enabled Social Change: Activism in the Internet Age* (Cambridge, MA: MIT Press, 2011).
26. Barry Wellman, Anabel Quan-Haase, Jeffrey Boase, Wenhong Chen, Keith Hampton, Isabel Díaz, and Kakuko Miyata, "The Social Affordances of the Internet for Networked Individualism," *Journal of Computer-Mediated Communication* 8, no. 3 (2003): JCMC834.
27. Andrew Jakubowicz, Kevin Dunn, Gail Mason, Yin Paradies, Ana-Maria Bliuc, Nasya Bahfen, Andre Oboler, Rosalie Atie, and Karen Connelly, "Racism and the Affordances of the Internet," in Andrew Jakubowicz, Kevin Dunn, Gail Mason, Yin Paradies, Ana-Maria Bliuc, Nasya Bahfen, Andre Oboler, Rosalie Atie, and Karen Connelly, *Cyber Racism and Community Resilience* (Cham, Switzerland: Palgrave Macmillan, 2017), 95–145.
28. Caiani and Parenti, *European and American Extreme Right Groups and the Internet*.
29. Winter, "Online Hate."
30. Perliger, *American Zealots*.
31. Anti-Defamation League, "With Hate in Their Hearts: The State of White Supremacy in the United States," July 13, 2015, https://www.adl.org/education/resources/reports/state-ofwhite-supremacy.
32. Ibid.
33. Ibid.
34. For a history of the Klan, see inter alia Sara Bullard, ed., *The Ku Klux Klan: A History of Racism and Violence* (Collingwood, PA: Diane, 1998); and Chester L. Quarles, *The Ku Klux Klan and Related American Racialist and Antisemitic Organizations: A History and Analysis* (Jefferson, NC: McFarland, , 1999).
35. Val Burris, Emery Smith, and Ann Strahm, "White Supremacist Networks on the Internet," *Sociological focus* 33, no. 2 (2000): 218.
36. Gerald R. Webster, "If First You Don't Secede, Try, Try Again: Secession, Hate, and the League of the South," in Colin Flint, *Spaces of Hate* (New York: Routledge, 2013), 149–176.
37. Kirsten Dyck, *Reichsrock: The International Web of White-Power and Neo-Nazi Hate Music* (New Brunswick, NJ: Rutgers University Press, 2016).
38. Burris, Smith, and Strahm, "White Supremacist Networks on the Internet."
39. John Pollard, "Skinhead Culture: The Ideologies, Mythologies, Religions and Conspiracy Theories of Racist Skinheads," *Patterns of Prejudice* 50, nos. 4–5 (2016): 398–419.
40. Burris, Smith, and Strahm, "White Supremacist Networks on the Internet."
41. Michael Barkun, *Religion and the Racist Right: The Origins of the Christian Identity Movement* (Chapel Hill, NC: UNC Press, 1997).
42. Anti-Defamation League, "With Hate in Their Hearts."
43. Caiani and Parenti, *European and American Extreme Right Groups and the Internet*.
44. Burris, Smith, and Strahm, "White Supremacist Networks on the Internet," 221.
45. Ibid, 216.
46. Ibid.
47. Ibid.
48. Author interview.
49. Author interview.
50. Author interview.
51. Author interview.
52. Author interview.
53. Author interview.
54. Author interview.
55. Author interviews.
56. Author interviews.
57. Author interview.

58. Author interview.
59. Author interview.
60. Author interviews.
61. Author interview.
62. For more on this history, see Walter Laqueur, *A History of Terrorism* (New York: Routledge, 2017).
63. For reference, see inter alia Susan Stern and Laura Browder, *With the Weathermen: The Personal Journal of a Revolutionary Woman* (New Brunswick, NJ: Rutgers University Press, 2007); Ron Jacobs, *The Way the Wind Blew: A History of the Weather Underground* (London: Verso, 1997).
64. For literature on the history of the now common term "electronic civil disobedience," see Stefan Wray, "On Electronic Civil Disobedience," *Peace Review* 11, no. 1 (1999): 107–111; Graham Meikle, "Electronic Civil Disobedience and Symbolic Power," (2008): 177–187; Mark Manion and Abby Goodrum, "Terrorism or Civil Disobedience: Toward a Hacktivist Ethic," *Acm Sigcas Computers and Society* 30, no. 2 (2000): 14–19.
65. Critical Art Ensemble, "Electronic Civil Disobedience and Other Unpopular Ideas." (1996).
66. Other works have engaged this idea in recounting the history of these artist resistance fighters, including Christian Beck, "Web of Resistance: Deleuzian Digital Space and Hacktivism," *Journal for Cultural Research* 20, no. 4 (2016): 334–349; Manion and Goodrum, "Terrorism or Civil Disobedience"; Abby Goodrum and Mark Manion, "The Ethics of Hacktivism," *Journal of Information Ethics* 9, no. 2 (2000): 51.
67. Karl Grindal, "Artist Collectives as the Origins of DDoS: The Strano Network to Electronic Disturbance Theater," unpublished ms., November 30, 2018.
68. Critical Art Ensemble, "Electronic Civil Disobedience and Other Unpopular Ideas."
69. Ibid.
70. Ibid.
71. Grindal, "Artist Collectives as the Origins of DDoS." Also see Molly Sauter, *The Coming Swarm: DDOS Actions, Hacktivism, and Civil Disobedience on the Internet* (New York: Bloomsbury, 2014); Dorothy E. Denning, *Information Warfare and Security* (Addison-Wesley Professional, Lebanon, IN, USA, 1998); T. Jordan and P. Taylor, *Hacktivism and Cyberwars* (London: Routledge, 2004).
72. See Grindal, "Artist Collectives as the Origins of DDoS," 2. For an early professional description, see Christos Douligeris and Aikaterini Mitrokotsa, "DDoS Attacks and Defense Mechanisms: A Classification," in *Proceedings of the 3rd IEEE International Symposium on Signal Processing and Information Technology (IEEE Cat. No. 03EX795)* (IEEE, 2003), 190–193.
73. Kirk L. Kroeker, "Celebrating the Legacy of PLATO," *Communications of the ACM* 53, no. 8 (August 2010): 19–20.
74. Grindal, "Artist Collectives as the Origins of DDoS," 2.
75. Nazrul Hoque, Dhruba K. Bhattacharyya, and Jugal K. Kalita, "Botnet in DDoS Attacks: Trends and Challenges," *IEEE Communications Surveys & Tutorials* 17, no. 4 (2015): 2242–2270.
76. WikiARTpedia, "Strano Network," May 15, 2010, http://www.wikiartpedia.org/index.php?title=Strano_network. Also see Julie Thomas, "Ethics of Hacktivism," *Information Security Reading Room* 12 (2001).
77. Grindal, "Artist Collectives as the Origins of DDoS," 5.
78. Ibid.
79. Ibid. Also see Tommaso Tozzi, "Netstrike (1995)," http://www.tommasotozzi.it/index.php?title=Netstrike_%281995%29.
80. Tozzi, "Netstrike (1995)."
81. Joseph Cox, "History of the DDoS Attack as a Tool of Protest," *Vice*, August 28, 2023, http://motherboard.vice.com/en_uk/read/history-of-the-ddos-attack.
82. "(eng) Netstrike for Mumia & Silvia," May 15, 1996, http://www.ainfos.ca/A-Infos96/5/0080.html. Also see Graham Meikle, "Hack Attacks and Electronic Civil Disobedience," in Graham Meikle, ed. *Future Active: Media Activism and the Internet* (Sydney: Taylor & Francis, March 2003).
83. Tommaso Tozzi, "Subject: Chiapas Net Strike," Ekphorie, September 7, 1996, http://www.ekphorie.de/museal/if95/chiapasn.htm.
84. Tozzi, "Netstrike (1995)."
85. Tommaso Tozzi, "Net Strike, No Copyright, etc.—Pratiche antagoniste nell'era telematica," 1996.
86. Grindal, "Artist Collectives as the Origins of DDoS," 5-6.

87. "29 gennaio 1998 Netstrike per il Chiapas," September 5, 1998. https://www.tmcrew.org/chiapas/chiapas2/netstrik.htm.
88. For good descriptions of the group, see Shannon Hurst, "Examining Hacktivism as Performance through the Electronic Disturbance Theater and Anonymous," Florida State University, Graduate thesis, (2013); Ricardo Dominguez, "Electronic Disturbance Theater: Timeline 1994–2002," *TDR: The Drama Review* 47, no. 2 (2003): 132–134.
89. Grindal, "Artist Collectives as the Origins of DDoS," 9.
90. The other book not yet mentioned is Critical Art Ensemble, *The Electronic Disturbance* (New York: , Autonomedia, 1994).
91. Grindal, "Artist Collectives as the Origins of DDoS," 9.
92. Brett Stalbaum, "The Zapatista Tactical FloodNet," Thing.net, http://www.thing.net/~rdom/ecd/ZapTact.html.
93. Grindal, "Artist Collectives as the Origins of DDoS," 9–10.
94. Ibid., 11–12.
95. Electronic Civil Disobedience, "Chronology of Swarm," Thing.net, http://www.thing.net/~rdom/ecd/CHRON.html.
96. Ibid.
97. Winn Schwartau, "Cyber-Civil Disobedience: Inside the Electronic Disturbance Theater's Battle with the Pentagon," NetworkWorldFusion, November 11, 1999, http://www.networkworld.com/news/0111vigcyber.html.
98. Grindal, "Artist Collectives as the Origins of DDoS," 12.
99. Ibid.
100. See, among other arguments, the consistent reference to these groups' perception that the use of these web technologies was an exercise in social mobilization, persuasion, and coordination more than it was capable of disruptive impact. Indeed, this was stated from the outset by EDT. See Critical Art Ensemble, "About CAE," http://critical-art.net/.
101. Grindal, "Artist Collectives as the Origins of DDoS."
102. Marco Deseriis, "Hacktivism: On the Use of Botnets in Cyberattacks," *Theory, Culture & Society* 34, no. 4 (2017): 131–152.
103. For a history of the group, see inter alia Burak Polat, Cemile Tokgöz Bakıroğlu, and Mira Elif Demirhan Sayın, "Hacktivism in Turkey: The Case of Redhack," *Mediterranean Journal of Social Sciences* 4, no. 9 (2013): 628–628.
104. Bülay Doğan, "Contextualizing Hacktivism: The Criminalization of Redhack." (2019).
105. From the outset, it's worth noting that a range of researchers have made the strong case that RedHack is far more representative of a resistance group fighting for nonviolent social transformation than a conventional hactivist outfit. See, for instance, Murat Akser, "The Revolution Will Be Hacktivated," *Digital Transformations in Turkey: Current Perspectives in Communication Studies* (2015); Altug Akin and Doğan Emrah Zıraman, "Power Struggle in/around the Turkish Online Realm and Three Forms of Opposition: Redhack, Alternative IS Association and Personal Resistances against YouTube Ban," *Global Media Journal: Mediterranean Edition* 10, no. 1 (2015).
106. For definitional work on hactivism, see Denning (2001).
107. Tim Maurer, "Cyber Proxies and Their Implications for Liberal Democracies," *Washington Quarterly* 41, no. 2 (2018): 171–188.
108. A number of works have delineated the ethical dimensions of hactivism. These, of course, note the general tendency of hactivists to adhere to a broad ethical code of conduct that emphasizes freedom from censorship, exploitation, and prohibition of access to the internet, among other things. This code was most famously advocated for by the Cult of the Dead Cow membership as a moral basis for cyber civil disobedience. The argument being made here is not that hacktivists lack a code of conduct writ large—the opposite tends to be true—but that RedHack is an example a group with a code of conduct defined by their specific sociopolitical struggle rather than a generic ethical base. For more on hacktivist culture and codes, see inter alia Kenneth Einar Himma, "Ethical Issues Involving Computer Security: Hacking, Hacktivism, and Counterhacking," *Handbook of Information and Computer Ethics* (2008): 191; Xiang Li, "Hacktivism and the First Amendment: Drawing the Line between Cyber Protests and Crime," *Harv. JL & Tech.* 27 (2013): 301; George O'Malley, "Hacktivism: Cyber Activism or Cyber Crime," *Trinity CL Rev.* 16 (2013): 137; Joseph Menn, *Cult of the Dead Cow: How the Original Hacking Supergroup Might Just Save the World* (London: Hachette UK, 2019).

109. Efe Kerem Sozeri, "Why RedHack Challenges Turkey's Political Establishment," *Daily Dot*, October 13, 2016.
110. Polat, Bakıroğlu, and Sayın, "Hactivism in Turkey."
111. Sozeri, "Why RedHack Challenges Turkey's Political Establishment."
112. Ibid.
113. Ibid.

Chapter 4

1. "A Brief Discussion on *falun gong*," *Renmin ribao* [*People's Daily*], July 23, 1999.
2. For a broad overview of Falun Gong, the organization's variation on *qigong* practices, and philosophical tenets, see James Tong, *Revenge of the Forbidden City: The Suppression of Falungong in China, 1999–2005* (New York: Oxford University Press, 2009); David A. Palmer, *Falun Gong Challenges the CCP. Qigong Fever: Body, Science, and Utopia in China* (New York: Columbia University Press, 2007); Mickey Spiegel, *Dangerous Meditation: China's Campaign against Falungong* (Washington, D.C.: Human Rights Watch, 2002).
3. "A Brief Discussion on *falun gong*."
4. Estimates vary. The most common hold is that between 70 million and 80 million adherents exist worldwide. See "Falun gong zhenshi di gushi" [The Real Story of Falun Gong], www.Mingui.ca, August 14, 1999. Other estimates have been as low as 2 million in the mid-1990s to between 40 million and 80 million at a peak in the early 2000s. See *Renmin ribao*, August 15, 1999, 1; *Nanfang ribao*, March 18, 1999, 11; *Xinhua*, October 27, 2001; Zong Hairen, "Zhu Rongji zai yijiujiujiu nian" [Zhu Rongji in 1999], 15.
5. See Sam Han and Kamaludeen Mohamed Nasir, *Digital Culture and Religion in Asia* (New York: Routledge, 2015), 4: 53.
6. *Renmin ribao*, August 13, 1999, 5.
7. See Richard Madsen, "Understanding Falun Gong," *Current History* 99, no. 638 (September 2000): 243–247.
8. See http://falundafa.org/fldfbb/news990502.htm, accessed August 14, 2001.
9. See Amnesty International, "The Crackdown on Falun Gong and Other So-Called Heretical Crganizations," March 23, 2000. Available at https://www.amnesty.org/en/documents/asa17/011/2000/en/.
10. See Bi Yun Huang, *Analyzing a Social Movement's Use of Internet: Resource Mobilization, New Social Movement Theories and the Case of Falun Gong* (Bloomington: Indiana University Press, 2009), 195–213.
11. James Tong, "An Organizational Analysis of the Falun Gong: Structure, Communications, Financing," *China Quarterly* 171 (2002): 643–645.
12. Ibid., 645. Also see Noah Porter, *Falun Gong in the United States: An Ethnographic Study* (Universal-Publishers, 2003); Madsen, "Understanding Falun Gong."
13. Around the events leading to banning, see *Xinhua*, October 21, 1999; *Xinhua, Beijing*, October 21, 1999. Otherwise, see "The Critical Masses: Officials Increasingly Ask People a Once Taboo Question: What They Think," *The Economist*, April 11, 2015.
14. Tong, *Revenge of the Forbidden City*, 81–82.
15. Discussed in "Huangyan mengbi buliao xueliang di yanjing" [Lies Cannot Deceive Bright Eyes]; "Suowei shijie mori" [So-Called End of the World]; and "A Brief Discussion of *falun gong*," all in *Minghui*.
16. Tong, *Revenge of the Forbidden City*, 56.
17. For a description of state sponsorship and oversight during this period, as well as changing opinions on the relationship between the government and Falun Gong, see David Ownby, *Falun Gong and the Future of China* (New York: Oxford University Press, 2008).
18. See David Palmer, *Qigong Fever: Body, Science and Utopia in China* (New York: Columbia University Press, 2007).
19. Ibid., 31.
20. Seth Faison, "In Beijing: A Roar of Silent Protestors," *New York Times*, April 27, 1999.
21. Ownby, *Falun Gong and the Future of China*, 43–45.
22. Ibid., 46.
23. For core claims, see Research Department, Ministry of Public Security, "Li Hongzhi." Also see the overview of such publications in Mingxia and Shiping Hua, eds., "The Battle between the Chinese Government and the Falun Gong," *Chinese Law and Government*, September–October 1999.

24. See Danny Schechter, *Falun Gong's Challenge to China: Spiritual Practice or "Evil cult"?* (New York: Akashic Books, November 2001), 56. Also see Ownby, *Falun Gong and the Future of China*, 171.
25. Schechter, *Falun Gong's Challenge to China*, 56; Ownby, *Falun Gong and the Future of China*, 171; Ethan Gutmann, "An Occurrence on Fuyou Street," *National Review*, July 13, 2009.
26. Gutmann, "An Occurrence on Fuyou Street."
27. *Renmin ribao*, July 23 and August 11, 1999, 1; *Guangming ribao*, August 13, 1999, 5.
28. Spiegel, *Dangerous Meditation*, 21.
29. Julia Ching, "The Falun Gong: Religious and Political Implications," *American Asian Review* 19, no. 4 (Winter 2001): 12.
30. In reality, there is no policy portfolio held by the organization or movement as a whole. Falun Gong does not focus on politics beyond the survival of the organization itself. However, since 1999 this has meant the adoption of a range of survival strategies that necessarily include decentralized resistance to and protest against the PRC. The main policy critique has to do with the outlawing of Falun Gong and related *qigong* organizations. Adherents criticize Beijing and have increasingly coalesced around the criticism that the PRC is not in a legitimate position to dictate the health of Chinese civil society.
31. See Tong, "An Organizational Analysis of the Falun Gong," citing "Demands on *falun dafa* Guidance Stations," (4/20/1994), Art. 1, "Regulations on Propagating the Doctrine and Method for *falun dafa* Disciples" (4/25/1994), Art. 4, "Norms for *falun dafa* Guidance Counsellors" (n.d.) Art. 5, and "What *falun dafa* Practitioners Ought to Know" (n.d.), Art. 4.
32. For perhaps the best outline of Falun Gong objectives and the evolution of group strategy, see Tong, *Revenge of the Forbidden City*.
33. See inter alia Kelly A. Thomas, "Falun Gong: An Analysis of China's National Security Concerns," *Pac. Rim L. & Pol'y J.* 10 (2000): 471.
34. Tong, *Revenge of the Forbidden City* notes that some Hong Kong–based protest publications estimate that arrests in 1999–2000 were as high as 50,000.
35. See Spiegel, *Dangerous Meditation*, 21.
36. Benjamin Penny, "The Past, Present and Future of Falun Gong," lecture the National Library of Australia, Canberra, 2001.
37. Ownby, *Falun Gong and the Future of China*.
38. See Porter, *Falun Gong in the United States*.
39. See Tong, "An Organizational Analysis of the Falun Gong," 637.
40. *Guangming ribao*, August 3, 1999, 1; *Xinhua, Beijing*, October 27, 2001.
41. "Norms for *falun dafa* Guidance Counsellors."
42. *Renmin ribao*, August 4, 1999, 1.
43. See "The Real Story of Falun Gong"; China Law Workers, "Incompatible with Law."
44. "Regulations on Propagating the Doctrine and Method for *falun dafa* Disciples."
45. See Tong, "An Organizational Analysis of the Falun Gong," 642.
46. Synonymous, as Tong notes, with Falun Gong in publications by the organization.
47. *Beijing wanbao*, August 7, 1999.
48. *Guangming ribao*, August 3, 1999, 1; *Xinhua, Beijing*, October 27, 2001.
49. See Tong, "An Organizational Analysis of the Falun Gong," 643.
50. Ibid., 646.
51. *Renmin ribao*, August 7, 8, 1999.
52. See *Fujian ribao*, August 5, 1999; *Haerbin ribao*, August 1, 1999.
53. *Renmin ribao*, August 4, 1999, 1.
54. For an overview of Falun Gong's committee structure, see Ye Hao, "An Explanation." For an overview of the functions of distributed committees among doctrinal, practice, and publication tasks, see Gongli-gongfa zu, Houqin banshi zu, Xuanchuan zu, see *Beijing wanbao*, August 7, 1999; *Beijing ribao*, July 25, 1999; *Renmin ribao*, August 7, 1999, 2.
55. See Tong, "An Organizational Analysis of the Falun Gong," 650–658.
56. See the brief discussion in Athina Karatzogianni, *The Politics of Cyberconflict* (New York: Routledge, 2006), ch. 3.
57. Porter reports Li's own description of group use of email encryption and burner mobile phones to maintain secrecy in intragroup communications (*Falun Gong in the United States*, 184).
58. See David Leigh, Luke Harding, and Charles Arthur, *Wikileaks: Inside Julian Assange's War on Secrecy* (New York: PublicAffairs, 2011), 183.

59. See Juha A. Vuori, *Critical Security and Chinese Politics: The Anti-Falungong Campaign* (New York: Routledge, 2014), 38–45.
60. See Patricia M. Thornton, "The New Cybersects: Resistance and Repression in the Reform Era, in *Chinese Society: Change, Conflict and Resistance*, 2nd ed., ed. E. J. Perry and M. Selden (London: RoutledgeCurzon, 2003), 265; Mark R. Bell and Taylor C. Boas, "Falun Gong and the Internet: Evangelism, Community, and Struggle for Survival," *Nova Religio: The Journal of Alternative and Emergent Religions* 6, no. 2 (2003): 277–293.
61. For a good overview of Dynaweb and Falun Gong's response, see Ethan Gutmann, "Hacker Nation: China's Cyber Assault," *World Affairs* (2010): 70–79; Brad Stone and David Barboza, "Scaling the Digital Wall in China," *New York Times*, January 16, 2010; Patricia M. Thornton, "Manufacturing Dissent in Transnational China: Boomerang, Backfire or Spectacle?," in Patricia M. Thornton, *Popular Contention in China* Cambridge, MA, USA, Harvard University Press, 2008; Stefan Johnsson, "China: The Silence behind the Wall," *Information Warfare* 2013.
62. See Gutmann, "Hacker Nation," Dynaweb can be downloaded at www.dongtaiwang.com.
63. See Bennett Gordon, "Iranian Protesters, Web Censors, and the Falun Gong," *UTNE Reader*, September 4, 2009.
64. See Bell and Boas, "Falun Gong and the Internet," 279–282.
65. Ibid., 284.
66. See Huang, *Analyzing a Social Movement's Use of Internet*, 146.
67. See, among others, Hong Kong Voice of Democracy, "Chinese Government Blocked E-Mails during Falun Gong Crackdown," July 1999, http://www.democracy.org.hk/EN/jul1999/mainland18.htm; Melinda Liu, "The Great Firewall of China," *Newsweek*, international ed., October 11, 1999, http://discuss.washingtonpost.com/nw-srv/issue/15_99b/printed/int/wb/ov13151.htm; Shanthi Kalathil, "A Thousand Websites Almost Bloom," *Asian Wall Street Journal*, August 29, 2000; "China Bolsters Censorship Tactics on the Internet," *San Jose Mercury News*, September 19, 2000; Associated Press, "China Tightens Internet Restrictions," November 7, 2000. For a fuller outline, see Ian Johnson, "The Survival of Falun Dafa Rests on Beepers and Faith," *Wall Street Journal*, August 25, 2000.
68. Derek E. Bambauer et al., "Internet Filtering in China in 2004–2005: A Country Study," 2005. Also see Matt Hartley, "How a Canadian Cracked the Great Firewall of China," *Globe and Mail*, October 3, 2008; David Bamman, Brendan O'Connor, and Noah A. Smith, "Censorship and Deletion Practices in Chinese Social Media," *Firstmonday* 17, nos. 3–5 (March 2012).
69. Gutmann, "Hacker Nation," 74.
70. Ibid., 75.
71. Ibid., 76.
72. See "On Important Matters, Practitioners Must Watch the Position of Minghui Net," http://www.clearwisdom.ca/eng/2000/July/16/AW071600 1.html; Kutolowski, "The Role of Clear Wisdom Net in My Cultivation," referencing http://www.clearwisdom.net/emh/articles/2000/6/17/9122.html and http://www.clearwisdom.net/emh/articles/2000/8/14/9117.html.
73. Simon van Zuylen-Wood, "MAGA-Land's Favorite Newspaper," *The Atlantic*, January 13, 2021.
74. Ibid.
75. Ibid.
76. Ibid.
77. Rodney Stark, "Why Religious Movements Succeed or Fail: A Revised General Model," *Journal of Contemporary Religion* 11, no. 2 (1996): 133–146.

Chapter 5

1. Dick Anthony, Thomas Robbins, and Steven Barrie-Anthony, "Cult and Anticult Totalism: Reciprocal Escalation and Violence," *Terrorism and Political Violence* 14, no. 1 (2002): 211–240.
2. Jean-François Mayer, "Cults, Violence and Religious Terrorism: An International Perspective," *Studies in Conflict and Terrorism* 24, no. 5 (2001): 361–376.
3. Though not unlike those typically thought of in the context of criminal and terrorist enterprise, as in Shah Mahmood, "Online Social Networks: The Overt and Covert Communication Channels for Terrorists and Beyond," in *2012 IEEE Conference on Technologies for Homeland Security (HST)* (Waltham, MA: IEEE, 2012), 574–579.
4. Haro-de-Rosario, Arturo, Alejandro Sáez-Martín, and María del Carmen Caba-Pérez. "Using social media to enhance citizen engagement with local government: Twitter or Facebook?" *New Media & Society* 20, no. 1 (2018): 29–49.

5. See inter alia Nicholas Tsagourias, "Cyber Attacks, Self-Defence and the Problem of Attribution," *Journal of Conflict and Security Law* 17, no. 2 (2012): 229–244; Thomas Rid and Ben Buchanan, "Attributing Cyber Attacks," *Journal of Strategic Studies* 38, nos. 1–2 (2015): 4–37; Victoria Rubin, Niall Conroy, Yimin Chen, and Sarah Cornwell, "Fake News or Truth? Using Satirical Cues to Detect Potentially Misleading News," in *Proceedings of the Second Workshop on Computational Approaches to Deception Detection* (San Diego, CA, 2016), 7–17.
6. The few previous scholarly write-ups of which include Evan Malmgren, "Don't Feed the Trolls," *Dissent* 64, no. 2 (2017): 9–12; Ella Guest, "(Anti–) Echo Chamber Participation: Examining Contributor Activity beyond the Chamber," in *Proceedings of the 9th International Conference on Social Media and Society* (New York: ACM, 2018), 301–304; Brady Robards, "Belonging and Neo-Tribalism on Social Media Site Reddit," in Anne Hardy, Andy Bennett, and Brady Robards, eds. *Neo-Tribes* (Cham, Switzerland: Palgrave Macmillan, 2018), 187–206.
7. This section is a paraphrase of work published in Christopher Whyte, "Of Commissars, Cults and Conspiratorial Communities: The Role of Countercultural Spaces in 'Democracy Hacking' Campaigns," *First Monday* (2020).
8. Reddit Metrics, "/r/The_Donald Metrics," archived from the original on July 12, 2017.
9. Narrative description of Russian influence in the case of r/The_Donald paired with interview evidence in this section is largely drawn from archived amateur evidence compiled by a series of Reddit users. All citation work originated with their compiled postings. See https://www.reddit.com/r/Keep_Track/comments/9hu52u/the_donald_is_actively_promoting_russian/, accessed January 8, 2019.
10. https://archive.is/D4iG2
11. https://archive.is/yGKmQ
12. https://archive.is/OkFxf
13. https://www.linkedin.com/company/usa-really
14. https://archive.is/5LbEG
15. https://archive.is/X9Pvt
16. https://archive.is/Do7rn
17. https://archive.is/GPqW1
18. https://archive.is/vRuo7
19. Media reports hold that the Trump campaign kept a watchful eye on r/The_Donald throughout the 2016 election via feeds at campaign headquarters. See Adrienne LaFrance, "Is Donald Trump a Secret Redditor?," *The Atlantic*, May 11, 2017.
20. Aaron Kessler, "Who Is @ TEN_GOP in the Mueller Indictment?," CNN, February 17, 2018.
21. For the original post, see https://www.reddit.com/r/conspiracy/comments/4s7mk8/al_sharpton_released_screaming_kill_police_and/
22. https://www.reddit.com/r/The_Donald/comments/6je3kn/sweden_national_police_chief_cries_for_help/
23. https://archive.is/FXHuc
24. https://www.reddit.com/domain/geotus.band/top/?t=all
25. Kevin Roose, "Is a New Russian Meddling Tactic Hiding in Plain Sight?," *New York Times*, September 25, 2018.
26. https://archive.is/vKL4A
27. https://www.linkedin.com/company/usa-really/
28. U.S. Department of Justice, "Internet Research Agency Indictment," February 16, 2018. Also see Mark Mazzetti and Katie Benner, "12 Russian Agents Indicted in Mueller Investigation," *New York Times*, July 13, 2018, https://www.nytimes.com/2018/07/13/us/politics/mueller-indictment-russian-intelligence-hacking.html.
29. Meaning the curation of debate to appear legitimate despite underlying content and tone manipulation.
30. A men's rights subculture dedicated to Men Going Their Own Way (MGTOW).
31. "Involuntary celibates."
32. A subculture community dedicated to the conspiracy that the political left is artificially promoting the false notion that, among other things, sexism exists.
33. A reference to the film *The Matrix*, "red pill" and "blue pill" are individuals who either buy into the façade of reality that is a societal mainstream constructed by malicious leftist political forces or accept the "truth." Other versions of the term (e.g., "green pill" or "black pill") are commonly used to reference more specific ideas about the manipulation of reality by forces of the mainstream.

34. Savvas Zannettou, Tristan Caulfield, Emiliano De Cristofaro, Nicolas Kourtelris, Ilias Leontiadis, Michael Sirivianos, Gianluca Stringhini, and Jeremy Blackburn, "The Web Centipede: Understanding How Web Communities Influence Each Other through the Lens of Mainstream and Alternative News Sources," in *Proceedings of the 2017 Internet Measurement Conference*. London, 2017, 405–417.
35. Ibid., 412.
36. Ibid., 413.
37. Ibid..
38. The communities of Gab provide an interesting and affirming counterpoint to the experiences being described here with reference to the subreddit r/The_Donald. A study of Alt-Tech (alternate technology) far-right interactions on the platform describes a series of affordances that seem to contrast with the restrictive mechanisms present in certain Reddit-based right-wing communities over the past several years, namely, the "lack of content moderation, culture of anonymity, microblogging architecture," and a crowdsourced model of funds generation. Even given these relatively loose shackles vis-à-vis information generation, curation, and presentation, the community has nevertheless leaned heavily toward self-victimization and a series of conspiratorial tendencies that mirror those seen on r/The_Donald. See Greta Jasser, Jordan McSwiney, Ed Pertwee, and Savvas Zannettou, "'Welcome to #GabFam': Far-Right Virtual Community on Gab," *New Media & Society*, 25, no. 7 (2021): 14614448211024546.
39. Ibid., 2.
40. Aji Romano, "Reddit Just Banned One of Its Most Toxic Forums. But It Won't Touch The_Donald," *Vox*, November 13, 2017.
41. Kathleen Hall Jamieson and Joseph N. Capella, *Echo Chamber: Rush Limbaugh and the Conservative Media Establishment* (New York: Oxford University Press, 2008).
42. Natascha Rietdijk, "Radicalizing Populism and the Making of an Echo Chamber: The Case of the Italian Anti-Vaccination Movement," *Krisis* (2021): 2.
43. Cass R. Sunstein, *Going to Extremes: How Like Minds Unite and Divide* (New York: Oxford University Press, 2009).
44. Such as Elizabeth Dubois and Grant Blank, "The Echo Chamber Is Overstated: The Moderating Effect of Political Interest and Diverse Media," *Information, Communication & Society* 21 (2018): 729–745; Frederik J. Zuiderveen Borgesius, Damian Trilling, Judith Möller, Balázs Bodó, Claes H. De Vreese, and Natali Helberger, "Should We Worry about Filter Bubbles?," *Internet Policy Review* 5 (2016).
45. C. Thi Nguyen, "Echo Chambers and Epistemic Bubbles," *Episteme* 17, no. 2 (2020): 141–161.
46. Cass R. Sunstein, *Republic.Com 2.0* (Princeton, NJ: Princeton University Press, 2009); Natalie Jomini Stroud, "Polarization and Partisan Selective Exposure," *Journal of Communication* 60, no. 3 (2010): 556–576.
47. Zannettou et al., "The Web Centipede."
48. Ibid., 405.
49. Ibid., 415–417.
50. These results have been replicated across other web contexts. See, for instance, Chengcheng Shao, Giovanni Luca Ciampaglia, Onur Varol, Kai-Cheng Yang, Alessandro Flammini, and Filippo Menczer, "The Spread of Low-Credibility Content by Social Bots," *Nature Communications* 9, no. 1 (2018): 1–9; Savvas Zannettou, Barry Bradlyn, Emiliano De Cristofaro, Haewoon Kwak, Michael Sirivianos, Gianluca Stringini, and Jeremy Blackburn, "What Is Gab: A Bastion of Free Speech or An Alt-Right Echo Chamber," in *Companion Proceedings of the the Web Conference 2018* (Lyon, France, 2018), 1007–1014.
51. Matteo Cinelli, Gianmarco De Francisci Morales, Alessandro Galeazzi, Walter Quattrociocchi, and Michele Starnini, "The Echo Chamber Effect on Social Media," *Proceedings of the National Academy of Sciences* 118, no. 9 (2021).
52. Kunihiro Miyazaki, Takayuki Uchiba, Kenji Tanaka, and Kazutoshi Sasahara, "The Strategy behind Anti-Vaxxers' Reply Behavior on Social Media," *arXiv preprint arXiv:2105.10319* (2021).
53. For the seminal description in the context of political messaging, see Kim Witte, "Putting the Fear Back into Fear Appeals: The Extended Parallel Process Model," *Communications Monographs* 59, no. 4 (1992): 329–349.
54. Christopher Whyte and Ugochukwu Etudo, "Cyber by a Different Logic: Using an Information Warfare Kill Chain to Understand Cyber-Enabled Influence Operations," in Christopher Whyte, Brian Mazanec and Trevor Thrall, eds. *Information Warfare in the Age of Cyber Conflict* (New York: Routledge, 2020), 114–131.

55. Rietdijk, "Radicalizing Populism and the Making of an Echo Chamber."
56. Ibid.
57. Whyte and Etudo, "Cyber by a Different Logic."
58. Ibid.
59. David M. Blei, Andrew Y. Ng, and Michael I. Jordan, "Latent Dirichlet Allocation," *Journal of Machine Learning Research* 3 (January 2003): 993–1022.
60. See Annalise Baines, Muhammad Ittefaq, and Mauryne Abwao, "# Scamdemic, # Plandemic, or # Scaredemic: What Parler Social Media Platform Tells Us about COVID-19 Vaccine," *Vaccines* 9, no. 5 (2021): 421; Tasmiah Nuzhath, Samia Tasnim, Rahul Kumar Sanjwal, Nusrat Fahmida Trisha, Mariya Rahman, S. M. Farabi Mahmud, Arif Arman, Susmita Chakraborty, and M. D. Mahbub Hossain, "COVID-19 Vaccination Hesitancy, Misinformation and Conspiracy Theories on Social Media: A Content Analysis of Twitter Data" (2020).
61. Andrea Grignolio, "A Brief History of Anti-Vaccination Movements," in Andrea Grignolio, ed. *Vaccines: Are They Worth a Shot?*(Cham, Switzerland: Copernicus, 2018), 25–40; S. Tafuri, Domenico Martinelli, Rosa Prato, and C. Germinario, "From the Struggle for Freedom to the Denial of Evidence: History of the Anti-Vaccination Movements in Europe," *Annali di igiene: Medicina preventiva e di comunita* 23, no. 2 (2011): 93–99.
62. Robert M. Wolfe and Lisa K. Sharp, "Anti-Vaccinationists Past and Present," *British Medical Journal* 325, no. 7361 (2002): 430–432.
63. Lauren R. Kolodziejski, "Harms of Hedging in Scientific Discourse: Andrew Wakefield and the Origins of the Autism Vaccine Controversy," *Technical Communication Quarterly* 23, no. 3 (2014): 165–183.
64. Ibid. Also see Brian Deer, "How the Vaccine Crisis Was Meant to Make Money," *British Medical Journal* 342 (2011); T. S. Sathyanarayana Rao and Chittaranjan Andrade, "The MMR Vaccine and Autism: Sensation, Refutation, Retraction, and Fraud," *Indian Journal of Psychiatry* 53, no. 2 (2011): 95.
65. Roberta Liggett O'Malley, Karen Holt, and Thomas J. Holt, "An Exploration of the Involuntary Celibate (Incel) Subculture Online," *Journal of Interpersonal Violence* (2020): 0886260520959625.
66. Bruce Hoffman, Jacob Ware, and Ezra Shapiro, "Assessing the Threat of Incel Violence," *Studies in Conflict & Terrorism* 43, Volume, 37, no. 7 (2020): 565–587.
67. Ibid. Also see Manoel Horta Ribeiro, Jeremy Blackburn, Barry Bradlyn, Emiliano De Cristofaro, Gianluca Stringhini, Summer Long, Stephanie Greenberg, and Savvas Zannettou, "From Pick-up Artists to Incels: A Data-Driven Sketch of the Manosphere," *arXiv preprint arXiv:2001.07600* (2020).
68. Thea Høiland, "Incels and the Stories They Tell: A Narrative Analysis of Incels' Shared Stories on Reddit" University of Oslo (master's thesis, 2019).
69. Hoffman, Ware, and Shapiro, "Assessing the Threat of Incel Violence."
70. Ibid.
71. Blei, Ng, and Jordan, "Latent Dirichlet Allocation."
72. For full details on the evolution of topic models, see Thomas L. Griffiths, Michael I. Jordan, Joshua B. Tenenbaum, and David M. Blei, "Hierarchical Topic Models and the Nested Chinese Restaurant Process," in Lawrence K. Saul, Yair Weiss and Léon Bottou, *Advances in Neural Information Processing Systems*Vancouver, Canada (2004), 17–24; David M. Blei and John D. Lafferty, "A Correlated Topic Model of Science," *Annals of Applied Statistics* (2007): 17–35; Daniel Ramage, Christopher D. Manning, and Susan Dumais, "Partially Labeled Topic Models for Interpretable Text Mining," in *Proceedings of the 17th ACM SIGKDD International Conference on Knowledge Discovery and Data Mining* (New York: ACM, 2011), 457–465; David M. Blei, "Probabilistic Topic Models," *Communications of the ACM*, Vol. 55, no. 4 (2012): 77–84.
73. Blei, Ng, and Jordan, "Latent Dirichlet Allocation."

Chapter 6

1. See, inter alia, John Arquilla and David Ronfeldt, "The Advent of Netwar" in *Networks and Netwars*, ed. John Arquilla and David Ronfeldt pp. 1–25 (Santa Monica, CA: RAND, 2001); John Arquilla and David Ronfeldt, "What Next for Networks and Netwars?," in Arquilla and Ronfeldt, *Networks and Netwars*, pp. 311–361; Anne Gehrett, vice president of Law Enforcement Program, CACI, personal interview, July 2004; Walter Enders, and Todd Sandler, "Patterns of Transnational Terrorism, 1970–1999: Alternative Time-Series Estimates," *International Studies Quarterly* 46, no. 2 (2002): 145.

2. For some of the most influential work forwarding this assertion, see Bruce Bimber, *Information and American Democracy* (Cambridge: Cambridge University Press, 2003); Bruce Bimber, "The Internet and Political Transformation: Populism, Community and Accelerated Pluralism," *Polity* 31, no. 1 (1998): 133–160; Lance Bennett and Shanto Iyengar, "A New Era of Minimal Effects? The Changing Foundations of Political Communication," *Journal of Communication* 58, no. 4 (2008): 707–731; Jennifer Earl and Katrina Kimport, *Digitally Enabled Social Change* (Cambridge, MA: MIT Press, 2011); Jan Van Dijk, *The Network Society* (Houton: Sage, 2012). For an overview of these perspectives, see Frank Webster, *Theories of the Information Society* (New York: Routledge, 2014). Some specific work on the relationship between the global information environment and nonstate actor operations has inevitably focused on the Islamic State and generally affirms this position of enhanced capability due to information framing and dissemination abilities. See, inter alia, J. Berger, "The Metronome of Apocalyptic Time: Social Media as Carrier Wave for Millenarian Contagion," *Perspectives on Terrorism* 9, no. 4 pp. 61–71 (2015); A. Zelin, "Picture or It Didn't Happen: A Snapshot of the Islamic State's Official Media Output," *Perspectives on Terrorism* 9, no. 4 pp. 85–97 (2015); S. Gates and S. Podder, "Social Media, Recruitment, Allegiance and the Islamic State," *Perspectives on Terrorism* 9, no. 4 pp. 111–116(2015); M. Berger, "The Metronome of Apocalyptic Time: Social Media as Carrier Wave for Millenarian Contagion" (2015); Jytte Klausen, "Tweeting the Jihad: Social Media Networks of Western Foreign Fighters in Syria and Iraq," *Studies in Conflict & Terrorism* 38, no. 1 (2015): 1–22; Daan Weggemans, Edwin Bakker, and Peter Grol, "Who Are They and Why Do They Go? The Radicalisation and Preparatory Processes of Dutch Jihadist Fighters," *Perspectives on Terrorism* 8, no. 4 (2014): 104; Rachel Briggs and Ross Frenett, "Foreign Fighters: the Challenge of Counter-narratives," policy brief (London: Institute for Strategic Dialogue, 2014).
3. See, for instance, Evgeny Morozov, *The Net Delusion: The Dark Side of Internet Freedom* (PublicAffairs, 2012); Matthew Hindman, *The Myth of Digital Democracy* (Princeton, NJ: Princeton University Press, 2008).
4. See, inter alia, Michele Zanini and Sean J. A. Edwards, "The Networking of Terror in the Information Age," in Arquilla and Ronfeldt, *Networks and Netwars*, pp. 29–60; Christopher Cox, "Digital Repertoires: Non-State Actors and ICTs," *Osprey Journal of Idea and Inquiry* (2006), paper 57. For a more specific description of how unprecedented physical disruption might occur in the digital age, see Michael Sechrist, "New Threats, Old Technology: Vulnerabilities in Undersea Communications Cable Network Management Systems," in *Science, Technology, and Public Policy Program Discussion Paper Series* (Cambridge, MA: Explorations in Cyber International Relations Project at Belfer Center for Science and International Affairs, 2012).
5. See Jeffrey Carr, *Inside Cyber Warfare Sebastopol* (Sebastopol, CA: O'Reilly Media, 2010); Derek Reveron, "An Introduction to National Security and Cyberspace," in *Cyberspace and National Security: Threats, Opportunities, and Power in a Virtual World*, ed. Derek Reveron (Washington, D.C.: Georgetown University Press, 2012), 3–20; Cox, "Digital Repertoires."
6. For good descriptions, see Thomas Rid and Peter McBurney, "Cyber Weapons," *RUSI Journal* 157, no. 1 (2012): 6–13; Brandon Valeriano and Ryan C. Maness, *Cyber War versus Cyber Realities: Cyber Conflict in the International System* (Oxford: Oxford University Press, 2015); Jason Healey, ed., *A Fierce Domain: Conflict in Cyberspace 1986–2012* (Washington, D.C.: Cyber Conflict Studies Association, 2013); Reveron, "An Introduction to National Security and Cyberspace."
7. See Christopher Whyte, "Dissecting the Digital World: Old Questions, New Answers," *International Studies Review* 20, no. 3 (2018): 520–532; Christopher Whyte, "Ending Cyber Coercion: Computer Network Attack, Exploitation and the Case of North Korea," *Comparative Strategy* 35, no. 2 (2015): 93–102.
8. See, for instance, Molly Sauter, *The Coming Swarm: DDoS Actions, Hactivism and Civil Disobedience on the Internet* (New York: Bloomsbury, 2014).
9. See Christopher Whyte, "Power and Predation in Cyberspace," *Strategic Studies Quarterly* 9, no. 1 (Spring 2015): 100–118; Brandon Valeriano and Ryan Maness, "A Theory of Cyber Espionage for the Intelligence Community," EMC Conference Paper, 2013.
10. See Jon Lindsay and Erik Gartzke, "Coercion through Cyberspace: The Stability-Instability Paradox Revisited," in *The Power to Hurt: Coercion in the Modern World*, ed. Kelly Greenhill and Peter Krause (NewYork: Oxford University Press, 2016); Benjamin Jensen, Ryan Maness, and Brandon Valeriano, "Cyber Victor: The Efficacy of Cyber Coercion," unpublished ms., 2016; Jon

Lindsay and Stephen Haggard, "North Korea and the Sony Hack: Exporting Instability through Cyberspace" (Washington D.C.: East-West Center, 2015); Whyte, "Ending Cyber Coercion."

11. See Sauter, *The Coming Swarm*, 2014.
12. See David E. Sanger, *The Reckoning: How President Obama Has Changed the Force of American Power* (New York: Crown, 2012); Symantec, "Advanced Persistent Threats: How They Work," 2014, Available at https://www.broadcom.com/404-symantec?sourceURL=http://www.symantec.com/business/theme.jsp?themeid=apt-infographic-1
13. It is important to note that the outcomes described here are entirely temporary in nature. Indeed, this is one of the main points made about cyber conflict potential by scholars studying cyberspace. Despite what some may argue or think, conflict potential with cyber is entirely limited by the limited nature of "victories" that can be won online. See, broadly, Thomas Rid, "Cyber War Will Not Take Place," *Journal of Strategic Studies* 35, no. 5 (February 2012): 5–32; David Betz, "Cyberpower in Strategic Affairs: Neither Unthinkable nor Blessed," *Journal of Strategic Studies* 35, no. 5 (October 2012): 689–711; Adam P. Liff, "Cyberwar: A New 'Absolute Weapon'? The Proliferation of Cyberwarfare Capabilities and Interstate War," *Journal of Strategic Studies* 35, no. 3 (June 2012): 401–428; Libicki, *Conquest in Cyber-space: National Security and Information Warfare*, Cambridge: Cambridge University Press, 2007; Jon R. Lindsay, "Stuxnet and the Limits of Cyber Warfare," *Security Studies* 22, no. 3 (August 2013): 365–404; Erik Gartzke, "The Myth of Cyberwar: Bringing War in Cyberspace Back Down to Earth," *International Security* 38, no. 2 (Fall 2013): 41–73; Jon R. Lindsay, "The Impact of China on Cybersecurity: Fiction and Friction," *International Security* 39, no. 3 (Winter 2014–2015): 7–47.
14. See J. Carr, The Myth of the CIA and the Trans-Siberian Pipeline Explosion, 2012, Avaibable at http://jeffreycarr.blogspot.com/2012/06/myth-of-cia-and-trans-siberian-pipeline.html.
15. For a broad policy discussion of the topic, see Richard Danzig, *Surviving on a Diet of Poisoned Fruit: Reducing the National Security Risks of America's Cyber Dependencies* (Washington D.C.: Center for a New American Security 2014). For a description of the first actual attack on such infrastructure, see Jose Bernat, "Inside the Cunning, Unprecedented Hack of Ukraine's Power Grid," *Wired*, March 3, 2016.
16. This argument is commonly cited by cyberwar skeptics to justify the analytic perspective that cyber conflict is of limited import in international relations. See, for example, Gregory J. Rattray, *Strategic Warfare in Cyberspace* (Cambridge, MA: MIT Press, 2001); Scott Borg, "Economically Complex Cyberattacks," *IEEE Security and Privacy Magazine* 3, no. 6 (November–December 2005): 64–67; Mike McConnell, "Cyberwar Is the New Atomic Age," *New Perspectives Quarterly* 26, no. 3 (Summer 2009): 72–77; Richard A. Clarke and Robert K. Knake, *Cyber War: The Next Threat to National Security and What to Do about It* (New York: Ecco, 2010); Timothy J. Junio, "How Probable Is Cyber War? Bringing IR Theory Back in to the Cyber Conoict Debate," *Journal of Strategic Studies* 36, no. 1 (February 2013): 125–133; Dale Peterson, "Offensive Cyber Weapons: Construction, Development, and Employment," *Journal of Strategic Studies* 36, no. 1 (February 2013): 120–124; Lucas Kello, "The Meaning of the Cyber Revolution: Perils to Theory and Statecraft," *International Security* 38, no. 2 (Fall 2013): 7–40.
17. This assumption is perhaps most clearly laid out in Audrey Kurth Cronin, *How Terrorism Ends: Understanding the Decline and Demise of Terrorist Campaigns* (Princeton, NJ: Princeton University Press, 2011).
18. The use of encryption for illicit purposes in Figure 6.1 and all subsequent figures is a collapsed index of three distinct categories of technique coded for in initial data collection, including the use of darknet sites and peer-to-peer or similar services.
19. See Gary D. Brown and Owen W. Tullos, "On the Spectrum of Cyberspace Operations," *Small Wars Journal* 11, no. 4 (December 2012).
20. See, for instance, Lora Saalman, "Little Grey Men: China and the Ukraine Crisis," *Survival* 58, no. 6 (2016): 135–156; Michael N. Schmitt, "Virtual Disenfranchisement: Cyber Election Meddling in the Grey Zones of International Law," *Chi. J. Int'l L.* 19 (2018): 30; Nigel Inkster, "Measuring Military Cyber Power," *Survival* 59, no. 4 (2017): 27–34; Nicholas D. Wright, "From Control to Influence: Cognition in the Grey Zone" Report for the Pentagon Joint Staff Strategic Multilayer Assessment Group (2017).
21. See Ramberto A. Torruella Jr., *Determining Hostile Intent in Cyberspace* (Washington, D.C.: National Defense University, 2014). Also see Andrew C. Foltz, *Stuxnet, Schmitt Analysis, and the Cyber Use of Force Debate* (Maxwell, AL: Air War College Maxwell Air Force Base, 2012).

22. Bryan Harris, Eli Konikoff, and Phillip Petersen, "Breaking the DDoS Attack Chain," *Institute for Software Research* (2013).
23. See Stefan Wray, "On Electronic Civil Disobedience," *Peace Review* 11, no. 1 (1999): 107–111.
24. Valeriano and Maness, *Cyber War versus Cyber Realities*.
25. See, for instance, Mark Carman, Mark Koerber, Jiuyong Li, Kim-Kwang Raymond Choo, and Helen Ashman, "Manipulating Visibility of Political and Apolitical Threads on Reddit via Score Boosting," in *2018 17th IEEE International Conference on Trust, Security and Privacy in Computing and Communications/12th IEEE International Conference on Big Data Science and Engineering (TrustCom/BigDataSE)* (New York: IEEE, 2018), 184–190.
26. For robust histories of the early development of the internet, see John Naughton, "The Evolution of the Internet: From Military Experiment to General Purpose Technology," *Journal of Cyber Policy* 1, no. 1 (2016): 5–28; Barry M. Leiner, Vinton G. Cerf, David D. Clark, Robert E. Kahn, Leonard Kleinrock, Daniel C. Lynch, Jon Postel, Larry G. Roberts, and Stephen Wolff, "A Brief History of the Internet," *ACM SIGCOMM Computer Communication Review* 39, no. 5 (2009): 22–31.
27. See inter alia Larry Diamond and Marc F. Plattner, eds., *Liberation Technology: Social Media and the Struggle for Democracy* (Baltimore: JHU Press, 2012); Rebecca MacKinnon, "Liberation Technology: China's 'Networked Authoritarianism,'" *Journal of Democracy* 22, no. 2 (2011): 32–46; Christian Christensen, "Discourses of Technology and Liberation: State Aid to Net Activists in an Era of 'Twitter Revolutions,'" *Communication Review* 14, no. 3 (2011): 233–253.
28. See Anita Breuer, Todd Landman, and Dorothea Farquhar, "Social Media and Protest Mobilization: Evidence from the Tunisian Revolution," *Democratization* 22, no. 4 (2015): 764–792.
29. See Blake Hounshell, "The Revolution Will Be Tweeted," *Foreign Policy* 187 (2011): 20; Sadaf R. Ali and Shahira Fahmy, "Gatekeeping and Citizen Journalism: The Use of Social Media during the Recent Uprisings in Iran, Egypt, and Libya," *Media, War & Conflict* 6, no. 1 (2013): 55–69; Susannah O'Sullivan, *Military Intervention in the Middle East and North Africa: The Case of NATO in Libya* (New York: Routledge, 2017).
30. Steven Heydemann, *Upgrading Authoritarianism in the Arab World* Saban Center, Brookings Institution, Washington D.C., No. 13, October 2007. Also see Marc Lynch, "After Egypt: The Limits and Promise of Online Challenges to the Authoritarian Arab State," *Perspectives on Politics* 9, no. 2 (2011): 301–310; Raymond Hinnebusch, "Syria: From 'Authoritarian Upgrading' to Revolution?," *International Affairs* 88, no. 1 (2012): 95–113; Jason Brownlee, Tarek E. Masoud, and Andrew Reynolds, *The Arab Spring: Pathways of Repression and Reform* (New York: Oxford University Press, 2015).
31. Gary LaFree and Laura Dugan, "Introducing the Global Terrorism Database," *Terrorism and Political Violence* 19, no. 2 (2007): 181–204.

Chapter 7

1. Though a full accounting of this literature would be unmanageable here, a number of resources for and surveys of the digital politics fields exist. These include, among many others, Barry Wellman, "The Three Ages of Internet Studies: Ten, Five and Zero Years Ago," *New Media & Society* 6, no. 1 (2004): 123–129; Mia Consalvo, Charles Ess, and John Wiley, eds., *The Handbook of Internet Studies* (Oxford: Wiley-Blackwell, 2011); William H. Dutton, ed., *The Oxford Handbook of Internet Studies* (Oxford: Oxford University Press, 2013); Mark Graham and William H. Dutton, eds., *Society and the Internet: How Networks of Information and Communication Are Changing Our Lives* (Oxford: Oxford University Press, 2019); Andrew Chadwick and Philip N. Howard, eds., *Routledge Handbook of Internet Politics* (Abingdon, UK: Taylor & Francis, 2010).
2. See Paul Joosse, "Leaderless Resistance and the Loneliness of Lone Wolves: Exploring the Rhetorical Dynamics of Lone Actor Violence," *Terrorism and Political Violence* 29, no. 1 (2017): 52–78.
3. There is a broad range of scholarship on the formation and dynamics of virtual communities across the business, economics, information systems, and international relations literatures. Here, the focus is on the audience cultivation and subcultural development mechanisms of online social communities. For prior work in this area, see inter alia Jessica L. Beyer, *Expect Us: Online Communities and Political Mobilization* (Oxford: Oxford University Press, 2014); Gabriella Coleman, "From Internet Farming to Weapons of the Geek," *Current Anthropology*

58, no. S15 (2017): S91–S102; Philip N. Howard, Saiph Savage, Claudia Flores Saviaga, Carlos Toxtli, and Andrés Monroy-Hernández, "Social Media, Civic Engagement, and the Slacktivism Hypothesis: Lessons from Mexico's 'El Bronco,'" *Journal of International Affairs* 70, no. 1 (2016): 55–73; Hans Asenbaum, "Cyborg Activism: Exploring the Reconfigurations of Democratic Subjectivity in Anonymous," *New Media & Society* 20, no. 4 (2018): 1543–1563.

4. Abrahms, Max. "Why terrorism does not work." *International Security* 31, no. 2 (2006): 42–78.
5. Among others, Robert A. Dahl, *Who Governs? Democracy and Power in an American City* (New Haven, CT: Yale University Press, 1961); Theodore J. Lowi, "American Business, Public Policy, Case Studies, and Political Theory," *World Politics* 16, no. 3 (July 1964): 677–715; Marvin Ott, "Mediation as a Method of Confict Resolution, Two Cases," *International Organization* 26, no. 4 (Autumn 1972): 613; John A. Vasquez, "The Tangibility of Issues and Global Conflict: A Test of Rosenau's Issue Area Typology," *Journal of Peace Research* 20, no. 2 (Summer 1983): 179; I. William Zartman, *Elusive Peace: Negotiating an End to Civil Conficts* (Washington, D.C.: Brookings, 1995).
6. For a description of such work, see inter alia Anthony F. Lemieux and Victor Asal, "Grievance, Social Dominance Orientation, and Authoritarianism in the Choice and Justification of Terror versus Protest," *Dynamics of Asymmetric Conflict* 3, no. 3 (2010): 194–207.
7. Among other works of the authors, David Ronfeldt, John Arquilla, Graham Fuller, and Melissa Fuller, *The Zapatista "Social Netwar" in Mexico* (Santa Monica, CA: RAND, 1999); Ian, Lesser, John Arquilla, Bruce Hoffman, David F. Ronfeldt, and Michele Zanini, *Countering the New Terrorism* (Santa Monica, CA: RAND, 1999).
8. Joshua Kilberg, "A Basic Model Explaining Terrorist Group Organizational Structure," *Studies in Conflict & Terrorism* 35, no. 11 (2012): 810–830; Dane Rowlands and Joshua Kilberg, "Organizational Structure and the Effects of Targeting Terrorist Leadership," Centre for Security and Defence Studies Working Papers, Norman Paterson School of International Affairs (Ottawa, Ontario: Carleton University, 2011).
9. Following Killberg (2011); Arquilla, John, David Ronfeldt, Dionne Barnes-Proby, Elizabeth Williams, and John Christian. *The Emergence of Noopolitik: Toward an American Information Strategy*. Rand Corporation, 1999; and Arquilla, John, and David Ronfeldt. "The advent of netwar (revisited)." *Networks and Netwars: The Future of Terror, Crime, and Militancy* (2001): 1–25.
10. Following Arquilla and Ronfeldt 1999; Arquilla and Ronfeldt 2001; Joshua Kilberg, "Organizing for Destruction: How Organizational Structure Affects Terrorist Group Behaviour" (PhD diss., Carleton University Ottawa, 2011).
11. Terrorism Knowledge Base, "Terrorist Organization Profile," hosted by START's Global Terrorism Database, University of Maryland, 2010. Available at https://www.start.umd.edu/news/terrorist-organization-profile-information-now-available-through-start.
12. Jane's World Insurgency and Terrorism, "Al-Qaeda in the Islamic Maghreb (AQIM)," Group Profile, March 8, 2011.
13. See, among others, Kilberg, "Organizing for Destruction"; Frederic S. Pearson, Isil Akbulut, and Marie Olson Lounsbery, "Group Structure and Intergroup Relations in Global Terror Networks: Further Explorations," *Terrorism and Political Violence* 29, no. 3 (2015): 1–23; A. Kiruthiga, S. Bose, and N. Buvaneswari, "An Experimental Simulation of Hub-Spoke Terrorist Organizational Structure," *Advances in Natural and Applied Sciences* 9, no. 9SE (2015): 41–45.
14. See inter alia Coleman, Gabriella. "Anonymous in Context: The Politics and Power behind the Mask." *Democracy* (2023).; Luke Goode, "Anonymous and the Political Ethos of Hacktivism," *Popular Communication* 13, no. 1 (2015): 74–86; Gabriella Coleman, "Anonymous and the Politics of Leaking," in *Beyond Wikileaks* (London: Palgrave Macmillan, 2013), 209–228.
15. Thomas Rid, *Cyber War Will Not Take Place* (New York: Oxford University Press, 2013).
16. Kilberg, "Organizing for Destruction."
17. See Russ Marion and Mary Uhl-Bien, "Complexity Theory and Al-Qaeda: Examining Complex Leadership," *Emergence* 5, no. 1 (2003): 54–76; Rohan Gunaratna and Aviv Oreg, "Al Qaeda's Organizational Structure and Its Evolution," *Studies in Conflict & Terrorism* 33, no. 12 (2010): 1043–1078; David Siddhartha Patel, "ISIS in Iraq: What We Get Wrong and Why 2015 Is Not 2007 Redux," *Middle East Brief* 87 (2015): 1–8.
18. Monty G. Marshall, Keith Jaggers, and Ted Robert Gurr, *Polity IV Project* (College Park: Center for International Development and Conflict Management at the University of Maryland, 2002).
19. S. Brock Blomberg, Gregory D. Hess, and Akila Weerapana, "Economic Conditions and Terrorism," in Tilman Bruck ed. *The Economic Analysis of Terrorism* (New York: Routledge, 2007), 45–62; Nicholas Sambanis, "Terrorism and Civil War," *Terrorism, Economic Development,*

and Political Openness (Cambridge: Cambridge University Press 2008): 174–206; and S. Brock Blomberg, Gregory D. Hess, and Akila Weerapana, *Terrorism from Within: An Economic Model of Terrorism*, Claremont Colleges Working Papers No. 2002-14, Claremont, California, 2002.
20. For the original description of the Gallup poll from which this data is drawn, see George Gallup, ed., *The Gallup Poll: Public Opinion 1993* (Lanham, MD: Rowman & Littlefield, 1994).
21. Information for which can be found at https://www.worldbank.org/en/publication/wdr2016/Digital-Adoption-Index.
22. Gary D. Brown and Owen W. Tullos, "On the Spectrum of Cyberspace Operations," *Small Wars Journal*| Dec 11, no. 4 (2012): 30am.

Chapter 8

1. H. Innes and M. Innes, "De-platforming Disinformation: Conspiracy Theories and Their Control," *Information, Communication & Society* (2021): 1–19.
2. Much of which took place in real time on Twitter and other social media platforms, as well as in the days that followed in think tank pieces and op eds. For instance, Daniel Byman, "The Assault on the US Capitol Opens a New Chapter in Domestic Terrorism (Washington D.C.: Brookings Institution, 2021); Brian Michael Jenkins, "Don't Muddy the Objectives on Fighting Domestic Extremism" (Washington D.C.: RAND, 2021); Michael German and Harsha Panduranga, "How to Combat White Supremacist Violence? Avoid Flawed Post-9/11 Counterterrorism Tactics" (New York: Brennan Center for Justice, 2021).
3. A reference to the famous and oft-revisited characterization of American politics by R. Hofstadter, *The Paranoid Style in American Politics* (New York: Vintage, 2012).
4. Including by the president of the United States. See "Jan. 6 a 'Violent Attempt' by 'Terrorists' to Hold 'Power': Biden," *Al Jazeera*, August 5, 2021.
5. Ben Sasse, "QAnon Is Destroying the GOP from Within," *The Atlantic*, January 16, 2021.
6. Susan Milligan, "Trump's GOP Drives Out Reagan Republicans," *U.S. News and World Report*, May 14, 2021.
7. S. Van der Linden, C. Panagopoulos, F. Azevedo, and J. T. Jost, "The Paranoid Style in American Politics Revisited: An Ideological Asymmetry in Conspiratorial Thinking," *Political Psychology* 42, no. 1 (2021): 23–51.
8. See A. K. Cronin, *How Terrorism Ends* (Princeton, NJ: Princeton University Press, 2009) for a robust history of such efforts.
9. See M. Kramer, "Guerrilla Warfare, Counterinsurgency and Terrorism in the North Caucasus: The Military Dimension of the Russian-Chechen Conflict," *Europe-Asia Studies* 57, no. 2 (2005): 209–290.
10. A. K. Cronin, "How al-Qaida Ends: The Decline and Demise of Terrorist Groups," *International Security* 31, no. 1 (2006): 30.
11. J. Jordan, "Attacking the Leader, Missing the Mark: Why Terrorist Groups Survive Decapitation Strikes," *International Security* 38, no. 4 (2014): 7–38.
12. A growing trend in the past five years that has only got more pronounced after January 6. See R. Rogers, "Deplatforming: Following Extreme Internet Celebrities to Telegram and Alternative Social Media," *European Journal of Communication* 35, no. 3 (2020): 213–229.
13. For instance, Haley Messenger, "Twitter to Uphold Permanent Ban against Trump, Even If He Were to Run for Office Again," NBC News, February 10, 2021.
14. Meghna Bali, "Why Did Major Tech Companies Deplatform Parler after the US Capitol Riots?," ABC News, January 12, 2021.
15. Adi Robertson, "Reddit Quarantines Trump Subreddit r/The_Donald for Violent Comments," *The Verge*, June 26, 2019.
16. Talia Lavin, "The Neo-Nazis of the Daily Stormer Wander the Digital," *The New Yorker*, January 7, 2018.
17. Elizabeth Culliford, "YouTube Cracks Down on QAnon, Banning Conspiracy Content Targeting Individuals," Reuters, October 15, 2021.
18. Brakkton Booker, "Facebook Removes 'Stop the Steal' Content; Twitter Suspends QAnon Accounts," NPR, January 12, 2021.
19. For initial work in this vein, see inter alia Rogers, "Deplatforming"; Innes and Innes, "De-platforming Disinformation"; Shiza Ali, Mohammad Hammas Saeed, Esraa Aldreabi, Jeremy Blackburn, Emiliano De Cristofaro, Savvas Zannettou, and Gianluca Stringhini. "Understanding the Effect of Deplatforming on Social Networks," in *13th ACM Web Science Conference 2021* (Southampton, UK, 2021), 187–195.

20. M. H. Ribeiro, S. Jhaver, J. Blackburn, G. Stringhini, E. De Cristofaro, and R. West, "Do Platform Migrations Compromise Content Moderation? Evidence from r/The_Donald and r/Incels," *Science Magazine*, October, 2021.
21. A. Zelenkauskaite, P. Toivanen, J. Huhtamäki, and K. Valaskivi, "Shades of Hatred Online: 4chan Duplicate Circulation Surge during Hybrid Media Events," *First Monday*, December 6, 2021.
22. A. Urman and S. Katz, "What They Do in the Shadows: Examining the Far-Right Networks on Telegram," *Information, Communication & Society* 25, no. 7, (2020); 1–20.
23. This is clear in data produced for a range of recent research projects, for instance R. Kor-Sins, "The Alt-Right Digital Migration: A Heterogeneous Engineering Approach to Social Media Platform Branding," *New Media & Society* 25, no. 9, (2021): 14614448211038810; Ali et al., "Understanding the Effect of Deplatforming on Social Networks."
24. This section is, in part, excerpted from Christopher Whyte, "Cyber Conflict or Democracy 'Hacked'? How Cyber Operations Enhance Information Warfare," *Journal of Cybersecurity* 6, no. 1 (2020): tyaa013.
25. The concept of a marketplace of democratic discourse is a common reference point for studies that examine drivers of public and foreign policy, broadly writ. Beyond the earliest cohesive articulations of the metaphor by John Stuart Mill and others, the model has been widely applied in prominent work on the determinants of great power conflict, on issues in conflict resolution and intervention studies, and more. For seminal uses, see inter alia Anthony Downs, *An Economic Theory of Democracy* (New York: Harper, 1957); Jack Snyder, *Myths of Empire: Domestic Politics and Political Ambition* (Ithaca, NY: Cornell University Press, 1991); Bruce Russett, *Grasping the Democratic Peace: Principles for a Post–Cold War World* (Princeton, NJ: Princeton University Press, 1993); Stephen Van Evera, *The Causes of War* (Ithaca, NY: Cornell University Press, 1999); Jack Snyder, *From Voting to Violence: Democratization and Nationalist Conflict* (New York: W. W. Norton, 2000); Dan Reiter and Allan C. Stam III, *Democracies at War* (Princeton, NJ: Princeton University Press, 2002).
26. For classical treatments of the concept, see John Milton, *Areopagitica: 1644* (London: Alex. Murray, 1868); John Stuart Mill, "On Liberty," in *A Selection of His Works* Edited by John Robson, (London: Palgrave, 1966), 1–147.
27. Karl S. Coplan, "Climate Change, Political Truth, and the Marketplace of Ideas," *Utah Law Review* (2012): 545.
28. Prominent work in this vein inevitably includes the program of work on the democratic or liberal peace in international relations. Examples include John M. Owen, "How Liberalism Produces Democratic Peace," *International Security* 19, no. 2 (1994): 87–125; Christopher Layne, "Kant or Cant: The Myth of the Democratic Peace," *International Security* 19, no. 2 (1994): 5–49; Bruce Russett, Christopher Layne, David E. Spiro, and Michael W. Doyle, "The Democratic Peace," *International Security* 19, no. 4 (1995): 164–184; Jack Snyder and Karen Ballentine, "Nationalism and the Marketplace of Ideas," *International Security* 21, no. 2 (1996): 5–40; David Kinsella, "No Rest for the Democratic Peace," *American Political Science Review* 99, no. 3 (2005): 453–457.
29. Maxwell E. McCombs and Donald L. Shaw, "The Evolution of Agenda-Setting Research: Twenty-Five Years in the Marketplace of Ideas," *Journal of Communication* 43, no. 2 (1993): 58–67.
30. As in Philip Mirowski, "A Visible Hand in the Marketplace of Ideas: Precision Measurement as Arbitrage," *Science in Context* 7, no. 3 (1994): 563–589.
31. See Kaufmann, Chaim. "Threat Inflation and the Failure of the Marketplace of Ideas: The Selling of the Iraq War." *International Security* 29, no. 1 (2004): 5–48; and Cramer, Jane Kellett. "Militarized Patriotism: Why the US Marketplace of Ideas Failed before the Iraq War." *Security Studies* 16, no. 3 (2007): 489–524.. Additionally, see Ronald R. Krebs and Chaim Kaufmann, "Selling the Market Short? The Marketplace of Ideas and the Iraq War," *International Security* 29, no. 4 (2005): 196–207; Tim Dunne, "Liberalism, International Terrorism, and Democratic Wars," *International Relations* 23, no. 1 (2009): 107–114; Jane K. Cramer and A. Trevor Thrall, "Introduction: Understanding Threat Inflation," in *American Foreign Policy and the Politics of Fear* (New York: Routledge, 2009), 19–33; Daniel W. Drezner, *The Ideas Industry* (Oxford: Oxford University Press, 2017).
32. Robert Schmuhl and Robert G. Picard, "The Marketplace of Ideas," *The Press: Institutions of American Democracy Series* 2 (2005): 141–155.
33. For discussion, see, for instance, Peter Burnell and Oliver Schlumberger, "Promoting Democracy—Promoting Autocracy? International Politics and National Political Regimes," *Contemporary Politics* 16, no. 1 (2010): 1–15.

34. See treatments in this vein in I. Klyamkin and L. Timofeev, *Tenevaya Rossiya* [Shadow Russia]: *Economic and Sociological Research* (Moscow: Russian State Humanitarian University, 2000), 224–225; Grigorii V. Golosov, "The 2012 Political Reform in Russia: The Interplay of Liberalizing Concessions and Authoritarian Corrections," *Problems of Post-Communism* 59, no. 6 (2012): 3–14; Ararat L. Osipian, "Loyalty as Rent: Corruption and Politicization of Russian Universities," *International Journal of Sociology and Social Policy* 32, nos. 3–4 (2012): 153–167.
35. Daniel Calingaert, "Election Rigging and How to Fight It," *Journal of Democracy* 17, no. 3 (2006): 138–151.
36. See Gary King, Jennifer Pan, and Margaret E. Roberts, "How Censorship in China Allows Government Criticism but Silences Collective Expression," *American Political Science Review* 107, no. 2 (2013): 326–343; Gary King, Jennifer Pan, and Margaret E. Roberts, "Reverse-Engineering Censorship in China: Randomized Experimentation and Participant Observation," *Science* 345, no. 6199 (2014): 1251722.
37. Jonathan Hassid, "Safety Valve or Pressure Cooker? Blogs in Chinese Political Life," *Journal of Communication* 62, no. 2 (2012): 212–230.
38. Rebecca MacKinnon, "Networked Authoritarianism in China and Beyond: Implications for Global Internet Freedom," *Liberation Technology in Authoritarian Regimes, Stanford University* (2010); Han, Rongbin, "Adaptive Persuasion in Cyberspace: The 'Fifty Cents Army' in China" (2013). APSA 2013 Annual Meeting Paper, American Political Science Association 2013 Annual Meeting, Available at SSRN: https://ssrn.com/abstract=2299744.
39. This is perhaps the most commonly cited requirement of democratic information systems metaphorically posed as marketplaces of ideas found in the most prominent treatments using the model in IR.
40. Kaufmann.

Index

For the benefit of digital users, indexed terms that span two pages (e.g., 52–53) may, on occasion, appear on only one of those pages.

'Tables and figures are indicated by an italic *t* and *f* following the page/paragraph number.'

Agnoli, Johannes, 47–48
Al Jihad électronique, 38, 178
Al Qaeda, 18, 23–24, 58, 195, 198, 225–27
Alien and Sedition Acts, 40–41
American Communist Party, 40–41
Andrew "weev" Auernheimer, 62–64
Anonymous Digital Coalition, 85, 86
Anti-Defamation League, 78–79
anti-vaxxer, 134–35, 137–38
Apple, Inc., 119–20
Aryan Nations, 80–82
Atomwaffen Division, 23–24
Aum Shinrikyo, 58

Beam, Louis, ix, 3, 57, 65
Beilenson, Laurence, 48–49
Biden, Joe, 1, 2, 25–26, 218, 221–22, 224
Birth of a Nation, 80
Black Lives Matter, 64*f*, 168–69, 180
Black pill, 136–42
Blackstock, Paul, 46, 47–49, 50–51
Blood & Honour, 23–24
Bolsheviks, 49
Bolsonaro, Jair, 218–19

Caiani, Manuela, 73–74, 75–76, 80
Capitol building, 1–2, 11–12, 39–40, 220–21, 223–24
Castells, Manuel, 27–28
Central Intelligence Agency, ix–x
Chinese Communist Party, 93, 94–95, 96–97, 98, 99, 103–5, 106–7, 109–10, 113, 115, 116, 177–78
Clinton, Hillary, 62–63, 124–25
CNN, 25–26
coercion, 4–5, 10–11, 32, 36, 52–55, 67, 121, 147, 226
Congress, 1, 2, 40–41, 124, 218, 222, 235
connective relationships, 26–28, 29–30, 35, 120, 134–35, 230, 231

conspiracy theory, 1–2, 15, 20, 25–26, 31, 39–40, 62–63, 73–74, 111–12, 139–40, 218, 221–23, 224
counterhegemony, 56
COVID-19, 25–26, 136–38, 139–40
cyber attack, vii, 4–5, 37–38, 77, 149, 156, 160–61, 162, 209, 236–37
cyber dissident, 10, 54–55
cyberterrorism, 65–67, 91–92, 142–43
cyberterrorist, 10, 52, 65, 71–72

darknet, 109, 121–22, 155*t*, 228
Denning, Dorothy, 26
digital activism, 10, 18–19, 52, 63–64, 84–85, 151–53, 157, 183–84, 191, 192, 196, 202–3, 239
digital antagonism, 16*f*, 18–19, 37–39, 52, 60–63, 65, 147, 148, 151–52, 158–59, 160, 161, 162–64, 164*f*, 165*f*, 167*f*, 168*f*, 170, 172–73, 174, 178–80, 182–84, 186–87, 189, 190, 191–92, 193–94, 202–13, 214, 215, 217
digital extremism, 31, 33–34, 35, 91–92, 142–43
discord, 2, 17, 128, 132–34, 223–24
disempowerment, 10–11̃, 65, 71–72, 83–87, 115–16, 120
Distributed Denial of Service (DDoS), 19, 85–86, 87, 148, 155, 155*t*, 158, 159–60, 166–69, 172–73, 213–14, 215
doxing, 121, 158–60, 165*f*, 166, 167*f*, 168*f*, 179*f*, 209
DynaWeb, 108–9

Earl, Jennifer, 26
Earth First!, 38, 54–55
Eastern Lightning, 15, 39, 94–95, 100, 106–7, 115, 154, 178
Electronic Disturbance Network, 85
Electronic Disturbance Theater, 16–17, 86
elite rhetoric, 4, 6–8, 61–62, 218–19

English School, 43–44
Epoch Times, 17, 105, 109–13
evil cult, 39, 94–95, 102, 104–5, 106–7, 171–72
external subversion, 49, 66–67

Facebook, 5–6, 25–26, 110–12, 113–14, 119–20, 121–22, 123–24, 134–36, 141–42, 143, 149, 221–22, 224, 227, 229–30
Fallaga Team, 38, 54–55
Falun Dafa, 99–100, 102
Falun Gong, 17–18, 91–92, 93–116, 117, 154, 171–72, 173
fifth column, 11
flat-eartherism, 39
fleeing in place, 10–11, 53
FloodNet, 86, 166
4chan, 130–31, 134, 138, 149, 221–22, 223–24
Freegate, 17, 108–9
Fringe 1.0, 15–16, 61–62, 68–92, 93, 94, 111, 112–13, 116, 117, 164–66
Fringe 2.0, 15–16, 17–18, 61–62, 71, 116, 117–46
Fringe 3.0, 218–37
front group, 57–58

Gab, 2, 130–31, 132–33, 221–22
Gallup, 25–26, 199–200
Giuliani, Rudy, 20
Global Digital Activism Data Set, 18–19, 151–52, 157
Golden Shield, 107–8
Google, 13–14, 119–20, 154–55, 229–30
Green Army, 63–64

hacker(s), 38–39, 52, 54–55, 62–64, 84–85, 87, 88, 109, 123, 158–59, 166–68, 169–70, 177–78, 180, 197–98
hacktivism, 4–5, 65–67, 72, 88–89, 180–83
Hamas, 58–59
hybrid warfare, 66–67
Hypertext Transfer Protocol, 70

illegitimacy, 16–17, 36–67, 115, 189, 193–94
incel, vii, 17–18, 128, 130, 137–38, 139, 141–42
information and communication technologies (ICT), 5, 15, 22–23, 35, 77, 90–91, 96–97, 149–50, 151–52, 154–55, 186–87, 187t, 191, 198–99, 201, 202–4, 204f, 205–7, 206f, 208–10, 211f, 213–14, 215, 217
Instagram, 121–22, 124–25, 227
internal subversion, 49, 50–51, 66–67
international relations (IR), 42–43, 49
Internet Research Agency, 112–13, 125
Irish Republican Army, 227

January 6th, 2021, vii, 1–2, 10, 11–12, 20–21, 23–24, 25–26, 39–40, 111–12, 142, 185, 218–19, 220–24, 225–26, 227, 228–29, 236–37

Kahin, Audrey, 43–44
Kahin, George, 43–44
Kimport, Katrina, 26
Kitson, Frank, 45–46, 56–57
Klan, Klu Klux, ix, 57, 78–79

leaderlessness, xi, 3–8, 7f, 9, 10, 12–13, 18, 20, 22–23, 25, 27, 29, 31, 37, 68, 142–46, 145f, 147–48, 183, 186–217, 218–37
leaderless resistance, ix–xi, 3–8, 7f, 37, 57–58, 59, 60f, 81–82, 143–44, 147, 189–90, 194, 210f, 211f, 215–16, 229
League of the South, 78–79
Le Pen, Marine, 6
LGBTQ, 38–39, 46, 57–58, 178
liberation technologies, 28, 172–73
Li Hongzhi, 95, 102, 103–4
lone wolves, x, 154

Make America Great Again (MAGA), 17
malware, 19, 107, 149–50, 155t, 160, 161f, 163f, 165f, 167f, 168f, 169–70, 173–74, 179f, 180–82, 187, 213–14, 215
meme-ification, 128
MeWe, 2
Morawiecki, Mateusz, 39
Muslim Brotherhood, 57–59, 63–64, 157, 164–66

National Democratic Party of Germany (NPD), 62–63, 158–59
National Socialism, xi, 55–56, 74–75, 79
neoclassical realism, 12–13
neo-Nazi, 2, 62–64, 73–74, 79, 93, 169–70, 227
New Tang Dynasty, 109–10
nomadic resistance, 71–72, 83–85, 86, 87, 90

Oath Keepers, 2
Obama, Barack, 79
Orbán, Viktor, 39

Parenti, Linda, 73–74, 75–76, 80
Parler, 2, 111–12, 221–22, 227
patriotic hackers, 52
People's Republic of China, 93, 95–96, 99–101, 102, 104–5, 106–7, 108–9, 171–72
Perliger, 73, 76
Pew, 25–26

phishing, 19, 155*t*, 160, 161*f*, 163*f*, 165*f*, 167*f*, 168*f*, 169, 179*f*
Pierce, Joseph, 52–53, 54
political warfare, 17, 66–67
Polity IV, 19, 174–76, 176*f*, 199–201
polysemic, 27
Proud Boys, 2
Putin, Vladimir, 49–50, 171–72, 234–35

QAnon, 2, 20, 39–40, 111–12, 222–24, 227, 228–29
qigong, 95–97, 98, 99, 101–2, 106, 107

Reddit, 2, 13–14, 121–22, 123–24, 125, 129–30, 131–32, 133, 134, 138, 140*f*, 149, 221–22, 229–30
RedHack, 16–17, 38, 88–90
RenRen, 96–97
Rid, Thomas, 56–57, 197–98
Rockwell, George Lincoln, 79
Rosenau, William, 56–57
r/The_Donald, 123–30, 131–34, 227
Russian Empire, 41–42
Russian Federation, 49–50
Russian Revolution, ix–x

SafeChat, 17, 111–12, 113–14
script kiddies, 85
sedition, 10, 41–42, 45–46, 49, 56–57, 65–66, 226, 227
Six Degrees, 80
Skype, 123
Snapchat, 96–97
Southern Poverty Law Center, 73–74, 78–79
Strano Network, 16–17, 85–86, 87

Three Percenters, 2, 23–24, 228
Tozzi, Tomasso, 85–87
Tree of Life, 23–24
Trump, Donald, 1, 2, 6, 20, 110, 123–24, 125, 128, 222–23, 227
Twitter, 5–6, 13–14, 25–26, 111–12, 121–22, 123–25, 130–32, 133, 134, 136–37, 138–42, 140*f*, 141*f*, 143, 149, 172–73, 227, 229–30

Ultrasurf, 108–9
United Islamic Cyber Force, 38
Unite the Right, vii, 39

Vu, Trung, 110–11

Wayback Machine, 80
Weathermen, 83–84
Web 1.0, 5–6, 16–17, 61–62, 67, 70–72, 80, 81–82, 88, 90–91, 116, 143, 229–30
Web 2.0, 3, 4–8, 12–13, 31, 61–62, 70–72, 87, 115, 117, 118–20, 130–31, 138, 143, 144, 145*f*, 147, 148, 186, 220, 225, 229–30
WeChat, 96–97
Weibo, 96–97, 149
WhatsApp, 96–97, 123–24
White nationalism, ix, 74–75, 78–79
White supremacy, ix, 73–76, 77–83, 90–91, 137–38
WikiLeaks, 62–63
Williams, Olivia R., 52–53, 54

YouTube, 121–22

Zeran v. America Online, Inc., 69–70

Made in the USA
Monee, IL
03 May 2026

49437402R00162